D0758120

DATE LOANED

SEP 1 0 1982

Nonproliferation
and U.S. Foreign Policy

JOSEPH A. YAGER, EDITOR

Nonproliferation and U.S. Foreign Policy

RICHARD K. BETTS

WILLIAM H. COURTNEY

HENRY S. ROWEN *and* RICHARD BRODY

JOSEPH A. YAGER

JOHN TAGGART HINCKLEY LIBRARY
NORTHWEST COMMUNITY COLLEGE
POWELL, WYOMING 82435

WITHDRAWN

BET 2/82 · 1951

THE BROOKINGS INSTITUTION
Washington, D.C.

Copyright © 1980 by
THE BROOKINGS INSTITUTION
1775 Massachusetts Avenue, N.W., Washington, D.C. 20036

Library of Congress Cataloging in Publication Data:

Main entry under title:

Nonproliferation and U.S. foreign policy.

  Includes bibliographical references and index.
    1. Nuclear nonproliferation. 2. United States—
Foreign relations—1945– I. Yager, Joseph A.,
1916–
JX1974.73.N66   327.1′74′0973   80-20483
ISBN 0-8157-9674-9
ISBN 0-8157-9673-0 (pbk.)

1 2 3 4 5 6 7 8 9

Board of Trustees

Robert V. Roosa
Chairman

Louis W. Cabot
Vice Chairman;
Chairman, Executive Committee

Vincent M. Barnett, Jr.
Barton M. Biggs
Edward W. Carter
Frank T. Cary
A. W. Clausen
William T. Coleman, Jr.
Bruce B. Dayton
John D. deButts
George M. Elsey
Huntington Harris
Roger W. Heyns
Carla A. Hills
Lane Kirkland
Bruce K. MacLaury
Robert S. McNamara
Arjay Miller
Herbert P. Patterson
Donald S. Perkins
J. Woodward Redmond
Charles W. Robinson
James D. Robinson III
Henry B. Schacht
Warren M. Shapleigh
Phyllis A. Wallace

Honorary Trustees

Arthur Stanton Adams
Eugene R. Black
Robert D. Calkins
Colgate W. Darden, Jr.
Douglas Dillon
John E. Lockwood
William McC. Martin, Jr.
H. Chapman Rose
Robert Brookings Smith
Sydney Stein, Jr.

THE BROOKINGS INSTITUTION is an independent organization devoted to nonpartisan research, education, and publication in economics, government, foreign policy, and the social sciences generally. Its principal purposes are to aid in the development of sound public policies and to promote public understanding of issues of national importance.

The Institution was founded on December 8, 1927, to merge the activities of the Institute for Government Research, founded in 1916, the Institute of Economics, founded in 1922, and the Robert Brookings Graduate School of Economics and Government, founded in 1924.

The Board of Trustees is responsible for the general administration of the Institution, while the immediate direction of the policies, program, and staff is vested in the President, assisted by an advisory committee of the officers and staff. The by-laws of the Institution state: "It is the function of the Trustees to make possible the conduct of scientific research, and publication, under the most favorable conditions, and to safeguard the independence of the research staff in the pursuit of their studies and in the publication of the results of such studies. It is not a part of their function to determine, control, or influence the conduct of particular investigations or the conclusions reached."

The President bears final responsibility for the decision to publish a manuscript as a Brookings book. In reaching his judgment on the competence, accuracy, and objectivity of each study, the President is advised by the director of the appropriate research program and weighs the views of a panel of expert outside readers who report to him in confidence on the quality of the work. Publication of a work signifies that it is deemed a competent treatment worthy of public consideration but does not imply endorsement of conclusions or recommendations.

The Institution maintains its position of neutrality on issues of public policy in order to safeguard the intellectual freedom of the staff. Hence interpretations or conclusions in Brookings publications should be understood to be solely those of the authors and should not be attributed to the Institution, to its trustees, officers, or other staff members, or to the organizations that support its research.

Foreword

THE continuing problem of checking the spread of nuclear weapons has entered a new phase. More nations are acquiring the technical knowledge, and in some cases the physical facilities, needed to produce nuclear weapons. Incentives to build such weapons are being strengthened by regional rivalries and declining confidence in the stability of the international order. An increase in the number of countries that have nuclear weapons in the final decades of this century is a real possibility.

Preventing, or even retarding, the further proliferation of nuclear weapons will not be easy. U.S. nonproliferation policy cannot be formulated in isolation. The endeavor must be integrated with other strands of foreign policy, and nonproliferation goals must sometimes give way to other foreign policy objectives. Moreover, nonproliferation policy cannot be applied uniformly everywhere but must be adapted to the differing circumstances of individual nations.

This study analyzes nonproliferation policy in the broader context of U.S. foreign policy. To obtain a better understanding of U.S. policy alternatives, the authors consider in some depth a number of countries that already have the capability of developing nuclear weapons. The principal focus of their study is on means of coping with the incentives that these countries may have to acquire nuclear weapons. Attention is also paid to civil nuclear energy policies, since those policies may affect the spread of facilities capable of producing the explosive component of nuclear weapons.

Richard K. Betts and Joseph A. Yager are members of the Brookings Foreign Policy Studies staff. William H. Courtney, a U.S. Foreign Ser-

vii

vice Officer, was a guest scholar at Brookings when he worked on the study. Henry S. Rowen is professor at the Stanford University Graduate School of Business; his collaborator, Richard Brody, was on the staff of Pan Heuristics at the time the study was prepared.

The authors are indebted to many persons in the United States and abroad for assistance and helpful suggestions. They are particularly grateful for comments on the manuscript by Justin L. Bloom, Richard Burt, Edward S. Milenky, Joseph S. Nye, Jr., George H. Quester, J. E. Spence, John Steinbruner, and Robert A. Stella.

The manuscript was edited by Elizabeth H. Cross and checked for accuracy by Clifford A. Wright. The index was prepared by Florence Robinson. Ruth Conrad and Jeanane Patterson typed the manuscript. Peter Woo provided research assistance on Part One of the study.

An early version of chapter 6 was published in *Asian Survey,* November 1979, and early versions of chapters 12 and 17 as one article in *International Security,* Fall 1979.

The Brookings Institution is grateful to the Departments of Defense, Energy, and State for financial support of this project. The views presented in this book are those of the authors and should not be ascribed to the persons or organizations whose assistance is acknowledged above, or to the trustees, officers, or other staff members of the Brookings Institution.

BRUCE K. MAC LAURY
President

July 1980
Washington, D.C.

Contents

Glossary   xiv

Introduction   1

PART ONE: NORTHEAST ASIA
Joseph A. Yager

1. The Region   7

2. Japan   9
   Defense Problems and Policies *10*
   The Civil Nuclear Energy Program *15*
   The Space Program *20*
   The Nuclear Ship Program *24*
   Present Policies on Nuclear Questions *25*
   Possible Future Policies on Nuclear Questions *30*

3. The Republic of Korea   47
   Civil Nuclear Energy *47*
   Nuclear Weapons *50*
   The Best of Both Worlds? *64*

4. Taiwan   66
   Civil Nuclear Energy *66*
   Nuclear Weapons *69*

PART TWO: INDIA, PAKISTAN, AND IRAN
Richard K. Betts

5. Nuclear Energy: Policies and Plans   85
   Economic, Technological, and Developmental Incentives *86*
   Present and Prospective Capabilities *95*
   Official Policies on Proliferation *105*

6. Incentives for Nuclear Weapons   116
   India *117*
   Pakistan *124*
   Iran *132*
   Domestic Determinants of Decision *135*

7. Nuclear Defense Options: Strategies, Costs,
   and Contingencies   145
   Deterrence Theory and New Frames of Reference *145*
   Defense Alternatives and Opportunity Costs *150*
   Prospective Nuclear Strategies *159*

PART THREE: THE MIDDLE EAST
Henry S. Rowen and Richard Brody

8. The Growing Nuclear "Overhang" in the Middle East   177

9. Regional Instabilities   182
   The Arab-Israeli Conflict *183*
   Relations among the Arabs *191*
   Interactions with Peripheral Powers *193*
   The Role of Other Outside Powers *195*
   Internal Instabilities *198*
   Implications of the Conventional Arms Rivalries *200*

10. Nuclear Potential and Possible Contingencies   203
    The Status of Announced Nuclear Plans *206*
    The Economics of Nuclear Power in the Region *209*
    Nuclear Desalting in the Middle East *212*
    The Shortage of Trained People *215*
    Prospects for an Arab Cooperative Nuclear Program *217*
    Possible Third World Nuclear Suppliers *220*
    NPT Status *225*
    Objectives, Types, and Costs of Possible Nuclear Forces *226*
    Nuclear-Relevant Delivery Capabilities *231*
    Control of Arab Nuclear Forces *232*
    Contingencies and Consequences *234*

PART FOUR: BRAZIL AND ARGENTINA
William H. Courtney

11. Nuclear Choices for Friendly Rivals   241
    Nuclear Programs *242*
    National Goals and Foreign Policy *250*
    Energy Policy *258*
    National Security Policy *261*
    Nuclear Options for the Future *270*
    Conclusions *277*

PART FIVE: SOUTH AFRICA
Richard K. Betts

12. A Diplomatic Bomb? South Africa's Nuclear Potential   283
    South African Nuclear Capabilities *284*
    Strategic Incentives and Military Options *290*
    Diplomatic Uses of the Nuclear Option *296*
    The Test That Wasn't, the Test That May Have Been *300*

PART SIX: U.S. POLICY CHOICES
*Richard K. Betts, William H. Courtney, Henry S. Rowen
and Richard Brody, and Joseph A. Yager*

13. Northeast Asia   309
    Japan *309*
    The Republic of Korea *313*
    The Republic of China *314*
    The Near-Nuclear Problem *318*
    Regional Problems *320*
    The United States and Northeast Asia *322*

14. India, Pakistan, and Iran   323
    Controlling Access to Fissionable Material *324*
    Controlling Fuel Supplies *329*
    Diplomatic Solutions *338*
    Offsetting Inducements *345*
    Direct Involvement *354*

15. The Middle East   366
    Helping to Change the Rules on Access to Nuclear Explosives *367*
    Helping to Promote Security in the Region *372*
    Consideration of a Broader Strategy *375*

16. Brazil and Argentina: Strategies for American
    Diplomacy   377
    Policies of Denial *385*
    Policies of Control *386*
    U.S. Nuclear Cooperation *390*
    U.S. Defense Policy *391*
    Comparisons with Other Near-Nuclear Countries *395*

17. Preventing the Development of South African
    Nuclear Weapons   397
    International Controls on South African Nuclear Activities *398*
    Leverage through Nuclear Cooperation: Carrot, Stick, or Boomerang? *401*
    Conclusions *404*

18. Influencing Incentives and Capabilities   407
    Measures to Reduce Incentives *408*
    Measures to Limit Capabilities *414*
    Problems of the 1980s and Beyond *418*

    Index   427

Tables

2-1. Comparison of Major Japanese Forces and Soviet Forces
     Deployed in the Far East, 1978   11
2-2. Estimated Japanese Demand for and Sources of Natural Uranium,
     Enriched Uranium, and Reprocessing Services, 1980–2000   19
2-3. Successful Launches of Japanese Satellites, 1970–78   22
2-4. Japanese Satellite Program, 1979–84   23
3-1. Conventional Military Forces of North and South Korea,
     1978–79   53
4-1. Conventional Military Forces of the People's Republic of China
     and the Republic of China, 1979   74
6-1. The South Asian Imbalance of Power and Pakistan's Defense
     Burden, 1977   125
7-1. Added Costs of Nuclear Force Building at Five Levels
     of Annual Effort   151
9-1. Major Weapons of Israel and Selected Arab Countries,
     1973 and 1979   201
10-1. Participation of Scientists from Countries Outside the Soviet Bloc
      in U.S. Atomic Energy Research from 1955 to 1976   216
10-2. Third World Nuclear Export Capabilities   221
11-1. Growth in Argentina and Brazil   251
11-2. Energy Consumption in Argentina and Brazil, Selected Years 261
11-3. Military Spending and Force Levels, Argentina and Brazil,
      Selected Years   268
14-1. Deliveries of Military Equipment to Pakistan and India
      by Various Countries, 1961–71   348

Nonproliferation
and U.S. Foreign Policy

Glossary

ASDF	Air Self Defense Force (Japan)
ASW	antisubmarine warfare
CANDU	Canadian deuterium and uranium nuclear reactor
COGEMA	Compagnie Générale des Matières Nucléaires
GSDF	Ground Self Defense Force (Japan)
HWR	heavy water reactor
IAEA	International Atomic Energy Agency
INFCE	International Nuclear Fuel Cycle Evaluation
IRBM	intermediate-range ballistic missile
KANUPP	Karachi nuclear power plant
LWR	light water reactor
MRBM	medium-range ballistic missile
MSDF	Maritime Self Defense Force (Japan)
NASA	National Space Development Agency (Japan)
NASDA	National Space Development Agency (Japan)
NATO	North Atlantic Treaty Organization
NPT	Treaty on the Non-Proliferation of Nuclear Weapons; nonproliferation treaty
NRC	Nuclear Regulatory Commission
PLO	Palestine Liberation Organization
PRC	People's Republic of China; China
ROC	Republic of China; Taiwan
ROK	Republic of Korea; South Korea
SAM	surface-to-air missile
SDF	Self Defense Forces (Japan)
SLBM	submarine-launched ballistic missile
SWU	separative work unit

Introduction

THE WORLD has lived with nuclear weapons for a third of a century. Despite earlier fears that these weapons would spread rapidly, the number of states with full-fledged and overt nuclear weapons capability has remained at five for sixteen years. If India with its "peaceful" nuclear device and Israel with its reported "bombs in the basement" are counted, the number is still only seven. Yet concern about the possibility of uncontrolled proliferation of nuclear weapons has recently increased.

This concern is based on the realization that a growing number of countries have the technological skills and the economic resources needed to produce nuclear weapons and the incentive to do so. Moreover, the development of civil nuclear energy has reached a stage at which it may significantly increase the risk of nuclear weapons proliferation. As more countries develop their own reprocessing or enrichment facilities, they will gain access to the explosive component of nuclear bombs and will be able to develop nuclear weapons quickly if some future domestic upheaval or international crisis overrides present inhibitions on their doing so.

In these circumstances, the problem of checking the spread of nuclear weapons has become more difficult. Reducing incentives to acquire such weapons continues to be of prime importance, but the threatened increase of sensitive fuel cycle facilities, which could give more and more countries what amounts to a near-nuclear weapons capability, must also receive attention.

Nonproliferation of nuclear weapons has been an important goal of U.S. foreign policy since the dawn of the nuclear age. After the failure of

1

the Baruch plan, which would have abolished nuclear weapons and placed intrinsically dangerous fuel cycle operations under international control, the United States adopted a policy of strict secrecy concerning nuclear technology. The limitations of this approach were revealed when the Soviet Union acquired nuclear weapons in 1949 (followed by the United Kingdom in 1952, France in 1960, and China in 1964).

Without completely abandoning the policy of secrecy, the United States next turned to a policy of promoting peaceful uses of nuclear energy in return for the application of safeguards to civil nuclear energy facilities. This policy was strengthened and internationalized when the Treaty on the Non-Proliferation of Nuclear Weapons, which was sponsored by the United States, came into force in 1970. Nations that adhered to the NPT and did not already possess nuclear weapons promised not to acquire them and to put their civil nuclear facilities under safeguards administered by the International Atomic Energy Agency. In return, they were assured of full access to nuclear technology for peaceful purposes.

The international regime established by the NPT and the IAEA safeguards had imperfections from the beginning. A number of important nonnuclear weapons states refused to abide by the treaty. Also, with the passage of time, doubts grew about the ability of safeguards to prevent the misuse of reprocessing and enrichment facilities for military purposes.

In the U.S. government, misgivings about the adequacy of the present nonproliferation regime have centered on the prospective rise of the so-called plutonium economy. Soon, it is feared, increasing amounts of spent nuclear fuel will be reprocessed to obtain plutonium for recycling as nuclear fuel. Dangerous quantities of plutonium, from which nuclear weapons can be made, will move in international trade. Moreover, some of the reprocessing will be done in nationally controlled plants in nonnuclear weapons states, which will as a result acquire a near-nuclear weapons capability.

The United States has tried to meet this perceived danger in two ways. First, it has used its influence (and in some cases its legal control over nuclear fuel of U.S. origin) to block the construction of reprocessing plants in nonnuclear weapons states and delay reprocessing everywhere. Second, it has initiated extensive multinational consultations (the International Nuclear Fuel Cycle Evaluation) on means of developing peaceful uses of nuclear energy without increasing the risk of nuclear weapons proliferation.

U.S. nonproliferation policy is at a turning point. On the one hand, the United States is trying to keep the existing nonproliferation regime from being overrun by trends that it views as dangerous. And at the same time, the United States appears to be groping toward the creation of a new nonproliferation regime in cooperation with other nations.

The problems of creating a new international regime to check the spread of nuclear weapons are the subject of a forthcoming Brookings study. This book, however, is concerned primarily with nonproliferation as an aspect of U.S. relations with specific countries. Multinational developments are by no means ignored, but the emphasis is on the interaction between nonproliferation policy and other components of U.S. foreign policy in concrete, largely bilateral relationships.

A number of countries were selected for analysis and grouped by region: Japan, South Korea, and Taiwan; India, Pakistan, and Iran; Israel and Egypt (and, less intensively, several other Arab countries); Brazil and Argentina; and South Africa. All these countries have the technical ability to build nuclear weapons in the next ten years or so, and all of them could have incentives for doing so, either now or in the future.[1]

The study examines the present policies of these countries on nuclear questions and the origins of those policies. Major attention is given to the factors that may determine their future policies. The concluding part of the book identifies and evaluates U.S. policy choices in pursuing the goal of nonproliferation both in these countries and more generally.

1. A number of countries with the technical ability to build nuclear weapons were not selected for study on the presumption either that their incentives were weak or that the likelihood of their taking independent action in this direction was small.

PART ONE

Northeast Asia

JOSEPH A. YAGER

CHAPTER ONE

The Region

GROUPING Japan, the Republic of Korea, and the Republic of China is justified by more than geography. The three share a common culture to some extent, they were part of the Japanese empire for most of the first half of this century, and their recent history has been marked by unusual economic dynamism. Perhaps more important for this study, none of them possess nuclear weapons, and all are subject to the pervasive influence of the shifting relations among the great powers—the United States, the Soviet Union, and China—that have substantial interests in the region. These similarities in their backgrounds and situations make it likely that changes in the nuclear policies of any one of them will have some effect on the other two.

The similarities should not be pushed too far, however. Of the three, only Japan is a major power whose nuclear policies have worldwide significance. The acquisition of nuclear weapons by South Korea or Taiwan would have important regional consequences, but neither could affect the global balance of power in the way that a nuclear-armed Japan could. And international schemes to check the spread of nuclear weapons could achieve useful results without the participation of South Korea or Taiwan, but Japanese support would be almost essential.

The security problems of the three also differ markedly. Japan perceives little or no immediate threat to its security but is concerned about a possible waning of U.S. power in the western Pacific and a concurrent growth of Soviet power. Both South Korea and Taiwan confront bitter domestic enemies, but the threats posed by those enemies are not the same. South Korea can roughly match North Korea militarily and is superior in population and economic achievement but nevertheless, with some reason, fears a surprise overland attack. Taiwan is vastly inferior in almost every respect to mainland China but has little fear of an all-out attack across the Taiwan Strait in the near future. Taiwan's anxiety about its longer run security, however, was greatly increased by the U.S. decision to terminate the mutual defense treaty with it at the end of 1979.

The distribution of nuclear capabilities, both civil and military, in the areas under study and the surrounding region is uneven. The three great powers have nuclear weapons, although the capabilities of the United States and the Soviet Union far exceed those of China. China also lags behind the superpowers in civil nuclear technology and does not yet have a civil nuclear energy program.

The only nuclear weapons known to be deployed in the areas under study are held by U.S. forces in South Korea. All, however, have civil nuclear energy programs. The Japanese program, as might be expected, is the largest and incorporates the most advanced technology.

The three governments have signed and ratified the Treaty on the Non-Proliferation of Nuclear Weapons. Adherence to the NPT does not predetermine their nuclear policies, of course, and it may not even preclude their acquiring nuclear weapons. The factors that will determine the nuclear policies of Japan, South Korea, and Taiwan will be explored in the three succeeding chapters.

CHAPTER TWO

Japan

THE INCLUSION of Japan among the countries to be given special attention in this study may seem surprising. Japan is the only country to have
suffered a nuclear attack, and partly as a consequence no country has
proclaimed a more sweeping or fervently held policy against the acquisition of nuclear weapons. But there are conceivable circumstances in
which this policy might be reconsidered and possibly abandoned, although
these circumstances seem remote today. Japan would not be just one
more state with nuclear weapons. Few nations that do not now have such
weapons could come close to equaling its ability to develop and deploy
sophisticated warheads and delivery systems. Moreover, a lightly armed
Japan has been a key part of the status quo in East Asia for a third of a
century. The consequences of Japan's sharply changing course and acquiring nuclear weapons are hard to foresee, but they would certainly be
major.

It is not necessary, however, to take seriously the possibility of Japan's
abandoning its current policy on nuclear weapons to justify a close examination of its policies on nuclear issues. The participation of Japan is
vital to the success of international efforts to check the spread of nuclear
weapons. It already has one of the world's largest civil nuclear energy
programs, and well-developed plans call for continued expansion of the
program. Moreover, Japan's economic strength and political potential
give it considerable weight in international deliberations on nuclear
problems.

To understand Japan's policies on nuclear questions, its security and
energy problems must be examined.

Defense Problems and Policies

No nation actively threatens Japan, although, based on history, geography, ideology, and military capabilities, the principal potential threat to its long-term security is the Soviet Union. A fully adequate defense of Japan should be able to deter or defeat four possible kinds of Soviet military action: interdiction of merchant shipping; conventional air bombardment; invasion; and nuclear attack. A defense that could deal with these threats could also cope with possible lesser threats from Japan's other neighbors.

The Japanese Self Defense Forces (SDF) have a limited capability against the first three of the threats listed above, but without nuclear weapons, they cannot deter nuclear attack. Under its mutual security treaty with the United States, Japan relies on U.S. forces to make up for the deficiencies in both its conventional and its nuclear capabilities.[1]

It is instructive to examine the current capability of the SDF to deal with the three Soviet conventional threats. Once some idea has been obtained of how far Japan is from possessing an adequate defense, Japan's options should it lose confidence in the protection now provided by U.S. forces can be considered.

Table 2-1 presents a comparison of the SDF and the conventional forces that the Soviet Union maintains in Siberia east of Lake Baikal. The table shows that Japan's Maritime Self Defense Force (MSDF) would be unable by itself to keep the Soviet Pacific fleet from gaining control of the sea around Japan and cutting off Japan's essential supplies of imported fuel, food, and industrial raw materials. The SDF are somewhat better equipped to deal with the threats of a conventional bombing attack or an invasion.

Most of the Soviet air force planes shown in table 2-1 do not directly threaten Japan but are maintained in eastern Siberia against a perceived Chinese threat. Moreover, even if the Chinese threat could be ignored, limitations of range and numbers of airfields would prevent the use of

---

1. For a detailed analysis of Japanese defense problems and the role of U.S. forces in the defense of Japan, see Stuart E. Johnson with Joseph A. Yager, *The Military Equation in Northeast Asia* (Brookings Institution, 1979).

Table 2-1. *Comparison of Major Japanese Forces and Soviet Forces Deployed in the Far East, 1978*

Forces	Japan	Soviet Union
Ground	155,000 men 12 infantry divisions 1 mechanized division	400,000 men[a] 37 motorized rifle divisions 5 tank divisions 1 airborne division
Naval	32 destroyers 15 frigates 13 submarines 125 antisubmarine warfare planes	7 cruisers 53 destroyers and frigates 73 submarines[b] 1 amphibious ship 340 naval aviation
Air	138 F-4EJs 150 F-104Js 100 F-86Fs, F-1s[a]	600 air defense 1,225 frontal aviation 202 long-range aviation

Sources: International Institute for Strategic Studies, *The Military Balance, 1979–1980* (London: IISS, 1979), pp. 9–11, 67; Robert P. Berman, *Soviet Air Power in Transition* (Brookings Institution, 1978), pp. 39–44; Barry M. Blechman and Robert P. Berman, eds., *Guide to Far Eastern Navies* (Naval Institute Press, 1978), pp. 31, 50; U.S. Department of the Army, *Handbook on Soviet Ground Forces* (Government Printing Office, 1975), pp. 4-9, 6-21, A-3, A-10.

a. Approximate number.

b. Does not include ballistic missile submarines.

more than a fraction of those planes in an attack on Japan. It is conceivable, however, that the bombers of Soviet long-range aviation in the Far East could be launched against Japanese cities and do heavy damage.

Soviet losses in a conventional air attack on Japan would probably be heavy, since most of the attacking force would be TU-16 Badgers, which are vulnerable to Japan's existing air defenses.[2] As the new TU-26 Backfire bomber is deployed to the Far East, however, the Soviet Union is gaining the advantage.[3] The Backfire can fly at low altitudes and thereby avoid detection and tracking by Japan's present radar system. Defenses against the Backfire will be improved as Japan carries out plans to acquire fifteen E-2C Hawkeye airborne early warning aircraft, which have a look-down monitoring capability. Japanese air defense capabilities will be further increased when the F-15 enters the inventory of the Air Self Defense Force (ASDF), which is scheduled to begin in 1980.

2. In addition to the fighter-attack planes shown in table 2-1, the SDF have eight HAWK and five Nike-J groups of surface-to-air missiles.

3. *Baltimore Sun,* April 29, 1979.

The Soviet ground forces in eastern Siberia are even less available for an attack on Japan than are the Soviet air units stationed in that area. Like the air units, the ground forces are deployed principally against China. Moreover, the Soviet amphibious lift capability in the Pacific is quite small—five amphibious ships and about twelve medium landing ships and fifty-five landing craft. This amphibious capability would clearly support an attack on only a limited objective, such as territory adjoining one of the straits linking the Sea of Japan and the Pacific Ocean. The Japanese Ground Self Defense Force (GSDF) could make an effective stand against such an effort if the Soviet Union was denied air control over the battlefield. Whether the ASDF could at present carry out this task unaided is at best uncertain.

If the protection of U.S. forces were suddenly withdrawn, Japan's own forces would be unable to deal with the existing Soviet threat, particularly that to Japan's vital sea lines of supply. But since the United States remains committed to the defense of Japan and maintains sufficient forces in the Pacific to back up that commitment, the security of Japan against external attack seems to be adequately provided for. It might even be asked why Japan needs any armed forces beyond those required to maintain domestic order.

The Japanese government has in fact not had an easy time formulating a convincing public explanation for its defense program. The initial difficulty was the clause in the postwar constitution under which Japan renounced the right to make war and declared that "land, sea and air forces as well as other war potential will never be maintained." This provision was subsequently interpreted as not prohibiting forces for self-defense, but it still imposes some constraints on the types of weapons with which those forces are armed.

More difficult to explain have been the reasons for spending money on a program that could not plausibly be depicted as directed against meeting any specific external threat. The Japanese authorities have responded to this problem by evading it. They do not deal publicly in even the general kind of threat analysis presented here. Until quite recently, the closest the Japanese government had come to justifying the forces being developed was to say that they were needed to check an unspecified (but clearly Soviet) "limited" attack until U.S. forces could be deployed to defeat the aggressor.

This concept of a holding force still appears in recent Japanese white papers on defense,[4] but it is overshadowed by the more sophisticated rationalization for the armed forces that Japan has developed since its defeat in World War II. This rationalization is the Standard Defense Force Concept, which was contained in the National Defense Program Outline adopted by both Japan's National Defense Council and its cabinet on October 29, 1976.[5]

The 1977 defense white paper, which was the first such paper to expound the new concept, stated that Japan's four defense buildup plans (the period of the fourth plan ended in 1976) had had the objective of dealing with "limited aggression," and declared this approach to have been incorrect. "In contrast the Standard Self Defense Force Concept does not necessarily estimate the quantity of defense capability simply in light of the scale of potential threat involved. Instead, quantitative strength was studied from the point of maintaining a flawless, balanced defense structure of organization and deployment; and of supporting a full surveillance posture during peacetime."[6]

The Standard Defense Force Concept calls for forces that are able to cope with aggression that is "small-scale" as well as "limited." The possibility of large-scale aggression is regarded as "extremely slight in view of the world and local geopolitical environments." Moreover, large-scale aggression would generally require "major advance preparation," which would reveal the aggressor's intent and permit effective deterrence within the current international environment.

The Standard Defense Force Concept rests explicitly on the assumption that there will be no basic structural changes in the international environment. Should "radical" changes occur, "the natural course would be an expansion and reinforcement of Japan's defense structure to conform to such changes. For this reason, the Standard Defense Force Concept includes the potential for smooth alteration of the defense structure

4. The 1978 white paper states: "In cases where the unassisted repelling of aggression is not feasible, due to scale, type or other factors of such aggression, Japan will continue an unyielding resistance by mobilizing all available forces until such times as cooperation from the United States is introduced, thus rebuffing such aggression." Japan Defense Agency, *Defense of Japan, 1978* (Tokyo: JDA, 1978), p. 202. The 1979 white paper contains similar statements. Japan Defense Agency, *Defense of Japan, 1979* (JDA, 1979), pp. 67, 75, 192.

5. *Defense of Japan, 1978*, especially pp. 67–80 and 199–206. See also *Defense of Japan, 1977*, pp. 51–57, and *Defense of Japan, 1979*, pp. 72–73.

6. *Defense of Japan, 1977*, p. 53.

as and when required." The concept calls for "a potentially alterable defense structure . . . capable of becoming the nucleus of a strengthened defense structure at the required time."

The 1977, 1978, and 1979 defense white papers list five areas in which structural changes would be considered important:

1. Maintenance of the Japan-U.S. security system.

2. Mutual deterrence between the United States and the Soviet Union.

3. Continuation of the Sino-Soviet dispute, possibly with some minor improvement in relations between the two communist powers.

4. Continued improvement in Sino-American relations.

5. Maintenance of the status quo in Korea and no major hostilities there.

Somewhat surprisingly, the present strength of the SDF corresponds closely to the requirements of the Standard Defense Force Concept.[7]

The authorized strength of the Ground Self Defense Force under the concept is to remain at approximately 180,000, but another composite brigade is to be created to permit the stationing of a ground force unit on Shikoku, the smallest of the four major islands, and the existing mechanized division and tank brigade are to be replaced by an armored division. The latter shift is explained, somewhat cryptically, as necessary to give the GSDF "at least one tactical unit of each of the various forces used mainly for mobile operations," thereby preventing "any potential shortfalls in mission-accomplishment capability."

No significant changes are required by the Standard Defense Force Concept in the Maritime Self Defense Force or the Air Self Defense Force. The MSDF is to acquire two additional submarines to improve "surveillance and defense" of Japan's major straits and ten additional shipborne helicopters to equip a helicopter destroyer now under construction. The ASDF will gain a squadron of early warning aircraft and one high-altitude surface-to-air missile unit.

The emphasis of the Standard Defense Force Concept is on continuous qualitative improvement, rather than on an increase in numbers of men or weapons. The SDF are to remain strictly defensive. Offensive weapons, such as intercontinental and long-range bombers, will not be acquired, nor will Japan acquire nuclear weapons.[8]

7. Ibid., p. 73, table 2; *Defense of Japan, 1978*, p. 77, table 2; and *Defense of Japan, 1979*, p. 227.

8. *Defense of Japan, 1979*, p. 64.

The Standard Defense Force Concept will not materially improve Japan's ability to cope with the four kinds of Soviet threats listed above. Although Japan must still rely on the United States to deter Soviet (and Chinese) nuclear attack or blackmail and to make up for deficiencies in its own forces in deterring or defeating various conceivable forms of Soviet conventional attack, the concept marks a significant shift in Japanese thinking about defense problems (or at least in the government's public explanation of its defense policies). The maintenance of armed forces is no longer rationalized by the need to meet some unspecified limited threat. Today's relatively small and purely defensive forces are seen principally as the nucleus of the larger forces that may one day be needed if Japan is to survive in a more hostile international environment.

This nucleus contains no basis for creating an independent nuclear weapons capability. The omission—if it can be so labeled—can easily be explained by the realities of Japan's domestic politics and international relations. At the same time, it is inconsistent with the underlying logic of the Standard Defense Force Concept. The question inevitably arises of whether this omission will be remedied, particularly if developments outside the defense establishment increase Japan's ability to create nuclear-armed forces.

In this connection, Japan's civil nuclear energy program is obviously of interest. Two other civil programs, the space program and the nuclear-powered ship program, deserve at least brief examination: the first, because the technology acquired in developing missiles for scientific research could be applied to the design of nuclear-armed strategic missiles; the second, because a Japanese nuclear deterrent might well take the form of nuclear-powered missile-firing submarines.

The Civil Nuclear Energy Program

Japan is one of the leading nations in the field of nuclear energy. Its installed nuclear generating capacity of 15,000 megawatts (electric) in late 1979 was greater than that of any other country except the United States.[9] By 1985 Japan is expected to have a nuclear generating capacity

9. International Nuclear Fuel Cycle Evaluation, *Fuel and Heavy Water Availability,* Report of Working Group 1, INFCE/PC/2/1 (INFCE, 1980), p. 44.

of 26,000 megawatts (electric) and to rely on nuclear power plants for 5.4 percent of its total energy requirements.[10] By 1990 nuclear generating capacity is projected to increase to 45,000 megawatts (electric).[11]

Japan's interest in nuclear energy is not surprising in view of its heavy dependence on imported oil and its unsettling experience with the 1973–74 Arab oil embargo. In 1977 imported oil accounted for 75 percent of Japan's total energy supply.[12] Prospects for reducing this dependence by developing domestic sources of energy are poor. All domestic energy sources combined—coal, hydropower, oil, natural gas, and geothermal power—currently provide Japan with only about one-tenth of its energy, and that fraction is expected to decline slowly.[13]

If Japan is to reduce its dependence on imported oil, it must shift some energy consumption to other imported energy materials, such as coal, liquefied natural gas, and nuclear fuel. Japan does plan to increase its imports of all three. It is especially attracted to nuclear energy, because the foreign exchange cost of fuel is a relatively small fraction of the value of the energy (electricity) produced and because nuclear fuel is more easily transported and stockpiled than hydrocarbons. Also, problems involved in obtaining and using increased amounts of imported coal and natural gas set limits on the substitution of these fuels for imported oil.

Thus far, the development of nuclear energy has to only a minor degree diversified Japan's dependence on imported energy materials but has in no way reduced that dependence. Japan must still buy virtually all of the natural uranium needed to fuel its nuclear power stations from other

10. Ministry of International Trade and Industry, *Energy in Japan: Facts and Figures* (Tokyo: MITI, 1978), table 8 (reference case), p. 20.

11. *Atoms in Japan*, vol. 21 (September 1977), table 2, p. 46. This is the minimum forecast in the interim report of the policy study group of the committee for energy that advises the minister of international trade and industry. The maximum forecast of the same group (on the assumption of "maximum efforts") is 60,000 megawatts (electric) of nuclear generating capacity in 1990. If the larger capacity is achieved, nuclear power could supply over 10 percent of Japan's energy requirements in 1990.

A recent, more pessimistic estimate by the U.S. Department of Energy projects a capacity for Japan of 17 gigawatts (electric) in 1985 and 27 gigawatts (electric) in 1990. U.S. Department of Energy, "International Energy Evaluation Series," Mid-Range Forecast (series C), May 1979.

12. Institute of Energy Economics, *Energy in Japan,* Quarterly Report 43 (December 1978), table 5, p. 15.

13. Ministry of International Trade and Industry, "Materials on Nuclear Industry" (February 1977), p. 3.

countries (principally Canada), and it must send that uranium elsewhere (principally to the United States) to be enriched. If Japan wishes to have its spent nuclear fuel reprocessed to extract the residual uranium and the plutonium, only a small part of the spent fuel generated each year can be reprocessed at home. The bulk of it must be sent to France and England.

Japan can do little to reduce its dependence on foreign natural uranium; its own uranium reserves are estimated to be only 9,000 tons (U_3O_8),[14] or less than one year's projected requirements in the mid-1980s. Official Japanese estimates of future sources of natural uranium through 2000 (see table 2-2) apparently make no allowance for domestic production.

As the table suggests, Japan plans to increase the proportion of its natural uranium supplies obtained from overseas development projects of Japanese firms. Recycled uranium from reprocessed spent fuel will provide a significant fraction of total requirements by the 1990s. Even though the recycled uranium was originally imported and would have to be enriched again before being recycled in light water reactors (LWRs), it can be regarded as a quasi-domestic source of fuel to the extent that the reprocessing is done in Japan.

Drastically reducing or even eliminating dependence on other countries for enrichment and reprocessing services is a feasible goal for Japan. There is no doubt about Japan's ability to develop the technology and mobilize the capital needed to build its own enrichment and reprocessing facilities. As shown in table 2-2, Japan plans to do all its own reprocessing and to reduce its dependence on foreign enrichment services by the mid-1990s.[15]

A pilot reprocessing plant with a capacity of 0.7 ton a day began oper-

14. *PNC* (Tokyo, n.d.), p. 20 (*PNC* is a brochure describing the programs of the Power Reactor and Nuclear Fuel Development Corporation).

15. The construction of some heavy water reactors (the Canadian deuterium and uranium reactor, CANDU) that use natural uranium was under consideration beginning in late 1978 (see "MITI Needs to Hold More Talks as to Employing CANDU," *Japan Economic Journal,* vol. 16 [November 21, 1978], p. 4; and "Report on HWRs Submitted but Reactor Policy Debate Continuing," *Atoms in Japan,* vol. 22 [December 1978], pp. 17–21). In August 1979, however, the Japanese Atomic Energy Commission recommended against the CANDU, apparently on the ground that it might interfere with development of the Japanese-designed advanced thermal reactor. " 'No' to CANDU Reactor," *Japan Economic Journal,* vol. 17 (July 24, 1979), p. 10; and "AEC Rules Against Import of CANDU," *Japan Times* (August 11, 1979), p. 5.

Table 2-2. *Estimated Japanese Demand for and Sources of Natural Uranium, Enriched Uranium, and Reprocessing Services, 1980–2000*

Item	1980	1985	1990	1995	2000
Assumed nuclear generating capacity[a] (gigawatts [electric])	15.5	33.0	60.0	100.0	150.0
Natural uranium[b] (short tons of U_3O_8)					
Annual demand	3,300	10,000	17,300	25,500	32,800
Annual supplies	9,800	11,100	10,100	13,100	17,200
Long-term foreign contracts	8,700	9,000	4,200	1,000	0
Overseas development projects	1,100	1,800	3,800	5,800	6,700
Recycled uranium	0	300	2,100	6,300	10,500
Enriched uranium[b] (tons SWU^c)					
Annual demand	1,600	3,800	6,600	10,000	13,700
Annual supplies	3,500	6,630	8,500	11,900	16,900
Foreign	3,500	6,600	5,500	5,500	5,500
Joint venture	0	0	1,000	1,000	2,000
Domestic	0	0	1,000	3,000	5,000
Recycled plutonium	0	30	1,000	2,400	4,400
Reprocessing services[d] (tons of uranium)					
Annual demand	280	450	1,100	2,140	3,200
Annual supplies	350	460	1,550	2,400	3,600
Foreign	230	260	890	0	0
Domestic	120	200	660	2,400	3,600

Source: Ministry of International Trade and Industry, Research Committee on Nuclear Fuel, "Interim Report on the Results of Study on the Nuclear Fuel Cycle," summarized in *Atoms in Japan*, vol. 22 (September 1978), pp. 27–34.

a. The assumed nuclear generating capacities shown are the maximum projections of the policy study group of the Advisory Committee for Energy, Ministry of International Trade and Industry. (See *Atoms in Japan*, vol. 21 [September 1977], p. 46.) To the extent that these projections are not realized, requirements for natural uranium, enriched uranium, and reprocessing services will of course be correspondingly reduced. As was indicated in the text, 26 gigawatts (electric) would be a more reasonable estimate for 1985 and 45 gigawatts for 1990.

b. The table indicates that Japan plans to add to its stockpile of natural uranium through 1985 and to its stockpile of enriched uranium through 2000. The gap between requirements for and supplies of natural uranium does not indicate a planned drawdown of stocks, but results from the table's showing only those supplies ensured under existing foreign contracts.

c. Separative work units (SWU) measure the amount of work of which an enrichment plant is capable. They are expressed in units of mass (tons or kilograms).

d. The table shows, under reprocessing services, that through 2000 Japan will be reducing an accumulation of spent fuel from the 1970s.

ations in late 1977.[16] Its principal function is to refine the reprocessing technology that will be used in a second plant scheduled to begin operations in 1990. A third plant is to open in 1993 and a fourth in 1998.

16. By agreement with the United States (see pp. 28–29), this plant was to operate at about half its capacity during the International Nuclear Fuel Cycle Evaluation. It was shut down for about a year because of a radioactive leak. *Japan Economic Journal* (March 6, 1976), p. 7.

These plants will be full-scale commercial facilities. Each will have a capacity of 5.0 tons a day.[17]

The Japanese are interested in reprocessing for two reasons: to facilitate the management of spent fuel and the disposal of nuclear waste by separating different categories of waste products; and to obtain plutonium and residual uranium for recycling in nuclear power plants. Recycling of residual uranium in existing light water reactors is to begin in 1984. Recycling of plutonium in the advanced thermal reactors (ATRs) currently under development is scheduled to begin in 1991.[18] Some experimental use of plutonium in LWRs is also contemplated in the next few years. Late in this century or early in the next century, the fast breeder reactors (FBRs) also under development will become both the major sources of plutonium in spent fuel and the major consumers of plutonium extracted from such fuel.[19]

The Japanese have been working on the centrifuge enrichment process since 1964. The first experimental cascade was operated successfully in the early 1970s.[20] A small pilot plant with a capacity of 70 or 80 tons separative work units (SWU) is scheduled to open in 1981. A demonstration plant with a capacity of 300–500 tons SWU should be ready by about 1984. A full-scale commercial plant with an annual capacity of 1,000 tons SWU is to begin operations in 1988. Capacity is to be progressively increased in subsequent years, reaching 5,000 tons SWU in 2000.[21]

In short, Japan today is firmly committed to a long-term program of developing and expanding its nuclear energy industry. A central feature of that program is the establishment of "a proper nuclear fuel cycle con-

17. Ministry of International Trade and Industry, Research Committee on Nuclear Fuel, "Interim Report on the Results of Study on the Nuclear Fuel Cycle," summarized in *Atoms in Japan*, vol. 22 (September 1978), pp. 27–34.

18. The prototype ATR "Fugen" reportedly achieved full power operation of 16.5 megawatts (electric) on November 13, 1978. " 'Fugen' Attains Full Power Operation," *Atoms in Japan*, vol. 22 (December 1978), p. 27.

19. Ibid., and author's conversations with Japanese officials in Tokyo, November 1977 and January 1979.

20. *PNC*, p. 19.

21. Summary of "Interim Report," p. 32; "Uranium Enriching with Domestic Process Starts," *Japan Economic Journal* (September 18, 1979), p. 1; and conversations with Japanese officials.

forming to Japan's own needs."[22] As in a number of other countries, local opposition to the construction of nuclear power stations has caused that central part of the program to fall behind schedule,[23] but this has not deflected the government from its objective of obtaining an increasing share of Japan's energy needs from nuclear power. Moreover, efforts to close the fuel cycle, reduce Japan's dependence on foreign enrichment and reprocessing services, and develop ATRs and FBRs using plutonium appear to be progressing.

The Space Program

The Japanese space program began on a modest scale in 1955 when the University of Tokyo decided to develop sounding rockets to conduct observations in the upper atmosphere as part of Japan's participation in the International Geophysical Year (1957–58). Fifteen years later, in February 1970, the university's Institute of Space and Aeronautical Science (ISAS, established in 1964) succeeded in putting Japan's first satellite into orbit. The Japanese space program is now a large, complex effort emphasizing both scientific research and practical applications.[24]

The ISAS is still entrusted with the scientific aspects of the program. Practical applications are carried out by the National Space Development Agency (NASDA). The Space Activities Commission is responsible for planning and coordinating the space program. In Japanese fiscal year 1976, the space activities budget exceeded 88 billion yen, or about $300 million.

A good overview of the Japanese space program can be obtained by examining the successful launches of satellites since the first one in

22. Summary of the December 1976 White Paper on Atomic Energy in "Two White Papers Issued," *Atoms in Japan,* vol. 20 (December 1976), pp. 24–37. See also "Contents of Report Made by Atomic Energy Department of the Energy Research Council," summarized in *Nihon Keizai,* October 25, 1978 (translated in American Embassy, Tokyo, "Daily Summary of Japanese Press," November 7, 1978, pp. 1–4).

23. Further delays may be caused by reactions to the accident at Three Mile Island. *Nihon Keizai,* August 1, 1979 (translated in "Daily Summary of Japanese Press," August 4–6, 1979, p. 1).

24. The principal source on the Japanese space program used in this study is Science and Technology Agency, *Space in Japan, 1976–77* (Tokyo: Federation of Economic Organizations [Keidanren], 1976).

February 1970 and the plans for more launches in the next few years. Table 2-3 shows that past launches have been for two broad purposes: scientific research and the improvement of rocket and satellite technology. The weight of satellites put into orbit by Japanese rockets between 1970 and 1976 increased nearly sixfold, from 24 kilograms to 139 kilograms. Table 2-4 indicates that the dual nature of the Japanese space program will continue into the 1980s, using M rockets for scientific satellites and N rockets for applications satellites.

The M (or Mu) rocket represents a further development of the L (or Lambda) rocket that put Japan's first satellite into orbit.[25] The M is a four-stage, solid-propellant rocket with an overall length of 23.567 meters and a launch weight of 43.8 tons. Its thrust at liftoff (including its eight strap-on boosters) is 200 tons. It is comparable to military rockets capable of carrying a 1,000-pound warhead 5,000 nautical miles. It is, however, only a semiguided rocket and cannot be controlled with any precision.

The N rocket is a three-stage, radio-guided rocket using a liquid propellant for the first and second stages and a solid propellant for the third stage.[26] The first stage is the U.S.-designed Thor Delta (1968 model), partially produced in Japan.[27] The N rocket is 32.57 meters long and weighs approximately 90 tons. Its thrust at liftoff (including three strap-on boosters) is approximately 150 tons. The N has a better guidance system than the M.[28]

The N rocket can put a 130-kilogram satellite into geostationary orbit; the NASDA is developing an improved version of the N rocket that will be able to place satellites weighing several hundred kilograms into geostationary orbit.[29] An effort to develop a "large liquid hydrogen launch vehicle" by the mid-1980s is also under way. It is hoped that further

25. For technical descriptions of the L and M rockets, see John E. Endicott, *Japan's Nuclear Option: Political, Technical, and Strategic Factors* (Praeger, 1975), pp. 247–51.

26. For a technical description of the N rocket, see Science and Technology Agency, *Space in Japan, 1976–77,* pp. 45–46; and National Space Development Agency of Japan, *NASDA, 1976–77,* pp. 15–16.

27. Endicott, *Japan's Nuclear Option,* p. 256.

28. The advanced N-1 and N-2 models contain significant improvements, including "black box" inertial guidance provided by NASA contractors with U.S. government approval (communication from American Embassy, Tokyo, July 17, 1978).

29. *NASDA, 1976–77,* p. 15.

Table 2-3. *Successful Launches of Japanese Satellites, 1970–78*[a]

Satellite	Launch date	Weight (kilograms)	Launching vehicle	Mission
Osumi	Feb. 1970	24	L-4S-5	Preliminary launching test for the following M launch vehicle
Tansei (MS-T1)	Feb. 1971	63	M-4S-2	Testing of housekeeping and function of the instrument system aboard satellites
Shinsei (scientific satellite 1)	Sept. 1971	65	M-4S-3	Observation of the HF solar radio wave emission, ionospheric plasma, and cosmic rays
Denpa (scientific satellite 2)	Aug. 1972	75	M-4S-4	Observation of plasma waves, plasma density, electron particle rays, electromagnetic waves, and geomagnetism
Tansei-II (MS-T2)	Feb. 1974	56	M-3C-1	Measurement of characteristic of launch vehicle and engineering test on satellite
Taiyo (scientific satellite 3)	Feb. 1975	86	M-3C-2	Observation of solar soft X-rays, solar vacuum, ultraviolet radiation, ultraviolet terrestrial corona lines, and so forth
Kiku (JETS-1)	Sept. 1975	83	N	Confirming launching technology, satellite tracking, and controlling technology; testing of antenna extension; and so forth
Ume (JISS)	Feb. 1976	139	N	Observation of worldwide distribution of critical frequencies of ionosphere, and so forth
Scientific satellite 5 (EXOS-A)	Feb. 1977	125	M-3H	Measurement of electron density and temperatures; observation of distribution of electron energies, aurora particles; and so forth
Kiku-2 (ETS-II)	Feb. 1977	130	N-3	Confirming technology for launching geostationary satellites; tracking and controlling geostationary satellites; and so forth
UME-2 (ISS-b)	Feb. 1978	141	N-4	Observation of worldwide distribution of critical frequencies of ionosphere, and so forth
CORSA-b	Feb. 1978	n.a.	M-3C	Study of X-ray stars, gamma ray bursts, and so forth
EXOS-B	Sept. 1978	80	M-3H	Measurement of electron density particles, plasma waves, and so forth

Source: Science and Technology Agency, *Space in Japan, 1976–77* (Tokyo: Federation of Economic Organizations [Keidanren], 1976), pp. 182–83; updated by information supplied by the Embassy of Japan, Washington, D.C., and by the American Embassy, Tokyo.

n.a. Not available.

a. Launches of Japanese satellites by the U.S. National Aeronautics and Space Administration are not shown.

Table 2-4. *Japanese Satellite Program, 1979–84*[a]

Satellite	Launching year (fiscal)	Approximate weight (kilograms)	Launching vehicle	Mission
Scientific				
MS-T4	1979	n.a.	M-3S	Testing spacecraft
ASTRO-A	1980	120	M-3S	Observation of solar hard X-ray flares, solar particles, X-ray bursts, and so forth
ASTRO-B	1982	120	M-3S	Observation of X-ray stars, gamma ray bursts, soft X-ray nebulae, and so forth
Application				
ETS-IV	1980	n.a.	N-II	Developing technology
GMS-II	1981	n.a.	N	Meteorological observations; geostationary orbit
ETS-III	1981	n.a.	N	Developing technology
GS	1982	n.a.	N	Geodetic surveys
MOS-1[b]	1984	n.a.	N-II	Testing temperature of sea surface and atmosphere

Source: *Space in Japan, 1976–77*, p. 183; modified and supplemented by information supplied by the Embassy of Japan, Washington, D.C.

n.a. Not available.

a. As of March 1978. Planned launches of Japanese satellites by the U.S. National Aeronautics and Space Administration are not shown.

b. Maritime observation satellite.

refinement of the technology acquired in developing this vehicle will yield an advanced vehicle capable of putting 10–15 tons into "low earth orbit" in the 1990s.[30]

Japan plans to use its improved space rockets to launch both larger satellites and manned spacecraft. Japan does not intend to be left behind other technologically advanced nations in the expansion of space activities. The long-range plans of the Space Activities Commission include Japanese participation on either a national or an international basis in a wide range of space projects, including the establishment of observation stations in space, a "space lighthouse," a "communications tower" in space, space laboratories, and plants in space to produce new materials.[31]

Two conclusions relevant to this study emerge from the brief review of the Japanese space program. First, the program is directed toward ra-

30. Special Committee on Long-Range Prospects, Space Activities Commission, *Long-Range Prospects of Japanese Space Development,* vol. 1: *General* (July 1977; unofficial translation), p. 25.

31. Ibid., especially pp. 21–24.

tional, nonmilitary goals. Second, the advances that Japan has already made in rocket technology and the further advances that it can be expected to make would be most useful in developing missiles to deliver nuclear weapons.

The Nuclear Ship Program

In 1963 the Japan Nuclear Ship Development Agency was established and charged with the design and construction of a nuclear-powered ship.[32] The first—and thus far the only—nuclear ship, the *Mutsu,* was launched in June 1969 and moved in the following year to its designated home port, Mutsu City in Aomori prefecture. Installation of the ship's nuclear reactor was completed in August 1972.

Testing of the reactor on shipboard was delayed by local opposition. In August 1974 the ship was moved 800 kilometers from shore and testing begun. When only 1.4 percent of capacity had been reached, a small amount of radiation "shine" was detected. The test was suspended, and the ship later returned to Mutsu City. The local authorities refused to permit operation of the reactor in the harbor and demanded that a new home port be found.[33]

Great difficulty was encountered in getting another port to accept the *Mutsu* for reinforcement of its defective shielding. In July 1978, however, the head of the Science and Technology Agency announced that the ship would be moved to a shipyard in Sasebo. This was done in October 1978.[34] The move to Sasebo was strongly opposed by local antinuclear elements, but the central government had considerable influence over the local government because its financial help was needed to save the shipyard in question from bankruptcy.[35]

The future of the nuclear ship program remains in doubt.[36] The Japa-

32. The information on the nuclear ship program presented here is drawn principally from Japan Atomic Energy Relations Organization, *Summary of Japan's Atomic Energy Development* (Tokyo: JAERO, 1977), pp. 38–40.

33. For a detailed account of the *Mutsu*'s problems, see Dane Lee Miller, "Drifting Ship, Drifting Government: The *Mutsu* Affair," *Japan Interpreter,* vol. 12 (Spring 1978), pp. 201–22.

34. *New York Times,* July 19, 1978; *Washington Post,* October 17, 1978.

35. *Nuclear Engineering International* (June 1978), p. 7.

36. Repairing the *Mutsu* will take three years, after which it must be moved to a new home port that will be difficult to find. "The NS 'Mutsu' Arrives at Sasebo Port,"

nese have presumably learned something about the application of nuclear power to ship propulsion. Further work would probably be required, however, to develop a power plant small enough for use on submarines.

Present Policies on Nuclear Questions

In January 1968 Prime Minister Eisaku Sato set forth four general principles that have continued to guide Japan's nuclear policies: (1) to develop nuclear energy for peaceful purposes only; (2) to encourage nuclear disarmament; (3) not to possess, produce, or bring nuclear weapons into Japan; and (4) to rely on the U.S. nuclear umbrella to deter nuclear attack.[37] Although these four principles are interconnected and are regarded as parts of an integrated policy, attention is usually focused both in Japan and elsewhere on the third principle, which is commonly referred to as the three nonnuclear principles.

The Japanese government has on a number of occasions declared that the three nonnuclear principles are not mandated by the constitution but represent a policy decision that could in theory be revised. Government spokesmen have argued that the constitution permits Japan to possess weapons only to the extent necessary for self-defense and that such weapons can be either conventional or nuclear. The government has always made clear that it has no intention of abandoning its policy against the possession, production, or introduction of nuclear weapons into the country.[38]

The three nonnuclear principles are so clear and unequivocal that applying them would appear to be quite easy. This has not always been the case, however. The declaration against bringing nuclear weapons into

---

Atoms in Japan, vol. 22 (October 1978), pp. 19–21. It would be premature, however, to conclude that the nuclear ship program is dead. On February 2, 1979, the Japanese Atomic Energy Commission established an Advisory Committee on Research and Development of Nuclear Ships. "Nuclear Ship Development in Japan," *Atoms in Japan,* vol. 23 (February 1979), p. 26.

37. Cited by Daniel I. Okimoto, "Japan's Non-Nuclear Policy: The Problem of the NPT," *Asian Survey,* vol. 15 (April 1975), pp. 313–27.

38. See, for example, "Government's Unified View Reveals Possession of Nuclear Weapons to Meet Minimum Requirements for Self-Defense Is Constitutional," *Yomiuri,* March 9, 1978, p. 1 (translated in "Daily Summary of Japanese Press," March 18–20, 1978, p. 15).

the country as applied to U.S. warships entering Japanese ports has proved especially troublesome. The U.S. government, following established policy, will neither confirm nor deny suspicions expressed by some Japanese (and occasionally supported by unofficial U.S. sources) that some of these ships carry nuclear weapons. The Japanese government has done its best to ignore the question, but if pressed would probably argue that nuclear weapons on U.S. warships are merely in transit and are not being introduced into Japan.

Contrary to what might have been expected, the three nonnuclear principles did not lead Japan to sign and ratify the Treaty on the Non-Proliferation of Nuclear Weapons quickly. Japan waited eighteen months before signing the treaty and in doing so registered a number of reservations. Another six years passed before the Diet ratified the treaty.[39]

Japan's hesitation about the NPT did not reflect vacillation on the part of the majority of the public or the members of the Diet on the question of acquiring nuclear weapons. A minority did argue that the nuclear option should be kept open, and there was a vague but pervasive uneasiness concerning the long-term consequences of renouncing nuclear weapons. The reasons for Japan's delay were indicated in the conditions for ratification that Japan specified in 1970 when it signed the NPT: (1) concrete steps toward disarmament by the states having nuclear weapons; (2) protection of the security interests of the states not having nuclear weapons; and (3) development of a fair and equal system of international safeguards.[40]

Whether the first of these three conditions has been satisfied is a matter for debate in Japan and elsewhere. The second condition focused on the U.S.-Japan security relationship, rather than on the security of non-nuclear weapons states in general. Thus in March 1975 key elements of the ruling Liberal Democratic party (LDP) agreed that the NPT would be submitted to the Diet for ratification if Foreign Minister Kiichi Miyazawa succeeded in a forthcoming trip to Washington in obtaining a reconfirmation of the U.S. commitment to the U.S.-Japan mutual security treaty. The reconfirmation was obtained and the treaty was submitted to

39. Two complementary articles give a good analytical review of Japan's handling of the NPT issue: Okimoto, "Japan's Non-Nuclear Policy," and John E. Endicott, "The 1975–76 Debate over Ratification of the NPT in Japan," *Asian Survey*, vol. 17 (March 1977), pp. 275–92.

40. Okimoto, "Japan's Non-Nuclear Policy," pp. 314–15.

the Diet, although, for a variety of reasons, it was not ratified until more than a year later.[41]

The third condition—the need for a fair and equal system of international safeguards—actually reflected concern that the NPT might in some way hinder Japan's civil nuclear energy program.[42] The specific Japanese condition about safeguards was satisfied by the development of less intrusive techniques by the International Atomic Energy Agency and by the negotiation of a safeguards agreement with the IAEA that gave Japan equality with Euratom. Concern about the effect of the NPT on the civil nuclear energy program was superseded by fear that Japan might have difficulty in obtaining nuclear fuel or exporting nuclear equipment if it did *not* adhere to the NPT. This fear was occasioned by renewed pressure on Japan to ratify the NPT by several nations, including the United States, the Soviet Union, and Canada, after the Indian nuclear test in May 1974.

In ratifying the NPT in mid-1976, Japan clearly thought that it was joining an international system within which it could continue to develop the peaceful uses of nuclear energy without external hindrance. Before the year was out, developments in the United States, from which Japan obtains most of its enriched uranium, made that assumption less certain. In October, President Ford issued a statement on nuclear policy that focused on the dangers of reprocessing, deferred reprocessing in the United States, and called on other countries to declare a three-year moratorium on the transfer of enrichment and reprocessing facilities and technology.[43] His opponent in the presidential campaign had previously been even more skeptical about the wisdom of moving into the plutonium economy and carrying out plans to deploy fast breeder reactors.

These positions by the leaders of the two chief U.S. political parties were seen in Tokyo as a direct challenge to the assumption underlying Japan's nuclear energy program, namely, that the nuclear fuel cycle would be closed and that breeder reactors, generating and using plutonium, would be a major future source of energy. The sudden shift in U.S.

41. Endicott, "Debate over Ratification," pp. 281–82.

42. In January 1975, when the LDP Security Affairs Research Council repeated the need for satisfying the 1970 conditions for ratification of the NPT, it broadened the third condition and called for "substantial equality in the field of utilizing atomic energy for peaceful purposes." Ibid., p. 277.

43. Press release, Office of the White House Press Secretary, "Statement by the President on Nuclear Policy," October 28, 1976.

policy was also a threat to Japan's political leadership and to its nuclear energy establishment, which had asked the Japanese people to accept a program, about which they were profoundly uneasy, on the ground that it would solve Japan's long-term energy problem. If there were to be no breeders and no plutonium economy, the age of nuclear energy might last only a few decades, and the government's rationale for the program would be destroyed.

The difference between U.S. and Japanese nuclear energy policies is much more than a matter for philosophical debate. The agreement for nuclear energy cooperation between the two countries requires Japan to obtain U.S. approval if it wishes to reprocess nuclear fuel of U.S. origin.[44] Therefore, when Japan let it be known in early 1977 that it proposed to begin operation of its French-designed pilot reprocessing plant at Tokai-Mura in July, the new Carter administration faced a difficult problem. President Carter repeated his concern about the dangers of using plutonium as a source of energy in a major policy statement in April 1977, in which he also called for an international nuclear fuel cycle evaluation to deal with the threatened spread of nuclear weapons.[45] Approving the opening of the Tokai-Mura plant could both undermine the credibility of the president's policy and set an undesirable precedent. On the other hand, blocking the opening of that plant—which had been built with U.S. encouragement—would be viewed by the Japanese as an arbitrary and unjustified interference with their efforts to develop nuclear energy as a means of reducing their heavy dependence on imported oil.

Tokai-Mura remained a major issue between Japan and the United States through the spring and summer of 1977.[46] President Carter and Prime Minister Takeo Fukuda discussed it twice. At one point, the differences between the two sides became so sharp that the chief Japanese negotiator publicly accused the United States of bad faith. In September, however, a compromise was reached that largely acceded to Japanese wishes.[47]

44. 19 U.S.T. 5214, article VIII, paragraph C.
45. White House press release of April 7, *Department of State Bulletin* (May 2, 1977), pp. 429–33.
46. The summary of the Tokai-Mura negotiations presented here is based principally on reporting in the Japanese press.
47. "Japan-U.S. Joint Communique on the Operation of the Tokai Reprocessing Facility," *Atoms in Japan,* vol. 21 (September 1977), pp. 17–20.

The two sides agreed that the Tokai-Mura plant could reprocess up to ninety-nine tons of spent fuel of U.S. origin for the next two years. (The Japanese had planned to operate the plant at about that level.) During the two-year period, the Japanese would conduct research on the co-processing method, which produces a mixture of uranium and plutonium oxides usable as nuclear fuel but not directly usable in nuclear weapons. If *both* Japan and the United States later agree that the coprocessing method is technically feasible and effective, the plant will be converted to that method. (Japanese agreement appears unlikely since in the course of the negotiations the Japanese side argued that converting the plant to another method would be prohibitively costly in both time and money.) The Japanese further agreed that for the two-year period they would not (1) use plutonium in commercial light water reactors, (2) construct a plutonium conversion plant, which would convert the plutonium nitrate produced by the Tokai-Mura plant to plutonium oxide, or (3) make any major moves toward the construction of a second, commercial-scale reprocessing plant. (The Japanese had never intended to take the first and third of these actions in the two-year period.) Deferring the second action is a significant inconvenience since plutonium oxide is needed in the ATR and FBR development programs. Also, tanks must be built to store plutonium nitrate, which is a liquid. Plutonium oxide is a solid.

The agreement reached in September 1977 in effect postponed a more definitive resolution of the Tokai-Mura problem until after completion of the International Nuclear Fuel Cycle Evaluation (INFCE), which was launched at a meeting in Washington in October 1977 and concluded in February 1980. Shortly before the conclusion, the U.S. government decided to extend the agreement for another year.[48]

Deferring resolution of the Tokai-Mura problem did not, however, ensure a period of peace on nuclear energy questions between the United States and Japan. In 1975 the Japanese electric utility companies had contracted jointly with British Nuclear Fuels, Limited (BNFL), and Compagnie Générale des Matières Nucléaires (COGEMA) for the reprocessing of 1,600 tons of spent fuel over the period 1977–82. In September 1977 and May 1978 the Japanese entered into separate contracts with BNFL and COGEMA under which the two European firms would

48. *Nihon Keizai* (February 15, 1980), p. 1 (translated in "Daily Summary of Japanese Press," February 26, 1980, p. 5).

reprocess a total of 3,200 tons of spent fuel over the period 1982–90.[49] Since the spent fuel in question is almost entirely of U.S. origin, the United States can, if it wishes, block execution of the reprocessing contracts, although this would precipitate a crisis in U.S. relations with the United Kingdom and France, as well as with Japan. The U.S. government has thus far handled this problem case by case without promulgating general criteria for approving or disapproving applications to ship spent fuel from Japan to France or the United Kingdom for reprocessing.

The Nuclear Non-Proliferation Act of 1978, which was signed by President Carter on March 9, threatens to create additional difficulties between Japan and the United States. The act requires the president to renegotiate agreements for cooperation with other countries to bring those agreements into conformity with the act's provisions.[50] The principal change reportedly sought by the United States is prior approval of the enrichment of nuclear material supplied by it.[51] The Japanese fear that the United States would use this authority to block construction of a national enrichment plant in Japan.[52]

Japan's problems in carrying out its nuclear program have not been limited to the United States. Canada, Japan's principal source of natural uranium, has demanded and obtained control over the disposition of natural uranium purchased from Canada. Canadian approval will be required both for reprocessing and for enrichment above 20 percent U-235.[53] Australia has also proposed that its agreement with Japan be revised to require its prior consent to the transfer of nuclear materials to a third country for enrichment or reprocessing.[54]

Possible Future Policies on Nuclear Questions

Japan's policies on both nuclear weapons and civil nuclear energy are well established and appear well suited to the nation's present situation

49. Ibid. (January 24, 1978), p. 2 (translated in "Daily Summary of Japanese Press," January 31, 1978, p. 3); and *New York Times,* May 25, 1978.

50. 92 Stat. 147.

51. *Atoms in Japan,* vol. 23 (February 1979), p. 34.

52. "U.S. Opposes Uranium Enrichment; Nuclear Fuel Cycle Plan in Pinch," *Yomiuri* (January 23, 1979), p. 1 (translated in "Daily Summary of Japanese Press," January 25, 1979, p. 6).

53. *Nihon Keizai* (January 24, 1978), p. 2 (translated in "Daily Summary of Japanese Press," January 31, 1978, p. 1); and *Toronto Globe and Mail,* January 27, 1978.

54. *Atoms in Japan,* vol. 23 (January 1979), p. 32.

in the world. All policies, however, are subject to change in response to shifting circumstances, and there is no reason to assume that Japan's nuclear policies are immutable.

Nuclear Weapons

Japan's firm commitment not to acquire nuclear weapons seems unlikely to be changed by purely domestic forces. All political parties and a majority of the public support this commitment.

If the slow erosion of electoral support for the ruling Liberal Democratic party continues—which is by no means certain—and if the LDP is forced into a coalition with elements of the political opposition, the policy against acquiring nuclear weapons would not be directly affected and might even be strengthened somewhat, at least in the short run. This is because the opposition parties are even more unified in their opposition to nuclear weapons than the LDP,[55] some of whose extreme right wing favor nuclear weapons. Also, a coalition government would have even more difficulty making a drastic shift of policy concerning nuclear weapons than a single-party government would.

A change in Japan's present policy against the acquisition of nuclear weapons would be opposed by a large majority of the Japanese public.[56] In a 1976 poll 64 percent thought that it would be undesirable for Japan to have its own nuclear weapons, and only 9 percent thought it would be desirable. About the same proportion (66 percent) in a 1973 poll thought it unnecessary for Japan to have its own nuclear weapons, but a much larger group (20 percent) thought it necessary. This difference in the two polls may be less significant than the increase in the number who were uncertain or did not know, from 14 percent in 1973 to 27 percent in 1976.

The 1973 and 1976 polls also revealed increasing uncertainty about whether Japan would have nuclear weapons in the future. The proportion expressing the view that Japan will have nuclear weapons remained

55. For a description of the positions of the opposition parties, see Endicott, *Japan's Nuclear Option*, pp. 78–86. Endicott also reproduces (p. 99) a 1972 *Mainichi* poll showing the percentages of the members of various parties absolutely opposed to Japan's acquiring nuclear weapons at any time: LDP, 45; Japan Socialist party, 65; Komeito, 68; Democratic Socialist party, 61; and Japan Communist party, 80.

56. The public opinion surveys cited here were conducted by *Sankei*. Information on the results of the surveys was provided by the U.S. Information Agency (now the International Communication Agency).

virtually unchanged—28 percent in 1973 and 27 percent in 1976—but the proportion of those taking the opposite view fell, from 42 percent to 29 percent, and the proportion of those that were uncertain or did not know rose, from 30 percent to 44 percent.

It is possible to read too much into the fact that over a quarter of the Japanese public has no opinion on the desirability of acquiring nuclear weapons and nearly half takes no position on the likelihood of Japan's acquiring such weapons. A large "can't say" or "don't know" response is not unheard of in polls in Japan.[57] Nevertheless, it is somewhat surprising to find this degree of public uncertainty on an issue as filled with emotion as the acquisition of nuclear weapons must be.

Uncertainty may in this case reflect uneasiness. Another 1976 poll asked respondents whether they felt uneasy that Japan did not have its own nuclear weapons. Forty-eight percent answered that they felt either "quite a bit" or "somewhat" uneasy. Forty-five percent felt little or no uneasiness, and only 7 percent did not know. The size of the uneasy group was much smaller (34 percent) in a similar poll taken in 1974, and the size of the undisturbed group much larger (63 percent). A 1972 poll, however, produced results closer to those of 1976, with 42 percent uneasy and 56 percent not.

Japanese public opinion on other defense issues appears to be undergoing some change. In 1973, 58 percent thought it was better to have the Self Defense Forces than not to have them. In 1977 this percentage had risen to a remarkable 83 percent. Over the 1972–76 period, support for an (unspecified) expansion of the SDF rose from 19 percent to 50 percent.

These and other polls that might have been cited suggest that, while the government's policy against the acquisition of nuclear weapons continues to command strong support, Japanese attitudes on this and other security-related issues could change in response to a major external shock. Or perhaps, to make the point more precisely, if the nation's political leadership decided that a different policy on nuclear weapons

---

57. For example, in a 1977 poll 27 percent took no position on the question of whether defense costs should be increased, decreased, or remain at present levels. On the other hand, in a 1976 poll only 15 percent were uncertain whether Japan would be better off with or without the Self Defense Forces. "JDA's Public Opinion Survey," *Sankei,* October 31, 1977 (translated in "Daily Summary of Japanese Press," November 3–4, 1977, p. 6, and June 20, 1976, p. 5).

was necessary to cope with a more threatening international environment, domestic public opinion would not necessarily stand in the way.

Changes in the International Environment

As noted earlier in this chapter, the 1977, 1978, and 1979 defense white papers listed five areas in which structural changes would be considered important. The possibility that radical changes in any of them would make the Japanese government change its current policy on the acquisition of nuclear weapons is considered below.

THE JAPAN-U.S. SECURITY SYSTEM. The most radical change conceivable in this area would be unilateral termination of the mutual security treaty by the United States. Japan would then have to cope by itself with the potential military threats from the Soviet Union and China. Japan would no doubt do its best to maintain good relations with both of the major communist powers but could not rely on diplomacy alone to ensure the nation's security. Seeking an alliance with either communist power would risk incurring the enmity of the other and would give rise to serious domestic political problems, especially if an alliance with the Soviet Union was proposed.

Under these circumstances, the possibility that Japan might have to provide for its own defense would be certain to receive serious consideration. One question would be whether an autonomous Japanese defense should include nuclear weapons, which could in theory be used either to deter the actual or threatened use of nuclear weapons against Japan (that is, to replace the U.S. nuclear umbrella) or to defend against various kinds of conventional attack—interdiction of sea lines of supply, aerial bombardment, and amphibious invasion. Japan would have to decide not simply whether or not to have nuclear weapons, but whether or not to develop nuclear forces that could perform one or more specific missions.

The most difficult mission would be strategic deterrence of the Soviet Union. This would require the ability to deliver a second strike that would inflict unacceptable damage on the Soviet population or economy.[58] Geography makes achieving such a capability difficult. All of Japan is within range of several existing Soviet nuclear delivery systems—manned

---

58. The evaluation of Japanese strategic options presented here is based largely on the more detailed technical analysis presented in Endicott, *Japan's Nuclear Option,* especially pp. 196–215.

bombers, land-based ballistic missiles, and submarine-launched ballistic missiles (SLBMs). Most of the Soviet centers of population and industry, however, are thousands of miles from Japan, beyond the reach of the planes now in the inventory of the ASDF.

A credible Japanese deterrent force could probably not be land-based, since its ability to survive a Soviet first strike would be questionable. A strategy of launch-on-warning would not be available because warning of an SLBM attack would be almost nonexistent. Japan might conceivably develop a long-range bomber force and keep part of it airborne, but the ability of Japanese bombers to penetrate Soviet air defenses and attack major targets far to the west would at best be doubtful. Stand-off bombers carrying cruise missiles would be more effective,[59] but this option would require Japan to develop propulsion and guidance technologies for such missiles more or less from scratch.

A more attractive option would be to develop nuclear-powered submarines armed with ballistic missiles similar to the U.S. *Polaris* submarines. Such submarines could stay on station for extended periods and would have a good chance of avoiding Soviet surveillance. In developing an SLBM deterrent system, the Japanese could build on experience and facilities acquired in the civil nuclear energy program (for nuclear explosives), the naval shipbuilding program (for experience in building modern teardrop-shaped submarines), and—to a limited extent—the nuclear-powered ship program (for nuclear propulsion).

Endicott has estimated that in eight to thirteen years Japan could develop a force of ten nuclear-powered submarines, each armed with sixteen one-megaton nuclear missiles with a range of 2,500 nautical miles. He put the total cost of such a force at $6.6 billion (1972 U.S. dollars), not including expenditures attributable to the civil nuclear energy program. Annual costs of the SLBM program would peak at about $2.0 billion halfway through the program.[60]

According to Endicott's analysis, four submarines of his hypothetical ten-boat force could be kept on station in the Arabian Sea, from which they could threaten Moscow and twenty-four other large cities.[61] Unless

59. Alton H. Quanbeck and Archie L. Wood, *Modernizing the Bomber Force: Why and How* (Brookings Institution, 1976), especially pp. 93–98.

60. Endicott, *Japan's Nuclear Option,* pp. 218–31. In 1976 dollars, estimated peak expenditures would be approximately $3.3 billion, which may be compared with the $5.1 billion actually budgeted for defense in Japanese fiscal year 1976.

61. Ibid., pp. 206–13.

advances in antisubmarine warfare technology enabled the USSR to destroy the boats on station at will, Japan would be able to deliver a second strike that would be unacceptable to the Soviet Union, especially in the context of its continuing competition with the United States and China. Security of the Japanese submarine force could be increased by the development of longer range missiles, which would permit aiming at the same twenty-five cities from larger patrol areas.[62]

The fact that an SLBM deterrent could be the answer to the loss of the U.S. nuclear umbrella does not mean that Japan would actually choose this course of action. Debate over how to adjust to the assumed termination of the mutual security treaty would be intense, and the advocates of an autonomous defense capability, including a nuclear deterrent, would not necessarily win. Strong sentiment in favor of a policy of lightly armed neutrality would undoubtedly continue to exist, and that point of view could become the dominant one.

Moreover, even those who saw the SLBM deterrent as the solution to Japan's strategic problem might hesitate to commit the nation to that course. The decision to build a force of nuclear-powered submarines armed with nuclear missiles could not be kept secret. For roughly a decade, Japan would therefore be vulnerable to pressure from the Soviet Union (and possibly also from China) to drop its nuclear weapons program. As some Japanese analysts have put it, this would indeed be "a time of danger."

Japan might therefore decide to concentrate on strengthening its defense against conventional attack and indefinitely defer the acquisition of a strategic nuclear capability against the Soviet Union and China. An increase in conventional defense would probably not be regarded as provocative by either of the communist powers. Such a buildup would gradually put an unaligned Japan in a better position to maneuver among the three nuclear-armed powers of the Pacific—the Soviet Union, China, and the United States—and reduce the danger of its being subjected to nuclear blackmail by any one of them.[63]

62. An SLBM deterrent would also be effective against China, since most of China's large cities would be within range of submarines armed with 2,500-mile missiles patrolling off China's east coast.

63. The potential value of conventional military strength to Japan may most clearly be seen by assuming that Japan becomes capable of determining the balance of naval power in the western Pacific. In that event, the Soviet Union would be restrained from applying nuclear pressure on Japan for fear that Japan would again

A somewhat riskier variant of this approach would also defer the acquisition of strategic nuclear weapons such as SLBMs but develop tactical nuclear weapons to strengthen defenses against conventional air bombardment and invasion. Japan could not be sure, however, that the Soviet Union and China (especially the former) would not see such weapons as only the first step toward achieving a strategic nuclear capability. Moreover, Japan could create adequate defenses against conventional air bombardment and invasion without possessing tactical nuclear weapons.[64]

MUTUAL DETERRENCE BETWEEN THE UNITED STATES AND THE SOVIET UNION. Exactly what is meant by the suggestion that a breakdown in mutual deterrence would call for a change in Japan's defense structure is not clear.[65] If nuclear war actually broke out between the superpowers, it would be too late for Japan to do anything about it. Perhaps what is meant is simply the increased likelihood of a U.S.-Soviet war. In that event, Japan would face two serious security problems. First, would the United States shift so much of its naval and air strength to the Atlantic and Western Europe—the main front against the Soviet Union—that it would be incapable of defending Japan, and Japan's supply lines, from conventional Soviet attack? And second, if a nuclear exchange between the United States and the Soviet Union occurred, how could Japan avoid destruction?

In principle, the first problem should lead Japan to build up its conventional forces, especially its antisubmarine warfare capabilities and its air defenses. Whether it would actually do this would depend on whether the public, as well as the government, perceived the problem as a real and urgent one. In any event, this problem does not strengthen the case for the acquisition of nuclear weapons, since Japan would remain allied with the United States and could continue to rely on the U.S. nuclear umbrella.

---

align itself with the United States, thereby both neutralizing the value of Soviet nuclear weapons and putting the Soviet navy in a position inferior to the combined U.S. and Japanese fleets.

64. Whether Japan alone could defend its long sea lines of supply is more questionable, but tactical nuclear weapons would add little to its ability to solve this problem.

65. The second of the five "structural areas" in which "changes would be considered important" is described somewhat obliquely as "efforts to avoid nuclear war and large-scale conflict apt to lead to nuclear war by the United States and the Soviet Union." *Defense of Japan, 1977*, p. 55.

The second problem is much more serious. If a U.S.-Soviet nuclear war were indeed inevitable, the only rational course for Japan would be to terminate its alliance with the United States and seek safety in neutrality. Japan would then face the same questions as those discussed above in connection with the assumed termination of the security treaty by the United States. Should Japan's neutrality be lightly or heavily armed? And if the latter, should Japan's defenses include nuclear weapons?

A lightly armed neutrality would seem most consistent with a policy of seeking safety in the face of an impending global catastrophe. Nuclear weapons would be viewed as more likely to invite destruction than to contribute to national security.

THE SINO-SOVIET DISPUTE. A worsening of relations between China and the Soviet Union to the point of actual war would be disturbing to Japan but would probably not cause any great change in defense policy. Japan's main fear would be interference with its sea communications. That problem could probably be handled successfully, however, with the diplomatic and naval support of the United States.

The Japanese are much more concerned about the possibility of a marked improvement in Sino-Soviet relations. If the two communist powers were to become military allies, the strategic situation in East Asia and the western Pacific would be fundamentally altered. Exploring the full consequences of such a shift in world politics would require a separate study at least as broad as this one. Some of the possible consequences, moreover, while major, would not directly affect Japanese defense policy.[66]

Three of these consequences deserve attention. First, the possibility of an attack by Communist China on Taiwan would increase. Second, the danger of war in Korea might decrease. And third, the strategic position of the Soviet Pacific fleet could be greatly improved.

If Peking did not have to fear war with the Soviet Union, it would be much more likely to seek a military solution of the Taiwan problem.[67]

66. For example, Soviet and Chinese efforts to gain influence in Southeast Asia now partly cancel one another and make it easier for small states there to maintain their independence. If the Soviet Union and China were to work together, their joint influence in the area would grow and might adversely affect Japanese economic interests. But no Japanese military response to such a development would be appropriate.

67. This contingency is explored at greater length in chapter 4.

Peking's most promising military strategy would probably be to try to cut Taiwan's sea and air links with the outside world, which would have an immediate and significant economic effect on Japan.[68] Japan would also fear the effect of military action in the vicinity of Taiwan on air and sea traffic between Japan and other important areas.

If the United States did not intervene to save Taiwan from economic strangulation, Japanese doubts about the permanence of the U.S. interest in East Asia and the western Pacific would be reinforced. The Japanese might derive some comfort from the fact that (after 1979) the United States would not be violating any formal security commitment in not coming to the aid of Taiwan. Their estimate of the long-term value of the U.S. security connection would nevertheless be reduced and the attractions of a more autonomous defense policy correspondingly increased.

If the United States did intervene, Japan would worry about being dragged into a confrontation with Peking because of its alliance with the United States. There would be understanding, even admiration, of a U.S. effort to break Peking's blockade of Taiwan, but only a minority would favor allowing the United States to use its bases in Japan in support of that effort. If the United States did not press the point, the U.S.-Japanese security relationship would survive a crisis over Taiwan, but attitudes on both sides might change in ways that would undermine its long-term prospects.

The American public might be impressed by the lack of mutuality in the relationship and disposed to question whether the security treaty was really in the interest of the United States. The Japanese public might have two somewhat inconsistent reactions. They might be impressed by the dangers inherent in the security relationship with the United States and at the same time disturbed by the fact that Japan had had to let a nation from the other side of the Pacific deal with a problem of primary importance to itself. These U.S. and Japanese reactions could weaken security ties between the two countries and make the emergence of an autonomous Japanese defense policy somewhat more likely.

In the case of Korea, the end of the Sino-Soviet dispute would spell

68. In 1978 the total value of Japan's exports to Taiwan was U.S.$3.8 billion (c.i.f.). Its imports from Taiwan in the same year came to U.S.$1.6 billion (f.o.b.). Directorate-General of Budget, Accounting, and Statistics, Executive Yuan, Republic of China, *Statistical Yearbook of the Republic of China, 1979* (Taipei, 1979), table 15, pp. 364–71.

the end of Pyongyang's ability to play Moscow against Peking and thereby maintain a considerable degree of independence from both. With the Soviet Union and China working together rather than competing for influence, North Korea would find it difficult to launch an attack on the South without their approval. However, the two powers appear reasonably content with the status quo on the Korean peninsula and not at all interested in a military confrontation with the United States. As long as the U.S. security commitment to South Korea remains credible, the Soviet Union and China can be expected to restrain North Korea from attacking South Korea. Since a new war in Korea would have a seriously unsettling effect on Japan, in this one respect the termination of the Sino-Soviet dispute would make any drastic change in Japan's defense policy less likely.

A Sino-Soviet reconciliation could greatly improve the strategic position of the Soviet Pacific fleet. At present, the main operating base for this fleet is at Vladivostok. To operate outside the Sea of Japan, Soviet naval units must pass through one of the straits leading to the Pacific Ocean. Those straits could fairly easily be mined or blockaded by U.S. and Japanese forces. The Soviet Union has attempted to offset this strategic disadvantage by developing a base at Petropavlovsk on the Pacific side of Kamchatka peninsula. However, since this base must be supplied largely by sea from Vladivostok, it too would be handicapped by the closing of the straits.

But if the Soviet Union and China were to become allies, China might conceivably allow the Soviet Pacific fleet to use Chinese ports. Countering the Soviet submarine threat to Japan's sea lines of supply would then be much more difficult. The problem would be further complicated by the likelihood that Chinese and Soviet naval forces would cooperate in a crisis, although this would be less important than the release of the Soviet Pacific fleet from its present geographical constraints, since the Chinese navy is principally a coastal defense force.

The Japanese reaction to an increased Sino-Soviet naval threat would depend largely on how the United States responded. If the United States appeared willing and able to counter any Sino-Soviet move against Japan's supply lines, Japan would probably be able to adjust to the new situation without any sharp changes of course. But if the United States appeared willing to accept Sino-Soviet naval superiority in the western Pacific, Japan would be forced to reconsider both its own defense posture and its security connection with the United States. The mutual security treaty would be seen as continuing to have some value, particularly in fending off nuclear threats from Moscow and Peking, and would probably not be abrogated. At the same time, Japan might fear that in the new situation its alliance with the United States was as likely to involve it in a confrontation with the communist powers as it was to deter those powers from threatening its supply lines.[69] Japan might therefore gradually increase its political distance from the United States, downgrade the importance of the security tie without actually cutting it, and pursue an increasingly autonomous defense policy—all this done cautiously to avoid giving the United States clear grounds for retaliation.

With a minimum of publicity, Japan might further strengthen its air defenses and antisubmarine warfare capability in anticipation of the day when it might have to survive without the backing of U.S. conventional forces. For a number of years, any move toward developing nuclear weapons would probably be avoided as both unnecessary and dangerously provocative. However, as Japan's conventional strength increased and the security connection with the United States became more attenuated, Japan would have to face the question of acquiring nuclear weapons for deterrence or defense.

SINO-U.S. RELATIONS. One of the assumptions underlying Japan's present security policy is continued improvement in Sino-American relations.[70] It is clear that Japan would be deeply disturbed if Sino-U.S. relations retrogressed and military confrontation became a real possibility. Japan therefore welcomed the normalization of relations between Washington and Peking.

Too close a relationship between Washington and Peking, however, might be even more disturbing to Japan than a reappearance of the animosity that characterized Sino-U.S. relations for a quarter of a century. Japan has carefully avoided becoming aligned with either side in the Sino-Soviet dispute[71] and clearly prefers that its ally, the United States,

---

69. This fear would be particularly strong (and well founded) if the Sino-Soviet rapprochement had been accompanied by a worsening of U.S. relations with one or both communist powers.

70. *Defense of Japan, 1979*, p. 73.

71. An example of this behavior was Japan's long delay in accepting China's demand that the peace treaty between the two countries contain a condemnation of regional "hegemony," a Chinese code word for the expansionist aims of the Soviet Union.

do likewise. If the United States were even to imply a commitment to help China repel a Soviet attack or agree to supply China with modern weapons, Japan would fear that its security connection with the United States could one day involve it in a clash with the Soviet Union. The more real this danger became, the more likely Japan would be to move away from the United States politically and to set forth on the road that leads to an autonomous defense policy.

DEVELOPMENTS IN KOREA. The last of the five assumptions underlying Japan's present defense policy is "generally unchanged Korean Peninsula situation along present lines and continued unlikelihood of at least major conflict there."[72] If hostilities did break out between North and South Korea, the possibility of the war's spreading to Japan would worry the Japanese deeply.

The United States would undoubtedly want to use its bases in Japan to support military operations in Korea. If the hostilities were clearly caused by North Korean aggression, the present and any future Liberal Democratic government would almost certainly acquiesce in the use of the bases. Nevertheless, many Japanese would oppose this decision, and even more would be uneasy that they might be involved even indirectly in a war. The dangers inherent in the alliance with the United States would be perceived more clearly, giving an impetus of uncertain force to the evolution of an autonomous defense policy.

If responsibility for starting the war was not clear and if Japan was ruled by a coalition government, permission to use the bases might be denied. The damage to the U.S.-Japanese alliance would then be more severe. Many Japanese would see the United States as trying to expose Japan to danger without adequate cause. Americans would question both Japanese good faith and the value of the alliance.

Another conceivable Korean contingency could pose the question of acquiring nuclear weapons more directly and more immediately—the acquisition of nuclear weapons by either South Korea or North Korea. Since South Korea appears to have a much greater capability, the discussion will proceed on the assumption that it is the South that acquires nuclear weapons.[73]

To say that the Japanese people and their leaders would be shaken by

72. *Defense of Japan, 1977*, p. 56.
73. The question of nuclear weapons in the Republic of Korea is discussed in chapter 3.

the rise of a new nuclear weapons state across the narrow Tsushima Strait would be a gross understatement. The fact that the possessors of this capability were Koreans, who were formerly ruled by Japan and are still viewed as inferiors, would arouse strong nationalist feelings. Even though relations between Tokyo and Seoul have been generally good for a number of years, the Japanese would remember past crises with the ROK and would feel both threatened and vulnerable.

As a matter of fact, it is most unlikely that the ROK would decide to acquire nuclear weapons with Japan in mind. The chief purpose of taking this step would be deterrence of a North Korean attack. Nevertheless, Japan would have real grounds for concern, since the development of a nuclear weapons capability in South Korea would be destabilizing to the entire region. Not only would the danger of a war between North and South Korea greatly increase, but relations between the outside powers with interests in Korea—the United States, the Soviet Union, China, and Japan—would be affected in potentially dangerous ways.

The attractiveness of nuclear weapons in Japan would certainly grow, at least for a time. Many Japanese would not want to be second best to Koreans. More thoughtful Japanese would see the South Korean acquisition of nuclear weapons as evidence that the world is an increasingly dangerous place, in which Japan may someday need nuclear weapons if it is to survive. Some might see the development as an excuse to step across the nuclear threshold with reduced risk.

It might be argued that Japan should respond by creating a minimal nuclear capability of its own. A limited number of fission bombs deliverable by fighter aircraft could neutralize the ROK capability in a future crisis without—it would be hoped—alarming the Soviet Union or China. The latter point would be crucial.

Moscow and Peking would not react only to the initial Japanese nuclear capability, against which effective defenses could be erected and which in any event would not give Japan a credible second-strike capability. They would also consider where the initial capability might lead. Moscow at least would probably try to nip the emerging Japanese nuclear force in the bud. Japan could not resist a Soviet ultimatum without U.S. backing, and that backing might not be forthcoming. The outcome could be disastrous for Japan: a public humiliation that would have serious domestic political consequences and a sharp deterioration in U.S.-Japanese relations and in the credibility of the U.S. security commitment.

Conclusions about Nuclear Weapons

Japan is clearly capable of developing nuclear weapons with sophisticated delivery systems. Few other nonnuclear weapons states can match its industrial base and advanced technology, including specifically relevant knowledge in the fields of nuclear energy, rockets, and naval design.

Japan's present policy against the acquisition of nuclear weapons, however, enjoys the support of all political parties, and no foreseeable domestic development seems likely to undermine it. But if external developments caused the Japanese government to reconsider its policy, public opinion would not necessarily exert an effective restraining influence.

One such development would be abrupt termination of the mutual security treaty by the United States. This is a remote possibility; it is used only as a means of more sharply defining the issues. Much more likely is a gradual weakening of the U.S.-Japanese security connection, which would eventually force Japan to decide whether or not it needed its own nuclear weapons.

Three other kinds of developments are more realistic.

—Disagreements with the United States over defense issues, such as the use of Japanese bases in the defense of South Korea.

—Loss of confidence in the U.S. security commitment, resulting, for example, from an excessive U.S. preoccupation with the security of Western Europe or a U.S. failure to respond adequately to the new strategic situation that would be created by Sino-Soviet rapprochement.

—Fear that the U.S. security connection exposes Japan to serious dangers, such as involvement in a war in Korea, a U.S.-Chinese confrontation with the Soviet Union, or a U.S.-Soviet nuclear exchange.

Also, a more specific contingency—the acquisition of nuclear weapons by the ROK—could precipitate a nuclear debate in Japan.

From today's perspective, it seems likely that if Japan gradually loosened its security ties with the United States it would not in the end decide to acquire nuclear weapons. They are not essential to meeting the conventional threats to Japan's security—interdiction, air bombardment, and amphibious invasion. A nuclear deterrent force would theoretically be desirable if Japan could no longer rely on the U.S. nuclear umbrella. In Japan's geographical situation, however, such a force would probably have to consist of nuclear-powered submarines armed with nuclear missiles, and creating it could take a decade or more, during which time

Japan would be exposed to Soviet or Chinese preventive measures. Even developing a minimal nuclear force to counter a South Korean nuclear capability might be blocked by the Soviet Union and possibly by China as well.

Lacking either the protection of the United States or its own nuclear deterrent, Japan could decide to remain only lightly armed and rely on a mixture of diplomacy and the constraints that the international system imposes on the nuclear powers to keep it out of danger. This policy could lead to an accommodation with the USSR resembling that of Finland. Alternatively, Japan could build up its conventional forces, especially its navy, to the point where it would once more be a factor in the balance of power in the Pacific. It could then more easily maneuver among the three nuclear powers of the area and might avoid being subjected to nuclear threats by any one of them.

One potentially important course of events remains to be considered: what might be called nuclear drift. Without any special effort on the part of the Japanese government, the "time of danger" may well shrink. If Japan reprocesses spent fuel from nuclear power plants, a supply of plutonium usable in nuclear weapons will be accumulated. The continued evolution of the space program will advance Japanese rocket technology. And the nuclear-powered-ship program may one day be revived to serve civil transport needs. A special effort by the government in these and other relevant areas of technology could further reduce the time needed to create a credible nuclear deterrent force.

In other words, Japan could, if it wished, quietly move very close to a nuclear weapons capability. Under present circumstances, it has little incentive to do so. If, however, Japan were moving toward an autonomous defense policy, such a capability could look quite attractive. Even so, the time of danger could not be eliminated altogether, and the final move to a full nuclear deterrent could remain too dangerous to attempt.

International Cooperation in Nuclear Matters

Japan's position is that the nonproliferation treaty and the system of safeguards administered by the International Atomic Energy Agency provide an adequate international framework for developing nuclear energy without increasing the risk of a further spread of nuclear weapons. Japan belongs to the London nuclear suppliers' group and regards its efforts to coordinate the export policies of countries that manufacture nuclear equipment as a useful adjunct to the more formal system of safeguards.

The Japanese government apparently does not see why all phases of the nuclear fuel cycle could not be effectively safeguarded. Japanese officials privately criticize the United States for worrying too much about the spread of sensitive fuel cycle facilities instead of pressing more nations to adhere to the NPT. They particularly object to the alleged failure of the United States to treat countries that have signed and ratified the NPT better than those that have not.

As noted, Japan plans to close the nuclear fuel cycle[74] and believes that this is essential to the solution of its long-term energy problems.[75] The U.S. decision to defer commercial reprocessing is seen as an abberation from wise energy policy that the United States can perhaps afford but that it should not force on others.

Despite these strongly held views, it does not follow that Japan will not cooperate in new international efforts to ensure that the continued development of nuclear energy does not bring about a further spread of nuclear weapons. Japan actively participated in the International Nuclear Fuel Cycle Evaluation and provided a cochairman of an INFCE working group on reprocessing, plutonium handling, and recycling. Japan is intent on solving its problems of nuclear fuel supply and of managing spent fuel, but it apparently does not insist that the solutions be purely national ones.[76]

For at least a decade, Japan has shown interest in participating in a multinational venture to produce low enriched uranium for light water reactors. Current Japanese projections of sources of enrichment services

74. Japan's representative at the INFCE organizing conference stated that his government was willing to consider new measures to check the spread of nuclear weapons, but made clear that "Japan's programme of establishing its nuclear fuel cycle should not be prejudiced by these measures." Statement of Yoshio Okawa at the Organizing Conference of the International Nuclear Fuel Cycle Evaluation, document 14, Washington, D.C., October 19, 1977.

75. In September 1978 the Atomic Energy Commission of Japan submitted a revision of the atomic development plan to the government. One of its main points was that there is no need to change the policy of establishing a full fuel cycle. "AEC Stresses Necessity of Reprocessing Spent N-Fuel," *Japan Economic Journal,* vol. 16 (September 19, 1978), p. 4.

76. The speculation on possible future Japanese policies presented here is based in part on conversations with Japanese scholars and officials.

show a "joint venture" that would provide 1,000 tons SWU in 1990 and 2,000 tons SWU in 2000 (see table 2-2 above).

Studies of the technical and economic feasibility of a joint Japanese-Australian enrichment plant, to be located in Australia, were conducted by the two governments in 1976–78.[77] If the project is carried out, a choice will have to be made between Japanese, Urenco (the British-Dutch-German uranium enrichment enterprise), and possibly U.S. centrifuge enrichment technology.[78]

Japan appears to have only a limited interest in participating in one or more of the various regional nuclear service centers that have been proposed in recent years. Such centers could in principle include enrichment and reprocessing facilities, but the Japanese would probably prefer to start more modestly with centers for the retrievable storage of spent fuel or for the permanent disposition of nuclear waste. Interest in the latter would be stronger than in the former, since current Japanese thinking envisages storing spent fuel in ponds next to power reactors for perhaps ten years and then reprocessing it, either domestically or in Western Europe.

In March 1979 the United States invited Japan to participate in establishing a spent fuel storage center on a sparsely inhabited Pacific island. Other possible participants would be South Korea, Taiwan, and the Philippines. In early 1980 Japan agreed to share with the United States the cost of a feasibility study of the project.[79]

Japan would be reluctant to give up its plans to build its first commercial-scale reprocessing plant, although it might be induced to shift thereafter to regional reprocessing if the venture proved to be economically sound and if there were no serious political complications. It would not want to join a reprocessing arrangement limited to itself, South Korea, and Taiwan, since it would not want to offend China or appear to be even remotely connected with possible efforts by its two partners to develop nuclear weapons.

77. *Nucleonics Week,* vol. 19 (March 23, 1978), p. 13.

78. "Japanese Help on Uranium Plant Suggested," *Nuclear Engineering International* (May 1978), p. 7; and "Japanese Expertise Studied for Enrichment," ibid. (February 1979), p. 7.

79. "U.S. Seeks Japan's Participation in Setting Up Nuclear Fuel Center," *Japan Economic Journal,* vol. 17 (March 20, 1979), p. 3; and *Nuclear Engineering International* (March 1980), p. 5.

CHAPTER THREE

The Republic of Korea

KOREA has long had a strategic importance out of proportion to its size. For centuries, China and Japan competed for influence there. In the nineteenth century, Russia joined in the competition, and in the twentieth century after World War II, the United States became involved. Today, Korea is one of the few places in the world where hostilities involving one or more of the great powers could conceivably break out at any moment. The future policy of the Republic of Korea on the acquisition of nuclear weapons is therefore a matter of considerable importance.

Korea is, however, more than an arena for competition among great powers. The Republic of Korea, which administers the southern half of the peninsula, is one of the world's rising middle powers. Its sustained economic growth and expanding trade have made it a significant factor in regional and global economic affairs. It is engaged in a substantial civil nuclear energy program, and its cooperation will be important in any future international efforts to direct the development of nuclear energy into channels that do not make the spread of nuclear weapons more likely.

Civil Nuclear Energy

The Republic of Korea has an ambitious civil nuclear energy program;[1] its domestic sources of energy are limited, its energy requirements are rising rapidly, and nuclear energy provides a partial alternative to expen-

1. The summary of the program presented here is based in part on conversations in Seoul in November 1977, June 1978, and January 1979.

sive and possibly unreliable imported oil. In 1975 imported oil accounted for 55 percent of the ROK's total energy consumption. Domestically mined coal, firewood, and charcoal supplied most of the remainder. By the early 1980s the share of imported oil in total energy consumption is expected to be about two-thirds. Thereafter it will decline as rising coal imports and increased production of nuclear energy more than make up for the falling output of domestic coal mines.[2]

The ROK entered the age of nuclear energy in June 1977, when its first nuclear power plant went critical. The installed capacity of this plant, 587 megawatts (electric), added about 9 percent to South Korea's electrical generating capacity. By the late 1980s nine nuclear power plants with a total capacity of 7,316 megawatts (electric) are expected to constitute about 25 percent of total capacity. In mid-1979 two nuclear power plants were under construction, and the site for two more plants was being cleared. Contracts for another two plants were awarded in August 1979.[3]

More nuclear fuel plants will probably be built, but how many and on what schedule has not yet been determined. Until recently, the Korea Electric Company estimated that a total of forty-four nuclear power plants would be built by the year 2000.[4] This projection is now described as only a computer exercise.

Except for the plant under construction at Wolsung, the ROK will probably build only light water reactors (LWRs) fueled by low enriched uranium through the 1980s. The plant in Wolsung will have a Canadian CANDU heavy water reactor (HWR), which uses natural uranium. More HWRs may be built during the 1990s.[5] Except for the Wolsung plant, all of the ROK's reactor business thus far has gone to the United States, although Canada has by no means given up efforts to sell more CANDUs, and European firms have shown a strong interest in the ROK's nuclear

2. Korea Development Institute, *Long-Term Prospect for Economic and Social Development, 1977–91* (Seoul: KDI, 1978), p. 84.

3. *Wall Street Journal*, August 4, 1979.

4. Korea Electric Company, "Long-Term Power Development Program," May 23, 1978, p. 5.

5. Heavy water reactors offer a means of diversifying sources of fuel supply and, in particular, of reducing dependence on foreign (currently U.S.) enrichment services. Their initial capital cost, however, is substantially greater than that of LWRs, and a mixture of LWR and HWR plants would be more difficult to staff and operate than a system consisting of only one type of reactor.

energy program. Some large South Korean firms may also enter the field in joint ventures with foreign corporations.[6]

The ROK does not at present have any fuel cycle facilities other than the power reactor mentioned above, two research reactors (one of 2-megawatt and the other of 0.25-megawatt capacity), and a small fuel fabrication plant. A commercial fabrication plant may be built in a few years, possibly as a joint venture with some other country.[7] All uranium is currently purchased in the United States and Canada and enriched by the U.S. Department of Energy.[8] South Korea has some deposits of low-grade uranium that would be commercially exploitable at about $60 a pound. The Korea Nuclear Fuel Development Institute is studying ways of using this domestic uranium (but not its enrichment).

The Korea Electric Company now plans to store spent fuel in pools next to nuclear power plants during the first fifteen years of operations. Thereafter, other arrangements will be required. In 1975 the ROK discussed with a French firm the purchase of a reprocessing plant. This project was dropped in early 1976, reportedly after discussions between the South Korean and U.S. governments.[9]

Along with other countries with civil nuclear energy programs, the ROK will face a number of problems in future years. Besides the management of spent fuel, arrangements for an assured supply of nuclear fuel and decisions on what kinds of reactors should follow the present generation of LWRs and HWRs must be made. Cutting across all of these problems is the question of whether to reprocess spent fuel and, if so, how to use the resulting supply of plutonium.

The general position of the ROK government appears to be to defer any major decisions until international consideration of how best to develop the nuclear fuel cycle has made further progress. This policy of waiting undoubtedly reflects both concern about the evolution of the

6. Tetsuo Tomura, "Big So. Korean Companies Take Strong Interest in A-Power Field," *Japan Economic Journal*, vol. 16 (October 31, 1978), p. 5.

7. Republic of Korea, Ministry of Science and Technology, *Korea, 1978: Atomic Energy Activities*, p. 12.

8. The ROK is interested in diversifying its sources of natural uranium and is looking into possibilities in Africa, Australia, and South America (especially Paraguay).

9. *New York Times*, January 30, 1976.

policies of countries such as the United States and Canada and an interest in seeing whether international solutions to some of these problems will become feasible.

The ROK was an active participant in the International Nuclear Fuel Cycle Evaluation and provided the cochairman of an INFCE working group on advanced fuel cycle and reactor concepts. The ROK is clearly interested in international approaches to fuel cycle problems. The South Korean representatives in the International Atomic Energy Agency have spoken in favor of proposals to establish multinational regional fuel cycle centers and an international nuclear supply authority.[10]

The ROK can well afford to delay decisions on its fuel cycle problems. The storage of spent fuel will not become a problem for well over a decade. The choice of the next generation of reactors is scarcely an urgent question in a program whose first power reactor did not begin commercial operations until 1978.

Nor does a national approach to reprocessing appear justified at this time. The civil nuclear energy program will not be able to support a reprocessing plant of efficient size for many years. Economies of scale are more likely to be realized by joining in a multinational venture should reprocessing become necessary or desirable. Moreover, the existing program does not require plutonium fuel. Recycling plutonium in the present generation of reactors is questionable from an economic point of view, and the ROK appears to have no plans at present to build advanced thermal reactors or breeders requiring plutonium.

Nuclear Weapons

On a number of occasions, the government of the ROK has declared that it has no intention of acquiring nuclear weapons. Most recently, the head of the South Korean delegation to the INFCE said: "It is a firm policy of the government of the Republic of Korea that the nuclear development program is solely for furthering the peaceful uses of atomic energy."[11] Consistent with its proclaimed policy, the ROK signed the

10. Statements by ROK representatives at the Eighteenth (1974), Twentieth (1976), and Twenty-first (1977) General Conferences of the International Atomic Energy Agency. Texts supplied by the Ministry of Science and Technology, Seoul.
11. Statement by Dr. B. W. Lee, Organizing Conference of the International Nuclear Fuel Cycle Evaluation, document 20, Washington, D.C., October 19, 1977.

Treaty on the Non-Proliferation of Nuclear Weapons and ratified it in March 1975.[12] Its only operating nuclear power plant is under IAEA safeguards, as future plants will be when they are completed and put into service.

The only nuclear weapons in Korea are held by U.S. forces stationed there.[13] These are tactical weapons that presumably could be delivered by fighter aircraft, field artillery, or missiles with a range of about fifty kilometers. They are reportedly being withdrawn on a schedule that would remove the last of them in 1982.[14] After the withdrawal, the U.S. Air Force units that will remain in Korea indefinitely could be resupplied with tactical nuclear weapons on very short notice in an emergency. Moreover, U.S. carriers in the Pacific presumably have a tactical nuclear weapons capability.

The failure of U.S. policy in Vietnam, followed by the announcement in 1977 of plans to withdraw U.S. ground combat forces from Korea over a five-year period, shook Korean confidence in the U.S. security commitment. As a consequence, interest in the question of whether the ROK should acquire nuclear weapons increased in South Korean academic circles and among foreign observers. One can only assume that the question was also being discussed in the ROK government. Confidence was presumably restored to some extent in July 1979 by President Carter's decision to defer further withdrawals of ground combat troops until at least 1981. At the time of this decision, only one infantry battalion had been withdrawn.[15]

The Case for Nuclear Weapons

In some countries, the acquisition of nuclear weapons may be thought to enhance national prestige or increase the influence of the technological or military elite. There is no evidence that these considerations play any

---

12. President Park Chung Hee affirmed the policy against acquiring nuclear weapons during his New Year's inspection of the Ministry of National Defense on January 28, 1977. Translated from *Seoul Shinmun*, January 28, 1977.

13. At a press conference on June 20, 1975, Secretary of Defense James R. Schlesinger confirmed that the United States has tactical nuclear weapons in South Korea. *New York Times*, June 21, 1975.

14. *Boston Globe*, July 28, 1978.

15. *Washington Post*, July 21, 1979.

significant role in South Korean thinking. The case for the ROK's acquiring nuclear weapons rests entirely on national security.[16]

Nuclear weapons are seen by their South Korean proponents as a means of deterring North Korean attack or ensuring a successful defense if an attack does occur. One variant of this argument regards the likelihood of a successful defense as an adequate deterrent. Another variant advocates a separate deterrent in the form of a strategic capability to inflict severe damage on North Korean cities and industries. The first variant points toward a need for low-yield, short-range nuclear weapons. The second appears to call for weapons of greater yield and longer range.

Either explicitly or implicitly, the case for nuclear weapons rests on the proposition that the South is militarily inferior to the North or that the balance is so close that a surprise attack could succeed. Support for this proposition can be found in the fact that the North is superior to the South in numbers of ground force divisions, aircraft, tanks, and artillery (see table 3-1 for a comparison of North and South Korean forces). Moreover, the attacker could have the advantage of surprise, which is particularly important because Seoul is only forty kilometers from the demilitarized zone. A successful defense, it is argued, would have to be a forward defense, north of Seoul. Space cannot be traded for time to mount a counteroffensive, when the space in question includes the nation's capital and its major concentration of population and industry.

One way to ensure a successful forward defense in the hope of deterring an attack would be the possession of nuclear weapons. Proponents of such weapons buttress their case by observing that the United States must have come to a similar conclusion when it positioned tactical nuclear weapons in Korea. Why, they ask, should not U.S. weapons be replaced by ROK weapons?

Proponents also see a similarity between the military situations in Korea and Europe. They note that the United States has deployed tactical nuclear weapons to Western Europe to remedy an imbalance in conventional firepower between NATO and Warsaw Pact forces and to deter an attack by the latter. Why, they again ask, should not the same action be taken in Korea, where the South is threatened by superior North Korean

16. The case for nuclear weapons presented here is based largely on private conversations with Korean scholars and is not meant to suggest that it would be supported by either the majority of Korean scholars or the government of the ROK.

Table 3-1. *Conventional Military Forces of North and South Korea,*
1978–79

Forces	North Korea	South Korea
Ground		
Personnel	560,000–600,000	520,000
Divisions	40	20
Infantry	35	19
Motorized	3	0
Armor	2	1
Tanks	2,300	840
Field artillery pieces	3,500	2,000
Rocket launchers	1,300	0
Mortars	9,000	5,300
Air		
Personnel	45,000	30,000
Jet fighters	460	300
Fighter bombers	20	0
Light bombers	85	0
Naval		
Personnel	27,000	46,000
Destroyers and frigates	3	9
Missile attack boats	18	0
Coastal patrol craft	330	68
Amphibious craft and		
minesweepers	90	18
Submarines	15	0

Sources: Estimates for North Korea are from International Institute for Strategic Studies, *The Military Balance, 1979–1980* (London: IISS, 1979), pp. 68–69. Those for South Korea were provided by the United Nations Command, Seoul, in June 1978.

forces and where the United States is reportedly withdrawing its tactical nuclear weapons and may withdraw its combat ground forces?

The prospect of a U.S. withdrawal not only heightens concern about the feasibility of a conventional forward defense, but also leads to discussion of the need for a strategic nuclear deterrent. Those who advocate such a deterrent argue that the principal value of U.S. ground combat troops and nuclear weapons in South Korea is their deterrent effect on North Korea. When these troops and weapons are withdrawn, some new force must take their place, if the same level of deterrence is to be preserved. Why not, then, deter North Korea in the same way that the United States deters the Soviet Union—by maintaining the ability to inflict unacceptable damage on the enemy's population and economy?

The Case against Nuclear Weapons

The case against nuclear weapons, stated briefly, is that they are not needed and that they would actually weaken the security of the ROK.

THE FEASIBILITY OF A CONVENTIONAL DEFENSE.[17] A simple comparison of numbers of divisions, planes, tanks, and artillery pieces can be misleading. North Korean divisions are much smaller than South Korean divisions, and the opposing ground forces are actually about the same size. Moreover, many North Korean planes and tanks are old and qualitatively inferior to planes and tanks in the ROK inventory. The North Korean tank force includes one model dating from World War II and another that is used only as a reconnaissance vehicle by the Soviet army. The main North Korean battle tank, the T-54, is of good quality, but it was first manufactured in 1948 and has been phased out of service by the Soviet army. The ROK tank force will soon consist entirely of refurbished U.S. M-48s, which are being fitted with a gun that is larger and more accurate than that of the T-54. The ROK also has large antitank defenses, including antitank guided missiles and fortifications and obstacles along the invasion corridors north of Seoul.

Although the combat aircraft of the North Korean air force outnumber those of the South by almost two to one, many of the North's planes are obsolescent and limited in performance. The 85 light bombers and 340 of the fighters (MIG-15s, -17s, and -19s) are subsonic and would be vulnerable to ROK air defenses, which include surface-to-air missiles as well as modern fighter aircraft. The F-4D/Es in the ROK air force are superior to any plane in North Korea's air force, and the ROK's F-5A/Es compare favorably with the North's best fighter aircraft, the MIG-21s. Eighteen more F-4Es and 60 more F-5E/Fs are on order. The qualitative superiority of the ROK aircraft is probably not enough, however, to compensate for its quantitative inferiority. This problem has been met by the decision of the United States to continue to station U.S. Air Force planes in Korea indefinitely.

Whether existing ROK forces supported by U.S. air units could turn back a North Korean attack north of Seoul would depend on the extent of tactical warning of the attack, the morale of the opposing forces, and

17. For a more detailed discussion of the defense policies of the ROK, see Stuart E. Johnson with Joseph A. Yager, *The Military Equation in Northeast Asia* (Brookings Institution, 1979).

the ability of the defending forces to direct sustained, heavy firepower against the invasion corridors. The last variable would depend in turn on the adequacy of forward-based ammunition stocks and the ability of the ROK-U.S. logistic system to move additional ammunition to the front from depots south of Seoul.

Prospects for a successful conventional defense north of Seoul are good and can be increased by measures planned or under way. In the event of an attack, the defending ROK forces would have the advantage of both terrain and prepared positions. North Korean tank forces would be forced to use the same invasion corridors that they used in 1950. But in a new invasion they would meet a strong ROK armored force and formidable antitank defenses, particularly at narrow choke points along the corridors. The defensive capabilities of the ROK forces will be further strengthened by the recently initiated five-year Force Improvement Plan, which will upgrade the tank force and modernize and expand the air force. The ROK's antitank capabilities will be further increased by U.S.-ROK coproduction of 100 helicopters in South Korea, some of which will be equipped with guided antitank missiles.

From a purely military point of view (which ignores political consequences), tactical nuclear weapons could contribute to a successful defense north of Seoul. It does not follow, however, that such weapons are essential to a successful defense or that some of the most important results sought through their use could not be achieved by other means. Minefields covered by artillery or other fire can halt and destroy advancing infantry, and conventional mobile weapon systems, such as tanks, guided antitank missiles, and tactical aircraft, can be effective against tanks.[18]

THE PROBLEM OF DETERRENCE. The ability of the ROK forces, with U.S. air and naval support, to stop an attack north of Seoul would not completely solve the ROK's national security problem. Even a successful defense would be extremely costly. Military and civilian casualties in the battle area would be heavy. The invaders might be kept out of Seoul, but

18. For a detailed analysis of the relative utility of nuclear weapons and conventional alternatives in checking a North Korean advance on Seoul, see Brian Jack and others, *Regional Rivalries and Nuclear Responses*, vol. 2: *The South Korean Case: A Nuclear Weapons Program Embedded in an Environment of Great Power Concerns*, DNA 001-77-C-0052, prepared for the Director, U.S. Defense Nuclear Agency (Los Angeles: Pan Heuristics, 1978), pp. 82–91.

the city and its people could not escape some damage from air, long-range missile, and artillery bombardment. Deterring an attack would clearly be much better than defeating it.

The possibility of failure might not be enough to deter the North Korean leadership. Their evaluation of the various military factors might be different from that above, and they might conclude that a surprise attack could overrun enough territory to make it worth the risk. They might further calculate that a UN-backed cease-fire would leave them in occupation of still more of the country and in a stronger military and political position.

Deterrence might fail even though substantial numbers of U.S. ground combat troops remain in Korea. The question is whether withdrawal of those troops would be viewed by Pyongyang as making U.S. involvement in the defense of the ROK less likely, thereby weakening the deterrent against a North Korean attack. Those who fear that this would be the effect argue that, since the U.S. troops are stationed north of Seoul, they would inevitably become involved in hostilities; they would act as a trip-wire, automatically ensuring U.S. participation in the defense of the ROK.

The validity of this line of argument depends not on what Americans or South Koreans think of it, but on the views of the North Korean leadership. Two considerations suggest that the trip-wire, as seen from Pyongyang, may not be a simple proposition. First, it may occur to the North Koreans that, if the United States must be trapped into honoring its security commitment to the ROK, that commitment cannot be worth much. The presence or absence of U.S. ground combat forces may therefore be no clue to what the United States would do if North Korea attacked. Second, if the Second Division of the U.S. Army is indeed a trip-wire, are not the U.S. Air Force units in South Korea trip-wires also? The fields on which those units are based would certainly be attacked in the first hours of a North Korean offensive, and the USAF would probably be involved before the fighting reached the Second Division.

But even if the withdrawal of U.S. ground combat troops did not weaken deterrence, might not the removal of U.S. tactical nuclear weapons do so? No clear-cut answer is possible. On the one hand, the probability that a president of the United States would authorize the use of such weapons was never high and has decreased over the years. Moreover, if the U.S. nuclear weapons were removed, they could be quickly reintroduced into Korea or brought to nearby waters. On the other hand, U.S.

nuclear weapons have long been part of the military status quo, the North Korean leaders cannot be certain that they would never be used, and it is virtually impossible to estimate how important those weapons are in the total deterrent.

If it is assumed, for purposes of this analysis, that withdrawal of U.S. ground combat troops and U.S. tactical nuclear weapons would significantly degrade the deterrent, it does not follow that the acquisition of a nuclear weapons capability by the ROK would be an effective remedy. When account is taken of the reactions of other powers, it becomes clear that this course could undermine support for the ROK and make a North Korean attack more likely.

Possible Reactions to South Korea's Acquisition of Nuclear Weapons

Reactions to a decision by the ROK to acquire nuclear weapons would vary somewhat, depending on the point at which the decision became known. If the world quickly became aware that the ROK had a nuclear weapons program, heavy pressure would be brought to bear by friend and foe for abandonment of the effort. The full significance of such a decision can, however, best be brought out by assuming—somewhat unrealistically—that it was kept secret until the program was far advanced and that the ROK ignored all outside efforts to make it change course. The question then becomes, what would the reactions be to the imminent appearance of a new nuclear weapons state? The most important reactions would be those of North Korea, the Soviet Union, China, Japan, and the United States.

NORTH KOREA. North Korea would be genuinely alarmed at what the development might mean for its own survival, but it would also see some new opportunities and could be expected to try to exploit them vigorously.

North Korea would at least consider a preemptive attack on the South aimed at destroying its adversary before the ROK's nuclear weapons tipped the military balance heavily against the North. The chances of success, and therefore the likelihood, of such an attack would increase if the South's nuclear decision had alienated the United States and Japan. Pyongyang might hope that the United States would give the ROK little or no help and that Japan would not permit the United States to use Japanese bases in support of military operations in Korea.

Pyongyang might further calculate that, even if an attack did not result in the total destruction of the ROK, it might still produce useful results. Some territory might be occupied, but more immediately important, the great powers might be induced to join in forcing Seoul to abandon its nuclear weapons program. The mere threat of an attack could of course produce the latter result.

Pyongyang would at a minimum try to create an atmosphere of international crisis in which it would hope to mobilize international support for its long-standing political initiatives, including the federation of North and South Korea on its own terms. A new diplomatic offensive designed to isolate the ROK would be a virtual certainty.

If North Korea decided that an attack was too risky, it could be expected to try to counter the emerging nuclear weapons capability of the South in several other ways. It would seek assurances from Peking and Moscow designed to neutralize the capability. It might ask one or both of the communist powers to help it develop its own nuclear weapons[19] and, in the interim, either provide it with such weapons or station nuclear-capable specialized units in North Korea.

THE SOVIET UNION AND CHINA. The problems created for these two countries by the new situation in Korea would be similar, but their responses would not necessarily be identical. Nor, for obvious reasons, would their actions be concerted. Their long-standing rivalry, including their competition for influence in Pyongyang, would shape their responses.

Both would denounce Seoul's decision to acquire nuclear weapons as a threat to peace. Both would probably respond positively to a request from Pyongyang for renewed security assurances, possibly including promises to retaliate with nuclear weapons if the South used such weapons against the North. And both would cooperate in the North Korean diplomatic campaign to isolate the ROK.

Both would probably refuse to provide North Korea with nuclear weapons, since to do so would set an undesirable precedent and reduce their ability to restrain Pyongyang from rash ventures.[20] The likely reactions of the Soviet Union and China to a North Korean request for

19. Little is known about North Korea's scientific and technological capabilities in the field of nuclear energy. People working in the field in Seoul have heard that North Korea has at least one research reactor and that North Korean scientists received some training in nuclear matters in the Soviet Union in the 1950s. North Korea apparently has no commercial nuclear power plants.

20. The Soviet Union would also be restrained by its adherence to the nonproliferation treaty.

assistance in developing nuclear weapons or for the stationing of nuclear-capable units in Korea are less predictable. Neither would want the other to gain any political or military advantage, and neither would be willing to cooperate with the other militarily or technologically. At the same time, North Korea would want to avoid alienating one of them by favoring the other as well as becoming excessively dependent on either one.

These complications might make it impossible for North Korea to work out arrangements for either technical assistance or military deployments. Conceivably, however, China could furnish technical assistance and the Soviet Union could deploy nuclear-capable units to North Korea. China is not known to have provided any other country with such assistance and is certainly not anxious to further the spread of nuclear weapons. At the same time, China—unlike the Soviet Union—has not adhered to the nonproliferation treaty and is less firmly committed, at least publicly, to opposing nuclear weapons proliferation. The Soviet Union, on the other hand, has a much more developed nuclear weapons capability than China and could more easily deploy units to North Korea.

The reactions of both powers to the prospect of a new war in Korea cannot easily be foreseen. In recent years, both have appeared reasonably satisfied with the situation on the peninsula and anxious to avoid the confrontation with the United States that a new outbreak of hostilities might bring. If the ROK's decision to acquire nuclear weapons had caused a breach between Seoul and Washington, the latter consideration would of course lose much of its force.

Peking would probably regret the breach and hope that the U.S. security relationship with the ROK could be quickly repaired, so that the U.S. military presence in Northeast Asia would continue to hinder the southward spread of Soviet influence. In the event of a North Korean attack the United States might forget its disagreement with Seoul over nuclear weapons policy and join in the defense of the ROK, or it might stand aside and let the ROK defend itself as best it could. Either outcome would be bad from Peking's point of view. The first would be highly dangerous, and the second would confirm a further withdrawal of U.S. power.

The second outcome (but not the first) would be welcomed by the Soviet Union. If Moscow were reasonably confident that the United States would not effectively support the ROK, it might encourage a North Korean attack by providing the modern equipment needed to increase the chances of success. Moscow might hope that in this way it could both remove Chinese influence (including perhaps a Chinese nuclear assistance program) from Korea and destroy the prospects for a return of U.S. influence.[21]

JAPAN. The Japanese would be alarmed by the prospect of both a new nuclear weapons state on their doorstep and the wider repercussions of this development. The first reaction of the Japanese government would be to denounce the ROK decision to acquire nuclear weapons. A suspension of diplomatic relations with Seoul would be a real possibility.

If North Korea launched a preemptive attack, some Japanese would blame the ROK for having provoked it. The preponderant Japanese sentiment would be an intense desire to avoid involvement in a Korean war, and this might lead the Japanese government, as has been noted, to refuse the United States permission to use bases in Japan to support military operations in Korea.

The developments in Korea would be certain to precipitate a reexamination of Japanese defense policy. This is clearly foreshadowed in the 1977, 1978, and 1979 Japanese white papers on defense, which state that Japan's present defense policy is based on the premise that the international environment will undergo no major changes for some time to come. As described in chapter 2, if radical changes do occur, "the natural course would be an expansion and reinforcement of Japan's defense structure to conform to such changes." One of the five structural areas in which changes would be considered important is "generally unchanged Korean Peninsula situation along present lines and continued unlikelihood of at least major conflict there."[22]

One question almost certain to be considered is whether Japan should follow the example of the ROK and develop its own nuclear weapons. As was concluded in chapter 2, Japan would probably decide that it was not in its interest to do so, although a Korea-oriented nuclear weapons capability might appear both more feasible and less dangerous than one designed to deter the Soviet Union or China. Some Japanese might argue that a modest arsenal of nuclear weapons deliverable by aircraft would be sufficient to neutralize the value of Seoul's nuclear weapons in a

21. Moscow could of course be proved wrong on at least the first count. After a war, if not sooner, Pyongyang would be likely to revert to its established policy of avoiding too great reliance on either the Soviet Union or China.

22. Japan Defense Agency, *Defense of Japan, 1977* (Tokyo: JDA, 1977), pp. 55–56. The same point is made in Japan Defense Agency, *Defense of Japan, 1978* (JDA, 1978), pp. 69–70, and *Defense of Japan, 1979* (JDA, 1979), p. 74.

future crisis and that Peking and Moscow would not feel threatened by such a limited Japanese capability.

THE UNITED STATES. A decision by South Korea to acquire nuclear weapons would put the United States in a difficult position. On the one hand, such a decision would run counter to the major U.S. objective of checking the further spread of nuclear weapons and could seriously destabilize a part of the world in which the United States has major interests. On the other hand, breaking with the ROK over its decision to acquire nuclear weapons could further endanger U.S. interests by making war more likely.

The U.S. government might try to resolve this dilemma by applying heavy pressure on the ROK to reverse its decision, stopping short of a rupture in diplomatic relations. The means of pressure available to the United States would be substantial. For example, shipments of nuclear fuel and equipment would almost certainly be suspended;[23] shipments of military items would probably be suspended; and Export-Import Bank financing might be terminated.

The danger would be that the process of U.S. pressure and ROK resistance would get out of hand and cause a serious deterioration in relations. This could encourage a North Korean attack on the ROK, to which U.S. public and congressional opinion might not support an adequate U.S. response.

Even if the immediate crisis in U.S.-South Korean relations were somehow surmounted, a serious problem would remain. An independent ROK nuclear weapons capability would bring about a fundamental change in the security relationship of the two nations. The United States would find it difficult to accept a situation in which its ally could expose it to a nuclear confrontation with the Soviet Union or China by using nuclear weapons against the ally of those two powers. The U.S. security commitment to the ROK would have to be qualified or procedures established that would give the United States a veto over the use, or threatened use, of ROK nuclear weapons.

23. U.S.-ROK agreement for cooperation in atomic energy matters would provide a legal basis for this action if the ROK nuclear weapons program was based on plutonium extracted from spent fuel of U.S. origin; 24 U.S.T. 2364, article VIII, paragraph C. Moreover, section 307 of the Nuclear Non-Proliferation Act of 1978 forbids the export of nuclear materials and equipment to states that have terminated or abrogated IAEA safeguards. The president can make exceptions to this prohibition, but he can be overruled by Congress if it acts within sixty days.

Other Problems

In view of its civil nuclear energy program and its corps of well-qualified scientists and engineers, there can be little doubt about the ability of the ROK to develop nuclear weapons if it decides to do so.[24] A number of significant problems would have to be solved, however, and the process would be time consuming and not without cost.

DOCTRINE. Before decisions are made on the types and sizes of weapons and on delivery systems, the circumstances in which the weapons would be used should be specified.[25] Although the discussion of deterrence earlier in this chapter is relevant here, there are more specific questions than whether to view nuclear weapons as a tactical means of defense or as a strategic deterrent. For example, design and delivery requirements for weapons aimed at North Korean airfields are different from those for weapons that might be used against concentrations of North Korean armor.

Some doctrinal questions involve difficult political and moral problems. If deterrence failed, would the ROK really use nuclear weapons against targets, such as industrial facilities or transportation choke points, that are in heavily populated areas? In particular, could nuclear weapons be used against North Korean forces advancing on Seoul without inflicting unacceptable casualties on civilians living along the invasion corridors?

TECHNICAL PROBLEMS AND COSTS. In theory, the ROK could acquire explosive material for nuclear weapons by enriching uranium to the required level or by extracting plutonium from uranium (either natural or slightly enriched) that had been irradiated in a reactor. The latter course would be easier, but some difficult technical problems would have to be solved in designing and building a reprocessing plant. The irradiated

24. In April 1977 the U.S. Energy Research and Development Agency listed the ROK among the countries "which appear technically capable of detonating a nuclear device in the intermediate term (within 4 to 6 years of a decision to do so)." *Nuclear Proliferation Factbook,* Joint Committee Print, House Committee on International Relations and Senate Committee on Governmental Affairs, 95 Cong. 1 sess. (Government Printing Office, 1977), p. 334.

25. In the early years of a nuclear weapons program, doctrine would of course be constrained by practical considerations: the amount of fissionable material available and the size and weight of the first explosive devices.

uranium could be spent fuel from power reactors or fuel irradiated in a reactor built specifically for the weapons program.

A country at the ROK's level of development in the field of nuclear technology might be able to build an adequate reprocessing plant in about four years at a cost of roughly $50 million (1976 dollars).[26] During the same period, work could easily be completed on reworking the fissile material for the first bomb, designing the bomb, fabricating it, and testing it. The total cost of these operations might be no more than $1 million.

An initial nuclear weapons capability might rely on the F-4s already in the inventory of the ROK air force as the delivery system. Configuring a number of F-4s to carry and release nuclear weapons would presumably be neither difficult nor expensive. The first primitive ROK nuclear devices might take the form of atomic demolition munitions and be emplaced in the invasion corridors, ready to be detonated in the event of an attack.

Developing even short-range nuclear missiles in hardened launching sites would be much more costly.[27] This step would be unnecessary, however, as long as South Korea did not have to worry about a preemptive North Korean nuclear strike. Under present conditions, aircraft are as effective a means of delivery as missiles over the short distance involved.

The economic and technological obstacles to an initial nuclear weapons capability do not appear to be very great. Time is a more serious consideration. From the moment that the existence of its nuclear weapons program became known, the ROK would be subject to the various pressures and dangers outlined earlier in this chapter.

LONGER RUN CONSEQUENCES. If the ROK's acquisition of nuclear weapons did not precipitate a new Korean war, it could affect the future of the Korean peninsula in one of two ways. North Korea might (despite predictable Soviet opposition) succeed in also developing nuclear weap-

26. Albert Wohlstetter and others, *Moving Toward Life in a Nuclear Armed Crowd?* ACDA/PAB-263, prepared for the Director, U.S. Arms Control and Disarmament Agency (Los Angeles: Pan Heuristics, 1976), p. 41.

27. As an interim measure, the ROK might develop nuclear warheads for the Nike-Hercules missiles already in its possession and prepare them for use in a surface-to-surface mode. On September 26, 1978, the ROK reportedly tested a surface-to-surface tactical missile resembling the Nike: *Aerospace Daily* (October 23, 1978), p. 242. There is no evidence, however, that the ROK plans to arm this missile with a nuclear warhead.

ons, leading to an uneasy and probably unstable relationship of mutual nuclear deterrence. Both North and South would be driven to spend more and more money on increasingly sophisticated delivery systems in an effort to maintain a credible second-strike capability.

Alternatively, North Korea might despair of matching the ROK's nuclear weapons capability and turn to the Soviet Union for protection. North Korea would then become a Soviet satellite rather than the autonomous regime, balanced carefully between China and the Soviet Union, that it is today.

Either alternative, it might be noted, would greatly reduce prospects for the eventual reunification of Korea.

The Best of Both Worlds?

Some Korean scholars have speculated on the possible advantages of moving closer to a nuclear weapons capability without actually acquiring such weapons. In this way, it might be possible to achieve some of the assumed deterrent value of these weapons without incurring any of the political and military costs. The model for such a policy is Israel, which is widely believed to possess disassembled "bombs in the basement" but which has largely avoided the adverse consequences of admitting that fact.

Duplicating Israel's reported policy is not open to the ROK, which has adhered to the nonproliferation treaty, has no unsafeguarded reactor, and cannot extract plutonium from its spent fuel without the permission of the country (the United States or Canada) that originally supplied the fuel. Israel has refused to sign the NPT, has a large unsafeguarded research reactor, and uses fuel of uncertain, but unrestricted, origin.

Moreover, when Israel was presumably developing its near-nuclear weapons capability, it was not difficult to import the components of a reprocessing plant, and Israel enjoyed a conventional military superiority over its enemies that largely relieved it of the fear that its nuclear program would precipitate an attack. The ROK could not easily circumvent the international controls on trade in sensitive nuclear equipment, and it would have to assume that, if Pyongyang learned of a South Korean nuclear weapons program, a preemptive attack would be quite possible.[28]

28. This inhibition would be reduced if the ROK were to acquire a clear conventional military superiority over the North—but the incentive for acquiring nuclear weapons would also be reduced.

A policy of moving closer to a nuclear weapons capability would have to be carried out in total secrecy, which would deprive it of one of its presumed advantages: the deterrent value of the bomb in the basement. But it is most unlikely that total secrecy could be maintained. Efforts to build an unsafeguarded reactor or to divert spent fuel from a safeguarded power reactor would probably be detected, as would efforts to assemble the components of a reprocessing plant.

There is some evidence that the ROK made some moves toward achieving a near-nuclear weapons capability in the early 1970s and abandoned the effort under U.S. pressure. An unidentified witness interviewed by the staff of a U.S. congressional committee reported that a secret Weapons Exploitation Committee formed by the ROK government had voted unanimously to proceed with the development of nuclear weapons.[29] The U.S. government reportedly learned of this project and persuaded South Korea to abandon it.[30]

THE present nuclear policies of the ROK appear to be well considered and consistent with the national interest. There is no reason to expect those policies to change under conditions likely in the foreseeable future.

The civil nuclear energy program will make an increasingly important contribution to meeting the country's rising energy requirements. In deferring some major decisions about the future of the nuclear fuel cycle, South Korea remains in a good position to take a leading role in creating new international institutions to facilitate the continued development of nuclear power without increasing the spread of nuclear weapons.

The ROK's decision not to acquire nuclear weapons is not only an important contribution to international peace and regional stability, but also promotes its own national security by avoiding the dangers that would follow the opposite decision.

29. *Investigation of Korean-American Relations,* Committee Print, Subcommittee on International Organizations of the House Committee on International Relations, 95 Cong. 2 sess. (GPO, 1978), pp. 79–80.

30. *Los Angeles Times,* November 4, 1978.

CHAPTER FOUR

Taiwan

FOR A GENERATION, the Republic of China on Taiwan has enjoyed a degree of domestic tranquillity, political stability, and economic progress rare among developing countries. Yet its future is uncertain. The question of whether Taiwan is to be reunited with mainland China—and, if so, by what means and under what terms—remains unanswered. And on January 1, 1979, the United States broke diplomatic relations with the ROC and gave notice that the U.S.-ROC mutual defense treaty[1] would be terminated at the end of the year. No one can say whether the next few years will bring the island war or peace.

Despite uncertainty over its future, Taiwan's nuclear policies appear to be unchanged. A massive investment is being made in nuclear energy as a means of generating electricity, and the government remains publicly committed to a policy of not acquiring nuclear weapons.

Civil Nuclear Energy

Taiwan has modest deposits of low-grade coal, some natural gas, and almost no oil.[2] Hydropower is useful principally for peaking purposes. In 1978, 81 percent of the island's total energy supply was imported, almost entirely in the form of oil. Over the period 1979–89, total energy

1. 6 U.S.T. 433.
2. The information on Taiwan's civil nuclear energy program presented here is based in part on conversations in Taipei in November 1977, July 1978, and January 1979.

requirements are expected to rise at an average annual rate of about 9 percent. Domestic energy production will not quite be able to keep pace, and by 1989 imported energy is expected to constitute 82 percent of total supply.[3]

It is not surprising that Taiwan plans to reduce its heavy and growing dependence on imported oil by importing coal and by developing nuclear energy. The government-owned Taiwan Power Company (Taipower) plans to build and put into operation by 1989 seven coal-burning plants with a total generating capacity of 4,450 megawatts (electric).[4] The first nuclear power plant began commercial operation in 1977 and the second in 1978. Four more plants are being built. By 1985 Taiwan will have six nuclear power plants with a total of 5,144 megawatts (electric), or about one-third of anticipated total capacity.[5] Taipower would like to complete six more nuclear power plants by 1993.

The two existing nuclear power plants and the four under construction have light water reactors (LWRs) fueled by low enriched uranium. The seventh and eighth plants are also expected to have LWRs. Other types of reactors may be considered for additional plants. Nuclear scientists on Taiwan have shown considerable interest in heavy water reactors (HWRs) that use natural uranium.[6] Several years ago, Taipower discussed the possible purchase of an HWR with Atomic Energy of Canada, Limited, which makes the CANDU reactor. The deal was blocked, however, by the Canadian government, presumably for fear of offending Peking.

Reactors for at least the first six nuclear power plants will be imported from the United States. But firms on Taiwan will probably play an increasing role in nuclear power projects on the island and perhaps in other areas. Plans to develop a nuclear "software" business[7] in cooperation with U.S. firms are well advanced. A joint effort by the Institute of Nuclear Energy Research (INER) and Taipower to design an LWR for

---

3. The energy data presented here are drawn from Ministry of Economic Affairs, Energy Policy Committee, *The Energy Situation in Taiwan, Republic of China* (March 1979), pp. 6, 18.

4. Taiwan Power Company, *Present Power System and Future Power Development in Taiwan, the Republic of China* (Taipei: TPC, 1978), p. 40.

5. Taiwan Power Company, *Taipower, 1978* (Taipei: TPC, 1979), pp. 14–16.

6. The director of the government's Institute of Nuclear Energy Research would like to design an HWR for use later in Taiwan's nuclear energy program.

7. Design of nuclear power plants, supervision of construction, and testing during construction and start-up.

both local use and export was being discussed in government circles in 1978.

That such ambitious projects can be seriously considered is an indication of the advanced competence of Taiwan in the field of nuclear energy. Taipower did not require a prime contractor for even its first nuclear power plant but used its own personnel to perform the overall managerial functions usually assigned to a prime contractor.

Two institutions on Taiwan are engaged in nuclear energy research. INER has a 40-megawatt reactor fueled by natural uranium and a 10-kilowatt reactor that uses 20–90 percent enriched uranium. The National Tsing Hua University has a 1-megawatt reactor that uses 93 percent enriched uranium (but is being converted to 20 percent enriched fuel) and two small reactors that use lightly enriched uranium.[8]

Taiwan has no nuclear fuel cycle facilities other than the power and research reactors mentioned above and a small plant that fabricates fuel for INER's largest research reactor. Taipower is interested in building a plant to fabricate fuel for its power reactors.

Natural uranium is obtained from the United States and, to a much smaller extent, from South Africa. The lack of diplomatic relations would make it difficult, though not impossible, for Taipower to enter into contracts for Canadian or Australian uranium.[9] Taipower is exploring the possibility of obtaining uranium from Paraguay or Bolivia.

Enrichment and fuel fabrication services for power reactors are obtained solely from the United States. Discussions with the French-sponsored Eurodif for enrichment services apparently ended inconclusively.

Taipower plans to store spent fuel at its reactors for at least ten years. Exploratory discussions with British Nuclear Fuels, Limited (BNFL), concerning reprocessing services were dropped when U.S. opposition to reprocessing became clear. Taipower believes, however, that reprocessing is the proper solution to the problem of spent fuel management.

The government of the ROC strongly favors a regional approach to fuel management.[10] It would join with other countries of the Pacific Basin

8. David S. L. Chu, "Taipower's Nuclear Power Program," paper prepared for the U.S. nuclear team, January 22, 1977, p. 10.

9. The Canadian and Australian authorities could be satisfied by the safeguards that would be applied by the United States after their uranium had been enriched in a U.S. facility.

10. Conversations with officials in Taipei in July 1978.

in establishing a regional nuclear service center that might at first provide storage facilities for spent fuel and later operate a reprocessing plant.[11] The government realizes that its participation would pose political problems for other potential participants that have no diplomatic relations with the ROC and do not want to offend the People's Republic of China (PRC). This is only one of a number of political risks the ROC must face in carrying out its civil nuclear energy program.

Even though the United States has withdrawn recognition, Taiwan's access to U.S. uranium and enrichment services can, and probably will, continue, but Taipei cannot be sure. Similarly, Taiwan may be able to arrange for reprocessing services in Europe or Japan before its problem of spent fuel storage becomes acute. But again, Taipei cannot be sure that such services will not be denied for political reasons.

Taiwan's civil nuclear energy program is fully justifiable on economic grounds, but it must be regarded as something of a political gamble. The leaders in Taipei would probably justify the gamble as being no more risky than relying largely on Middle Eastern oil. They may also see political advantages in an energy policy that increases the economic stake of the United States in Taiwan.

Nuclear Weapons

There can be little doubt of the ROC's ability to develop nuclear weapons if it decided that was in its interest. Taiwan has a large and diversified industrial capacity and has been training nuclear scientists and engineers both at home and abroad for over twenty years. A recent study ranked Taiwan's capability in the field of nuclear weapons alongside that of a number of industrialized countries "that have full access to the special nuclear material needed for weapons and have a broad nuclear technology manpower base."[12]

11. This concept was first presented by the president of Taipower, David S. L. Chu, "Regional Spent-Fuel Reprocessing in Asia," paper prepared for the First Pacific Basin Conference on Nuclear Power Development and the Fuel Cycle, 1976.

12. Albert Wohlstetter and others, *Moving Toward Life in a Nuclear Armed Crowd?* ACDA/PAB-263, prepared for the Director, U.S. Arms Control and Disarmament Agency (Los Angeles: Pan Heuristics, 1976), p. 201. See also *Nuclear Proliferation Factbook,* Joint Committee Print, House Committee on International Relations and Senate Committee on Governmental Affairs, 95 Cong. 1 sess. (Government Printing Office, 1977), p. 334, which lists the Republic of China among the countries technically capable of detonating a nuclear device "within less than 1—up to 3 years of a decision to do so."

In this discussion, it will be assumed that an initial ROC nuclear weapons capability would consist of a few rather bulky fission devices in the 10- to 40-kiloton range. Although these devices might at first be deliverable only by commercial aircraft, they would constitute a threat to urban targets throughout east China. Smaller weapons that could be delivered with greater accuracy by fighter aircraft[13] on tactical targets such as military airfields would come later, as would medium-range missiles with nuclear warheads.

Present Policy

The government of the ROC has often declared that it has no intention of acquiring nuclear weapons, it signed and ratified the Treaty on the Non-Proliferation of Nuclear Weapons, and all of its nuclear facilities are subject to International Atomic Energy Agency safeguards.[14] The ROC's policy against possessing nuclear weapons was strongly reaffirmed by Premier (now President) Chiang Ching-kuo on January 27, 1977, who pointed out that "although the Chinese Government has the capability of developing nuclear weapons it will never engage in the production of such weapons."[15] As recently as December 20, 1978—five days after President Carter's announcement that U.S. diplomatic relations with the ROC would be ended—Vice Foreign Minister Frederick Chien told reporters that the ROC was "not going into the nuclear arms field."[16]

This policy is usually justified in Taipei on the grounds that such weapons are immoral and that they could not in any case be used against fellow Chinese. The cost of both the weapons and the means of delivering them is also sometimes mentioned. A more sophisticated justification was given by a senior ROC official in a private conversation with the author in November 1977. He cited an ancient Chinese proverb to the effect that "he who has no jade, has no guilt. When he acquires jade, he becomes

13. The ROC has no F-4s and would have to use F-104Gs, which have a more limited range and carrying capacity.

14. The ROC lost its membership in the IAEA as a consequence of the loss of its seat in the United Nations. Safeguards on Taiwan are applied pursuant to the ROC-U.S.-IAEA trilateral agreement and a bilateral ROC-IAEA agreement, both of which predate the NPT.

15. Press release, Republic of China, Government Information Office, January 27, 1977.

16. *New York Times,* December 21, 1978.

guilty." In other words, acquiring nuclear weapons would draw the opprobrium of the world.

In a formal sense, the question of nuclear weapons has been treated as a closed issue in Taipei. ("The position of the President is very firm." Period.) It apparently is not discussed much, as it is in Seoul.[17] Nevertheless, some military officers and some scientists are believed to favor the weapons, and the general public would probably applaud a decision by the government to develop them.

If the present policy is reversed, it will be because the government sees military or political advantages in possessing nuclear weapons. It is also possible that the government will decide that the best policy would be to move closer to a nuclear weapons capability without taking the final step and actually assembling an explosive device.

The Military Utility of Nuclear Weapons

The ROC faces four kinds of military threats from the armed forces of the People's Republic of China: (1) nuclear attack; (2) invasion of Taiwan; (3) seizure of the major ROC-held offshore islands; and (4) interdiction of Taiwan's sea and air lines of supply. At the present time, none of these threats is imminent.

The PRC's main security concern is not with the Taiwan problem, but with the threats posed by the USSR from the north and its ally Vietnam from the south. The PRC is therefore unlikely to open a new front along its eastern sea frontier, particularly since to do so might involve it in a military confrontation with the United States. Not only would such a confrontation be highly dangerous, but it would also run counter to the PRC's policy of seeking improved relations with the United States as a means of strengthening its position in the struggle against the Soviet Union.

The ROC cannot assume that these circumstances will continue indefinitely. The PRC's relations with the Soviet Union and Vietnam may not always be as bad as they are today, and the strength of the U.S. deterrent is clearly on the decline. It is true that, in announcing the shift

---

17. This situation could change. On January 20, 1979, the English-language *China News* carried an editorial endorsing the government's policy against the acquisition of nuclear weapons but calling for "open discussion about nuclear possibilities and prospects."

of U.S. diplomatic recognition from Taipei to Peking, President Carter declared that the United States "will continue to have an interest in the peaceful resolution of the Taiwan issue," and Secretary of State Cyrus R. Vance has stated that despite the termination of the mutual defense treaty the United States will continue to sell "carefully selected defensive weapons" to Taiwan.[18] These declarations, however, are not regarded by the ROC as an adequate substitute for the treaty.[19] Increasingly, the ROC must ask whether standing alone it could deal successfully with the potential military threats from the mainland and whether nuclear weapons would make a substantial contribution to its security.

THE NUCLEAR THREAT. From a strictly military point of view, the ROC has no answer to the threat presented by the PRC's inventory of several hundred nuclear weapons, ranging from 20 kilotons to 2–3 megatons in explosive force. Means of delivery include forty to fifty medium-range ballistic missiles with a range of 600–700 miles, and fifty to seventy intermediate-range ballistic missiles with a range of 1,500–1,750 miles. The PRC's air force also includes intermediate- and medium-range bombers capable of delivering nuclear weapons.[20] The ROC has no defense against the PRC's nuclear-armed missiles and could not be sure of 100 percent results against the PRC's bombers, even though they are obsolescent and fly at subsonic speeds.

If the PRC had no fear of U.S. retaliation, it could conceivably deliver an ultimatum, demanding that the ROC surrender or suffer nuclear destruction. For several reasons, however, Peking is unlikely to take this action. First, despite the termination of the mutual defense treaty, the PRC could not be sure that the United States would not intervene or that the United States and the Soviet Union would not join in seeking to block a resort to nuclear weapons that both would view as a dangerous precedent. Second, the PRC would hesitate to weaken its deterrent against the Soviet Union by expending some of its limited number of

18. Department of State, Bureau of Public Affairs, "U.S. Policy Toward China, July 15, 1971–January 15, 1979," *Selected Documents,* East Asian and Pacific series, no. 9 (State Department, January 1979), pp. 46, 56.

19. Conversations in Taipei, January 1979.

20. Unclassified sources on PRC nuclear weapons capabilities include International Institute for Strategic Studies, *The Military Balance, 1979–1980* (London: IISS, 1979); General George S. Brown, *United States Military Posture for FY 1979* (GPO, 1978); and Defense Intelligence Agency, *Handbook on the Chinese Armed Forces,* DDI-2680-32-76, July 1976.

nuclear weapons on Taiwan. Third, by threatening to kill thousands of innocent people to settle a domestic quarrel, the PRC would severely damage its international standing. Fourth, the PRC has declared that it would not be the first to use nuclear weapons; if this is credible for foreign enemies, it is probably even more credible for fellow Chinese. And fifth, the ROC might refuse to capitulate, in which case, would the PRC actually carry out its threat and use nuclear weapons against Chinese whom it merely wished to reunite with the rest of the nation?

One event that could make the PRC nuclear ultimatum more likely would be a decision by the ROC to develop nuclear weapons. Peking might well regard the prospect of a nuclear threat from the east, in addition to that already faced from the north, as intolerable and move to eradicate it before it achieved dangerous dimensions. The PRC would justify its action as an effort to eliminate a threat to peace. Many people in other countries would agree. One or both superpowers would be much less likely to intervene than if the ROC had not provided the PRC with an excuse.

INVASION OF TAIWAN BY CONVENTIONAL FORCES. Table 4-1 presents in summary form a comparison of the conventional military forces of the PRC and the ROC. If the ROC faced its domestic adversary across a land frontier, its situation would clearly be hopeless. However, the PRC has only a limited capability to project military force across the Taiwan Strait.[21]

The PRC's navy includes perhaps fifteen U.S.-built LSTs (landing ships, tank) of World War II vintage that were captured from the ROC. The navy's major surface combatants could not provide the heavy firepower that would be needed to support an amphibious landing on Taiwan. The PRC's air force is far larger than that of the ROC, but it (and the air component of the navy) consists largely of short-range and obsolescent fighter planes that are best suited for air defense. The ROC has better planes with better armament, and its pilots are believed to be better trained than those of the PRC. Only part of the PRC's air force could be deployed against Taiwan because of limited airfield capacity and the need to station large numbers of planes along the Soviet border.

---

21. For a more detailed discussion of PRC and ROC military capabilities, see Stuart E. Johnson with Joseph A. Yager, *The Military Equation in Northeast Asia* (Brookings Institution, 1979).

Table 4-1. *Conventional Military Forces of the People's Republic of China and the Republic of China, 1979*

Forces	People's Republic of China	Republic of China
Ground		
Personnel	3,600,000	400,000
Divisions	129	22
Infantry	115	18
Armored	11	2
Airborne	3	0
Marine	0	2
Air		
Combat aircraft	4,700	388
Naval		
Major surface combatants[a]	25	33
Submarines	93	2
Patrol craft (all classes)	826	9
Shore-based aircraft	800	9

Source: International Institute for Strategic Studies, *The Military Balance, 1979–1980* (London: IISS, 1979), pp. 64 and 65.
a. Destroyers, destroyer escorts, and frigates.

An invasion of Taiwan would be a hazardous undertaking. By accepting disproportionate losses of planes and pilots to the qualitatively superior—though badly outnumbered—ROC air force, the PRC could probably achieve air superiority and with it control of the waters of the Taiwan Strait. The issue would then be decided on the beaches, and the outcome would be uncertain.

If the PRC did not already have nuclear weapons, the ROC might conclude that by developing its own it could deter or defeat an invasion of Taiwan. Certainly, the thought that launching an invasion could lead to the destruction of several major cities would have an inhibiting effect on the leaders in Peking. Besides which, ROC tactical nuclear weapons could severely damage an invasion force in its assembly areas on the mainland or on the landing beaches on Taiwan.

Since the PRC does have nuclear weapons, the ROC would have to assume that, if it threatened to use such weapons against mainland cities, the PRC might strike first. Were Taiwan actually to use nuclear weapons against either mainland cities or an invasion force, the PRC might retaliate with devastating nuclear attacks on targets on Taiwan, possibly including its major cities.[22]

The fundamental difficulty from Taiwan's point of view is that it could not easily create a credible second-strike capability, a problem similar to that faced by Japan (discussed in chapter 2). The answer is also similar: a force of submarines armed with nuclear missiles. These submarines would not have to be nuclear powered to maintain stations threatening the major cities of mainland China, and they could be equipped with cruise missiles rather than ballistic missiles. Nevertheless, the cost and the technological problems to be solved in designing and building the submarines and equipping them with missiles would be formidable. Long before a program creating a force of nuclear missile submarines could be completed, the PRC could be expected to act decisively to bring it to an end.

Developing nuclear weapons to deal with a possible invasion of Taiwan therefore does not at first sight appear to be a rational course of action. It might be asked, however, whether displaying a convincing determination to meet an invasion attempt with nuclear weapons, despite the potentially suicidal consequences, might not be an effective deterrent.[23] The ROC might calculate that, if it somehow got its initial nuclear weapons force in place without precipitating a nuclear showdown with the PRC, it would present the PRC with a paralyzing dilemma. On the one hand, to launch an invasion before destroying the ROC's nuclear force would be to risk severe damage to several cities or destruction of part of the invasion force in the assembly areas, or both. On the other hand, delivering a first strike sufficiently large to ensure destruction of the ROC nuclear force would probably cause heavy civilian casualties and seriously damage the international standing of the PRC.

It must be emphasized that this justification of the deterrent value of nuclear weapons rests on two unprovable assumptions: that the PRC

22. For an analysis of possible nuclear exchanges between the PRC and the ROC, see Beverly Rowen and others, *Regional Rivalries and Nuclear Responses,* vol. 3: *Region of the South China Sea,* DNA 001-77-C-0052, prepared for the Director, U.S. Defense Nuclear Agency (Los Angeles: Pan Heuristics, 1978), pp. 38–56.

23. A parallel might be drawn with the U.S. deployment of tactical nuclear weapons to Western Europe, which is justified as a deterrent of a Soviet attack, even though use of those weapons would almost certainly set in motion a sequence of catastrophic events.

could be made to believe that the ROC would respond to an invasion attempt by initiating a nuclear exchange and that the PRC would not resolve its dilemma by striking first. In other words, the value of nuclear weapons in deterring an invasion of Taiwan would depend on the ROC's success in projecting an image of desperate willingness to take great risks that would paralyze the PRC rather than stimulate it to take devastating preemptive action.

SEIZURE OF OFFSHORE ISLANDS. The PRC might conceivably decide to try to seize one or more of the major ROC-held offshore islands, either as a prelude to the invasion of Taiwan or as a means of undermining morale on Taiwan. Quemoy would be the most likely objective, because it is closer to the mainland than Matsu and has a much larger garrison (60,000 men, or more than one-seventh of the ROC ground forces).

A direct assault against the heavily fortified ROC positions on Quemoy would be costly and might not succeed. The PRC would therefore be more likely to try to starve out the garrison by cutting off resupply from Taiwan. Large stocks of food and ammunition are believed to be stored underground on Quemoy, but in time a blockade would undoubtedly succeed. Against PRC artillery, fighter planes, and patrol boats armed with torpedoes and antiship missiles, the ROC navy and air force probably could not break the blockade. Nuclear weapons would not be much use against the blockading forces; they could not be used against close-in PRC artillery positions without endangering the troops on Quemoy. Nor could nuclear weapons be relied on to deter an attack on Quemoy. Loss of Quemoy and its garrison would be a serious, though by no means fatal, blow to the ROC. The PRC is therefore unlikely to believe that the ROC would resort to nuclear weapons to save Quemoy.

INTERDICTION OF TAIWAN'S LINES OF SUPPLY. If Peking should decide to try to solve the Taiwan problem by force, it might well adopt the strategy of interdicting the island's sea and air lines of supply. The PRC's navy and air force might be unable to maintain an effective blockade, as the term is used in international law, but that would not be necessary. Peking could simply announce that all the ports and airfields of the rebellious province of Taiwan had been closed. If foreign merchant ships disregarded the order, one or more could be seized or even sunk. Civil aircraft trying to reach Taiwan could be forced to land on the mainland or shot down if they refused to land.

Nations such as Japan and the United States that trade heavily with Taiwan would be certain to protest the closure order, but unless their merchant ships and civil aircraft were given effective protection, they would obey it.[24] The ROC navy and air force unaided could not cope with the problem.

Without foreign intervention (which would mean the United States), the economy of Taiwan would be slowly strangled. The problem would not be providing a minimum level of subsistence for the island's population. Taiwan grows much of its food requirements, and needed supplements, largely of grain, could be brought in under convoy or possibly with the acquiescence of the PRC. The problem would be economic stagnation, unemployment, inflation, and a precipitous fall in living standards. Taiwan's highly industrialized economy depends on heavy imports of fuel, raw materials, and semifinished goods. It pays for these essential imports by exporting a wide variety of manufactured and agricultural products. Without access to foreign markets and sources of supply, Taiwan's economy would collapse.

Nuclear weapons probably would not increase the ability of the ROC to deal with the threat of interdiction. Breaking the noose around Taiwan by direct military means would call for expanded conventional anti-submarine and air defense capabilities. Threatening a nuclear attack on mainland China cities unless the closure order were lifted would risk a preemptive PRC nuclear strike on Taiwan.

The PRC might be restrained from issuing a closure order by the fear that it would eventually cause the ROC to lash out in desperation against mainland targets. But it would be more likely to calculate that, long before the point of desperation was reached, the slow strangulation of Taiwan's economy would force it to the bargaining table.

The Political Utility of Nuclear Weapons

Although the military utility of nuclear weapons to the ROC must be rated quite low, its leaders might conclude that, in some circumstances, nuclear weapons could improve their political position, both domestically and internationally.

24. A further reason for compliance would be the increase in insurance rates and hazardous-duty pay that would follow issuance of the closure order.

The loss of U.S. diplomatic recognition was a blow that had long been anticipated[25] but that Taipei proved powerless to prevent. For seven years, it concentrated on preserving what was left of the U.S. connection. This policy was entirely realistic, but many people on Taiwan may now see it as futile and defeatist. Even those who are not secretly critical of their government's past effectiveness may harbor doubts about its ability to cope with an uncertain future.

The ROC leaders might see nuclear weapons as at least a partial answer to this problem. By announcing that Taiwan had quietly developed nuclear weapons (or even a near-nuclear capability), they might hope to reassure the public and demonstrate that they had indeed been doing something to ensure the island's future.

They might also see nuclear weapons as useful internationally. By joining the select group of nuclear weapons states, Taiwan would be proclaiming that it was still a power to be reckoned with. Also, it would incidentally add to the credibility of a future claim, should it decide to make it, that Taiwan is a separate and independent state and should be recognized as such.[26]

The Adverse Consequences of Nuclear Weapons

Not all the consequences of Taiwan's developing nuclear weapons would be perceived as positive. The PRC would of course denounce the action and might take preemptive military action. Japan would also deplore the action, although it would be less shaken than it would be by a South Korean nuclear capability (in part, as a matter of geography, but also as a reflection of the different views that Japanese hold of Chinese and Koreans). While the Soviet Union might also publicly denounce the ROC's action, it would probably secretly welcome it as a new complication for the PRC.[27]

25. The U.S. policy of seeking to normalize relations with the PRC dates from the communiqué signed by President Richard M. Nixon and Premier Chou En-lai in Shanghai on February 27, 1972. *Department of State Bulletin* (March 20, 1972), pp. 435–38.

26. This point is made by George H. Quester, "Taiwan and Nuclear Proliferation," *Orbis,* vol. 18 (Spring 1974), pp. 140–50.

27. In fact, the action might marginally increase the possibility of informal cooperation between Taipei and Moscow. The latter might see some advantage in increasing the nuclear threat to the PRC by helping the ROC improve the sophistication of its nuclear weapons delivery systems.

In deciding whether to acquire nuclear weapons, the ROC would have to give great weight to the probable response of the United States. The United States would almost certainly cut off the fuel and equipment needed to operate and expand Taiwan's nuclear power plants.[28] Shipments of military weapons, ammunition, and spare parts would probably be suspended and Export-Import Bank financing terminated. Perhaps more important in the longer run, adverse public and congressional reaction would make less credible U.S. declarations of continued interest in the peaceful resolution of the Taiwan problem.

The Near-Nuclear Option

Taipei may have seriously considered a policy of moving close to a nuclear weapons capability but deferred a decision on whether to assemble such weapons. In late August 1976 the press reported that the ROC was secretly reprocessing spent nuclear fuel to obtain plutonium usable in nuclear weapons. These reports were promptly denied by Taiwan.[29] On September 17 the ROC delivered a formal diplomatic note to the American embassy in Taipei that included the statement: "The government of the Republic of China has no intention whatsoever to develop nuclear weapons or a nuclear explosive device, or to engage in any activities related to reprocessing purposes."[30]

But U.S. suspicion did not completely subside. Apparently it centered on the Institute of Nuclear Energy Research at Lungtan.[31] INER was originally part of the Chungshan Institute of Science and Technology, which conducts research of interest to the ROC armed forces. Several years ago, INER was detached administratively from the Chungshan

28. Section 307 of the Nuclear Non-Proliferation Act of 1978 provides in part that "no nuclear materials and equipment or sensitive nuclear technology shall be exported to (1) any non-nuclear-weapon state that is found by the President to have . . . (b) terminated or abrogated IAEA safeguards." The president can authorize the continuation of such exports if he determines that their cessation "would be seriously prejudicial to the achievement of United States non-proliferation objectives or otherwise jeopardize the common defense and security." This determination must, however, be submitted to Congress, which can overrule it by a concurrent resolution if it acts within sixty days.

29. *Washington Post*, August 29, 1976, and *New York Times*, August 30, 1976.

30. *Washington Post*, September 23, 1976.

31. The account of developments at Lungtan is based principally on private conversations with Chinese officials in Taipei in November 1977 and July 1978.

Institute and put under the ROC Atomic Energy Council. How completely INER has been removed from military influence may be questioned, however, and this seems to have increased U.S. suspicion.[32]

In early 1977 a U.S. team, including nuclear scientists, inspected INER. Exactly what they found has not been made public, but as a result of their visit INER's largest research reactor was shut down.[33] The reactor was not started again until mid-1978, and it is subject to restrictions proposed by the United States. A second U.S. inspection team visited INER in July 1978. Although the available facts concerning the developments at INER are too sketchy to support any definite conclusions, they do justify an exploration of the ROC's near-nuclear option.

In theory, moving close to a nuclear weapons capability would give the ROC more freedom of choice. That is, if nuclear weapons appeared advantageous at some future time, they could be put together with little delay. In the interim, the ROC could hope to avoid the costs and dangers of actually possessing nuclear weapons.

In the real world, executing a near-nuclear policy would not be easy. The practical obstacles to be overcome were pointed out in chapter 3 in the discussion of the feasibility of such a policy for the Republic of Korea. For the ROC, secrecy would be especially important to the success of a near-nuclear policy and difficult to maintain. Rightly or wrongly, the suspicion of the United States has been aroused, and it can be expected to act vigorously to block any efforts by the ROC to move closer to a nuclear weapons capability. Moreover, the commitment not to engage in reprocessing that the ROC made to the United States in 1976 would rule out one of the important steps in a near-nuclear policy.

The fact that a near-nuclear policy may not be feasible for the ROC, however, is of largely academic interest because it probably would not be desirable either. Being secret, it would not even have the limited deterrent value that the possession of finished nuclear weapons would have. And if it were exposed, the political costs and military dangers would be as serious as those that would be incurred in openly developing a nuclear weapons capability.

32. INER is still located next to the Chungshan Institute, the director of Chungshan is the second-ranking member of the AEC, and some members of INER's scientific staff hold military commissions.

33. A reprocessing laboratory was dismantled before the team's visit as a token of good faith by the ROC.

THE ROC has made a major commitment to developing nuclear power to meet a substantial part of its future energy needs. That commitment rests on a sound economic and technological foundation, but it is vulnerable both to the political and military hazards that threaten the island's future and to possible difficulties in obtaining needed fuel, equipment, and services.

Taiwan has made no effort to close the nuclear fuel cycle by acquiring enrichment or reprocessing facilities. Apparently it intends to continue to rely on the United States for enrichment services, but it would welcome an opportunity to join a regional nuclear service center that would initially store spent fuel and later reprocess it.

At present the ROC appears to have no intention of acquiring nuclear weapons. From both the military and the political points of view, the disadvantages of possessing such weapons outweigh the advantages. The ROC may in the recent past have considered adopting a policy of moving closer to a nuclear weapons capability. It may give renewed consideration to such a policy as a result of its loss of U.S. recognition. However, for Taiwan a near-nuclear policy is probably not feasible, nor would it bring gains commensurate with its risks.

PART TWO

India, Pakistan, and Iran

RICHARD K. BETTS

CHAPTER FIVE

Nuclear Energy: Policies and Plans

MUCH of American concern about prospective proliferation centers on the diffusion of nuclear energy facilities for peaceful purposes that can provide a country with the ability to produce nuclear weapons, whether or not the country has any incentive for or intention of doing so at present. Energy strategy may allow nuclear adaptations in military strategy. Since a nuclear infrastructure of some sort (though not necessarily an electric-power-generating capacity) is the minimal prerequisite for indigenous nuclear weapons, the energy-related incentives for nuclear facilities and the present and projected extent of such facilities are the first considera-tion for assessment of prospects for a bomb program. But the full sig-nificance of physical capabilities emerges only when economic rationales for energy production and government policies on nuclear weapons are considered. If the economic case is strong and government commitments against weapons acquisition are solid, the growth of capabilities is less worrisome than if energy benefits and weapons policies are ambiguous or suspect. Plans, infrastructure, and policies vary a great deal among the three countries examined here.

In this chapter the situation in the three countries is compared in each of these dimensions, which are taken up in ascending order of importance for nonproliferation: (1) prevalent internal views about the economic value of nuclear energy generation and the political value of fuel-cycle in-dependence; (2) current and projected investment in nuclear equipment;

(3) official attitudes on weapons-related matters. On all of these questions data for India are both more extensive and more reliable than for the other countries. The relevant aspects of Pakistan's plans have changed rapidly, and Iran's nuclear program could either remain stalled or be reenergized, depending on the evolution of the political situation in Tehran. Economic rationales, physical capabilities, and weapons policies should therefore all be considered variables whose significance depends on the interactions between them and on changeable political decisions.

Economic, Technological, and Developmental Incentives

Analysis in this section emphasizes needs for nuclear energy as perceived or asserted by leaders in the three countries rather than objective calculations, because these beliefs are what will govern decisions. Most American analysts agree that nuclear energy plans have been more ambitious than pure cost-benefit analysis would justify. To the extent that calculations considered objective by Americans contradict native views of the necessity for more nuclear power, they may help change those views —and hence decisions—in the future, but so far there is little evidence to support this expectation.

Countries in South Asia—indeed, most developed countries as well as many in the third world—still see the expansion of nuclear power as necessary to ensure sufficient long-term energy resources. In recent years American analysts have offered a number of compelling arguments for rethinking the economic rationality of massive nuclear energy programs in developing countries, and especially for reconsidering the cost-effectiveness of indigenous enrichment and reprocessing facilities. These analyses buttressed the Carter administration's initiatives to prevent precipitate movement toward a global plutonium economy. Such arguments, however, have not yet convinced many of their targets. A 1976 Pan Heuristics report, for instance, noted that annual energy savings attributable to plans for the expansion of nuclear power, even under the optimistic assumption of a cost advantage of 5 mills per kilowatt-hour, amount in most cases to less than $1 per capita. But the highest projected savings rates were in some of the countries considered to be potential proliferators, such as Iran, where it was $3.28[1] (although other estimates differ, and Iran's nuclear plans are now in limbo). Moreover, even a $1 per capita saving is substantial for a less developed country with low per capita income. The Pan Heuristics estimates, however, were well within the margin of error, so it is not certain that there would be any savings for some countries.

The relative energy profligacy of the industrial nations makes many in the third world skeptical of American remonstrances. An Indian official writes that his country spends 50 percent of its exchange earnings to import oil and notes further:

The combined nuclear programs of the developing countries seek to generate a total of 130,000 billion kilowatt hours per year. This amount of electricity can be produced with 550,000 barrels of oil per day, which is 9 percent of United States oil imports, or 3.3 percent of United States oil consumption. It seems that nonproliferation could be more easily achieved by less consumption of oil by the developed countries.[2]

Nuclear sophistication is not simply a matter of energy opportunity costs to many in India, but an essential component of modernization and independence in general. Global interdependence and varying opportunity costs in nuclear power, which lead some Western economists to see heavy investment in elaborate nuclear establishments as a misallocation of resources for poor countries, are less appealing to those countries, which see such calculations as a rationalization for maintaining the scientific superiority of the industrial states. The pioneering head of India's atomic energy program, Homi Bhabha, put it simply: "What the developed countries have and the underdeveloped lack is modern science and an economy based on modern technology. The problem of developing the underdeveloped countries is therefore the problem of establishing modern science in them and transforming their economy to one based on modern science and technology."[3] In a view that may seem paranoid

1. Albert Wohlstetter and others, *Moving Toward Life in a Nuclear Armed Crowd?* ACDA/PAB-263, prepared for the Director, U.S. Arms Control and Disarmament Agency (Los Angeles: Pan Heuristics, 1976), pp. 84–85.

2. Rikhi Jaipal, "The Indian Nuclear Explosion," *International Security,* vol. 1 (Spring 1977), pp. 46, 50.

3. Quoted in William R. Van Cleave and Harold W. Rood, "A Technological Comparison of Two Potential Nuclear Powers: India and Japan," *Asian Survey,* vol. 7 (July 1967), p. 483. Promotion of advanced research and development efforts in developing countries is also justified "as a watch dog against the import of obsolete

to Americans but more reasonable to policymakers who remember the Moghul conquest and British imperium, Subrahmanyam argues that Indians attribute their colonization to technological inferiority and that the Treaty on the Non-Proliferation of Nuclear Weapons (NPT) is a device to promote "technological hegemony."[4] Others see nuclear investment as both a way to leapfrog from underdevelopment to modernity faster than the European countries did and a way to generate significant industrial spin-off benefits in nonnuclear sectors of the economy.[5]

Such arguments are political as much as economic, assuming a national stake in autonomy and reflecting a visceral insistence on scientific equality for its own sake. But past American policy is not blameless in this regard; the rhetoric of economic development was abetted by the rhetoric of the United Nations Atoms for Peace program.[6] In any case, such arguments indicate that Indian decisionmakers' cost-benefit calculations will attach a value to autonomy and technical equality that may cancel some portion of the diseconomies of nuclear power cited by Western critics. Even though the Indian nuclear program (like most others) has proved costlier and produced less power than anticipated,[7] the economic auton-

---

technology"; "Transfer of Technology: An Indian Viewpoint at Shiraz, Iran," *Nuclear India*, vol. 15 (May–June 1977), p. 2. Bhabha also maintained that buying foreign expertise meant that an underdeveloped country would be paying a share of the cost of research and development, and that "more permanent benefit would result to the country if this money were made available for supporting research and development for India." Quoted in O. P. Dwivedi, "India's Nuclear Energy Policy," paper prepared for the Edinburgh International Political Science Association Congress, August 16–21, 1976, p. 11.

4. K. Subrahmanyam, "India's Nuclear Policy," in Onkar Marwah and Ann Schulz, eds., *Nuclear Proliferation and the Near-Nuclear Countries* (Ballinger, 1975), p. 143.

5. Vikram A. Sarabhai and others, "Impact of Nuclear Technology in Developing Countries," *Nuclear India*, vol. 10 (September 1971), pp. 3–5. An example of industrial spin-offs is the impetus to develop the Indian mining industry and metallurgy provided by facilities needed to process ores for the nuclear program. Van Cleave and Rood, "Technological Comparison of Two Potential Nuclear Powers," pp. 485, 487.

6. Roberta Wohlstetter, *'The Buddha Smiles': Absent-Minded Peaceful Aid and the Indian Bomb*, PH 77-04-370-23, monograph 3, prepared for the U.S. Energy Research and Development Administration (Los Angeles: Pan Heuristics, April 1977), p. 4.

7. Efficiency was purposely sacrificed for construction of the second CANDU reactor at Kalpakkam (longer construction time and higher costs) in order to maximize its self-sufficiency. P. D. Henderson, *India: The Energy Sector* (Oxford University Press for the World Bank, 1975), p. 83.

omy theme was still being touted by the end of the 1970s, perhaps because American pressure on fuel supplies accentuated the dependence problem. Many Indians have justified full-cycle nuclear energy capabilities and breeder reactor construction with statements to the effect that the third world missed the industrial revolution and will not make the same mistake by missing the nuclear revolution. Yet they still offer purely economic justifications as well for the same programs. Marwah states that the developing countries have a greater need for breeders because their nuclear generating capacities will not be fully matured until the year 2000. As with oil, "It appears . . . one more case of a new technology whose exploitation by advanced societies will deplete a world resource (uranium), making it necessary for later-developing parts of the world to utilize still more advanced technology."[8] Western analyses that project sufficient stocks of natural uranium, despite major uncertainties, are regarded with skepticism, as are assurances that access to Western enrichment facilities eliminates justification for indigenous full-cycle capabilities. As a Pakistani analyst pointed out, in terms that should be persuasive to Americans anxious to escape dependence on Middle East oil, "So long as uranium enrichment remains a near monopoly of certain countries . . . the supply of enriched uranium is less secure than the supply of oil."[9]

Of the three countries, India has the most persuasive economic case for an ambitious nuclear program. First, its nuclear capabilities are already exceptionally advanced and it is questionable (at least to many Indian analysts) that heavy nuclear investment detracts from other development programs. Budgetary data for Indian nuclear expenditures are hard to pin down, because different observers apparently use different accountings, but Jaipal claims that expenditures by the Department of Atomic Energy between 1951 and 1973 were $370 million (an average of $16.8 million a year). The five-year plan inaugurated as a result of the rise in oil prices budgeted an average $63 million a year—only 0.7 percent of total expenditures for development.[10] Others claim that

8. Onkar Marwah, "India's Nuclear and Space Programs: Intent and Policy," *International Security,* vol. 2 (Fall 1977), p. 110n.

9. Tariq Osman Hyder, "Islamic World and Peaceful Nuclear Energy," in *Proceedings of the International Conference on Defence and the Muslim World* (London: Islamic Institute of Defence Technology, 1979), p. 112.

10. Jaipal, "Indian Nuclear Explosion," p. 45.

total Indian expenditures were much higher[11] but still consumed only a
third of the government's research and development budget.[12] It is not
clear that such accountings give full weight to the capital costs of nuclear
plants, which are higher than those of thermal plants. Nevertheless,
Indian planners consider nuclear power cost-effective because of deficiencies in other resources. Hydropower fluctuates with the monsoon
season and is already used to capacity in many areas. Coal resources are
located in the eastern and central portions of the country, and when
transportation costs were taken into account uranium emerged as the
least expensive energy source for many other areas. (Here again such
rationales are suspect since they do not mention the possibility of using
cheaper imported coal.) Other more traditional sources of energy are
also derided or seen as insufficient: "Firewood and cow-dung cannot
possibly continue to provide the same level of energy as they do now;
further dependency on these two sources will make India a land with no
forests, and perhaps more animals than people."[13]

The weapons-applicable aspects of India's energy plans that alarm
nonproliferation advocates are rationalized by economic independence
criteria, too. Choice of heavy water reactors (HWRs) that run on natural uranium (which are better adapted to plutonium production than
light water reactors) is justified by the logic of self-sufficiency since they
do not require enriched uranium; original plans to move toward burning
plutonium were motivated by the high cost of enrichment and the need
to build stocks of plutonium for the fast breeder program; and the plan
for the thorium-based breeders is reinforced by India's massive deposits
of thorium.[14] In fact the commitment to the breeder is cited as a reason

11. *Nucleonics Week,* vol. 18 (June 23, 1977), p. 12, cites expenditures of $99
million in 1976–77 and a budget of $182 million for 1977–78. Onkar Marwah gives
a figure of slightly more than $1 billion for past expenditures over a twenty-year
period; "India's Nuclear Program: Decisions, Intent, and Policy, 1950–1976," in
William H. Overholt, ed., *Asia's Nuclear Future* (Westview Press, 1977), p. 168.
The different figures of Jaipal ("Indian Nuclear Explosion") may be attributable to
variations in the exchange rate for the rupee or programming of some atomic energy
expenditures outside the account of India's Department of Atomic Energy (not the
same as the Indian Atomic Energy Commission), or both.

12. Marwah, "India's Nuclear Program," p. 168.

13. Dwivedi, "India's Nuclear Energy Policy," p. 7.

14. See Robert Gillette, "India and Argentina: Developing a Nuclear Affinity,"
Science (June 28, 1974), p. 1351; and Marwah, "India's Nuclear and Space Programs," p. 101.

for the West not to be alarmed by the acquisition of plutonium; diversion of the plutonium stockpiles to a weapons program would retard the breeder program, according to one Indian argument, and enough fissile material from the breeders to make a significant number of weapons will not be available until the next century. India's plans for the breeders are of long standing: Jawaharlal Nehru discussed them, and the related need for plutonium, in parliament two decades ago.

Many Western analysts regard such economic rationales for the development of nuclear power on a large scale as unfounded. For example, avoiding dependence for fuel enrichment is less obviously an advantage if the country lacks sufficient natural uranium of its own to run its HWRs. While India does mine uranium, analysts recognized by the early 1970s that indigenous supplies would not last long. Criticism of Indian plans as cost-ineffective goes back to the 1950s. Such criticism, however, was not the conventional wisdom—even in the West—in either the crucial formative years of the Indian program or later. By the middle 1960s, for instance, defects were apparent in a 1963 appraisal by Burns and Roe, Incorporated, of the Tarapur power project (the report had concluded the nuclear project would be competitive with conventional alternatives), yet as late as 1974 the report was still undisputed as the authoritative source.[15] Americans also share the responsibility for India's early commitment to plutonium reprocessing: the vagueness of India's plans for plutonium in relation to realistic programs for power production was hardly different from the way the United States and Britain thought about the utility or necessity for plutonium through the 1950s.[16] Much of Bhabha's early interest in reprocessing was attributable to the influence of U.S. scientists, and in the 1950s and early 1960s American training programs for foreign nuclear engineers took for granted the economic necessity of reprocessing. Reprocessing was integral to the three-phase nuclear development plan envisioned in 1961, which aimed ultimately to exploit India's indigenous thorium supplies in fast breeders that would run on U-233.[17] It is hardly surprising, then, that the Indian nuclear establishment developed a devotion to and a vested interest in both nuclear power for electricity and plutonium for fuel.

In Iran the revolution makes any prediction of energy or defense

15. Wohlstetter, 'The Buddha Smiles,' pp. 39–53, 65–67, 127–28.
16. Ibid., p. 1.
17. Shyam Bhatia, India's Nuclear Bomb (Sahibabad: Vikas, 1979), p. 102.

policies there problematic. The Khomeini government canceled reactor purchases and took steps to end construction on projects in progress. It is not certain, however, that nuclear generation of energy will be completely abandoned. If a more pragmatic government emerges, it might see value in salvaging some of the nuclear program. The prerevolutionary background of Iranian nuclear plans, then, may be instructive.

The shah's ambitious development plans were coupled with the prospect that the country's oil resources would be nearly depleted before the end of the century. Indeed, Iranians have maintained that their oil is too valuable to be burned for power. Planners under the shah assumed oil prices would keep rising while nuclear power costs would stabilize. The best purposes for oil were for export for foreign exchange and for use in chemical and petrochemical industries. By the last year of the shah's rule, however, sharp escalations in capital and operating costs made nuclear power hardly more cost-effective than oil or coal. Also, neither the shah nor the succeeding revolutionary government attempted to acquire indigenous enrichment or reprocessing facilities. A prior question, in any case, will be what to do with spent fuel. It is notable—and was of concern to those suspicious of Iranian intentions about nuclear weapons—that Iran under the shah refused to return spent fuel to suppliers and even offered to accept Austria's nuclear waste for storage. But this offer angered leaders of the Muslim clergy (many of whom came to power in 1979) because it made Iran a "dumping ground" for Western waste.[18] Like India, Iran also has some indigenous sources of uranium. Of the three countries, Iran's nuclear policies, both before and after the shah's fall, have been the least alarming from a nonproliferation perspective; however, its policies have also been the least articulated and discussed in public, and civil convulsions make future policies conjectural at best.

Until recently Pakistan planned a major infrastructure: twenty-four power reactors, mostly of the heavy water variety, by the turn of the century, as well as reprocessing and enrichment facilities. Of the three coun-

18. Zalmay Khalilzad and others, *Regional Rivalries and Nuclear Responses,* vol. 1: *Competition and Conflict in the Arabian Sea and the Prospects for Nuclear Proliferation,* DNA 001-77-C-0052, prepared for the Director, U.S. Defense Nuclear Agency (Los Angeles: Pan Heuristics, 1978), p. 115; Bijan Mossavar-Rahmani, "Iran's Energy Options: Nuclear Power Versus Natural Gas in an OPEC Developing Country," paper prepared for the University of Chicago Workshop on Energy Options and Risks, November 1978, pp. 3, 5, 8.

tries, Pakistan had the least plausible economic justification for such an ambitious program. Construction of such an establishment, given Pakistan's relatively low levels of nuclear expertise and equipment and the strained state of its economy, would mean significant financial sacrifices and investment trade-offs. Pakistan has less wherewithal to indulge in maximizing autonomy, and it is not clear that energy needs justify such a program. Some Pakistanis pointed out in 1976 that the country imported over 85 percent of its fuel (spending for oil increased sevenfold after 1973, taking up a major portion of the national budget) and cited a study by the International Atomic Energy Agency that suggested the need for the twenty-four reactors.[19] Interest in nuclear power was also spurred in late 1973 when the chairman of the Pakistan Atomic Energy Commission announced that large uranium deposits had been discovered in the southern Punjab and speculated that Pakistan would become a uranium exporter.

At least one analyst, however, persuasively contradicts the economic justification by pointing to more cost-effective energy alternatives. Khalilzad notes that Pakistan has large amounts of natural gas. Coal reserves were estimated as of 1976 at 482 million tons (or about five hundred years' output at production levels of the early 1970s), and the country could make greater use of hydroelectric power.[20] (Use of water for irrigation rather than power, however, has been cited as a competing demand of higher priority.[21]) The government was predicting that 40 percent of oil requirements would be met domestically within a few years. Moreover, members of the Organization of Petroleum Exporting Countries were subsidizing Pakistan's oil purchases: Pakistan spent $385 million on oil at the same time it received $580 million in grants and aid from Iran and Arab countries. Before the 1973 oil price increase Pakistan

19. *Nucleonics Week,* vol. 17 (May 27, 1976), p. 5. For the official technical rationale for Pakistan's high projections, see Mohammad Ahmad, "Long Term Plan for Nuclear Power in Pakistan," *The Nucleus: Quarterly Journal of the Pakistan Atomic Energy Commission,* vol. 11 (October–December 1974), pp. 3–13; and *Nuclear Power Planning Study for Pakistan* (Vienna: International Atomic Energy Agency, 1975).

20. Zalmay Khalilzad, "Pakistan: The Making of a Nuclear Power," *Asian Survey,* vol. 16 (June 1976), pp. 582–86.

21. John J. Stobbs, Judith B. Fox, and James H. Allen, *International Data Collection and Analysis,* vol. 4, EN-77-C-01-5072, prepared for U.S. Department of Energy (Atlanta: Nuclear Assurance Corporation, 1978), p. PAKISTAN-1.

received little aid from Middle Eastern countries, but in 1974–75 it received the second largest amount of aid to emanate from OPEC, and Saudi Arabia and other Persian Gulf states decided to take up the slack when the United States cut aid to Pakistan in 1979.[22] The IAEA recommendations for the pace of the Pakistani reactor buildup also assumed substantial increases in the nation's demand for energy because of a direct relation between growth in gross national product and increases in energy consumption. Khalilzad challenges this notion, pointing out that in 1973 Pakistan's per capita GNP was substantially higher than India's yet per capita energy consumption was only marginally higher and that in the same year Pakistan's energy production declined substantially but its per capita GNP grew. Pan Heuristics estimates also suggested that Pakistan's annual per capita savings from the nuclear power plants on order might amount to only 5 cents.[23] And though the economic logic of substantial reactor investments is questionable, the energy rationale for indigenous reprocessing and enrichment, which Pakistan has also been pursuing, is even weaker.

So the economic logic of major nuclear investments by these countries remains in dispute, and the weight of argument has shifted in the negative direction since the early 1970s. American economists have presented reasonable arguments debunking the necessity for massive nuclear power programs and even more persuasive arguments against the prospective cost-effectiveness of the plutonium reprocessing. Unanticipated cost increases are leading some planners in the countries themselves to reevaluate the desirable scale of nuclear energy investments. But uncertain data and predictability prevent antireprocessing arguments from being conclusive, at least to local leaders. In any case, the linkage of political and psychological considerations of self-sufficiency and equality, in the view of many planners in the region, prevent purely economic arguments from being compelling, even if these planners are genuinely uninterested in a nuclear weapons option. The country with the least persuasive economic justification for a large nuclear energy program (Pakistan) is also the one, as subsequent discussion will indicate, with the clearest strategic incentives for nuclear weapons, which may make the economic case even

22. U.S. Foreign Broadcast Information Service (FBIS), *Daily Report: Middle East and North Africa* (April 13, 1979), p. S3.

23. Khalilzad, "Pakistan," pp. 581–82; Wohlstetter and others, *Moving Toward Life in a Nuclear Armed Crowd?* p. 85.

less relevant. For all the countries, the next step in appreciating their prospective options is to move from their nuclear power incentives to their capabilities.

Present and Prospective Capabilities

Declared interest in nuclear power and fuel-cycle autonomy in India and Pakistan have been similar, but there is a wide gap in their actual capabilities. Iran's interest evaporated in 1979, which makes capabilities a nonissue unless the authorities in Tehran reconsider their policies. Such reversal is possible if the revolutionary situation evolves in a less puritanical direction and leaders begin to focus on internal economic and external strategic alternatives. Actual capabilities are therefore a significant factor in assessing New Delhi's nuclear weapons potential, and policies have, comparatively, much more effect on the judgment about Islamabad and Tehran.

India

Only India now has a highly developed nuclear industry, but the extent of its sophistication and autonomy, compared with any other third world countries, is not widely appreciated in the West. Atomic energy research in India actually began in 1944, when Homi Bhabha obtained private support for a group of nuclear scientists from the Tata Institute of Fundamental Research in Bombay, more than a year before the first atomic detonation at Alamogordo.[24] India obtained crude uranium oxide for research from Canada in 1947, with American and British concurrence (reportedly motivated in part by the hope of ensuring access to Indian thorium resources in the future). Desiring to match a glamorous Soviet aid project (a steel mill), Canada sold India a research reactor (CIRUS) in 1955. At about the same time a pool-type reactor, built almost entirely by the Indians, went critical at Apsara.[25]

24. Marwah, "India's Nuclear and Space Programs," p. 98.
25. Barrie Morrison and Donald M. Page, "India's Option: The Nuclear Route to Achieve Goal as a World Power," *International Perspectives* (July–August 1974), p. 25; H. N. Sethna, "India's Atomic Energy Programme—Past and Future," *International Atomic Energy Agency Bulletin,* vol. 21 (October 1979), p. 4.

India has four operational research reactors and two test reactors under construction or planned, including an experimental fast breeder at Kalpakkam. There are ten commercial nuclear power plants, existing or projected: four operational (two at Tarapur and two at Rajasthan); two under construction at Madras; two planned and located (Narora-1 and -2); and two planned but, as of 1979, not located. The Tarapur reactors are of the light water variety, and the others are heavy water reactors. Cumulative generating capacity in megawatts (electric) projected in 1978 for 1985 is 1,660 and for the year 2000 it is 10,160.[26] Mining and milling operations at Jaduguda provide natural uranium for the heavy water CANDU reactors, and fuel is fabricated at the Hyderabad Nuclear Fuel Complex (NFC), which contains seven plants "for sequential processing of Zircon Sand, uranium ore concentrate and imported enriched uranium hexafloride into finished fuel assemblies."[27] Except for the enrichment of fuel for the two light water reactors at Tarapur, all of the processing of Indian reactor fuel is done at the NFC. There is a pilot-scale plutonium plant at Trombay (apparently used to obtain the fissionable material for India's 1974 explosive test) for reprocessing spent fuel from the research reactors. A newer power reactor fuel reprocessing plant at Tarapur is designed to handle spent fuel from the Tarapur and Rajasthan reactors. (Commissioning of this plant was delayed by disputes with the United States, but by 1978 it was operating with fuel wastes from unsafeguarded research reactors.) A third plant is planned for Madras to reprocess spent fuel from the Madras and Narora reactors. Finally, India has four heavy water plants in various phases of operation, construction, or commissioning and two more in the planning stage.[28]

The program is, compared with those in other third world countries, remarkably self-sufficient. Estimates differ but all agree that the general technical manpower base and the nuclear component within it have increased rapidly over the years since independence. Even in the 1960s

26. "Two More N-Plants to Be Built," *Nuclear Engineering International* (June 1979), p. 9; Stobbs, Fox, and Allen, *International Data Collection and Analysis,* vol. 3, pp. INDIA-8, -9, -24.

27. Stobbs, Fox, and Allen, *International Data Collection and Analysis,* vol. 3, p. INDIA-12.

28. Ibid., pp. INDIA-13, -15–16; "India Commences Operation of Tarapur Reprocessing Plant," *Nuclear Engineering International* (June 1978), p. 9; *Nucleonics Week,* vol. 21 (April 17, 1980), p. 9.

the Indian research effort engaged over 3,000 scientists, and by the late 1970s the Bombay research center alone had 7,000 scientists and technical personnel.[29] India's level of overall scientific and technical manpower is, in fact, *the third largest in the world* (behind only the United States and the Soviet Union)—about 1.5 million by the end of the 1970s and growing more slowly after having increased at a rate of 150 percent every ten years.[30] The Trombay chemical separation plant was engineered, built, and commissioned by indigenous personnel.[31] A substantial portion of nuclear equipment is produced domestically; for example, 75 percent of all instrumentation for power plants.[32] Fueling machine carriages are manufactured for less than half the cost of importing them from Canada.[33] India has also entered the export market, selling nonsensitive equipment or discussing sales with countries like Argentina, Brazil, Libya, and Vietnam.

Self-sufficiency is far from complete. For example, although indigenous scientific expertise on nuclear matters is impressive, the Indian industrial base is not sufficient to provide all the necessary machinery and tooling for nuclear facilities.[34] But sources of external nuclear aid or interchange are diversified. There are nuclear cooperation agreements with the United States, the United Kingdom, the USSR, France, West Germany, Hungary, and Spain. Canada, most intensely involved in India's program in the early years, halted nuclear sales and cooperation with India after the 1974 test explosion and made the termination "permanent" in May 1976 after unsuccessful negotiations for full-scope safeguards, but agreed a year later to resume cooperation.[35] The Cana-

29. Wing Commander Maharaj J. Chopra, "India's Nuclear Path in the 1970s," *Military Review*, vol. 54 (October 1974), p. 38; Jaipal, "Indian Nuclear Explosion," p. 45.

30. Marwah, "India's Nuclear and Space Programs," p. 112n; F. A. Long, "Science and Technology in India: Their Role in National Development," in John W. Mellor, ed., *India: A Rising Middle Power* (Westview Press, 1979), p. 225.

31. Van Cleave and Rood, "Technological Comparison of Two Potential Nuclear Powers," p. 486.

32. S. P. Seth, "India's Atomic Profile," *Pacific Community*, vol. 6 (January 1975), p. 276.

33. *Nucleonics Week*, vol. 17 (September 2, 1976), p. 6.

34. Ibid., vol. 20 (March 8, 1979), p. 10.

35. Don Oberdorfer, "Soviets Agree to Sell India Heavy Water for Reactors," *Washington Post*, December 8, 1976; *Nucleonics Week*, vol. 18 (June 23, 1977), p. 12.

dian cutoff caused problems; for instance, the start-up of the second Rajasthan power reactor was delayed by lack of heavy water. (The Soviet Union agreed to supply the heavy water but held up delivery while insisting on multiple-point safeguards similar to what Canada had demanded.[36]) Problems with heavy water, such as an explosion that shut down the Baroda plant, place constraints on the production and stockpiling of unsafeguarded plutonium. One reporter suggests that the civilian power program needed the Soviet heavy water so that the small amount of indigenous production could be used to run the research reactor (unsafeguarded) that yielded the plutonium for the 1974 explosion.[37] There are other indications of weaknesses in the Indian program, such as questionable compromises on safety, greater than the foregoing list of accomplishments implies,[38] and a number of projects are several years behind schedule. Energy results are still modest, too. By the end of the 1970s only 3 percent of gross electrical consumption was being supplied by nuclear power.[39]

As more of the country's new power reactors that are not internationally safeguarded (built without external assistance and the restrictions attendant on such contracts) come on line—the two at Madras and two at Narora—there will be more freely disposable plutonium. (This assumes that India will not accede to demands for full-scope safeguards.) Availability of unsafeguarded plutonium, "for a weapons program worthy of the name" in the view of most Indians, depends on the operation of the large (600 megawatts) domestically built reactors, and it will be some time before sufficient amounts begin to accumulate from them. But if safeguards and power generation requirements are not taken into

36. *Nucleonics Week,* vol. 18 (March 24, 1977), p. 8.

37. Thomas O'Toole, "Soviet Sale Raises Question on India's Nuclear Plans," *Washington Post,* December 12, 1976.

38. Seth, "India's Atomic Profile," pp. 273, 276; Paul F. Power, "The Indo-American Nuclear Controversy," *Asian Survey,* vol. 19 (June 1979), p. 578. In June 1978 *Hindu,* a Madras newspaper, revealed a number of inadequacies in the nuclear program. The report was linked with hawkish criticism of Prime Minister Morarji Desai's policies by elements of the nuclear establishment. The report included allegations that the 1974 explosive test had a disappointingly low yield and followed two earlier failures. See Simon Winchester, "India's Big Blast Shrinks a Bit in Course of Nuclear Debate," *Washington Post,* June 23, 1978. Excessive exposure of workers to radiation was also reported. See Milton R. Benjamin, "Atomic Power," *Washington Post,* December 3, 1978.

39. Power, "Indo-American Nuclear Controversy," p. 578.

account, India already has an impressive amount of fissile material for a bomb program and will soon have a massive amount. On the assumption that the IAEA's 1974 projections of installed capacity will only be realized by half, India will annually produce enough plutonium for over five hundred "minimum" bombs (5 kilograms each) by 1990. Within a few years India may have enough plutonium for almost two hundred minimum bombs, or a still appreciable number of larger devices.[40]

Pakistan

Although Pakistan's nuclear capabilities are dwarfed by those of India, they are frightening in their potential for the development of weapons. The nuclear program did not begin until the mid-1950s, when the government decided to take advantage of the UN Atoms for Peace initiative. The first nuclear research institute was established in January 1955.[41] Pakistan's supply of trained technical manpower is much smaller than India's. While West Pakistan kept much of the country's nuclear equipment in the 1971 partition, Bangladesh kept many of the nuclear scientists.[42] Although technical staff strength increased by a factor of more than seventeen in the 1950s, by 1972 Pakistan had fewer than 600 nuclear scientists trained to the M.A. and Ph.D. levels.[43] Many of the scientists sent abroad for training by the Pakistan Atomic Energy Com-

40. G. S. Bhargava, *India's Security in the 1980s,* Adelphi Paper 125 (London: International Institute for Strategic Studies, 1976), p. 22. On the IAEA 1974 projections and more conservative calculations of prospective plutonium accumulation, see Richard J. Barber Associates, *LDC Nuclear Prospects, 1975–1990: Commercial, Economic and Security Implications,* UC-2, report 52, prepared for the U.S. Energy Research and Development Administration (Washington, D.C.: Barber Associates, 1975), fig. V-1.

41. Pakistan Atomic Energy Commission, *Atomic Energy in Pakistan, 1958–68* (Karachi, 1968), p. 5.

42. *Nucleonics Week,* vol. 18 (September 15, 1977), p. 8. This case study does not consider in any detail the prospects for the development of nuclear weapons in Bangladesh. The country's preoccupation with internal economic problems, its weakness, and the comparative mildness of its external antagonisms makes it seem an unlikely candidate. The possibility, however, should not be ruled out. While there is at present no prospect of enrichment or reprocessing capability in Bangladesh, the country's projected accumulation of plutonium from reactors is not significantly less than Pakistan's.

43. PAEC, *Atomic Energy in Pakistan,* p. 32; Khalilzad and others, *Regional Rivalries,* vol. 1, p. 43.

mission stayed abroad, although fewer have done so in recent years because of the decline in job opportunities in the West and more energetic recruiting by the PAEC.[44] Pakistan has one power reactor (KANUPP, a CANDU heavy water reactor of 125-megawatt capacity constructed by the Canadian General Electric Company on a turnkey contract) in operation near Karachi. This reactor may be capable of producing up to 137 kilograms of plutonium a year at full capacity (although it has never operated at full capacity). Other estimates of the plutonium production rate, such as those by Barber Associates,[45] are lower. A 5-megawatt training reactor using low enriched uranium is at the Pakistan Institute of Nuclear Science and Technology, and a 500-megawatt power plant at Chashma Barrage is planned. There is also a pilot plant for the concentration of uranium ore with the capacity to handle 10,000 pounds a day, which was designed in large part by Pakistani scientists at the Lahore Atomic Energy Centre, but Pakistan has no fuel fabrication facilities.[46] The PAEC had attempted to acquire such facilities from Canada but was refused when Pakistan would not accede to Canadian pressure to renegotiate safeguards agreements.[47] A heavy water production plant is under construction.[48]

Production from the KANUPP reactor has been curtailed since the beginning of 1977 because Canada suspended fuel supply, with resumption contingent on Pakistan's signing the NPT or accepting full-scope safeguards. Minister of State for Foreign Affairs and Defense Aziz Ahmad refused such conditions and maintained that spare parts to keep KANUPP running could be obtained elsewhere (though he admitted there would be trouble in getting "intricate" parts).[49] Fuel supply could also be a problem, although press reports claim that Libya may have

44. Shirin Tahir-Kheli, "Pakistan's Nuclear Option and U.S. Policy," *Orbis,* vol. 22 (Summer 1978), p. 358.

45. *LDC Nuclear Prospects.*

46. PAEC, *Atomic Energy in Pakistan,* p. 10; Khalilzad, "Pakistan," p. 587; Stobbs, Fox, and Allen, *International Data Collection and Analysis,* vol. 4, pp. PAKISTAN-1, -11; Khalilzad and others, *Regional Rivalries,* vol. 1, p. 42; Charles K. Ebinger, "Pakistan: Energy Planning in a Strategic Vortex" (Washington, D.C.: Conant and Associates, Ltd., October 1979), p. 136.

47. Charles K. Ebinger, "U.S. Nuclear Non-proliferation Policy: The Pakistan Controversy," *Fletcher Forum,* vol. 3 (Summer 1979), pp. 4, 10–11.

48. Zalmay Khalilzad, "Pakistan and the Bomb," *Survival,* vol. 21 (November–December 1979), p. 245.

49. *Nucleonics Week,* vol. 18 (January 6, 1977), p. 6.

supplied Pakistan with diuranate (yellowcake) hijacked across the border in Niger.[50] If supply and maintenance obstacles can be overcome, Pakistan may soon have enough separable plutonium for up to fifty small bombs. Recent officially projected cumulative generating capacity for 1985 is 725 megawatts (electric) and for 2000, 5,525 megawatts.[51] This projection is unrealistic, especially since Pakistani projections have steadily exceeded the pace of implementation. Despite failure even to contract for many of the projected reactors on schedule, the PAEC in 1975 published an ambitious electricity plan for the rest of the twentieth century.[52]

The relevance of the plutonium accumulation depends on the acquisition of separation facilities. Islamabad contracted with France in 1976 for the construction of such a reprocessing plant at Chashma, at an expected cost of approximately $150 million. At the beginning of 1978 the French Foreign Ministry announced its desire to amend the contract by introducing technical modifications—whereby the end product would be a mixture of uranium and plutonium—that would make military use of the product physically more difficult.[53] Introduction of this "coprocessing" system was unacceptable to Pakistan. This might not be surprising even if Pakistani lack of interest in nuclear weapons were genuine. At the time of the demand *Nucleonics Week* reported: "Paris sources say there are many problems still to be resolved before coprocessing becomes an industrially viable process." The report went on to quote an observer: "*In theory* it could be good, but *the process still needs development.* If you don't get the right mix [of uranium and plutonium], then coprocessing will be no good."[54] Pakistan also objected that the project would have to be redesigned, which meant writing off the engineering work already

50. Colin Smith and Shyam Bhatia, "Stealing the Bomb for Pakistan: Nuclear Proliferation and Dr. Khan's 'Mission Impossible,'" *World Press Review* (March 1980), p. 27.

51. Stobbs, Fox, and Allen, *International Data Collection and Analysis,* vol. 4, p. PAKISTAN-9. On near-term Pakistani plutonium accumulation, see Wohlstetter and others, *Moving Toward Life in a Nuclear Armed Crowd?* p. 36.

52. Khalilzad and others, *Regional Rivalries,* vol. 1, p. 44.

53. Ibid., p. 43; "Pakistan Sticks to French Nuclear Deal," *Washington Post,* January 4, 1977; Jonathan Kandell, "French Seek to Add Safeguards to Nuclear Pact with Pakistan," *New York Times,* January 10, 1978. Kandell's sources indicated the French believed this could add as much as twenty years to the time Pakistan would need to use the plutonium for weapons.

54. *Nucleonics Week,* vol. 19 (January 12, 1978), pp. 4–5; emphasis added.

done and delaying the start-up date for the plant. To the Pakistanis, then, the French request to renegotiate might have seemed a demand to buy a pig in a poke. They demanded that Paris carry out the reprocessing agreement "as it presently stands without any modification."[55] Subsequently, President Valéry Giscard d'Estaing made the coprocessing demand formal, which amounted to de facto cancellation of the contract, but Pakistan tried to keep discussions on the matter open and President Mohammed Zia ul-Haq had not given up hope by the autumn of 1979.[56]

Whatever the contractual merits of Pakistan's case, nonproliferation advocates still have obvious reasons for concern. No persuasive case has been made for the economic logic of reprocessing in that country. (By late 1978 even the Pakistani press had begun to admit this.[57]) All the options seem cost-ineffective, especially since reprocessing from HWRs (which Pakistan plans to install) is even less economical than from light water reactors (LWRs). Apparently Pakistan began negotiations with France before the 1973 OPEC oil price increase, although the increase was later cited as justification for ambitious plans for nuclear power.[58] Moreover, some analysts believe that "5 percent covert diversion of fissionable materials would not be difficult." Seven and one-half kilograms of plutonium could be diverted from current accumulation, with an additional 17.5 kilograms by 1985 and up to 10 kilograms annually "after 1985, if the Chashma-Barrage reactor becomes operational." At this rate, Pakistan could divert enough for three bombs by 1985, and "more than one bomb a year thereafter."[59]

Construction of the enrichment plant near Kahuta, however, is the most obvious sign of interest in a weapons option. First, Pakistan's original plan was to rely on HWRs (which run on natural uranium). Even if a few LWRs were built, a domestic enrichment facility for an operation of that size would not be an efficient investment. Second, Pakistan tried to build the plant clandestinely. Working with plans acquired by Abdul Qader Khan, a Pakistani physicist working at the British-German-Dutch enrichment plant at Almelo, the Netherlands, the Pakistanis placed equip-

55. "Pakistan: France Must Hold to Nuclear Deal," *Washington Post,* January 12, 1978.

56. Milton R. Benjamin, "Pakistan Says France Killing Controversial Nuclear Deal," *Washington Post,* August 24, 1978.

57. "Re-processing Leaves One Cold," *Pakistan Economist,* October 21, 1978.

58. Ebinger, "U.S. Nuclear Non-proliferation Policy," p. 4.

59. Khalilzad and others, *Regional Rivalries,* vol. 1, pp. 75, 80.

ment orders through front-companies and intermediaries with various subcontracting firms in Europe and the United States. Inverters to be used for centrifuges were purchased with the explanation that they were for use in textile plants. Many items were purchased before Pakistan's plans were discovered and the exporting countries could apply full controls. Only after the United States publicly charged Pakistan with covert attempts to build the plant and terminated foreign aid did President Zia ul-Haq admit that the project existed, and then he said it would not produce weapons-grade uranium.[60]

Iran

Proportionally, Iran, with its oil wealth, has the greatest objective potential to invest quickly in a high level of nuclear technology and production, but the Khomeini government brought the country's program to a halt. For a while there was great confusion, as most reactor purchases were canceled and the new government spoke with several voices about whether current projects might be continued. Some of the new officials denounced interest payments for overdue installments on the construction of two reactors at Bushehr as "un-Islamic" and told the German firm (Kraftwerk Union) behind the project that it would be canceled. KWU received contradictory signals from other officials, however, and held up the recall of its last workers in the country.[61] By the first anniversary of the shah's ouster the nuclear program appeared to be dead, with the prospect for resurrection dependent on major political changes.

Even before the revolution, Iran's nuclear program lagged behind those of India and Pakistan. The Iranian Atomic Energy Organization was not formally created until 1974. Projections, however, were very ambitious.[62] Although a large number of reactors were planned, they

60. *Nucleonics Week,* vol. 19 (October 12, 1978), p. 13; David Binder, "How Pakistan Ran the Nuke Round the End," *New York Times,* April 19, 1979; Salamat Ali, "Pakistan: A Spate of Early Warnings," *Far Eastern Economic Review* (July 20, 1979), p. 34. Sensitivity about the areas where the project was under way was suggested by a series of incidents in which diplomats and a journalist venturing near the site, or the home of Abdul Qader Khan, were assaulted. "A Clue to the Bomb Mystery," *The Economist* (July 14–20, 1979), pp. 60–61.

61. *Oil and Gas Journal Newsletter,* vol. 77 (June 11, 1979); "KWU Still Has Hopes for Bushehr," *Nuclear Engineering International* (July 1979), p. 4.

62. When the shah fell there were four LWRs under construction at Bushehr and Ahvaz, another four planned, and an agreement in principle to buy six to eight more

were all LWRs, and while there was some uncertainty about signing away rights to reprocessing forever, there were no plans to acquire separation facilities.[63] Thus even if a Thermidor in the revolution leads to reinstatement of old plans, applying them to weapons-related functions would run into major obstacles. The supply of enriched fuel for LWRs was to be handled by the shah through the purchase of interests in the European Eurodif and Coredif projects. In June 1979 the revolutionary government indicated it wished to withdraw from this arrangement; at the end of 1979 a French court froze Iran's stake in Eurodif pending negotiation of the withdrawal with the European partners; and early in 1980 the head of the Iranian Atomic Energy Organization reportedly denied his country's intent to withdraw.[64]

Any hypothetical attempt by a postrevolutionary government to get back into this business or to seek reprocessing facilities might meet skepticism from suppliers. The shah's sources of equipment supply were well diversified,[65] but if authorities in Tehran have second thoughts about demodernizing their energy programs they may find that the development of the London nuclear suppliers' group and foreign doubts about their own responsibility have lost them the opportunity to recant. If the gov-

---

from the United States. Earlier projections of electricity-generating capacity were for 6,930 megawatts by 1985 and 43,330 megawatts by 2000. Stobbs, Fox, and Allen, *International Data Collection and Analysis*, vol. 3, pp. IRAN-8, -9; "Update: Iran—Half of Generating Capacity Nuclear by 1992," *Nuclear Engineering International* (March 1978), p. 13. Plans were scaled down, however, in the months before the shah fell as a result of second thoughts about cost-effectiveness as well as attempts to divert funds to social expenditures in order to placate popular opposition to the regime. *Nucleonics Week*, vol. 19 (August 24, 1978), pp. 1–2, and vol. 19 (September 14, 1978), p. 6; "Iran: Reductions in Defense and Nuclear Spending," *Strategic Middle Eastern Affairs*, vol. 26 (October 18, 1978), p. 2.

63. There were tentative initiatives in 1974 and 1976 to obtain reprocessing plants from France and Japan, and the shah agreed not to seek such facilities only if the future possibility of reprocessing abroad or in a multinational regional center was left open. *Nucleonics Week,* vol. 17 (June 17, 1976), p. 7; vol. 18 (September 29, 1977), p. 8; vol. 19 (January 12, 1978), p. 2; and vol. 19 (July 20, 1978), p. 1.

64. "Iran Weighs More Limits on Gas Exports; Pipeline to Russia, Europe Is in Jeopardy," *Wall Street Journal,* June 8, 1979; Paul Lewis, "Iran Curbed on French Atom Plant," *New York Times,* December 4, 1979; *World Business Weekly* (March 17, 1980), p. 19.

65. Reactors were ordered from the United States, France, and West Germany. Technical assistance and training agreements were made with England and considered even with the USSR. "Iran Plans World's Fourth Biggest Nuclear Programme," *Nuclear Engineering International* (March 1977), pp. 32–33.

ernment were to regain interest in nuclear energy, however, while maintaining a xenophobic orientation, it might seek autonomy with full-cycle capabilities. If unable to purchase reprocessing or enrichment facilities it would have few options other than recruiting "scientific mercenaries."[66] Even before the convulsions of 1978–79 Iran's nuclear program was heavily dependent on foreign staff. A related possibility is nuclear espionage and clandestine commerce in sensitive technical components. (Pakistan has already taken advantage of these means. Dutch security officials concluded that Abdul Qader Khan pirated secret data from the Almelo enrichment facility, and Dutch companies apparently violated strategic export standards in selling special steel tubing for centrifuges.)[67] Alternatively, Iran could seek a cooperative partnership in Pakistan's struggle to develop sensitive technology. But relations between Islamabad and Tehran deteriorated after the revolution (President Zia ul-Haq supported the shah, and although Zia's regime is Muslim, it is not Shiite as was the anti-shah movement). The extremely hypothetical quality of all these speculations on whether interest might be renewed and how options might be pursued suggests how unlikely it is that Iran's nuclear capabilities will become threatening or that a clandestine effort to produce weapons would be practical.[68]

Official Policies on Proliferation

Capabilities alone are not reason for concern. If they were, West Germany would be considered a much greater proliferation risk than any of the countries in this study. Evidence of reassuring intentions can reduce the anxiety provoked by high capability, and evidence of dangerous ultimate intentions should be alarming even when it concerns a country whose present capabilities are weak.

66. See Lewis A. Dunn, "Nuclear 'Gray Marketeering,'" *International Security,* vol. 1 (Winter 1977), p. 109. Dunn notes elsewhere that the worldwide slowdown in nuclear energy programs could be increasing the pool of such mercenaries by increasing unemployment among nuclear engineers and technicians; "Half-Past India's Bang," *Foreign Policy,* no. 36 (Fall 1979), pp. 79–80.

67. "Pakistan Helped by Dutch Leak," *Nuclear Engineering International* (April 1980), p. 6.

68. George H. Quester, "The Shah and the Bomb," *Policy Sciences,* vol. 8 (1977), p. 25; Anne Hessing Cahn, "Determinants of the Nuclear Option: The Case of Iran," in Marwah and Schulz, eds., *Nuclear Proliferation,* p. 192.

The NPT

Iran signed the Treaty on the Non-Proliferation of Nuclear Weapons almost immediately and deposited ratification soon thereafter. The post-shah regime has not yet shown any interest in the NPT and may well maintain Iran's adherence to it. But having declared virtually all of the shah's undertakings illegitimate and void, the regime may not consider itself legally bound by the earlier ratification.

Neither India nor Pakistan has signed the treaty, although both have officially renounced any intention of acquiring nuclear weapons. (India persists in insisting that the "peaceful" device detonated in 1974 was not a nuclear weapon. According to Indian Atomic Energy Commission chairman H. N. Sethna, "the explosion was an experiment to study the cratering and cracking effects on rocks.[69]) Pakistan's opposition to the NPT has been equivocal, and it has indicated that it would consider ad-hering to the treaty if India did so, if nuclear fuel supplies were assured, and if Pakistan's security could be credibly guaranteed. India has de-nounced the treaty vociferously on grounds of international principle and national sovereignty.[70]

The official Indian position has been that all nuclear weapons should be abolished and that until they are the NPT is a discriminatory covenant that legitimates the current hierarchy of international power and per-petuates the second-class status of nonnuclear weapons states.[71] The angriest of the Indian critics have characterized the treaty as either a

69. Quoted in Wohlstetter, *'The Buddha Smiles,'* p. 120.

70. Stockholm International Peace Research Institute, *The Near-Nuclear Coun-tries and the NPT* (Stockholm: Almqvist and Wiksell, 1972), pp. 26–27: "At the Conference of Non-Nuclear-Weapon States in September 1968, the initiative for which had come from Pakistan, Pakistan proposed that an effective security guaran-tee should contain the following provisions:

"1. Prohibition of first use of nuclear weapons by nuclear-weapons states against non-nuclear weapon states.

"2. Immediate assistance to be given to non-nuclear-weapon states which are the victims of nuclear aggression.

"3. Assistance should be forthcoming before the Security Council can act.

"4. The security guarantee should include all non-nuclear-weapon states which have renounced the manufacture or acquisition of nuclear weapons, irrespec-tive of whether they sign the NPT or not."

For a detailed review of India's position on the NPT, see ibid., pp. 19–22.

71. Shelton L. Williams, *The U.S., India, and the Bomb,* Washington Center of Foreign Policy Research, Studies in International Affairs 12 (Johns Hopkins Press, 1969), chap. 3; William Epstein, *The Last Chance: Nuclear Proliferation and Arms Control* (Free Press, 1976), pp. 64–66, 73–75, 77–78, 81, 84, 109, 117, 122, 195.

condescending example of cryptoracism or an imperialistic plot to maintain the subordination of the third world to the influence of the superpowers and to frustrate the technological development and economic competitiveness of the developing nations. One critic sees "atomic apartheid" in article III of the treaty.[72] Rikhi Jaipal, permanent representative of India to the United Nations, maintains: "It is the nuclear Brahmins that advocate the maintenance of the purity of their caste at the expense of the lesser breed. . . . Such a concept implies a grave abridgement of the sovereignty of developing countries and is tantamount to a sort of nuclear colonialism. The notion that some states are inherently more responsible than others is totally rejected by India."[73]

Opposition to stringent or comprehensive inspection safeguards has often been couched in similar terms. India viewed the "peaceful-uses-only" clause in its original agreements with Canada more loosely than the Canadians did. This was not apparent to the Canadians, who did not place the agreements in the context of Nehru's previously stated opposition to external control. Nehru told parliament in 1954 that international controls were another example of the major powers' attempts to dominate the world and would not be accepted if they were not advantageous to India. In the 1956 agreement with Canada, "Bhabha insisted that India's word was a sufficient safeguard to members of the Commonwealth and expressions of Canadian doubts only served to call into question Indian credibility, a subject diplomats found easy to avoid."[74]

When India detonated its device in 1974 Canada considered the act a breach of agreements. The Indian government rejected this interpretation. The United States was assured that no American-supplied materials were used in the explosion and that therefore no safeguards for which the United States was responsible had been transgressed. Later it came to light, however, that American-supplied heavy water had been used in the project, constituting a violation in the view of most U.S. observers.[75]

72. M. L. Sondhi, "India and Nuclear China," *Pacific Community*, vol. 4 (January 1973), p. 273.

73. Jaipal, "Indian Nuclear Explosion," p. 47. Unidentified Pakistani sources interpreted U.S. opposition to the French contract for a reprocessing plant in the same terms: "What the West is trying to do is erect an economic caste system with itself as Brahmin." Quoted in *Nucleonics Week*, vol. 17 (May 27, 1976), p. 6.

74. Morrison and Page, "India's Option," p. 25.

75. Wohlstetter, *'The Buddha Smiles,'* pp. 150–55. See also Ashok Kapur, "The Canada-India Nuclear Negotiations: Some Hypotheses and Lessons," *The World Today*, vol. 34 (August 1978), pp. 311–20.

In the long period before the detonation the United States and Canada had announced publicly that "peaceful applications" excluded by definition explosives of any kind, and the Canadians made many private reminders on this point. "However, in advance of the actual Indian explosion, neither Canada nor the United States insisted that the Indians themselves publicly agree with them."[76] Indians were also irritated that international reaction to the underground Pokharan test was extreme while China's atmospheric tests have caused little comment.

India opposed the formation of the International Atomic Energy Agency, and at the October 1956 United Nations conference on the IAEA statute the USSR supported the Indian position.[77] In recent years Soviet policy has approached the American position, and it was reportedly the Soviet delegation that introduced the proposal at the November 1976 meetings of the London nuclear suppliers' group to require full-scope safeguards.[78] This shift, in conjunction with new U.S. pressure, looked as if it might lead to greater Indian flexibility. When British Prime Minister James Callaghan visited New Delhi early in 1978, there were initial reports that the Indian government might consider modifying its refusal to accept such comprehensive coverage. Immediately after the visit, however, Prime Minister Morarji R. Desai dispelled such hopes, saying that India would not accede to full-scope safeguards unless the United States and the USSR agreed to forswear all nuclear explosive testing and stop adding to weapons inventories, "and also come to an agreement to have gradual reduction with a view to complete destruction of atomic weapons."[79] Desai stated publicly in mid-1978 that India's condi-

76. Wohlstetter, '*The Buddha Smiles,*' p. 164. American intelligence, almost a decade before the Pokharan test, not only estimated that India already had sufficient plutonium for an explosive device and could detonate one within a year of deciding to do so, but also warned that there were no longer prohibitive safeguards applying to CIRUS uranium or heavy water. Donald F. Chamberlain, Director of Scientific Intelligence, Central Intelligence Agency, Memorandum for NSC, "The Indian Nuclear Weapons Capability," October 18, 1965 (Box 16, National Security Files, Vietnam Country File, Southwest Asia Special Intelligence Material File, Lyndon Baines Johnson Library, Austin, Texas, vol. VII).

77. Ashok Kapur, *India's Nuclear Option: Atomic Diplomacy and Decision Making* (Praeger, 1976), p. 108.

78. Oberdorfer, "Soviets Agree to Sell India Heavy Water."

79. Simon Winchester, "Indian Approval Is Seen for Nuclear Inspections," *Washington Post,* January 10, 1978; William Borders, "Desai Denies India Eases Nuclear Policy," *New York Times,* January 13, 1978. Desai's disarmament moralism, of

tions for accommodation on safeguards included the opening of military reactors to inspection[80]—something not contemplated by the current nuclear weapons states. Many of the standard Indian arguments of principle are pithily encapsulated in an article by the Indian ambassador to the United States:

> The great weakness of the nonproliferation effort has been its almost total preoccupation with those countries which do not possess the weapons and do not want them. . . . [it is] a vigorous policy of trying to disarm the unarmed. . . . Countries like India, which have no interest in making bombs, are penalized [by the U.S. Nuclear Non-Proliferation Act] for their voluntary restraint. They are asked to subject themselves to full-scope safeguards, which the nuclear-weapons powers reject for themselves.[81]

India has accepted some unwanted safeguards out of necessity. A Soviet transfer of heavy water in 1976, to overcome problems for a CANDU reactor at Kota arising from Canadian disengagement from cooperation, entailed an accord with the IAEA the following year that covered RAPP-II but not other new CANDU reactors. This amounted to "creeping, partial safeguards." But New Delhi continued to resist demands for full-scope safeguards even when the rationale was presented as a matter of self-interest. After Pakistan's work on enrichment facilities was revealed, Zia offered a proposal for a joint renunciation of nuclear weapons coupled with international inspection of all nuclear facilities in both countries, but India refused—in part because the future of the Zia regime seemed uncertain, but also on principle.[82] Some commentary in India suggested that the Americans were trying to use alarm about Pakistan's activities to force India into accepting full-scope safeguards.[83] Viewed from Washington, however, Pakistan's position on safeguards has remained reasonable in principle but no more reassuring in practice while its technical capabilities are becoming more threatening.

---

course, was nothing new in India policy. See Bhabani Sen Gupta, "India and Disarmament," in B. R. Nanda, ed., *Indian Foreign Policy: The Nehru Years* (Delhi: Vikas, 1976), pp. 228–51.

80. *Nucleonics Week,* vol. 19 (June 22, 1978), p. 7.

81. Nani A. Palkhivala, "Disarming the Unarmed," *Newsweek* (International Edition), June 19, 1978, p. 45.

82. Simon Barber, "The Islamic Atomic Bombshell," *Far Eastern Economic Review* (April 27, 1979), p. 12.

83. *Bombay Times* editorial, "Pak Bomb," April 9, 1979, reprinted in FBIS, *Daily Report: Middle East and North Africa* (April 13, 1979), p. S2.

The 1974 Indian explosion rudely awakened Canada to the inadequacies of its safeguards requirements, so Ottawa pressured Islamabad as well as New Delhi to renegotiate. Pakistan resisted, and Canada terminated nuclear assistance. When it came to the reprocessing plant to be obtained from France, however, Islamabad was accommodating. In 1976 Pakistan objected to French restrictions requiring safeguards for twenty years on domestic copies of French-supplied installations. Islamabad nevertheless acceded to stringent limitations in the tripartite agreement in March of that year (between Pakistan, France, and the IAEA). Pakistani sources claimed that the agreement "covers not only the technical equipment, but the furniture, telephones, everything. Under the safeguards we wouldn't even be able to use our chairs in a prejudicial manner." The safeguards "cover all imported materials in perpetuity," and the technology is covered for a finite period long enough to make it obsolete before the safeguards lapse.[84] The fact that Pakistan had yielded to virtually all France's demands also incensed Zulfikar Ali Bhutto when President Ford's letter requesting that Pakistan cancel the plant purchase arrived on the same day the tripartite safeguards pact was announced.[85] (The severity of these safeguards is also what led some Indian analysts, such as Subrahmanyam, to appear unalarmed about Pakistani nuclear potential.[86] Such views, of course, ignore the fact that safeguards inhibit diversion but constrain little else in a weapons program short of testing.) When controversy arose over efforts to obtain an enrichment plant, Pakistan's Foreign Office said the country would accept full safeguards on its "peaceful program of nuclear research" if such safeguards were not discriminatory and were applied to every other country, including India, Israel, and South Africa.[87]

The shah of Iran evinced irritation about U.S. proposals for controls, saying, "You are asking us for safeguards that are incompatible with our sovereignty."[88] When options for joint ownership of reprocessing facilities for Iranian spent fuel were being considered (before the U.S. de-

84. *Nucleonics Week,* vol. 17 (May 27, 1976), p. 6.

85. Ebinger, "U.S. Nuclear Non-proliferation Policy," p. 13.

86. Subrahmanyam, "India's Nuclear Policy," p. 138.

87. FBIS, *Daily Report: Middle East and North Africa* (April 9, 1979), p. S3; Peter Niesewand, "Pakistan Denies It Is Developing Nuclear Arms," *Washington Post,* April 9, 1979.

88. Quoted in Norman Gall, "Atoms for Brazil, Dangers for All," *Foreign Policy,* no. 23 (Summer 1976), p. 176.

cision to hold all reprocessing in abeyance), it was also noted that the conditions for controls were more demanding than any in the previous bilateral cooperation agreements undertaken by the United States. According to indications publicly available, however, the shah raised no obstacle to the imposition of the safeguards demanded by the United States for Iranian nuclear facilities. But the anti-Western nationalists now in power may not be so reasonable.

At present, the country with the most advanced nuclear establishment (India) has the highest potential for accumulating unsafeguarded plutonium and is staunchly resisting initiatives to modify its autonomy; the country with the next highest potential for domestic plutonium production (Pakistan) grudgingly accepted (when contracting with France for a reprocessing plant) safeguards designed to cover all of its facilities until the turn of the century, and many of them even after that (if the Pakistanis proceed to build the reprocessing plant by themselves using the original French plans but without further supplies or assistance from France, it is uncertain whether they would still consider themselves bound by the safeguards, and it is apparent from their covert approach to the enrichment facility that they did not envision having to submit it to safeguards); and the country with a substantial potential for the production of unseparated plutonium (Iran), which would have the highest potential if it went back to earlier plans for reactor purchases, accepted safeguards on its power reactors and has not entered into any arrangement to acquire facilities for indigenous reprocessing.

Explosions

Declaratory policy aside, it is normally assumed (in the United States) that the best index of nuclear weapons capability is the explosion of a nuclear device. By this criterion, India has had nuclear weapons status since May 1974. In 1965 Prime Minister Lal Bahadur Shastri took Homi Bhabha's advice and authorized preliminary preparations for a peaceful nuclear explosion. At the time, there was a respectable body of opinion in the international nuclear community that such explosions would be legitimate and useful means of carrying out earth-moving and mining purposes. Indira Gandhi then postponed preparations, probably to avoid endangering Canadian cooperation in developing the second power reactor in Rajasthan. The project was reinstated sometime around the crisis of 1971,[89] and India's AEC estimated the costs of the peaceful nuclear explosion as around $400,000.[90] The Indian government denied that the device detonated at Pokharan was a bomb; indeed, Prime Minister Desai argued before the United Nations General Assembly, "We are the only country which has pledged not to manufacture or acquire nuclear weapons even if the whole of world did so. I solemnly reiterate that pledge before this august Assembly."[91] Indian policy continues to assume that peaceful nuclear explosions have significant potential benefits, such as stimulating higher yields from gas and oil reserves or tapping geothermal heat. Jaipal, for instance, cites support from a 1970 IAEA report that peaceful nuclear explosions are particularly valuable for increasing India's freedom from dependence on imports of metals because they can facilitate exploitation of low-grade nonferrous ore deposits.[92] Another argument advanced for continued testing is its usefulness in helping Indian scientists keep track of Chinese explosions.[93]

As with the nonproliferation treaty, American opposition to peaceful nuclear explosions is criticized as a discriminatory double standard. The NPT "seeks to prohibit the conduct of PNEs underground *except by nuclear weapons states!*" according to Jaipal, who continues:

India's policy is what might frankly be regarded as normal, and one might hope that its example would be emulated by the nuclear weapon states. . . . The ultimate mockery is the threshold test ban which permits them [the nuclear weapons states] to test underground nuclear weapons yielding 150 kilotons capacity, whereas India's 10-kiloton test of a device intended for peaceful uses is regarded as opening the door to nuclear proliferation![94]

89. Power, "Indo-American Nuclear Controversy," pp. 575–77.

90. George H. Quester, "Enlisting Post-1974 India to the Cause of Nonproliferation," in Mellor, ed., *India: A Rising Middle Power*, p. 194.

91. Morarji Desai, "Disarmament: Choice Between Life and Death," *Indian & Foreign Review* (June 15, 1978), p. 12.

92. Jaipal, "Indian Nuclear Explosion," p. 46. For a catalog of multiple benefits foreseen from peaceful nuclear explosions and arguments against critics of the Pokharan explosion, see Chopra, "India's Nuclear Path," pp. 43–44; R. Ramanna, "Peaceful Nuclear Explosions (PNEs)," in T. T. Poulose, ed., *Perspectives of India's Nuclear Policy* (New Delhi–Stockholm: Young Asia Publications, 1978), especially pp. 47–51; and K. T. Thomas, "Peaceful Applications of Underground Nuclear Explosions," *Nuclear India*, vol. 13 (July 1974), pp. 4–8. For a more recent Indian analysis that recognizes but does not dismiss the limited utility of peaceful nuclear explosions, see T. T. Poulose and C. Raja Mohan, "Peaceful Nuclear Explosions," *IDSA Journal* (New Delhi), vol. 9 (July–September 1976), pp. 14–38.

93. Sondhi, "India and Nuclear China," p. 272 (exactly how it would do this is not spelled out); Ebinger, "U.S. Nuclear Non-proliferation Policy," p. 5.

94. Jaipal, "Indian Nuclear Explosion," pp. 48–49; emphasis in the original.

American efforts later in the decade were aimed at persuading India not to undertake a second peaceful test. The government did not formally agree to forgo a second explosion, but Desai announced that he saw no present need for one. This statement was criticized by some members of the opposition as "nuclear surrender" to the United States.[95] Desai, however, explicitly told parliament that he did not rule out the use of peaceful nuclear explosions for mining and oil and gas exploration.[96] When Indira Gandhi returned to power, she repeated her commitment to peaceful uses of nuclear energy but said that if national interests required it India would "not hesitate from carrying out nuclear explosions."[97]

Pakistan's official position, including that of the post-Bhutto government, has been that it does not intend to develop nuclear weapons. The acceptance of strenuous safeguards requirements for the reprocessing plant France was supposed to supply and the offer to accept full-scope safeguards if other threshold countries did too were cited as supporting the credibility of that policy. The intention to remain nonnuclear, however, seems far from sincere. The most obvious indications are the secret moves toward enrichment and the fact that Pakistan has not signed the NPT, both for reasons of principle similar to India's and because India has not signed it either. And for years Pakistan's leaders gave evidence of ambivalence even before the Pokharan event, loaded statements of intent to remain nonnuclear with major conditions, and made the impact of India's nuclear test on Pakistan's policy clear. Former Prime Minister Bhutto revealed in an interview that much earlier, as foreign minister, he had urged Mohammed Ayub Khan to develop a security-oriented nuclear program, unconstrained by considerations of economic viability.[98] Bhutto was also famous for his often-quoted statement, "If India builds the bomb, we will eat leaves or grass, even go hungry but we will have to get one of our own."[99] According to Munir Khan, chairman of the PAEC, national interests vis-à-vis India were factored into nuclear development policy at the prime minister's direction in 1971.[100] In 1969 Bhutto wrote,

95. "Mr. Desai: No Need for Nuclear Test Now," *Indian & Foreign Review* (August 1, 1977), p. 8; Khalilzad and others, *Regional Rivalries,* vol. 1, p. 17.

96. *Nucleonics Week,* vol. 19 (August 3, 1978), p. 8.

97. "Gandhi Says National Interest May Require Nuclear Blasts," *Washington Post,* March 14, 1980.

98. Ebinger, "U.S. Nuclear Non-proliferation Policy," p. 7.

99. Quoted in G. W. Choudhury, *India, Pakistan, Bangladesh, and the Major Powers: Politics of a Divided Subcontinent* (Free Press, 1975), p. 240.

100. Ebinger, "U.S. Nuclear Non-proliferation Policy," p. 7.

"All wars of our age have become total wars. . . . It would be dangerous to plan for less and our plans should, therefore, include the nuclear deterrent. . . . Our problem, in its essence, is how to obtain such a weapon in time before the crisis begins."[101]

After the Indian explosion Bhutto told the National Assembly, "A more grave and serious event . . . has not taken place in the history of Pakistan."[102] Soon after, the government appealed to Pakistani nuclear experts abroad to come home to undertake vital work.[103] Not long before his ouster he told the national assembly that Pakistan would abandon its contract with France to obtain reprocessing facilities only when all nuclear weapons had been destroyed[104]—an implicit acknowledgment that the plant was not needed for purely economic reasons, but to maintain a weapons option. After his imprisonment Bhutto implied that under his administration the country came close to nuclear weapons capability because the French trusted him and would have gone through with the reprocessing deal if he had not been ousted. "We know that Israel and South Africa have full nuclear capability," he said from his cell. "The Christian, Jewish and Hindu civilizations have this capability. The Communist powers also possess it. Only the Islamic civilization was without it, but that position was about to change."[105]

Bhutto's successor, Zia, has continued to deny that Pakistan intends to develop nuclear weapons while continuing to develop the requisite capabilities. Reports in the summer of 1979 suggested American officials had indications that Pakistan was preparing an underground test site.[106] Zia and other officials repeated denials,[107] and foreign affairs adviser Agha Shahi told members of the U.S. Congress in October 1979 that Zia was willing to pledge there would be no detonations during his current ad-

101. Quoted in Maj. Gen. D. K. Palit and P. K. S. Namboodiri, *Pakistan's Islamic Bomb* (New Delhi: Vikas, 1979), p. 15.

102. Quoted in Ebinger, "U.S. Nuclear Non-proliferation Policy," p. 6. Such rhetoric was matched by the former chief of staff of the Pakistan army, General Tikka Khan, who said Pakistan "will have to beg or borrow to develop our own nuclear capability."

103. Ibid., p. 8.

104. *Nucleonics Week,* vol. 18 (June 16, 1977), p. 5.

105. Quoted in Palit and Namboodiri, *Pakistan's Islamic Bomb,* p. v.

106. Richard Burt, "U.S. Aides Say Pakistan Is Reported to Be Building an A-Bomb Site," *New York Times,* August 17, 1979.

107. See the statement by Khalid Ali, press counselor of Pakistan's embassy, in a letter to the editor, *New York Times,* August 28, 1979; and "Pakistan President Denies Planning to Make A-Bomb," *Washington Post,* August 21, 1979.

ministration, although he could not bind future governments.[108] During Deputy Secretary of State Warren Christopher's visit after the Soviet invasion of Afghanistan, Pakistani officials refused to rule out the testing of a peaceful nuclear device.[109]

Iran may be the despair of the rest of U.S. foreign policy, but on the issue of nonproliferation, at least, it prompts the fewest anxieties of the three countries under discussion. As a party to the NPT, it renounced nuclear weapons. Shortly after the 1974 Indian test the shah was asked if Iran would acquire nuclear weapons and replied, "Without a doubt, and sooner than one would think,"[110] but this assertion was denied several days later. In a September 1976 interview with Mohamed Heikal, the shah said that if confronted by other countries in the region with nuclear weapons, "Iran must, of necessity, have them as well."[111] There was no evidence that the shah intended to abrogate or circumvent the NPT, but there is enough evidence to suggest that he envisioned the need to do so under certain conditions. The new regime could well react to such conditions similarly, although nothing indicates positively that it has any interest in nuclear weapons.

Declaratory policy in all three countries renounces nuclear weapons development. In India and Pakistan energy policy and nuclear capabilities—present in India, planned but not certain to be obtained in Pakistan—leave open the physical option for fabrication of nuclear weapons. If the Iranian revolutionary government's apparent lack of interest in nuclear issues were to change—which is quite possible in view of the extreme fluidity of the political situation in the country—Iran's wealth could facilitate the acquisition of such facilities, either from foreign contractors if the suppliers' group does not maintain solidarity (it has not flatly banned such exports, anyway) or hypothetically from a corps of internationally recruited and lavishly paid scientists and engineers. Thus in all three countries, the development of weapons capability, as well as a decision on whether or not to exercise the capability, hinges to a large extent on strategic incentives and internal political interpretations and reaction to those incentives.

108. Don Oberdorfer, "Effort to Block Pakistan from A-Bomb Faltering," *Washington Post*, October 20, 1979.

109. Richard Burt, "Pakistani Nuclear Effort May Imperil U.S. Aid Plan," *New York Times*, February 28, 1980.

110. Quoted in Quester, "The Shah and the Bomb," p. 22.

111. Quoted in Lewis A. Dunn, "India, Pakistan, Iran . . .: A Nuclear Proliferation Chain?" in Overholt, ed., *Asia's Nuclear Future*, p. 210.

CHAPTER SIX

Incentives for Nuclear Weapons

INCENTIVES are harder to judge and predict than capabilities. For one thing, motivations are subjective. The leaders of the three countries may not themselves have a clear or steadfast view of their interests, which makes it risky for an outside analyst to try to discern them. And motives can change quickly, either from a reassessment by government or from a change of government. Such ambiguities are probably greater in the South and West Asia region than in any other. The domestic politics of India, Pakistan, and Iran have undergone extreme turbulence in recent years and are likely to remain in flux for some time.

The jarring leadership changes that have occurred in all three countries since 1977 might imply that previous evidence about incentives is outdated. This is true in part for Iran, less so for India and Pakistan. For the three countries, however, the external balance-of-power considerations that could impel decisions toward nuclear weapons have remained or intensified while the governments have changed. For Iran, in fact, while dissociation from the West and aggravated tension with neighbors after the shah's fall reflected reactionary sentiments that are not congenial to nuclear development, it increased the relevance of the nuclear option to realpolitik (as long as a pro-Soviet government does not take over). Because of the salience of traditional balance-of-power incentives, the historical background of these countries and the orientations of their leaders are worth considering even though the particular leaders or regimes have passed from the scene. Finally, previous evidence is relevant because the region is, in a sense, already "quasi-proliferated." How it got that way is important for appreciating the context of future decisions even though political fluidity makes specific predictions impossible.

For much of the postwar period the only nations with the technical capability to manufacture nuclear weapons (principally the advanced industrial states of Europe and Japan as well as China) had weak incentives to do so. Their security problems were subsumed under the competition between the superpowers. The strength of the United States and the Soviet Union, which provided nuclear umbrellas for their allies, and the solidity of the alliances gave most of these countries sufficient reason to feel they could do without independent nuclear capabilities. The exceptions were the countries—France and China—whose leaders decided they could not or should not place their security in the hands of one of the superpowers. For most of the candidates for proliferation, the bipolarity of international strategic competition reduced incentives. These conditions do not apply in South and West Asia, for two reasons.

First, alliance ties with the superpowers, both formal and tacit, have existed in the region. But even at their best these ties have been weak, conditional, and unreliable when compared with NATO, the Warsaw Pact, and the U.S.-Japanese mutual security treaty. None of the great powers since the 1940s have stationed combat forces in India, Pakistan, or Iran, and none have pledged unequivocally to engage in combat to defend any of those countries in a regional war. Indeed, India and Pakistan have fought three wars, with no direct military involvement by the United States, the USSR, or China. In any case, superpower ties with India, Pakistan, and Iran are now in disarray.

Second, the Nixon doctrine, the retrenchment of American commitments, and the phenomenon referred to as the international "diffusion of power" have made the states in the region aware that they must plan to rely primarily on themselves in the event of local war. Increases in incentives parallel increases in capabilities. India can already build nuclear weapons; Pakistan is developing the requisite facilities; and Iran's oil would provide the wealth to acquire the capability if policy were to change.

India

In analyzing strategic intentions in the region, India is the pivot. It has the highest levels of both conventional military and nuclear energy capabilities, and has already demonstrated that it can build and detonate nuclear explosives. What the New Delhi government does in moving closer to or away from nuclear weapons status will have a strong influence on Pakistan's decisions and might affect Iranian calculations.

India is the dominant power in the region and one of the principal "emerging middle powers" in the world. Prima facie this suggests that prestige incentives for nuclear weapons would be high or at least as important as they might be for a country like Brazil. Nonalignment rhetoric, which, in view of India's geography and economy, is a realistic and self-interested stance,[1] has in the past obscured the extent of Indian nationalism. And nationalism is likely to be a more potent force in government policy since the Desai government has fallen. A number of Indian analysts foresee if not a global role for the country, at least a wider one than Washington has wanted to accept even at times of greatest "tilt" toward New Delhi. "What emerges conclusively from the posture of the Carter administration," according to Nayar, "is that it forthrightly acknowledges India to be the preeminent power *in* South Asia—a recognition of what India has already accomplished against American opposition—but simultaneously requires that South Asia remain a regional 'ghetto' without influence in, or relevance to, the larger international system. . . . This is nothing but containment in a new form."[2]

The reality of India's national power is seldom appreciated in the West, where it is often stereotyped as a primitive, hopelessly poor, and dependent giant. But although low per capita income supports this stereotype and prospective problems in economic development are staggering, India's absolute gross national product—which has approached $100 billion in recent years—is substantial. And low national per capita income masks the industrial enclaves with much higher per capita production and income. While India ranks low on the global scale of power, regionally it is a leviathan. Its GNP is almost seven times the size of

1. "There is no basis for the view that the policies of a sovereign India during the 1947–62 period constituted a unique approach to national security distinct from the traditional one of power politics. Given India's geographical contiguity to the Soviet Union and China and her need for the greatest number of sources from which economic aid might be obtained, India's leaders opted for a policy of nonalignment toward the two power blocs." Lorne J. Kavic, *India's Quest for Security: Defense Policies, 1947–1965* (University of California Press, 1967), p. 208.

2. Baldev Raj Nayar, "Regional Power in a Multipolar World," in John W. Mellor, ed., *India: A Rising Middle Power* (Westview Press, 1979), p. 173.

Pakistan's and a third larger than Iran's was at its peak before the shah's fall.[3] In an interview in which she interpreted American policy as aimed at destroying India's self-reliance, Indira Gandhi said the United States could not have its cake and eat it too by considering dependent third world countries such as Bangladesh basket cases and self-reliant ones such as India arrogant.[4]

The prestige incentive for nuclear weapons can also be seen as compensatory. The 1974 explosion showed that, despite the modesty of industrial and economic progress, in the nuclear field India is first class.

Government policy, however, has never indicated that prestige incentives are important. India has traditionally been the leading international exponent of nuclear disarmament. Internal arguments in favor of a bomb have been principally strategic and defensive ones. Nine days after the first Chinese nuclear test in 1964 Homi Bhabha argued in a broadcast that the only defense against nuclear attack "appears to be a capability and threat of retaliation."[5] There have also been two sets of contrasting arguments that the policies of the superpowers make it expedient for India to have its own weapons capability. On one hand, extreme nationalists argue that India faces nuclear threats from the United States:

The experience in Vietnam, and the circumstances that led to the use of nuclear weapons on Japan when compared with the experiences of confrontation in the central European line and the Sino-Soviet border, suggest that mass destruction agents like nuclear weapons, ecocidal agents, etc., tend to be used only when there is no fear of retaliation and when there is no sense of mutual deterrence.[6]

Deployment of the U.S. carrier *Enterprise* to the Bay of Bengal during the 1971 Indo-Pakistani war is cited by such spokesmen as evidence of the reality of the threat of American coercion. After Kissinger's secret visit to Peking in 1971, facilitated by Yahya Khan's assistance as intermediary, some Indians also perceived the emergence of a "United States-

3. U.S. Arms Control and Disarmament Agency, *World Military Expenditures and Arms Transfers, 1967–1976* (Government Printing Office, 1979), pp. 46, 56.

4. Shirin Tahir-Kheli, "Pakistan's Nuclear Option and U.S. Policy," *Orbis,* vol. 22 (Summer 1978), p. 367.

5. Quoted in A. G. Noorani, "India's Quest for a Nuclear Guarantee," *Asian Survey,* vol. 7 (July 1967), p. 490.

6. K. Subrahmanyam, "India's Nuclear Policy," in Onkar Marwah and Ann Schulz, eds., *Nuclear Proliferation and the Near-Nuclear Countries* (Ballinger, 1975), pp. 128, 135.

China-Pakistan axis."[7] Indian strategists have long opposed American
military presence in the Indian Ocean and have not been comforted by
the upgrading of the base at Diego Garcia, including increasing runway
lengths to a degree that some of them believe could accommodate B-52s
and KC-135s.

On the other hand, more moderate observers worry about the implications of détente and the imprudence of relying on superpower protection:

In a world where the two Super-powers have the same general intention to reduce their risks of injuring one another, the Indians have watched with particular concern the Russian acceptance of the "humiliation" of the United States
mining of Haiphong coincidentally with the Moscow summit . . . the symbolic
demonstration of how the new code of conduct among the two Super-powers
will work in the future. In facing China as an adversary armed with medium-
and short-range missiles, any capability of counter-balancing through adherence to "international stability" would appear meaningless.[8]

Another observer suggests that mutual deterrence between the superpowers means that, until such states develop their own counters, the only
use for their arsenals would be against other states like India.[9]

China is the principal threat that has driven Indian interest in a weapons option. To Americans, Sino-Indian hostilities may seem less significant, intense, or enduring than the East-West confrontation, but it is
notable that Indians and Chinese have killed each other on the battlefield
(in the 1962 border war), which cannot be said of NATO and Warsaw
Pact forces. (This difference also can be seen by pro-nuclear exponents
as supporting the view that possession of a nuclear deterrent enhances
security by reducing the risk of war.) There was a synergistic quality in
the perceptions of danger from China: the trauma of the border conflict
was followed in only two years by China's nuclear explosion. The first
event reified the threat; the second emphasized its nuclear dimension.
Less than a year later, in the 1965 Indo-Pakistani war, China reportedly
threatened to open a second front on Pakistan's behalf; the People's

7. G. S. Bhargava, *India's Security in the 1980s,* Adelphi Paper 125 (London:
International Institute for Strategic Studies, 1976), p. 16.

8. M. L. Sondhi, "India and Nuclear China," *Pacific Community,* vol. 4 (January 1973), p. 276.

9. Rohit Handa, *Policy for India's Defence* (New Delhi: Chetana Publications,
1976), p. 76.

Liberation Army did in fact shoot at Indian outposts in the Himalayas during the war.[10]

Many Indians are not convinced that the PRC's designs on the subcontinent are limited, especially in view of previous Chinese support of Maoist and other insurgent or secessionist groups such as the Naxalites and Naga and Mizo tribal rebels.[11] China also might have complex motives for the border conflict. The most direct routes from China to Tibet, the "province" that Peking had difficulty pacifying in 1959–60, are almost impassable. An easier route passes from Sinkiang through the disputed Aksai Chin area. In one view, the PRC needs this territory in order to feel that its claim to Tibet is certain and unambiguously recognized. The Chinese may have interpreted Indian opposition to a compromise agreement on the border as evidence of unwillingness to accord full legitimacy to PRC sovereignty over Tibet, instead "following the old British policy of seeking to make it a buffer state. The outrage expressed by the Indian press, the public, and some members of Parliament over suppression of the Tibetan revolt in 1959 had already made China suspicious."[12] The border question has not yet been resolved.

In the conventional military balance, India is not perilously insecure against the PRC. After the humiliation in the 1962 border fighting, New Delhi drastically overhauled its defense establishment. Within two years armed forces manpower more than doubled, from 400,000 to 860,000.

10. Ashok Kapur, "Peace and Power in India's Nuclear Policy," *Asian Survey,* vol. 10 (September 1970), p. 784; Allen S. Whiting, *The Chinese Calculus of Deterrence: India and Indochina* (University of Michigan Press, 1975), p. 233. According to the U.S. Central Intelligence Agency, China did make ambiguous threats to India during the 1965 war, protesting Indian " 'military works of aggression' which are alleged to be on the Chinese side of the Sikkim border or on the boundary itself. It seems likely that the Chinese, having set a deadline, are planning to follow through with military action of some sort. . . . This threat appears calculated to bring maximum psychological pressure to bear on the Indians with the object of diverting attention from the Kashmir front and easing the pressure on Pakistan." CIA, Office of Current Intelligence, Intelligence Memorandum: "Communist China Issues New Threat Against India," September 15, 1965 (Box 16, National Security Files, Vietnam Country File, Southeast Asia Special Intelligence Material file, Lyndon Baines Johnson Library, Austin, Texas, vol. VII, item 13, p. 1).

11. Bhargava, *India's Security in the 1980s,* p. 9; William J. Barnds, *India, Pakistan, and the Great Powers* (Praeger for the Council on Foreign Relations, 1972), pp. 317–18.

12. Ibid.

More specifically, India now has eleven mountain divisions, trained for combat in the most likely area of confrontation. Major improvements were made in training, equipment, communications, and logistics. Given limitations in Chinese logistical capacities and the probability that in a conflict with India Peking would have to maintain large reserves guarding flanks (principally the Soviet border, which would require a larger proportion of Chinese forces than the proportion that India would have to hold in reserve against Pakistan), the Indian army would be in a favorable position to cope with another limited war on its northeastern border. In that case the principal PRC edge against India would be its nuclear forces. China's fifty to seventy IRBMs, forty to fifty MRBMs, and about ninety TU-16 medium bombers[13] are enough to inflict unacceptable destruction on Indian targets. Indians have considered numerous situations in which the PRC might use its nuclear card. For example, if there were a partly successful leftist coup in Nepal, India intervened at the request of democratic opponents, and the leftists asked for Chinese help, the Chinese would have to use nuclear weapons because it could not get enough of its conventional power to Nepal to match the Indian army.[14]

It might be argued that India should not be alarmed by Chinese nuclear capabilities for several reasons. The Chinese have always argued for a restrictive concept of nuclear weapons, deemphasizing their utility (although they argued for nuclear superiority by the socialist states to deter the use of nuclear forces by the imperialist powers), and they would be inhibited from expending nuclear ordnance against India by the desire not to weaken their deterrent against the USSR. The PRC has also made a "no-first-use" pledge, and the primary target of its nuclear forces is almost certainly the Soviet Union.[15] No-first-use declaratory policy, however, should not be any more reassuring to New Delhi than comparable Soviet pledges would be to Bonn or Washington. (The same lack of trust in enemy rhetoric applies to Pakistan's unwillingness to take present Indian nuclear policy at face value.)

13. International Institute for Strategic Studies, *The Military Balance, 1979–1980* (London: IISS, 1979), p. 60.

14. Subramanian Swamy, "A Weapons Strategy for a Nuclear India," *India Quarterly,* vol. 30 (October–December 1974), p. 274.

15. Jonathan D. Pollack, "China as a Nuclear Power," in William H. Overholt, ed., *Asia's Nuclear Future* (Westview Press, 1977), pp. 42–44.

The Indian nuclear program as it stands—having demonstrated weapons capability and keeping the option but not developing a deployable nuclear force—is a political rather than a military response to the China challenge.[16] Maintaining a weapon-threshold capability may give India the best of both worlds diplomatically: the ability, as a state without weapons, to promote disarmament and chastise the nuclear powers and the ability to wield a latent deterrent. Moreover, some reason that by not foreclosing its own option India retains its only leverage for disarmament; without the option as a latent alternative, other powers have no reason to take Indian proposals seriously.[17] But if Indo-Chinese relations should worsen, New Delhi would have more incentive for implementing the option and making the deterrent manifest. Exercising the option might also be considered a means of improving relations with Peking. If serious rapprochement is undertaken, "possession of nuclear weapons will make it possible to secure better terms."[18] Some Indian analysts even argue that an independent force would be a means of convincing the PRC that New Delhi is not in collusion with Moscow.[19] The contrary arguments, nevertheless, still carry substantial weight with many Indians: forgoing a nuclear weapons program enhances the possibility of détente with China by avoiding provocation and reduces Pakistan's incentives to develop nuclear weapons. (One analyst, though, suggests that a Pakistani nuclear force could benefit New Delhi because it would reduce Islamabad's dependence on Peking.[20])

The most encouraging fact for U.S. nonproliferation policy in recent years was that Prime Minister Desai, a disciple of Mahatma Gandhi, continued to adhere to his lifelong opposition to nuclear weapons. Atomic Energy was one of the portfolios he kept for himself. His views were well expressed by a namesake, Manilal Jagdish Desai, who as secretary general

16. Ashok Kapur, *India's Nuclear Option: Atomic Diplomacy and Decision Making* (Praeger, 1976), p. 21.

17. Col. R. Rama Rao, "India's Security Perceptions and the Nuclear Issue," in T. T. Poulose, ed., *Perspectives of India's Nuclear Policy* (New Delhi–Stockholm: Young Asia Publications, 1978), p. 97.

18. John Maddox, *Prospects for Nuclear Proliferation,* Adelphi Paper 113 (London: International Institute for Strategic Studies, 1975), p. 18.

19. Sondhi, "India and Nuclear China," p. 272.

20. Jayashree Jayagopal, "India's Nuclear Policy and Pakistan's Nuclear Responses," in Poulose, ed., *Perspectives of India's Nuclear Policy,* p. 197.

of the Ministry of External Affairs in 1965 summed up arguments against an Indian bomb:

India will be playing straight into the hands of China if because of fear or emotional reaction or prestige considerations, it enters into a nuclear race with China.The enormous diversion of resources and talents required will retard India's economic and social development programmes indefinitely and by creating scarcity and economic dislocation and social discontent [will] not only weaken India internally but eliminate it as a political factor in Asia and Africa.[21]

Desai's nuclear pacifism, however, provided no lasting comfort for American nonproliferationists, since he was ousted from office in mid-1979. His immediate successor, Charan Singh, announced a firmer policy, and warned that, if Pakistan continued its efforts to develop nuclear weapons capability, India would reconsider its own policy.[22] Indira Gandhi is likely to look even more favorably on nuclear weapons options.

Pakistan

India's decision on whether or not to exercise its nuclear option will directly affect Pakistan's plans. But even if India refrains from a nuclear weapons program, leaders in Islamabad still have some compelling strategic reasons to get a bomb. In contrast to the situation that exists between India and China, Pakistan devotes proportionally larger resources to defense expenditures yet remains hopelessly inferior to its primary antagonist in important gross indexes of conventional military power and potential (see table 6-1). In three categories, Pakistan's effort in recent years has been between twice and four times that of India (only in per capita GNP does Pakistan have an advantage). And although the gaps in capabilities have narrowed since the nadir of the early 1970s, Pakistan's armed forces are less than half the size of India's, expenditures barely one-fourth, and military power potential (GNP) less than one-

21. Shelton L. Williams, *The U.S., India, and the Bomb,* Washington Center of Foreign Policy Research, Studies in International Affairs 12 (Johns Hopkins Press, 1969), p. 74.
22. Mario Bianchi, "Singh to Seek a More Firm Defense Policy," *Korea Times,* August 18, 1979; Mohan Ram, "New Twist Given to India-Pakistan Nuclear Race," *Christian Science Monitor,* August 17, 1979.

Table 6-1. *The South Asian Imbalance of Power and Pakistan's Defense Burden, 1977*

1977 dollars

Item	India (1)	Pakistan (2)	Col. 2 as percent of col. 1[a] (3)
Capability			
Military expenditures (millions of dollars)	3,081	882	0.28
Armed forces (thousands)	1,270	588	0.46
GNP (billions of dollars)	95.3	14.36	0.15
Effort			
Military expenditures as percent of GNP	3.2	6.1	1.9
Military expenditures per capita (dollars)	5.00	11.00	2.2
GNP per capita (constant dollars)	140.5	180.3	1.28
Armed forces per 1,000 population	1.98	7.79	3.93

Source: U.S. Arms Control and Disarmament Agency, *World Military Expenditures and Arms Transfers, 1968–1977* (Government Printing Office, 1979), pp. 46, 56, 89, 99.

a. The top three rows of column 3 show Pakistan's capability as a proportion of India's capability; the bottom four rows show Pakistan's effort as a proportion of India's effort.

fifth. The significance of the disparity is lessened by India's need to keep forces in reserve against the Chinese border, and the disparity also narrowed after the mid-1970s. But Pakistani planners are unlikely to depreciate the threat very much because the gap is still huge and the possibility of war remains significant. Pakistanis were alarmed by large increases in India's defense budget after 1974, which was already past the time when Pakistan's dismemberment had eliminated most of the threat to India. Nuclear weapons could come to seem the only means by which to assure deterrence of Indian conventional attack or to defend Pakistani territory if deterrence failed. (One argument to calm Pakistan's anxieties is that its borders have become more defensible since it lost the eastern wing—forces can be concentrated. This is not necessarily more comforting to leaders in Islamabad, though, than the argument that German defense would be more "practical" on the Weser-Lech line would be to Bonn.) Given the unwillingness of allies (the United States and the PRC) to intervene militarily on its behalf in the last two years, the Carter administration's diplomatic tilt back toward New Delhi, and the difficulty of obtaining modern military equipment abroad, Pakistan may also feel it has little to lose in undertaking a nuclear weapons program. Of the three countries considered here, Pakistan has the most compelling positive incentives for a bomb and the fewest and weakest negative incentives. And if Pakistan implements a weapons program, India—and perhaps even Iran at a future date—might decide to go in that direction.

The enmity between India and Pakistan has roots in the old communal violence between Hindus and the Muslim minority that led to partition of the subcontinent in 1947. The depth and intensity of historic visceral animosity between the two groups, for cultural, political, and religious reasons,[23] are similar to the conflict between Arabs and Jews in Palestine. Pakistanis have feared irredentism—"Akhand Barat" or "undivided India" sentiment—since partition. Conflict over Jammu and Kashmir, and India's unwillingness to accept self-determination as a basis for resolving that conflict, kept the fear alive.

Since the defeat in the 1971 war, Islamabad has seen in New Delhi's annexation of Sikkim and diplomatic pressure on Bangladesh and Nepal additional reasons to remain suspicious of Indian designs. After losing the eastern wing of the country, fears of further dismemberment were not allayed. There are regional and ethnic separatist movements in Pakistan, and some diplomats in the early 1970s claimed to have evidence that the USSR was supporting secessionists in Baluchistan and the North-West Frontier Province.[24] Tension increased in late 1973 with activities by Baluchi guerrillas, and Baluchistan and the North-West Frontier Province were placed under central administration. A bloody counterinsurgency campaign lasted until the new government accepted a truce in 1977 after ousting Bhutto. Since the Soviet invasion of Afghanistan, the prospect of Baluchi secession, supported by Moscow, has come to the fore again. Such problems suggest that in one sense the threat to Pakistan's security is internal and not remediable by nuclear weapons. But the internal instability is linked to external strategy by the possibility that upheaval could catalyze Indian intervention just as it did in 1971. There was also tension between Pakistan and Afghanistan after the 1973 coup that installed Muhammed Daud Khan as president. Daud had earlier supported the creation of Pushtunistan, a new entity that would include sections of Pakistani territory. An alarming prospect to Pakistani planners was that a crisis over the Pushtunistan issue might ignite a two-front war with

23. See Barnds, *India, Pakistan, and the Great Powers,* pp. 13–43.
24. Anwar H. Syed, "Pakistan's Security Problem: A Bill of Constraints," *Orbis,* vol. 16 (Winter 1973), p. 971.

India and Afghanistan.[25] The Pushtunistan issue festered for decades. The United States even became involved in November 1950, trying to promote negotiations on the problem between Afghanistan and Pakistan.[26] According to one report, the Afghan government considered marching on Peshawar during the Indo-Pakistani war in 1971 but was dissuaded by the Soviet Union.[27]

Pakistani anxiety deepened after the April 1978 coup in Kabul and the installation of pro-Soviet authorities. The first head of government, Nur Mohammed Taraki, and his deputy prime minister and foreign minister, Hafizullah Amin, who succeeded him in a 1979 coup, were both Pushtuns, from a clan "which has its deepest roots on the Pakistani side of the border."[28] The 1978 coup also occurred shortly after the previous government, under pressure from the shah, had agreed to deny anti-Pakistani Baluchi guerrillas and Pushtun dissidents the use of Afghan territory as a base. Since the Soviet invasion and installation of the Babrak Karmal government, the Pushtunistan issue has lost significance (though it could become important again in the future) because the biggest source of conflict became Pakistan's support of the Muslim rebellion against the Marxist government in Kabul. Even before the invasion Pakistan's tolerance of refugee military activities prompted warnings in *Pravda* that war between the two countries was possible and that the Soviet Union might not stand aside if it occurred.[29] A mass rally was held in the Afghan capital to support secessionists in Pakistan.[30] Since December 1979, with Soviet military forces on Pakistan's doorstep, President Zia ul-Haq has walked a tightrope between provocation and accommodation of Moscow and the Karmal government.

It is no simple task to present obviously persuasive arguments as to

25. Stephen Oren, "The Afghani Coup and the Peace of the Northern Tier," *The World Today*, vol. 30 (January 1974), pp. 26–32.

26. U.S. Department of State, *Foreign Relations of the United States, 1951*, vol. 6: *Asia and the Pacific*, pt. 2 (GPO, 1977), pp. 1929–2003.

27. Zalmay Khalilzad and others, *Regional Rivalries and Nuclear Responses*, vol. 1: *Conflict and Competition in the Arabian Sea and the Prospects for Nuclear Proliferation*, DNA 001-77-C-0052, prepared for the Director, U.S. Defense Nuclear Agency (Los Angeles: Pan Heuristics, 1978), p. 58.

28. Selig S. Harrison, "Nightmare in Baluchistan," *Foreign Policy*, no. 32 (Fall 1978), pp. 146–47.

29. "Afghan-Pakistan War Looms: Soviet," *New York News*, June 2, 1979.

30. Michael T. Kaufman, "Afghanistan Regime Keeps Control with Core of Loyalists," *New York Times*, September 9, 1979.

why Pakistan does not need nuclear weapons, especially if American strategic planners put themselves in Pakistani shoes. "Mirror-imaging" of course has many drawbacks as a technique of strategic analysis. Indeed, the most ardent U.S. proponents of arms control have been heavily criticized by hard-liners for assuming that Soviet strategists view the East-West nuclear competition in the same terms as Americans do. But it may be useful to speculate on the extent to which Pakistan's nuclear incentives might correspond to the original rationales behind Western reliance on nuclear weapons. For much of the cold war, both before and after the USSR achieved its own nuclear capability, American and NATO policy was based on the premise that nuclear retaliatory power was needed to counterbalance superior Soviet conventional forces. Thus it can be plausibly argued that Pakistan has as much legitimate need for a nuclear deterrent as the United States did in the late 1940s, or as the United States, Britain, France, and China do today.[31] Pakistan's conventional capabilities compared with those of India are far weaker than NATO's capabilities compared with those of the Warsaw Pact, Pakistan has had little luck in using stronger allies to maintain a balance of power on the subcontinent, and the hostility between Islamabad and New Delhi has never been less than that between Moscow and Washington. Indeed, former Pakistani Prime Minister Bhutto pointed out after the Indian nuclear test, "No two among the five great nuclear-weapon powers . . . have had a history of confrontation and wars between them in contemporary times or in [the] past remotely comparable to the relations between India and Pakistan."[32] At a minimum, many Pakistanis feel it only reasonable to have an unimplemented threshold option—fissionable material, weapon designs, or components untested but ready for use as bombs—comparable to India's.

New Delhi has done little to reduce Pakistan's incentives. Since the 1971 victory Indian officials have made numerous statements amounting to a demand that Islamabad recognize and resign itself to the new reality of Indian predominance on the subcontinent. India has also demanded that Pakistan neither rearm to a degree that could threaten India nor seek

31. The son of the former prime minister wrote an interesting and thoughtful analysis supporting a Pakistani nuclear weapons program. Mir Murtaza Bhutto, "A Modicum of Harmony" (Honors thesis, Harvard University, March 1976).

32. Statement in U.S. Arms Control and Disarmament Agency, *Documents on Disarmament, 1974* (GPO, 1976), p. 147.

allies from outside the region. From Islamabad this may seem the equivalent of a demand for a South Asian version of "finlandization." When this is combined with U.S. demands and France's cancellation of its contract to build the plutonium reprocessing plant, Pakistan is wedged between a neighbor's politico-military hegemony and the great powers' technological hegemony.

The prestige value of either a nuclear weapons program or the option for one could complement its strategic value for Pakistan. It would be one means of deflating Indian predominance or showing that Pakistan has to be taken seriously as an independent international actor. While the desire for a large degree of technical or economic autonomy is understandable for formerly colonized nations, and while such autonomy is possible for India, it is probably beyond Pakistan's reach; near autonomy in at least one important area—nuclear energy—might therefore be all the more important as a symbol of national sovereignty. For Pakistan, pressed to accept second-class statehood on the subcontinent, national status and recognition are part of its security problem. Shirin Tahir-Kheli quotes a Pakistani official: "The Iranians have oil, Indians have Carter as well as the Device—it's only fair that Pakistanis should have at least the Bomb."[33] Nuclear status could enlarge Pakistan's role in the pan-Islamic movement and give it a position of military leadership with conservative Arab states.[34] Prestige motives in a strategic sense may also be compounded by internal political interests. Zia may have believed unveiling a nuclear weapon could be a gesture to rally declining popular support as the economy worsened and Bhutto's Pakistan People's Party maintained its strength. The PPP has been most strongly supported in areas where anti-India sentiment is highest.[35]

Counterarguments based on norms of global stability are not persuasive from Islamabad's viewpoint. Indian spokesmen complain about the discriminatory double standard in the nonproliferation treaty, but to

33. Tahir-Kheli, "Pakistan's Nuclear Option," p. 367.

34. As early as 1977 Karachi's *Defence Journal* (vol. 3 [1977], pp. 8–11) promoted Pakistan's strategic identification in this direction, with an article titled "Need for an Islamic Strategic Studies Group." Early hopes for support from the Muslim world were disappointed, but revived again after the 1973 Middle East war and the 1974 Islamic Summit Conference in Lahore.

35. William J. Barnds, "Pakistan's Foreign Policy: Shifting Opportunities and Constraints," in Lawrence Ziring, Ralph Braibanti, and W. Howard Wriggins, eds., *Pakistan: The Long View* (Duke University Press, 1977), p. 388.

Pakistanis the problem is a triple standard. The United States has demanded concessions from them (giving up reprocessing capability) that
are not demanded from India: "For Pakistan, selective application of
sanctions—i.e., no sanctions against India—has weakened the moral case
against proliferation."[36] The United States extended a commodity loan
and economic aid in August 1978 despite India's refusal to accept full-
scope safeguards, but it terminated aid to Pakistan in 1979 even before
that country's facilities for producing fissionable material were complete.
Indeed, in view of the Indian example and the American administration's
decision to provide fuel despite Desai's refusal to accept full-scope safeguards, Pakistani strategists may believe they have more to gain by
defiance. They might even cite what Indians noted as a softening of U.S.
attitudes and a reversal of the decline in Indo-American relations after
India's 1974 nuclear test.[37] Such reasoning was certainly not confirmed
by the American decision in 1979 to cut off economic and military aid in
response to Pakistan's secret initiatives to build enrichment facilities, but
optimistic Pakistani decisionmakers may hope for a revision of U.S.
policy and laws (which mandate such a cutoff) once the storm blows
over. This gamble might be rationalized by the fact that the U.S. sanctions were limited. Food aid was not terminated, and though military
grants were stopped, equipment purchases were not proscribed. And since
the Soviet invasion of Afghanistan, the United States has been more
solicitous and has more reason not to mortgage its entire Pakistan policy
to the proliferation issue. Planners might also calculate that a nuclear
deterrent would prevent Indian attack on Pakistan proper and thus provide more room for maneuver "in small wars or insurrections in, for example, Kashmir."[38] This possibility is reflected in Indian strategists' ap-
preciation of the impact of a Pakistani nuclear force: "Our national
strategy would have to adjust to the condition that Indian arms must not
launch an offensive against Pakistan; even perhaps that in a defensive
battle Indian arms must not inflict a decisive defeat on Pakistan."[39]

The essential incentives and justifications perceived by many Paki-

36. Tahir-Kheli, "Pakistan's Nuclear Option," p. 371.
37. Sitanshu Das, "President Carter's Visit in Retrospect," *Indian & Foreign Review* (February 1, 1978), p. 13.
38. Stephen P. Cohen, "Perception, Influence, and Weapons Proliferation in South Asia," report for the Department of State, August 1979, p. 46.
39. Maj. Gen. D. K. Palit and P. K. S. Namboodiri, *Pakistan's Islamic Bomb* (New Delhi: Vikas, 1979), p. 117.

stanis for pursuing nuclear autonomy—national security requirements, superpower indifference to Pakistan's vulnerability, international double or triple standards, and the need for diplomatic leverage—have been encapsulated by one analyst:

The commotion over the sale of the French reprocessing plant has dramatized the nervousness of countries that in previous years, when Pakistan drew attention to potential sources of conflict on the subcontinent, remained largely unmoved. It has also shaken up the accepted principle of Indian superiority over Pakistan. . . . Moreover, it signifies that the big powers are alert only to the nuclear threat. . . . The big powers have somehow come to accept the occurrence of conventional wars, the accompanying defeats and territorial occupation. . . . The use of nuclear "devices," on the other hand, is totally unacceptable. . . . To hold this weapon, then, is automatically to involve the major powers in the problems that may lead to its use, or in the solutions that may preclude its use.[40]

Despite the straits in which Pakistan finds itself vis-à-vis India and the Soviet Union—or in part because of them—prudent planners in Islamabad, of course, also have to consider the disincentives for acquiring nuclear weapons. Such a move might provoke India to (1) harden its stance toward Pakistan; (2) develop a nuclear force of its own large enough to increase the threat to Pakistan; (3) possibly attempt preemptive or preventive war before the Pakistani nuclear force is fully developed and deployed. Pakistani strategists might not see these costs as outweighing the benefits of a nuclear force but are unlikely to ignore them. The new Soviet threat, on the other hand, which places Pakistan in a vise between superior powers on its eastern and western borders, makes conventional defense even less feasible. A small nuclear force—a finite or proportional deterrent—may seem the only alternative to becoming a servile protectorate.

Ironically, resort to theories of strategic deterrence for arguments to dissuade Pakistan from proliferation reveals that the theories of American hawks, who favor high levels of nuclear arms for the United States, should prove most useful. Analysis that stresses the value of nuclear superiority should give Pakistani officials pause, because provoking India into a nuclear arms race would leave Pakistan consistently on the short end, and it would always be dwarfed by Soviet nuclear capabilities. If, however, they believed the deterrence theories of doves, who dismiss the utility of nuclear superiority and argue the sufficiency of an assured de-

40. Tahir-Kheli, "Pakistan's Nuclear Option," p. 362.

struction capability as a deterrent, especially theories of "finite" deterrence, a small and inferior nuclear force would be much more appealing.
Even prudent planners, however, may see any of the risks as lower and
bearable if Pakistan develops only the weapons option without actually
testing explosive devices or deploying a nuclear force.

Iran

In the mid-1970s Iran was often cited as an example of a state that
might be motivated to acquire nuclear weapons by the desire for national
prestige. This was implied by the shah's ambitious programs of modernization, economic development, and investment in sophisticated conventional military forces, and the increased acceptance by the West of Iran
as the dominant power in the Persian Gulf area. Symbolic of these potential motives was the official name of the country: the Empire of Iran.
Although the reactionary and leftist forces that overthrew the shah repu-
diated his works, it is by no means certain that foreign policy in the long
run—after the confused transition period of the revolution ends—will be
much different. What might have appealed to the shah as a means of
achieving grandeur could appeal to successors as a means of achieving
independence from both East and West. Iranians have reasons—the
humiliation of occupation by the British and the Russians in this century
—to be aware of the fragility of their national sovereignty. If pro-Soviet
forces do not secure power, the dictates of realpolitik may ultimately
produce some similarities between the foreign policy of the shah and
those of subsequent rulers. My analysis, in any case, suggests how a more
stable government in Tehran—following the resolution of the country's
current internal political problems—might approach the nuclear question.

Iran's security priorities are in the south and west (the Persian Gulf
and Iraq) and north (the USSR), but several factors link its interest to
the region to the east. Like Islamabad, Tehran has a stake in controlling
unrest in Baluchistan (the Baluchi population spills over into Iran). As a
result, Iran has reason to value the integrity and stability of Pakistan;
this interest is compounded by Pakistan's value as a buffer state against
India. These goals are also related to Iran's interests in the Persian Gulf
and the Gulf of Oman. An observer who had close ties with the shah notes

that he feared the potential combination of a hostile regime (Baluchistan) on the northern shore of the approaches to the Persian Gulf with a radical coup in Oman, which could threaten Iran's oil lifeline by pinching access to the critical Strait of Hormuz.[41] Reactionary forces, and certainly Iranian leftists, may be less concerned about this problem, although regional dissidence has been one of the Khomeini regime's principal internal problems. The geography will not change, however, and any Iranian government that is less than fully isolationist—or suicidal—will keep its eye on the region.

The danger of internal instability is also linked to Iran's on-and-off antagonism with Iraq. This was temporarily moderated by a détente in 1974 involving resolution of the immediate dispute concerning jurisdiction over the Shatt-al-Arab waterway and withdrawal of Iranian support for Kurdish rebels. With the advent of the Khomeini government the conflict heated up again. Before the détente there were ten border clashes between Iraq and Iran from 1972 to 1974, some of them severe (forty-one Iranians were reported killed in one, sixty in another).[42] The Baluchi Liberation Front was established in Baghdad. In February 1973 arms caches in the Iraqi embassy in Pakistan, apparently intended for the Baluchis, were revealed, precipitating Pakistan's severance of diplomatic relations with Iraq. At that time, at least, there was speculation that "for the Shah, aware that Iran lies between the USSR and her coveted warm-water ports, a feeling of encirclement may be growing."[43] If xenophobic elements control Iran and overcome internal challenges and the confrontation with the United States, they could become even more concerned about encirclement. Only a pro-Soviet government in Tehran would regard such dangers as negligible.

Also, although Iraq has signed and ratified the NPT, suspicious Iranian strategists could fear a crude Iraqi nuclear option. France negotiated to sell Baghdad an Osiris research reactor designed to use uranium enriched (according to one report) to 93 percent.[44] This would be oralloy, weapons-grade material. France assured other nations that the Iraqi con-

41. Alvin J. Cottrell, "The Foreign Policy of the Shah," *Strategic Review*, vol. 3 (Fall 1975), pp. 32–44.

42. R. M. Burrell and Alvin J. Cottrell, *Iran, Afghanistan, Pakistan: Tensions and Dilemmas*, Center for International and Strategic Studies, Georgetown University, Washington Papers, vol. 2, no. 20 (Sage, 1974), p. 5.

43. Oren, "Afghani Coup," p. 30.

44. *Nucleonics Week*, special edition (November 18, 1976), p. 3.

tract conformed to nuclear suppliers' group guidelines,[45] but the deal
sparked concern in the region. Damascus subsequently sought "bids for
a feasibility study of nuclear research and energy" in Syria.[46] In 1979
France was building two research reactors for Iraq when the factory was
sabotaged, and some officials suspected an Israeli commando operation.
Theoretically, the Iraqis could divert the reactors' highly enriched uranium fuel charges for a few small bombs. Withholding only part of this
amount from use in the reactor would provide a "finite" deterrent capable of destroying Tehran or Tel Aviv. (Naim Haddad, senior member of
Iraq's Revolutionary Command Council, accused the United States of
helping Israel produce nuclear weapons and said, "If Israel owns the
atom bomb, then the Arabs must get an atom bomb."[47]) An American
journalist, Jack Anderson, wrote in 1978 on the basis of leaks from
intelligence sources that the Iraqis had asked for a two-year fuel supply
of perhaps 70 to 80 kilograms, but there were reports that the French
were developing a new low enriched "caramel" fuel for the Osiris, which
would eliminate its weapons potential.[48] By early 1980, however, alarm
was increasing again as the French decided to proceed with the contract
for high enriched uranium and there were reports of Italian and Brazilian
involvement in Iraq's nuclear program that might produce spin-offs
applicable to weapons technology.

Iran has a geographically wide-ranging sphere of potential politico-
military interests, many of which can be pursued with assurance with its
conventional power alone if revolutionary chaos finally yields to more
disciplined internal organization. Indeed, the shah's first successors appeared uninterested in ambitious military capabilities, and Iran has more
to lose by stirring up local rivals with the introduction of nuclear weapons than it has to gain. If it should decide that it needs a completely
independent and impressive deterrent against Soviet attack, however, the
nuclear option could become more attractive. The attitude of the revolu-

45. *Nucleonics Week,* vol. 19 (January 19, 1978), p. 10.
46. Ibid. (March 2, 1978), p. 11.
47. Quoted in J. P. Smith, "Oil Wealth Causing a Shift in Iraq's Foreign Policy,"
Washington Post, August 8, 1978.
48. Jack Anderson, "France to Push Iraqi Nuclear Deal," *Washington Post,* January 12, 1978; Smith, "Oil Wealth Causing a Shift." The Iraqi reaction to the caramel proposal "is said to have been that that was not what they had contracted for."
Ronald Koven, "Saboteurs Bomb French Plant Constructing 2 Reactors for Iraq,"
Washington Post, April 7, 1979.

tionary government does not seem to make this likely, but its confrontation with the United States and the ensuing alienation, which is likely to outlive the hostage crisis, reduce the defensive options against Soviet power. A reactionary government without allies might be antinuclear by instinct, but more equivocal when considering alternatives for defensive self-sufficiency.

Iran shares a border of 1,250 miles with the USSR. There is a history of Russian pressure and Iranian suspicion: traditional Russian interest in access to the Persian Gulf, confirmed by Molotov in negotiating the Nazi-Soviet nonaggression pact of 1939; the World War II occupation; the 1946 crisis over Azerbaijan; and the Soviet flanking movement through its 1979–80 invasion of Afghanistan. In relative capabilities, Iran's position against the Soviet Union is even more hopeless than Pakistan's against India. To infer that Iran has equally strong incentives for nuclear weapons, however, would be unwarranted. Soviet-Iranian tension exists, but it has been less intense than the hostility on the subcontinent; until recently, at least, Iran had less reason to foresee the probability of war than Pakistan. This relative security was reinforced in the past by the shah's alliance relationship with the United States. If Soviet pressure were exerted in the future, an Iranian government without this tie would be more vulnerable. If a xenophobic Iran were to suffer some humiliation or coercion by the Soviet Union, a shift toward nuclear weapons would become more likely, although fear of strong Soviet reaction would also rise. At present, however, Iran's relations with the superpowers give it more reason to forgo nuclear weapons than to acquire them. Pursuing a nuclear force would provoke the Soviet Union without necessarily achieving a deterrent both credible and secure, and—because the revolutionary regime has taken on the image of a "crazy state" in the course of the hostage crisis—nuclear plans could provoke covert Western intervention to derail weapons development.

Domestic Determinants of Decision

The preceding discussion of incentives is a strategic analysis. In reality, of course, government policy decisions are based on other considerations as well. The distribution of disagreements and influence within foreign policy and defense bureaucracies, parliamentary and party politics, public opinion, and the idiosyncrasies of particular leaders often impinge on policymaking in a way that may or may not be consistent with an "objective" assessment of strategic requirements. India displays the most evidence of domestic debate on nuclear matters, and Iran the least. Information on the Pakistani nuclear policy process is limited, but reasonable inferences can be made.

In view of the security threats perceived by India and Pakistan, it is perhaps not surprising that there is relatively little domestic opposition in either country to national defense programs: "In neither Pakistan nor India is there a substantial body of public opinion opposed to increased arms spending."[49] This does not automatically imply popular support for nuclear weapons, but there is remarkably little opposition to this variant of preparedness either. The stereotype in the West of India as a pacifist culture, fostered by Mahatma Gandhi's personal philosophy, is misleading in this respect. On the other hand, the professional military establishments in these two countries have not been united pro-bomb lobbies. (In several nations, in fact, the army, the largest and most prestigious of the three military services in most cases, has been the least enthusiastic of the services about investment in nuclear forces.[50]) At the level of popular discussion in the nuclear-prone countries of South Asia gross perceptions of external threats may be more significant than detailed analyses of alternative defense options, and in the government professional strategic planners' disagreements about priorities and doctrines may complicate the resolution of debate over the strategic value of a serious nuclear weapons program.

Originally there were two basic schools of thought on nuclear weapons in the government of post-independence India: the dominant view, personified in Prime Minister Jawaharlal Nehru, with his orientation to

49. Stephen P. Cohen, "Security in South Asia," *Asian Survey,* vol. 15 (March 1975), p. 202.

50. In the 1950s the U.S. Army's leaders were energetically opposed to decisions adapting defense strategy to heavy reliance on strategic nuclear forces, although they were agreeable to the development of battlefield tactical nuclear weapons. See Samuel P. Huntington, *The Common Defense: Strategic Programs in National Politics* (Columbia University Press, 1961), pp. 300ff. In France the army was reluctant to proceed with the nuclear program in 1958. Wilfrid L. Kohl, *French Nuclear Diplomacy* (Princeton University Press, 1971), p. 25n. In Britain the Royal Navy too opposed the drain on resources for an independent deterrent. Andrew J. Pierre, *Nuclear Politics: The British Experience with an Independent Strategic Force, 1939–1970* (London: Oxford University Press, 1972), pp. 192–93.

disarmament and "world order" solutions to international conflict, and the pro-bomb lobby personified in Atomic Energy Commission chief Homi Bhabha. After 1962, and especially in the 1964–68 period, a third school, a synthesis, emerged, which supported an unexercised weapons option. This remains official policy, and since the 1950s the nuclear establishment has been organized for conversion to a weapons program if policy changes.[51] When China exploded its first bomb in October 1964 almost a hundred members of parliament signed a petition in favor of nuclear weapons. A vigorous public debate followed.[52] The last serious spurt of discussion on the issue before the 1974 test was provoked by China's 1970 launching of a satellite.[53] This was, in a sense, the equivalent of the 1957 shock to the United States of *Sputnik*. In the early 1970s the New Delhi government perceived strong domestic pressure in favor of the bomb, and this "pushed India's leadership further along the nuclear road than they might otherwise have chosen to go."[54] In 1971 the nuclear energy and space program known as the "Sarabhai profile" was inaugurated, as a means, according to some, of diverting public pressure for a weapons program. But in the same year, according to the defense minister, the decision was made to prepare for the peaceful nuclear explosion.[55] Other internal issues (inflation, food scarcity, economic disruptions) eroded support for Indira Gandhi's policies during the next two years. The 1974 test placated public opposition to some extent; in this interpretation the explosion was designed to influence internal rather than international opinion.[56]

That conclusion is supported by Indian public opinion data. In 1966

51. Kapur, *India's Nuclear Option,* pp. 122, 125.

52. Barrie Morrison and Donald M. Page, "India's Option: The Nuclear Route to Achieve Goal as a World Power," *International Perspectives* (July–August 1974), p. 26.

53. Bhabani Sen Gupta, "How Close Is India to the Bomb?" in Geoffrey Kemp, Robert L. Pfaltzgraff, Jr., and Uri Ra'anan, eds., *The Superpowers in a Multinuclear World* (Heath, 1974), pp. 107, 121n.

54. Frank T. J. Bray and Michael L. Moodie, "Nuclear Politics in India," *Survival,* vol. 20 (May–June 1977), p. 111.

55. B. K. Wariavwalla, "South Asian Security System," paper for the conference on Prospects for Nuclear Proliferation in Developing Countries, Institute for Far Eastern Studies, Kyungnam University, Seoul, Korea, January 1979, p. 16.

56. "The awareness that India is making tangible progress in nuclear development, as evidenced by the nuclear test, is an effective way of deflating the pro-bomb lobby." S. P. Seth, "India's Atomic Profile," *Pacific Community,* vol. 6 (January 1975), p. 278.

and 1968, 70 percent of literate Indians favored production of nuclear weapons. Other surveys confirmed this percentage, with the distribution of opinion roughly consistent across lines of age, education, income, and cities.[57] The 1971 victory over Pakistan temporarily deflated elite pressure for a bomb; Gandhi said in a news conference, "We seem to have got what we wanted without the bomb."[58] Other data suggest an overlapping of prestige and security incentives in the attentive public. A survey of elite attitudes just before the decision for the explosion showed that pro-bomb sentiments correlated positively with both optimism about India's future and isolationism in foreign policy.[59] To say the least, U.S. nonproliferation policy cannot rely on popular pressure to dissuade the Indian government from building a nuclear force. Most hopeful for nonproliferation goals, perhaps, is that public opinion has had only limited influence on foreign policy.

Decisions by Indian officials have been more important in forestalling the move from weapons option to weapons program. The Atomic Energy Commission, which contains many bomb proponents, has been unusually independent, a "state within a state" in Marwah's characterization.[60] Yet the AEC remains under the direct charge of the prime minister, and none of them, from Nehru to Desai, have supported a weapons program (the 1974 test, again, was rationalized as distinct from a weapons program). In the foreign policy and defense bureaucracies as a whole there have been substantial disagreements on the issue. Some important officials (Rajeshwar Dayal, Jagat Mehta, and Rikhi Jaipal) even favored adherence to the NPT, and atomic energy head Vikram Sarabhai was ambivalent. The cabinet, however, was reported to be unanimously opposed.[61] Nationalistic Indian strategists have usually been guardedly optimistic at best about the eventual likelihood of a high-level decision

57. Gerald Braunthal, "An Attitude Survey in India," *Public Opinion Quarterly*, vol. 33 (Spring 1969), p. 81, cited in Kapur, *India's Nuclear Option*, p. 179; Indian Institute of Public Opinion, *Public Opinion Survey*, vol. 13 (February 1968), cited in George Quester, *The Politics of Nuclear Proliferation* (Johns Hopkins University Press, 1973), p. 71; Indian Institute of Public Opinion, *Monthly Public Opinion Surveys*, October 1968, cited in Kapur, *India's Nuclear Option*, p. 180.

58. Sen Gupta, "How Close Is India to the Bomb?" p. 108.

59. Ashis Nandy, "Between Two Gandhis: Psychopolitical Aspects of the Nuclearization of India," *Asian Survey*, vol. 14 (November 1974), pp. 969–70.

60. Onkar Marwah, "India's Nuclear Program: Decisions, Intent, and Policy, 1950–1976," in Overholt, ed., *Asia's Nuclear Future*, p. 169.

61. Kapur, *India's Nuclear Option*, p. 196.

for the bomb. Subrahmanyam, for instance, complained the year before the Pokharan explosion:

The present generation of decision makers and elite marks a marginal improvement over the previous generation in regard to Indocentricity. . . . Still they are too much influenced by their conditioning by the liberal West. . . . But this attitude is bound to change as the newer generation of decision makers move into positions of influence. Mrs. Gandhi is at present the only practitioner of *real politik* among a whole lot of confused Westernised elite.[62]

Desai opposed a weapons program, but the anti-Gandhi coalition was unstable and contained many who favor nuclear weapons. The Congress for Democracy–Janata party coalition that defeated Gandhi in 1977 did so with only a plurality: slightly over 43 percent of the vote.[63] At least three principal figures in the coalition, and the ones whose portfolios would logically be central in policymaking on nuclear weapons (the ministers of defense, external affairs, and finance), had supported a bomb program. Thirty-five percent of Janata's parliamentary representation was made up of a militant Hindu party, the Jana Sangh, which has demanded nuclear weapons at least since 1964, and perhaps earlier, before the Chinese inaugural detonation of that year. Other elements of the coalition, for example, the Socialists, favored the bomb as well.[64] Of all Indian parties, only the Communist party of India explicitly opposes a nuclear weapons program. Within months of returning to power, Indira Gandhi made statements that explicitly left the bomb option open.

There are also differences in the executive bureaucracy, but they are difficult to trace. The Indian defense policy process is relatively "closed" compared to policymaking in Western countries. Few groups are involved, tight security limits available data, and leaks are also restricted by the belief that disputes should be kept within the bureaucracy.[65]

---

62. K. Subrahmanyam, "Indian Nuclear Force in the Eighties?" *Institute for Defence Studies and Analyses Journal* (New Delhi), vol. 5 (April 1973), p. 468.

63. U.S. Central Intelligence Agency, *National Basic Intelligence Factbook* (GPO, July 1979), p. 90.

64. Onkar Marwah, "India's Nuclear and Space Programs: Intent and Policy," *International Security*, vol. 2 (Fall 1977), p. 120; Selig S. Harrison, "Troubled India and Her Neighbours," in K. P. Misra, ed., *Studies in Indian Foreign Policy* (Delhi: Vikas, 1969), p. 212; G. G. Mirchandani, "India and Nuclear Weapons," pp. 60–62, and Ashok Kapur, "India's Nuclear Politics and Policy: Janata Party's Evolving Stance," pp. 170–75, both in Poulose, ed., *Perspectives of India's Nuclear Policy*.

65. Stephen P. Cohen, "The Security Policy-Making Process in India," in Frank B. Horton III, Anthony C. Rogerson, and Edward L. Warner III, eds., *Comparative Defense Policy* (Johns Hopkins University Press, 1974), pp. 156–57, 159.

Moreover, it is uncertain how significant the influence of these differences on high-level decisions is. Lateral communication, intellectual cross-fertilization, or bargaining between ministries is limited. The defense establishment is not interlocked with the atomic energy program; there is no rotation of scientists and engineers between the two. On general, non-operational politico-military issues the Defense Ministry is not permitted to initiate consultations with the Ministry of External Affairs or the prime minister's secretariat. When consulted by political bureaus, Defense Ministry advice is supposed to be limited to the military implications of the question at hand; "there is no real two-way dialogue between the military and political staffs in India on matters involving long-term strategic planning. . . . the services lack the authority or the political clout to initiate analyses or make representations. . . . In questions relating to atomic energy and the NPT the consultative process did not touch the defense services even marginally. In nuclear energy matters, the budgetary process revolves around the Indian Atomic Energy Commission and the budgets of Defence and Atomic Energy are not competing with each other."[66]

Finally, the limited influence of the defense bureaucracy does not unambiguously increase the influence of the anti-bomb case. As mentioned earlier, the military is not a united lobby in favor of nuclear weapons. Many Indian soldiers did not press for the bomb because, given likely trade-offs in the defense budget, such a program might drain resources away from conventional forces, and because the innovation could be "institutionally disruptive."[67] Most important defense decisions in India involve the army, the least pro-nuclear of the services, because of its size and traditional prestige. Military disunity on the nuclear issue broke into the open in 1973 when Field Marshal Manekshaw opposed the bomb.[68] The navy used to be starved for funds, although its allocations increased from 3 to over 10 percent of the defense budget after 1971. A naval buildup might be competitive wtih nuclear weapons in defense budget trade-offs, implying that that service is not enthusiastic

66. Kapur, *India's Nuclear Option*, p. 149.
67. Cohen, "Security in South Asia," p. 209n. See also Quester, *Politics of Nuclear Proliferation*, p. 69, and T. T. Poulose, "India's Nuclear Policy," in Poulose, ed., *Perspectives of India's Nuclear Policy*, p. 110.
68. Sen Gupta, "How Close Is India to the Bomb?" p. 116; see also p. 124n.

about nuclear weapons. There are indications, however, that the navy may be more interested in nuclear capability than the other services.[69] This would make sense, since the navy is the only one of the services that could plausibly foresee having to face one of the two superpowers as a combatant in the Indian Ocean. The dispatch of the U.S. carrier *Enterprise* to the Bay of Bengal in 1971 strengthened this belief. And the navy has an aircraft carrier, the *Vikrant,* which conceivably could serve as a platform for a nuclear strike force.

Available information on Pakistani policymaking and military thought is sparse. Pakistan's more authoritarian political system and its less developed scientific community have yielded less open discourse on nuclear energy issues than can be found in India. Professional soldiers in Pakistan are reluctant to discuss their strategic views in public (the principal forum for discussion, the *Pakistan Army Journal,* is not available to outsiders). An important contrast to India, with its relatively stable constitutional system, is that the military services in Pakistan have usually dominated policymaking; in fact, they have often—as at present—*been* the government. One researcher's interviews, however, indicated that the military was less adamant than the last civilian head of government, Ali Bhutto, about purchasing the plutonium reprocessing plant from France. According to some reports, a number of high officers regretted Bhutto's decision to reject Henry Kissinger's August 1976 offer to trade U.S. approval of the sale of one hundred A-7 attack aircraft for Pakistani cancellation of the reprocessing deal wtih France.[70]

Bhutto so successfully invested the reprocessing issue with significance as a test of national sovereignty and resolve, however, that it is now difficult for the military, which ousted him, to back out of the contract even were it so inclined. And revelation of recent plans for enrichment capability indicate that it is not inclined to forgo a weapons option. The Pakistani air force's difficulty in modernizing its inventory and acquiring the new aircraft it wanted from the United States conceivably could cut either way in the strategic debate: on the one hand, it inhibits the prospective efficacy, and hence the credibility, of its nuclear delivery capabil-

69. Kapur, *India's Nuclear Option,* p. 148n; Cohen, "Security in South Asia," p. 210; Mohan Ram, "India Debates Development of a Blue-Water Navy," *Christian Science Monitor,* May 11, 1978.

70. Tahir-Kheli, "Pakistan's Nuclear Option," pp. 368–69.

ity; on the other hand, it may make the "nuclear-as-offset-for-conven-tional-inferiority" incentive that much more potent. The navy, like that of India, has traditionally been the minor and neglected service, al-though recently closer ties with the rest of the Muslim world might work to reverse this pattern.[71] But without a carrier and lacking the resources and technology to convert its submarines to carry SLBMs, the navy would have to develop some ingenious or exotic delivery vehicles to per-form a substantial nuclear mission.

No matter how the Pakistani armed services see the attractiveness or drawbacks of a nuclearized strategy, the views of military leaders will be crucial in the policy decision—either largely determining, as in the present regime, or at least highly influential in any likely successor civil-ian government. And despite the disadvantages of going nuclear that Western nonproliferationists point out to them, they are unlikely to be much less persuaded of the value of a nuclear deterrent than American or Soviet civil political leaders have been, or any more convinced of the "unthinkability" of strategic or tactical nuclear warfare than American or Soviet military leaders have been.

Of all three countries, Iran's defense decisionmaking process on major issues used to be the least complex. The process was, quite simply, the shah's personal deliberations. The roles of the foreign ministry, legisla-ture, and other government institutions were negligible; there were no competing bureaucracies, parties, associations, or lobbies that had sig-nificant influence on matters of high policy; and there was virtually no public debate.[72] Monarchical rule and lack of public discussion discour-aged popular awareness of issues. Now, however, Iran's national decision process is probably the most complex—chaotic might be more accu-rate—of the three countries. It is not yet clear what enduring changes may flow from recent unrest. As of this writing there is no evidence that an authoritative government exists in Tehran, let alone a decisive and coherent reformulation of external defense policy.

However simple or complex the structural constraints on policymak-

---

71. Lorne J. Kavic, "Force Posture: India and Pakistan," in Horton, Rogerson, and Warner, eds., *Comparative Defense Policy,* p. 385.

72. Shahram Chubin and Sepehr Zabih, *The Foreign Relations of Iran: A De-veloping State in a Zone of Great Power Conflict* (University of California Press, 1974), p. 18.

ing are, the future decisions likely to be made in each of the three nations are both uncertain and interdependent because all three countries face cross-pressures on the nuclear issue. Nonproliferation planners cannot count on the continuity of decisional patterns. Indira Gandhi's return to power with a large mandate and the fractionation of the Indian opposition suggest that the government in New Delhi will have wide latitude to pursue whatever policy seems strategically sensible to the prime minister. Renewed warmth in Indo-Soviet relations should discourage India from moving toward a nuclear force, but increased American support of Pakistan and China creates pressure in the other direction. Serious threats to security and distrust of American offers of support (which are limited and equivocal anyway) leave little reason for the fragile regime in Islamabad to stop developing the requisite capabilities for fission weapons, but the danger of provoking a now more militant India and more proximate Soviet Union should dissuade Pakistan from testing or deploying weapons. With a history of coups, military government, recent Muslim zealotry, and a fractious combination of domestic interests, Pakistan has an unpredictable political future, and this makes nuclear decisions even less predictable. It would be foolhardy to forecast what sort of government will eventually emerge in Iran, let alone what its procedures and policies will be. The volatility of the whole situation in the Near East leaves a wide range of possibilities open. A nonproliferation rationale or "solution" to pro-nuclear incentives that might be persuasive in any of the three capitals at the moment may not prove persuasive a few years later.

Decisionmaking will always take place within a certain range of limitations implied by external threats and opportunities. All three countries have many good reasons not to seek nuclear weapons. But in general strategic incentives, Pakistan has the most to gain and the least to lose by seeking weapons capability; Iran's potential gains and losses are uncertain and depend on the evolution of both its government and its relations with the superpowers; and India's contradictory interests—hedging against a moderate Chinese threat versus propelling Pakistan into a crash program for nuclear force deployment—appear to be best served by its recent policy: maintenance of the weapons option through demonstrated explosive capability and threshold bomb-production capability. The incentives of all three countries are contingent and interconnected. One major diplomatic or military surprise could change all of them.

There is no sure way to persuade any of them, in terms of their own individual national security interests rather than global nonproliferation interests and in the absence of new countervailing incentives, that they do not need deliverable nuclear explosives. An American foreign policy that places high priority on nonproliferation will have to offer these countries much more than the unconvincing moralistic homilies or heavy-handed economic and technical threats proffered so far.

CHAPTER SEVEN

Nuclear Defense Options: Strategies, Costs, and Contingencies

THE EMPHASIS in this study is on American options for checking the spread of nuclear weapons. Because most of those options would mean appreciable costs for the United States—in aid, commitments, and detraction from interests and policies outside the issue of nuclear weapons—it is well first to consider what the costs of not controlling proliferation might be. This involves analysis of how strategic interactions in the region might evolve if one or more of the nations deployed nuclear weapons, how the individual nations might calculate their own defensive alternatives to nuclear weapons, what crises could lead to the use of such weapons, and what nuclear doctrines and tactics might appear logical to strategic planners in the three countries. To move from the general to the specific, the first step is to consider theoretical arguments offered by third world strategists and others that the spread of nuclear weapons may actually yield more security and stability, not less.

Deterrence Theory and New Frames of Reference

Paradoxically, progress in devising more realistic and effective nonproliferation strategies is sometimes impeded by the axiomatic quality of most American observers' opposition to proliferation. Understanding of the problem is limited if all motives for acquiring nuclear weapons are assumed to be either diabolical or stupid. Many analyses postulate that it is self-evident that the spread of nuclear weapons would be extremely dangerous, destabilizing, and counterproductive even for those who obtained them. But while this may be true, it is not self-evident; the previous discussion of incentives shows why. If it were both true and self-evident, there would be no problem, because no nation would want to proliferate. As it is, a number of foreign strategists see the antiproliferation arguments of the nuclear weapons states as disingenuous, ethnocentrically naive, or inconsistent with the logic of their own defense policies. These critics have two arguments that have seldom been persuasively countered. First, the development of massive inventories of nuclear weapons by the great powers for over thirty years has not produced disaster; indeed, some American arms controllers attribute the absence of a third world war in the 1950s and 1960s in great part to the existence of these weapons.[1] Second, even if nuclear forces are not benign, they are—contrary to prevalent arguments in the U.S. arms control community—very useful for deterrence and defense. Otherwise, why would the great powers have gone to such lengths to acquire them and been so recalcitrant in negotiating their reduction?

To be more compelling, the movement against nuclear spread has to demonstrate that it is not simply a cynical or neo-imperial attempt by the "haves" to maintain the inequality of international power and the weakness and subservience of the "have nots." More important, the movement must demonstrate that it is not in the self-interest of the have-nots to become haves. To do this, it is necessary to show in strategic terms why the development of nuclear weapons in new regions will yield more danger and instability than it has on the European continent, and in cost-benefit terms why prospective proliferators have more to gain or preserve by not procuring such weapons. This implies adapting theories of nuclear deterrence, previously developed almost exclusively in the context of superpower competition, to the different insecurities and the strategic balances in the nuclear-prone regions.

1. See, for example, Michael Mandelbaum, "International Stability and Nuclear Order: The First Nuclear Regime," in David C. Gompert and others, *Nuclear Weapons and World Politics* (McGraw-Hill for the Council on Foreign Relations, 1977), pp. 15–80.

Two revolutions—political and technological—occurred in 1945: the congealing of global bipolarity and the emergence of nuclear weapons. In most of the postwar era, despite the many complexities and uncertainties of the major powers' defense policies, the coincidence of these developments lent clarity to the problem of nuclear strategy. The evolution of theories and strategies of deterrence (and of rationales for arms control based on principles of "stability" and "parity") was facilitated by the dyadic character of nuclear interaction. There has been no international consensus, it is true, on how to stabilize the nuclear relationship between the superpowers. American strategic superiority in the first two decades of the cold war and doctrinal differences that have persisted between the United States and the USSR in the more recent period of parity have led to major disagreements between and dilemmas for analysts who seek ways to reduce the danger of nuclear war. The quest for arms control has nevertheless benefited from the relative simplicity of conceptualizing the strategic problem where there are only two significant competitors. As long as both nuclear powers concern themselves mainly only with each other, it is possible to construct a theory of stable mutual deterrence, and ultimately to devise plans for reducing levels of nuclear weapons, by calculating what configuration of forces represents parity, equivalence, or the denial of unilateral advantage to either side. Bipolarity makes cooperative resolution of the traditional "security dilemma" more feasible than under conditions of multipolarity. The first phase of the strategic arms limitation talks (SALT) was successful to some extent apart from the wider political interests involved, because the United States and the Soviet Union each had only one military standard (the other's aggregate strength) by which to judge the threat, the adequacy of its own forces, and the advisability of limiting them.

Nuclear proliferation complicates this calculation of stable deterrence, eroding the basis for realistic agreement on arms limitations, even for the superpowers. Some argue that the Soviet Union needs a margin of greater nuclear strength than the United States because it must counter the nuclear forces of Britain, France, and China. It becomes much more complicated for proliferation-prone regions such as South and West Asia, where there are several overlapping antagonisms and major disparities in military power. Devising a logic for stable multipolar deterrence, should several countries in such a region become nuclearized, is extremely difficult. (Refined theories of "stability" between opposing nuclear forces are in fact almost uniquely American.) Trying to avoid instability in a nuclearized multipolar environment is challenging because of ambiguities about what the targets of any one of the nuclear forces are, what combinations of opponents certain states feel they have to hedge against, and the relationship of nuclear options to conventional war in the respective strategies of the nations in the region.

In South and West Asia there is no hope of basing a nonproliferation or arms control regime on equivalence of military power because there are insurmountable inequalities in the region and because all three countries have adversaries outside the region. As noted earlier, India has overwhelming superiority over Pakistan in almost every dimension. This superiority cannot unilaterally be diminished, significantly reducing the threat to Pakistan, as long as Indian planners believe they need to counter Chinese military capabilities. The forces required to deter Peking are more than enough to alarm Islamabad. China, in turn, cannot significantly reduce Indian apprehension without reducing its capability for deterring the Soviet Union. Pakistan now confronts the Soviet Union as well as India. Iran also has potential opponents on several fronts: in a situation similar to the China-India-Pakistan triangle, the military power the shah cultivated primarily for Persian Gulf or other contingencies (much of which has been damaged by the chaos of the revolution, but some of which remains intact) cannot automatically be subtracted from the amount Iran could commit in South Asia if it decided to do so. More coherent organization and cooperation with Western suppliers to repair equipment and keep it serviceable would be necessary to mobilize and project these forces. Alternatively, a new military aid relationship with the USSR—a mirror image of Egypt's shift from Soviet to American patronage—would be necessary. Prudent Indian defense planners might foresee a worst-case situation of having to combat China and Pakistan (and possibly Iran)—all supported by one of the superpowers—simultaneously.[2] The simplest and most significant fact affecting prospects for regional arms control is that India, Pakistan, and Iran each has adver-

2. One example of the Indian version of "encirclement" anxiety is Baldev Raj Nayar, "Regional Power in a Multipolar World," in John W. Mellor, ed., *India: A Rising Middle Power* (Westview Press, 1979), p. 177: "The encompassing strategic reality for India in the 1970s has been a continued encounter with the policy of containment . . . operated through the mechanism of interregional balances rather than the mere regional balance created before."

saries that are superior to it in military power and against which it perceives the need for credible defense capabilities:

Defender or aggressor	Perceived adversaries	
	Probable	Possible
India	China	Iran
	Pakistan	United States?
Pakistan	India	
	Afghanistan	
	USSR	
Iran	Iraq	India
	United States	Saudi Arabia?
	USSR	Afghanistan

India and Iran—at least if the latter maintains a nonaligned stance—may perceive the need for a defense capability similar to the *"tous azimuts"* (all directions) strategy proposed by French General Ailleret.[3] The azimuths along which either of these countries may feel it necessary to project a defensive or retaliatory capability are ambiguous, so calculations of "balance" between any two of them cannot be made in the way they traditionally have been between the United States and USSR.

Nuclear deterrence theory, as it developed in the West from U.S.-Soviet interaction, rarely grappled directly with the complexity of a muddled multipolar nuclear environment. One strategist who did develop a rationale with some potential relevance to the India-Pakistan-Iran complex was French General Pierre Gallois. He argued a theory of "proportional deterrence"—that a weak state with a modest nuclear force can deter a stronger power by threatening retaliation severe enough to outweigh the value of the aggressor's potential gains.[4] In this argument nuclear proliferation would be positive and moderating rather than destabilizing. Most analysts in the United States and the USSR have considered this view on the one hand unrealistic and unnecessary and on the other hand terribly dangerous. For the latter to be the determining consideration, however, the former must be demonstrated. This was less difficult in the 1960s, when Americans argued that the *force de frappe* was unnecessary because France had a sufficient alternative for deterring

3. Charles Ailleret, "Défense 'Dirigée' ou Défense 'Tous Azimuts,' " *Revue de Défense Nationale,* December 1967.

4. Pierre Gallois, *The Balance of Terror: Strategy for the Nuclear Age,* Richard Howard, trans. (Houghton Mifflin, 1961).

Soviet invasion: the NATO alliance and the U.S. nuclear umbrella. In the 1970s, however, it is not as easy to refute strategists in South Asia who see Gallois's theory as applicable to their defense problems. The old counterargument rests on the traditional bipolar frame of reference and the assumption that the weaker nations' defense problems can be subsumed in an alliance with a superpower. This argument does not apply in regions where vulnerable states are not guaranteed such military protection. And there is the danger that a small force invites preemption. But the simple fact that these arguments—whether or not they were correct—did not convince the French should be considered. Should Iran, India, or Pakistan have more reason to feel that they can or should rely on nonnuclear defense options than France did? Should the United States expect them to be any more sensitive to the dangers of developing a weak nuclear force than China was?

Defense Alternatives and Opportunity Costs

The strategic value of a nuclear force must be assessed in conjunction with conventional defense options. What can nuclear weapons add to other defense capabilities? Is the marginal cost of building a nuclear force less than the cost of improving conventional capabilities enough to provide the same increment of security? Or would a nuclear force fundable within the bounds of current levels of gross military expenditures offset the amount of conventional power that would have to be reduced to free the needed resources? The last question is especially relevant for a country such as Pakistan, whose resources allocable to defense are stretched close to the limit; if it appeared that a nuclear force could economically compensate for a substantial reduction in conventional capability—as the Eisenhower administration's New Look of 1953 was designed to do for U.S. defense policy—it would be attractive.

Answers to these questions can be imprecise and tentative at best—rough educated guesses based on gross calculations and weak data. Assessments of the costs of nuclear forces at different levels of sophistication are highly uncertain. But before the specific problems of the three nations are discussed, these rough estimates can be used to illustrate the general range of alternatives that defense planners in the region might perceive. Table 7-1 presents added defense costs for the three countries at five levels of annual investment in a nuclear force. The annual costs

Table 7-1. *Added Costs of Nuclear Force Building at Five Levels of Annual Effort*

Percent unless otherwise specified

Item	India (1)	Pakistan (2)	Iran under the shah (3)	Postulated minimal Iranian defense budget (4)
Defense budget, 1979 (billions of dollars)	3.7	1.15	9.199	1.5
Increase for nuclear program[a]				
1. $10 million (miniforce)	0.3	0.9	0.1	0.7
2. $100 million	2.7	9.6	1.1	6.7
3. $300 million	8.1	26.1	3.3	20.0
4. $500 million	13.5	43.5	5.4	33.3
5. $700 million (massive force)	18.9	60.9	7.6	46.7

Sources: Defense budgets for columns 1 and 2 from U.S. Central Intelligence Agency, *National Basic Intelligence Factbook* (Government Printing Office, July 1979); for column 3 from CIA, *National Basic Intelligence Factbook* (GPO, January 1978). The figures in column 4 are hypothetical, for illustrative purposes; data on postrevolutionary defense budgets are not available.

a. All percentages assume available fissionable material.

for the five levels are arbitrary and heuristic. The add-on nuclear force cost figures, especially at the low end, are also less than the "full system" costs would presumably be, assuming that some components of the force—such as delivery aircraft—are already funded within the conventional expenditure totals. However, the marginal cost of a nuclear force, rather than the full cost, will probably loom largest to decisionmakers. For India and Pakistan it can also be assumed that much of the necessary fissile material is already covered by atomic energy budgets (although if Pakistan's installed reactor capacity falls far short of projections, as is likely, additional expenditures may be required if more than a few weapons are to be built). If plutonium is available, a "desperation" force of crudely "weaponized" devices slung under stripped-down aircraft or rigged for dumping from a C-130 could be slapped together by any country at negligible financial cost. This option is not represented in the table. Beyond that minimal and dangerously unstable sort of force,[5] the

5. Even such a minimal capability might make sense under some circumstances. If there were only a few bombs and they were not kept visibly and consistently located with one obvious delivery system, it would be difficult for an opponent to destroy them. At the same time, the opponent could not be sure the bombs would not be used in extreme straits. This could be a reasonably attractive form of finite deterrence for a weak state.

table assumes a general linear relationship between expenditures and size or quality of the force developed. More exact estimates are not made because the range of real total costs of various force-building programs presented in other attempts at more rigorous projection is so wide that it would be unrealistic to pretend that precise projections can be made.[6] Similarly, specification of exactly what such amounts would buy is of questionable usefulness here because of the many available choices of force mix and posture (for example, would strategic planners who received an incremental allocation of $100 million for improvements in the nuclear force posture spend it to acquire five or ten more strike aircraft, to buy more avionics to improve the penetrativity of existing aircraft, to shelter or harden offensive forces, or on other combinations of qualitative or quantitative improvements?). The presentation in table 7-1 is useful, however, not only because the rough ranges are plausible but especially because it demonstrates the relative difference between the three countries in the burdens that would be imposed by developing progressively stronger nuclear forces. Finally, it should be noted that the figures for Iran are less indicative because the new regime has cut defense expenditures drastically. But the figures do suggest what Iran could spend—given its declining but still substantial oil wealth—if the situation changed and major commitments to military forces again became

6. At the low end is Leonard Beaton's often-quoted 1966 estimate of a ten-year cost of $230 million for a modest force, including rocket development; "Capabilities of Non-Nuclear Powers," in Alastair Buchan, ed., *A World of Nuclear Powers?* (Prentice-Hall for the American Assembly, 1966), p. 33. At the higher end are 1967 United Nations estimates of ten-year costs for India of $1.7 billion for a minimum force of thirty to fifty B-57 bombers, fifty soft medium-range ballistic missiles, and one hundred plutonium warheads, and $5.6 billion for a bigger and less vulnerable force including hardened intermediate-range ballistic missiles and two missile-firing submarines, all with thermonuclear warheads. Cited in Emile Benoit, *Defense and Economic Growth in the Developing Countries* (Heath, 1973), p. 208. Benoit maintains that the UN model understates the costs and that the high option would be economically disastrous. However, this is questionable, as subsequent discussion of Onkar Marwah's opportunity cost analysis will suggest (though that analysis is itself highly questionable), especially since Benoit makes the peculiar statement that the $5.6 billion option "would cost nearly as much as two years of total national product" (p. 209). Even in 1967 India's GNP was over $47 billion in current dollars! (Benoit may have meant two years of *growth* in GNP.) And as noted, some components of the forces (such as the B-57s and newer replacement aircraft) already exist in the conventional force structure or will be acquired. On wide variations in projected costs from an Indian point of view, see Sampooran Singh, *India and the Nuclear Bomb* (New Delhi: Chand, 1971), chap. 7.

attractive, or what additions to an austere revolutionary defense budget would be necessary to acquire nuclear forces.

The table assumes that for an average annual expenditure of $10 million a weak, vulnerable, but reasonably reliable force, with warheads mated to existing delivery systems, could be constructed in a year or two. For $100 million to $500 million and more years of investment, progressively more sophisticated and secure capabilities could be developed; and with a program of $700 million a year a powerful and diversified force (by regional standards) could be built, adding more advanced delivery systems and more concealment, mobility, or hardening. Although this capability would be puny compared to those of the major nuclear powers, it would be both imposing and credible within the region. (The percentage of conventional expenditures that would have to be reduced if the programs were to be undertaken without surpassing current defense budget ceilings would be comparable.) The low-option programs could probably be consummated in a few years; the highest option would probably take more than a decade.

The figures in the table suggest that by adding little more than 8 percent ($300 million) to its defense budget (or reducing conventional expenditures by a comparable amount) India could undertake a moderate weapons delivery program. If military applications spun off from the separately funded space program were substantial, this force might eventually even include an MRBM capability of some sort against China.[7] Even the high-option Indian force, requiring a defense budget increase of almost 19 percent, would probably remain inferior to China's but would at least go well beyond the "finite deterrence" level. To make the $300 million investment (and without an equivalent prospect for missile development), Pakistan would have to divert more than a quarter of its

7. The Indian space program, under the jurisdiction of the Department of Atomic Energy since 1961, accelerated substantially in mid-1972. Barrie Morrison and Donald M. Page, "India's Option: The Nuclear Route to Achieve Goal as a World Power," *International Perspectives* (July–August 1974), p. 27; Onkar Marwah "India's Nuclear and Space Programs: Intent and Policy," *International Security*, vol. 2 (Fall 1977), p. 103. The program still has a long way to go. With Soviet assistance, India built an earth satellite in 1975, but the Russians had to launch it, and after a few days its power system failed. In June 1979 the USSR launched a second satellite for India, but its cameras did not work. In August 1979 India used its own launcher, but the rocket crashed five minutes after lift-off. Peter Niesewand, "Indian Space Shot Fails, Setting Back Program," *Washington Post,* August 11, 1979. In the summer of 1980 India did successfully launch an earth satellite.

resources from conventional forces, as it would undoubtedly be infeasible to add that amount to recent military expenditures and any higher levels of effort would be fiscally unrealistic. By dedicating less than one-tenth of its defense budget, however, Pakistan could pursue the annual $100 million option, which would probably yield a force substantial enough to give India reason for concern. This smaller force would still rely mainly on aircraft (if they could be purchased) though possibly also on ship-to-shore missiles or unsophisticated ground-launched rockets or cruise missiles. Iran, however, if it placed a high priority on military power, could undertake even the ambitious program ($700 million a year) with less than an 8 percent increase over the shah's last defense budget. If the revolutionary government maintains a much lower level of military spending (and if the country's economy does not improve), it will be difficult for Iran to afford more than a modest program. But the emotional, irrational tenor of recent Iranian policy may make a small force attractive even if it does not make good strategic sense.

All this makes Iran's lack of indigenous plutonium reprocessing an especially critical constraint on its options. But based on a 1976 Pan Heuristics estimate that an inefficient plutonium production facility designed only for making bombs could be built for $50 million,[8] Iran could hypothetically still pursue the miniforce option for about one-half of 1 percent of its 1979 military budget, although cutbacks in plans for reactors might cause problems in accumulating reprocessable fuel. Even on the assumption that a large force-building program would require three times as much additional investment (about $150 million) in reprocessing capacity for fissile material, Iran could undertake the high option and still add less than 10 percent to 1979 defense expenditures, or it could pursue the low option for a comparable proportion of a much more austere budget.

India probably has little to gain from significant increases in conventional military force levels—indeed, military manpower declined in the late 1970s—although more modernization would be desirable. It has already built its defense establishment to impressive levels. Military spending increased after the 1971 war, despite the weakening of Pakistan. India has the world's fourth largest armed force and the third

8. Albert Wohlstetter and others, *Moving Toward Life in a Nuclear Armed Crowd?* ACDA/PAB-263, prepared for the Director, U.S. Arms Control and Disarmament Agency (Los Angeles: Pan Heuristics, 1976), p. 14.

largest army (bigger than the U.S. Army). Building this military establishment does not seem to have placed an excessive burden on the country's overall economic development. Over time defense expenditures and
the rate of economic growth in India have been positively correlated,
although this does not prove positive cause and effect. Even if economic
modernization spinoff benefits from military programs are ignored,
freezing India's defense burden at the level of 1950 real expenditures
would have produced "a tangible but not large improvement in the
civilian growth rate."[9] After 1980 India's GNP will probably be higher
than those of Britain, France, or China were when those nations began
nuclear weapons programs. By one Indian's estimate, dedication of
1 percent of GNP would be sufficient to match France's recent military
nuclear program.[10] These comparisons, of course, suggest only absolute
capabilities and ignore the severity of domestic economic problems—
such as low per capita income and development imperatives—which
militate against diversion of any substantial proportion of national resources to military expenditures.

Some analysts like to emphasize that the country's domestic purchasing power is much greater than a comparison with U.S. per capita income
suggests: "For less, therefore, the Indians can buy more goods and services from their economy and therefore their effective budgets may in
fact be much larger than their dollar equivalent budgets."[11] Much of the
research, development, and testing costs that would contribute to a
nuclear force are also covered by nonmilitary accounts, particularly
energy and space budgets; in the same way, expenditures for the space
program are partially discounted as investments in communications and
education. By Marwah's calculations, "in opportunity cost analysis,
civilian-allocated expenditures do not *add* to, but rather *replace* an investment that would have to be made otherwise . . . reimbursements
from the expenditures undertaken are a countervail to costs." Given an-

9. Benoit, *Defense and Economic Growth,* pp. 162, 168.
10. K. Subrahmanyam, cited by James E. Dougherty, "Nuclear Proliferation in
Asia," *Orbis,* vol. 19 (Fall 1975), p. 927.
11. Wayne Wilcox, "Strategic Reinsurance for India," *Survival,* vol. 14 (July–
August 1972), p. 180. Comparisons at official exchange rates are deceptive, and
divergences are exaggerated by methodological weaknesses in national income statistics, such as "the inability to take adequate account of the greater cheapness of
essential consumption items in rural areas of the poorer countries." Benoit, *Defense
and Economic Growth,* p. 153.

nual and projected expenditures (1950–80) in nuclear energy and space programs of $1.6 billion to $2 billion, and profits averaging $33.3 million a year since 1970–71 from sales of commercial nuclear power, heavy water, isotopes, fuel fabrication, and consultancy services (scheduled to rise to $227 million a year by 1985)—8 percent rate of return— the net investment cost for a military nuclear program appears less than meets the eye.[12] Such calculations are questionable, to say the least, but in considering the probability of an Indian decision for a weapons program, all that matters is whether *Indian* decisionmakers believe them.

Pakistan has fewer potential economies of scale, a less advanced technical base, and a GNP less than one-fifth as large as India's. Since it has a higher conventional defense burden as well, Pakistan would find it much more difficult to undertake a significant nuclear weapons program without major sacrifices. Although its economy improved after it lost the eastern wing and defense expenditures declined as a percentage of the national budget, the economy has suffered recently.[13] Per capita income declined 2 percent in 1976. External debt climbed from $3 billion to $7 billion between 1971 and 1977. At recent rates a third of Pakistan's exports were being used for debt service.[14] In 1977 the deficit worsened because world cotton prices fell and government spending increased; as 1978 began, General Zia ul-Haq, the chief executive, announced a 10 percent tax surcharge. But since Pakistan has more incentives for a nuclear force than India, the financial barriers might be perceived in Islamabad as no more constraining than they seem in New Delhi— especially if Pakistan chose a small-force nuclear strategy, some variant of finite or proportional deterrence.

Though financial barriers to a nuclear weapons program are not insurmountable for either India or Pakistan, they do constitute a disincen-

12. Marwah, "India's Nuclear and Space Programs," pp. 107, 108.
13. In 1971 the Embassy of Pakistan in Washington reported that defense appropriations were 40.6 percent of total revenues and estimated that they would be 38.7 percent in 1971–72. The 1973 Pakistan Economic Survey estimated the military budget as 59.33 percent of total government expenditures for 1971–72 and 56.89 percent for 1972–73. Anwar H. Syed, "Pakistan's Security Problem: A Bill of Constraints," *Orbis,* vol. 16 (Winter 1973), p. 960. By the fiscal year ending June 30, 1979, however, the CIA reported that military expenditures were about 28 percent of the central government budget. U.S. Central Intelligence Agency, *National Basic Intelligence Factbook* (Government Printing Office, July 1979), p. 153.
14. Shirin Tahir-Kheli, "Pakistan's Nuclear Option and U.S. Policy," *Orbis,* vol. 22 (Summer 1978), p. 369.

tive. The marginal cost of a nuclear force for India would be less than for Pakistan, but possibly high enough to be dissuasive since India's positive incentives for such a force are also marginal. If New Delhi planned more than a modest force, the marginal cost would also be significant and would require major trade-off decisions on other items either in the defense budget or in other expenditures—such as those for economic development—if the defense budget were increased. For Pakistan, with its economic problems and shortage of capital, the most plausible choice would be a small nuclear force, and a small force might be viewed as likely to aggravate the external threat more than it countered it. In short, economic constraints are not disabling in either country, but with competing economic demands and indirect social and political costs, they are likely to weigh heavily in a nuclear decision.

Compared to the countries of the subcontinent, the financial constraints on an Iranian nuclear force program are currently severe but potentially insignificant. In the future, however, it is unlikely that the constraints introduced around the time of the fall of the Pahlavi regime will be reversed. During the unrest before the shah's departure, wage increases promised to workers amounted to almost a third of Iran's prospective oil revenues. Conventional defense options are also important. If the residual capabilities from the shah's massive defense buildup were revivified or replaced by Soviet matériel, Iran might still consider itself a major military power in the region and remain uninterested in nuclear options. The conventional buildup took less than 15 percent of GNP and less than a third of the national budget in the shah's later years. These are substantial proportions, certainly not to be sustained in the future, but not greatly out of line with comparable defense allocations of the United States in the 1950s and 1960s or the Soviet Union today. Even in 1977, a record-breaking year by the CIA's higher estimates (a $10.15 billion defense budget), the percentages for Iran were 15.4 of GNP, or 34.9 of budget.[15] Iran will not be pushed into a nuclear posture, as Pakistan could be, by its inability to afford conventional power, unless autonomous deterrence of the Soviet Union or a continuing "pox on both superpowers" stance becomes firm policy.

15. CIA, *National Basic Intelligence Factbook* (GPO, July 1977), p. 95. On the wage increase, see William Claiborne, "Iran Launches Probe of Royal Family's Finances," *Washington Post*, November 10, 1978.

The foregoing argument, however, understates the financial trade-offs that an Iranian nuclear program would entail. First, defense budget totals in the late 1970s were atypically high even for the shah's regime.[16] Second, the hidden costs of the Iranian military investment program and future operations, maintenance, and logistics expenditures may be very high if the revolutionary government decides to try to keep much of its hardware in operational condition. A Senate staff study on military sales to Iran was especially critical of the overextension of domestic technical supervision resources, and suggested that absorptive capacity was reaching, if not exceeding, its boundaries.[17] There may be limits to the proportion of expenditures that could be diverted to a nuclear force without degrading the readiness of conventional forces. This was the case earlier when Iran relied heavily on U.S. technical personnel for training, maintenance, and logistics, and is even more so now with the cessation of modernization and economic development. Removal of American assistance crippled the effectiveness of the most advanced components of the Iranian conventional defense posture. Third, unlike Pakistan, it is improbable that Iranian military planners would choose a small, weak, and vulnerable nuclear force unless it was for symbolic rather than credible operational purposes. If they decided to risk provoking the Soviet Union as well as India—especially if Iran was still at loggerheads with the United States—it would be more logical to attempt to establish a significant and credible force as quickly as possible, unless they believed that a meager nuclear force, capable of inflicting heavy damage only on Arab neighbors, would not try the limits of Moscow's patience, an option that could have some appeal. What would be a massive deterrent against regional competitors would be only a modest deterrent against the USSR. Thus if Iran should undertake any nuclear weapons program, it could be one toward the upper end of the options presented in table 7-1.

16. Shahram Chubin, *Iran's Military Security in the 1980s*, Discussion Paper 23 (Santa Monica: California Seminar on Arms Control and Foreign Policy, 1977), p. 23.
17. Robert Mantel and Geoffrey Kemp, *U.S. Military Sales to Iran*, Committee Print, A Staff Report to the Subcommittee on Foreign Assistance of the Senate Committee on Foreign Relations, 94 Cong. 2 sess. (GPO, 1976), pp. viii–x, 1, 23, 33–37, 52.

Prospective Nuclear Strategies

The continuing general incentives for nuclear weapons have already been discussed. More specific speculation about how planners in the region might use nuclear weapons for either deterrence or defense involves considering the potential crisis situations that might lead to war and the probable effects of a nuclear force on the resolution of such crises or the outcomes of such wars. (For this purpose, the analysis in this section presumes acquisition of nuclear weapons.) As in Western nuclear strategies, matching battlefield scenarios with nuclear doctrines may be seen as enhancing deterrence and simultaneously offering hypothetical alternatives to surrender if deterrence fails. Indeed, if one considers options for use and contingencies relevant to the regional candidates in the same way as American strategists have traditionally considered the relation of strategic and tactical nuclear options to European defense, some of the sets of circumstances that might lead to nuclear use in South and West Asia that otherwise seem unreal or bizarre to nonproliferation advocates may actually seem hardly more so than U.S. defense policy itself. Nor is the fact that any prospective nuclear doctrine in the region has serious, even apparently suicidal, drawbacks a definitive counterargument to reliance on a nuclear deterrent as an important component of defense policy. There are major underlying dilemmas, contradictions, and inconsistencies in U.S. nuclear doctrine—especially regarding tactical or theater nuclear weapons—that have never been fully resolved. In short, while speculation on scenarios has an air of unreality to many opponents of proliferation, one should remember that this kind of speculation is a linchpin of American defense planning. Unless policymakers in South and West Asia can be expected to be more down to earth in developing their national security strategies than Americans are about their own, analysis of hypothetical circumstances is fundamental to deducing the importance that Indians, Pakistanis, or Iranians may attach to acquiring nuclear forces.

On the assumption that all three have nuclear weapons, each country would face several questions about how they should be integrated into a deterrent posture or into military operations if deterrence failed. The simplest choice is between planning to use a force preemptively and planning to use it in retaliation against conventional or nuclear aggression. (Most of this analysis will focus on the latter.) A related choice at the strategic level is between a targeting strategy of counterforce (aiming at enemy nuclear or military assets) and one of countervalue (aiming at population concentrations or economic assets). A third important choice is whether to plan a tactical battlefield option.

At a high level of generality there are numerous nuclear postures each of the nations could assume, such as the following.[18]

—Deterrence by uncertainty. Maintenance of any level of nuclear force, perhaps with policy on use unarticulated, with reliance on the enemy's unwillingness to test the defender's will to use the weapons recklessly and the enemy's lack of confidence in its own first-strike capabilities.

—Proportional deterrence (à la Gallois). Maintenance of a force capable of targeting population, assets, or forces, the destruction of which would exceed in cost the prospective gains from aggression.

—Superiority. Ability to inflict greater damage on the adversary than it could inflict on the defender, preferably even after absorbing a preemptive attack.

—"Assured heavy damage." Similar to the American conception of assured destruction, but without the certainty that the damage inflicted would thoroughly cripple the target country's society or economy. The damage would clearly be formidable but not "unacceptable" beyond doubt.

The first of these is the crudest and perhaps the most appropriate for a minimal force. It would be least practical if the opponent had a significant counterforce option. By American standards, reliance on a vulnerable and unsophisticated force, especially if its command and control technology was rudimentary, would be destabilizing. This is true, however, only if the enemy knows what the means of delivery are. If the warheads are separated from the delivery systems and the identity of the delivery systems is ambiguous, the capability is not very vulnerable. In this sense a force that lacks high readiness may still offer effective deterrence. And even if the force is more visible, such a posture might appear more realistic than it would between superpowers. Forces that would be

18. These four examples draw on Lewis A. Dunn, Herman Kahn, and others, *Trends in Nuclear Proliferation, 1975–1995: Projections, Problems, and Policy Options,* HI-2336/3-RR, prepared for the U.S. Arms Control and Disarmament Agency (Croton-on-Hudson, N.Y.: Hudson Institute, 1976), pp. 97ff.

vulnerable to preemption by a major power may be less so if the opponent's capabilities are limited. A major part of France's deterrent—its eighteen fixed-site IRBMs—could be criticized today on the same grounds; those IRBMs could easily be obliterated by a Soviet first strike. In today's terms American and Soviet postures in the 1950s—forward-based bombers and soft missile emplacements—were also potentially destabilizing in their vulnerability, yet the superpowers relied on them. When recognized, the vulnerabilities were gradually corrected, but it should not be assumed that third world decisionmakers, few of whom have been educated in U.S. strategic theory, will perceive the problems of force stability as acutely as Americans do or that they will not be inventive enough to find a way to adapt a weak force to stable deterrence. Currently available modes of delivery or new ones, some of which seem perhaps too exotic or speculative to be taken seriously at present, may be within the reach of the South and West Asian contenders and might seem secure enough by regional standards to offer a credible deterrent. These include aircraft, drones, clandestine insertion, torpedoes, unguided rockets, and 1950s-style cruise missiles.[19] Also, the credibility of such crude postures would be greater if rationalized by a countervalue doctrine. Such a doctrine may not be sensible, but a planner in the region may think it is. If the force is not vulnerable to preemption, American critics would be hard put to discredit the strategy because many of them have supported such a doctrine (assured destruction) for the United States, maintaining that it is reliably stable.

Below are illustrative discussions of conflict situations that might affect decisionmakers' perceptions of the utility of nuclear forces, as well as alternative plans and doctrines for deterrent postures, strategic retaliation, or battlefield use of nuclear weapons.

India

Potentially, conflict with China could arise from a number of circumstances. As with situations that could lead to a U.S.-Soviet nuclear exchange, none seem probable under current conditions. But the possibility of unanticipated major changes in policy or of crisis generated by third parties makes the case for contingency planning based on capabilities rather than on the intentions of an adversary as perceived at present. One

19. Ibid., pp. 79–86.

possibility envisioned by some in India "is a Soviet-American military showdown in Europe or elsewhere, leaving China free to settle military scores with India."[20] Another variant, which assumes less premeditated aggressive intent on the part of China, would be an initially low-intensity crisis in the border area—perhaps arising from domestic instability or insurrection on the Indian side, with limited Chinese support for separatist forces—that escalated into more serious confrontation than Peking or New Delhi foresaw at the outset. Either of these two variants would be a more plausible precipitant of war if Soviet ties and tacit security assurances to India weakened. A third possibility is an aggressive move by India. Internal chaos, economic reverses, domestic political polarization, and a rise in secessionist activities conceivably could lead a beleaguered New Delhi government to turn to external initiatives as a way of fostering internal unity and distracting contending factions. This possibility is perhaps the least likely, and if it occurred, the initiatives would probably be taken against Pakistan rather than against China. If Pakistan had no nuclear weapons, India's nuclear capabilities would not be important in this case (except to help deter pro-Pakistani Chinese intervention), since conventional power would probably suffice to batter the Pakistanis. If Pakistan did have nuclear weapons by that time, nuclear contingencies would be relevant. In either case it can be assumed that any Indian nuclear force would be configured against the PRC and that no important changes or additions would be required to cope with contingencies involving Pakistan. (Some hawkish Indian strategists, such as Subrahmanyam, have hinted at an antisuperpower role for an Indian nuclear force, perhaps to deter local intervention. This may seem fanciful to most observers in this country, although one American analyst suggested a rationale that might support such a theory. Brennan noted that a minor nuclear power could secure its forces from preemption by other minor powers, and though they would remain vulnerable to a massive counterforce strike by a superpower, the latter would be dissuaded because such an attack would require it to expend a substantial proportion of its own forces—weakening its position in relation to the other superpower.[21])

20. G. S. Bhargava, *India's Security in the 1980s,* Adelphi Paper 125 (London: International Institute for Strategic Studies, 1976), p. 16.
21. Donald G. Brennan, "Some Remarks on Multipolar Nuclear Strategy," in Richard Rosecrance, ed., *The Future of the International Strategic System* (Chandler,

India could not realistically plan to achieve an effective counterforce capability against China under any circumstances. The PRC's nuclear forces are much more advanced, and its resources for staying ahead in a strategic arms race with India are greater. This in itself presents a slight impediment to an Indian decision to undertake a nuclear defense strategy, because New Delhi's traditional official stance on the immorality of nuclear weapons would make it harder to plan—at least explicitly or without a radical change in the philosophy of the governing elite—a strategy of retaliation against population as opposed to military forces. On the other hand, the American liberal tradition did not prevent the adoption of a massive retaliation strategy.

Even without this inhibition, there are still operational barriers—though they are prospectively surmountable—to a credible countervalue posture. Canberra medium bombers in India's inventory have a short range (800 miles). India has a negligible capacity for offensive air operations against the PRC at present. Plans are under way to purchase modern deep-strike aircraft—Anglo-French Jaguars—to replace five of the seven squadrons of obsolescent Canberras and Hunters. But even if a "worst case" in delivery capability is assumed—that is, if the Indian air force could not replace the older planes—nuclear strikes could be made feasible. If the aircraft were based in the northern and northeastern parts of the country and if one-way missions were excluded, they could probably threaten cities with less than 2 percent of China's population.[22] But

---

1972), p. 20. In regard to the Pakistan contingency it should be noted that on one index—deep-strike aircraft—India's capabilities are inferior to Pakistan's. The Indian air force is heavily weighted with interceptors and has no aircraft that match Pakistan's Mirages—one reason they are buying more advanced attack planes with the hope of eventually being able to produce them domestically. Mohan Ram, "India Looking to Britain, France for Warplanes," *Christian Science Monitor,* January 18, 1978. In net capacity, however, India's force of 620 combat aircraft is more impressive than Pakistan's 256; International Institute for Strategic Studies, *The Military Balance, 1979–1980* (London: IISS, 1979), pp. 66, 71. Critical Pakistani targets—especially for interdiction—are within easy range of Indian bases. Indian Air Chief Marshal Pratap C. Dal made a special point of noting in March 1975, when the U.S. arms embargo against Pakistan ended, that the only major seaport (Karachi) and the roads and railways for moving supplies inland could be struck and cut by India as they were in 1971. Bhargava, *India's Security,* pp. 11–12.

22. Frank Bray, "Notes on Alternative Indian Nuclear Targeting Options," in Geoffrey Kemp, Robert L. Pfaltzgraff, Jr., and Uri Ra'anan, eds., *The Superpowers in a Multinuclear World* (Heath, 1974), pp. 247–48.

options could be expanded significantly if deployment and flight constraints were compromised. Range would increase if the bombers were
based as far east as possible, in Assam. However, this area is internally
unstable, and bases there would also be more vulnerable to attack. But on
the assumption that the PRC would preempt with missiles in any case, the
difference in distance means little. If one-way missions were planned, the
Canberras' range would increase to 1,600 miles. This would put most of
the important Chinese targets south of Manchuria, including Peking,
within reach. Planning for one-way missions—or "one-and-a-half-way"
—is also not unthinkable, in view of all the other risks and sacrifices
implied by a nuclear strategy in general. In the 1950s some U.S. aircraft
were programmed for such missions against the USSR (and even today
few B-52 crews have much confidence that in a general war they would
get home). For some high-value targets (such as Canton), plans might
call for the crews to have enough fuel left, after making the strike, to
head for the coast and recover in, or to bail out over, non-PRC territory
(such as Hong Kong).

In any case, civilian jet aircraft with ample range are available and
could be configured to deliver weapons (though they would be more
vulnerable to air defenses). Commercial airliners do not have bomb bays
or racks, of course, but these could be built in or the "hard point" in-
board of the first left engine on many such aircraft (such as the Boeing
747) could be used. These hard points are for the purpose of attaching
pod packs for ferrying replacement engines, but they can carry 6,000 to
8,000 pounds—more than the 2,000 pounds a first-generation nuclear
weapon is likely to weigh. Iran, India, and Pakistan all have 747s. Even
more plentiful are Boeing 727s, and bombs could be dumped from the
rear ventral staircase on those craft. Another option that has been suggested is to hide nuclear weapons on merchant ships in crowded sea-
lanes along the China coast.[23]

If India acquired longer-range military aircraft as part of its nuclear
force development, the problems of range and penetrativity would be
reduced. Development of 2,500-mile-range MRBMs, especially if they
were hardened or mobile, would enhance striking power and eliminate

---

23. Harold W. Maynard, "In Case of Deluge: Where Nuclear Proliferation Meets
Conventional Arms Sales" (Los Alamos Scientific Laboratories, July 1977), pp. 16–
17. The merchant ship option is proposed in Pran Chopra, *India's Second Liberation*
(MIT Press, 1974), pp. 220–21.

penetration problems. (This development is probably well in the future, however.) Recent plans are to develop satellite-launching rockets by the mid-1980s that could be transmuted to launch surface-to-surface missiles with a range of 1,000 miles—and a payload of only several kilograms—which is substantially less ambitious.[24] Guidance problems would limit the effectiveness of such missiles, at least in the near future, against anything but cities. Another option, though less realistic, would be to use the aircraft carrier *Vikrant* as a nuclear platform. New aircraft, such as the American A-4 (which the United States considered selling to India in 1976), would have to be procured.[25] This option would require substantial warning for the *Vikrant* to reach the South China Sea. This option is improbable on several counts: India's lack of experience and doubtful capacity for mounting such a long-range projection of naval force, and uncertainty about whether the ship could launch its planes before being attacked by Chinese forces even if it could reach the coastal area. A more desirable naval platform, of course, would be SLBM-carrying submarines, but developing this capability would be a major technical and financial challenge to India.

Battlefield use of tactical nuclear weapons is plausible. If conflict were in the mountainous border area, collateral damage from such use might be low. The terrain, however, could limit the destructive efficiency of nuclear explosives. And if the conflict is limited to that area, India's conventional capabilities make the prospect of a necessary resort to tactical nuclear weapons—as U.S. planners have envisioned this necessity in Europe—unlikely. Given the conventional balance of force and the probable area in which military engagements with China would occur, it is difficult to foresee an important operational role for Indian nuclear weapons other than to deter or retaliate against Chinese strategic nuclear forces. Nevertheless, Indian officers have given some attention to useful tactical applications for nuclear weapons in the Himalayas, such as "extra-powerful land mines: nuclear barricades to invasion."[26]

24. Zalmay Khalilzad and others, *Regional Rivalries and Nuclear Responses,* vol. 1: *Competition and Conflict in the Arabian Sea and the Prospects for Nuclear Proliferation,* DNA 001-77-C-0052, prepared for the Director, U.S. Defense Nuclear Agency (Los Angeles: Pan Heuristics, 1978), p. 22.

25. George C. Wilson, "U.S. Moves to Sell Jets to India," *Washington Post,* December 9, 1976.

26. Stephen P. Cohen and Richard L. Park, *India: Emergent Power?* (Crane, Russak for the National Strategy Information Center, 1978), p. 49.

Pakistan

The threatening situations to which nuclear weapons might seem relevant from Islamabad are more significant and more likely to arise than the Chinese contingencies New Delhi faces. The old possibility of war with India remains, and the probability of adequate conventional defense cannot be assumed. War could start over issues similar to those that precipitated it in the past, such as Kashmir. The new possibility of direct conflict with Soviet forces, spurred by the situation in Afghanistan, is even more frightening. During an April 1980 visit to France Soviet Foreign Minister Andrei Gromyko made veiled threats against Pakistan's very existence.[27]

India could wage an unlimited war and crush Pakistan, rather than simply making inroads along the border as in past wars. Pakistan may doubt that it can rely on its wartime strategy of the past: to hold Indian forces near the border long enough to draw the superpowers into mediation. In 1971—despite Washington's tilt toward Pakistan—mediation occurred too late to prevent the loss of East Pakistan. For the Pakistanis even a weak nuclear force and a crude posture of deterrence by uncertainty could seem politically valuable as a way of limiting a future conventional conflict—this would make New Delhi reluctant to force Islamabad to the wall. Even if Pakistan valued this war-limiting nonuse option as action policy, it could also seek to enhance deterrence by maintaining a first-use declaratory policy analogous to the U.S. position that first use of tactical nuclear weapons, and ultimately of strategic forces, is reserved as an option to prevent the defeat of NATO forces by conventional Warsaw Pact forces.

Since India is likely to invest more heavily in air defenses if its neighbor to the west goes nuclear, Pakistan would be unable to deploy a nuclear force capable of inflicting assured destruction at levels that American theorists have usually considered sufficient for assured deterrence (Robert S. McNamara's standard in the mid-1960s was 20–25 percent of enemy population and 50 percent of industry),[28] but it could

27. See Flora Lewis, "Gromyko, Visiting France, Sharply Criticizes Pakistan," *New York Times*, April 26, 1980.

28. Henry S. Rowen, "Formulating Strategic Doctrine," in *Appendices: Commission on the Organization of the Government for the Conduct of Foreign Policy, June 1975*, vol. 4 (GPO, 1975), p. 227.

still threaten substantial damage. For example, a 10-kiloton bomb dropped in the center of Bombay would kill over a quarter of a million Indians.[29] Deployment of ballistic missiles would boost the credibility of a countervalue retaliatory posture. There is little prospect of Pakistan's developing such capability, however, despite dubious indications of some progress in rudimentary missile research. The facility at Sonmiani Beach, which in the past launched weather research vehicles with French components, recruited additional scientists in 1975, chiefly propulsion experts.[30] But without substantial—and unlikely—foreign assistance, it would probably be an arduous process for Islamabad to develop a missile program with reliable military applications.

Problems in designing a secure deterrent, or at least one invulnerable to preemption by *conventional* strikes, are also taxing. One hypothetical option, though even less realistic than an Indian plan to use its carrier against China, might be nuclear torpedoes.[31] Pakistan has four *Daphne*-class and two *Agosta*-class submarines.[32] A *Daphne* is not a *Trident*, to be sure, but Indian capacity for antisubmarine warfare is probably limited enough to make it a secure launch platform, and torpedoes are at least closer to being a Pakistani option than SLBMs are. Bombay, Madras, and smaller coastal cities might then be vulnerable to retaliation. Calcutta lies too far up an estuary to be attacked by torpedoes, but even unguided cruise missiles mounted on surface ships could reach such nearby inland targets. Such capabilities might also be seen as supporting the possibility of a Pakistani first use of tactical nuclear weapons on the battlefield—to force a "pause" in a way similar to what some U.S. strategists have seen as their applicability in Europe—by posing a reserve countervalue option to deter devastating Indian retaliation in response to the use of the tactical nuclear weapons. This sort of calculation, of course, is extremely speculative. Moreover, the skillful design, engineering, and testing necessary for deploying warheads on torpedoes is probably beyond Pakistani means in the near future, and surface ships would be vulnerable platforms.

29. Zalmay Khalilzad, "Pakistan and the Bomb," *Bulletin of the Atomic Scientists,* vol. 36 (January 1980), p. 14.

30. "Islamabad's Missile Programme," *Far Eastern Economic Review* (December 19, 1975), p. 5.

31. See Dunn, Kahn, and others, *Trends in Nuclear Proliferation,* pp. 81–82.

32. IISS, *Military Balance, 1979–1980,* p. 71.

Battlefield use of nuclear weapons is probably more plausible for Pakistan than for India against China. One American has even suggested that global proliferation of tactical nuclear capabilities would be a stabilizing reinforcement of the territorial status quo: "With the defense of its borders entrusted to forces structured around the firepower of nuclear weapons, any nation . . . could walk like a porcupine through the forests of international affairs: no threat to its neighbors, too prickly for predators to swallow."[33] This view is overoptimistic: first, because technical resources for development of a refined force of "mininukes" exceed the capacities of most nations[34] (although pre-positioned atomic demolition mines would be more feasible), and second, because, given the equally limited strategic defense capabilities of most states and the short ranges involved for strategic targeting in many areas, it would be impossible in most cases to differentiate a tactical force from a strategic force. For Pakistan, nevertheless, nuclear border defense could seem reasonable in extremis, or at least as thinkable as tactical nuclear warfare in central Germany has seemed to American strategists. Unlike Germany, for instance, the part of northern Rajasthan around the axis between the Pakistani town of Surtanahu and the Indian town of Anupgarh is a thinly populated near desert. In this area at least, Pakistan's use of tactical nuclear weapons over its own territory does not seem impossible, although it might simply prompt Indian military planners to design an attack through more populated areas, in a manner similar to what one American observer sees as an incentive for the Soviet Union—if contemplating an attack on Germany in the face of U.S. tactical nuclear weapons—to employ a "city-hugging" strategy.[35]

Any prospect of the use of nuclear weapons in South Asia is fraught with imponderables, complexities, and dilemmas that suggest that the option could be suicidal and thus make such contingency planning seem unreal. However, that does not rule out the possibility that military strategists in the region would see value in postures and plans based on

33. R. Robert Sandoval, "Consider the Porcupine: Another View of Nuclear Proliferation," *Bulletin of the Atomic Scientists,* vol. 32 (May 1976), p. 19.

34. Lewis A. Dunn and others, *Changing Dimensions of Proliferation Policy, 1975–1995,* prepared for the U.S. Arms Control and Disarmament Agency (Hudson Institute, 1977), p. 16.

35. Paul Bracken, "Urban Sprawl and NATO Defence," *Survival,* vol. 18 (November–December 1976), pp. 254–60.

nuclear use. Most of the criticism that could be leveled at such plans has also been directed at American nuclear plans for the defense of NATO. Scenarios implying the utility of Pakistani nuclear strikes against India are no more improbable than the scenarios that have driven U.S. nuclear doctrine. Moreover, war is more likely in South Asia than in Central Europe; Pakistan is weaker in conventional defenses against India than NATO is against the Warsaw Pact; thus tactical nuclear weapons, if they were available, could seem even more relevant to planners in Islamabad than to those in Washington. One difference that mitigates the comparison is that Europeans have had more trepidation than Americans about planning to use battlefield nuclear weapons, since the destruction would occur over their territory, and have been more in favor of relying on *strategic* nuclear retaliation against a Soviet attack. The "suicidal" dangers implicit in theater nuclear doctrine are also present in U.S. strategy. In some ways the American posture increases Soviet incentives to *begin* any attack with nuclear weapons rather than wait for retreating NATO forces to use them first.[36] After all, if the United States plans to use tactical nuclear weapons only if NATO is losing, and the Soviet Union would not launch an attack unless it assumed it would be winning, there would be nothing to gain and everything to lose by waiting to absorb the first nuclear blow. If Pakistani planners were more sensitive to this dilemma, it might prompt them to reject the tactical nuclear option, realizing that it might encourage Indian first use.

Iran

There are several azimuths along which an Iranian nuclear capability might be projected. To the west lies Iraq, perhaps the most likely target, and to the north is the USSR, the most powerful enemy. If India begins to dismember Pakistan, especially if the latter does not have nuclear weapons and the former does, Iran might feel compelled to bolster its eastern neighbor's integrity. The shah supported Pakistan; his successors have the Islamic affinity with the country, as well as the strategic interest, to encourage them to do the same. If the Soviet Union threatened Iran and U.S. leaders remained aloof or were preoccupied by simultaneous

36. See Jeffrey Record, "Theatre Nuclear Weapons: Begging the Soviet Union to Pre-empt," *Survival,* vol. 19 (September–October 1977), pp. 208–11.

Soviet initiatives elsewhere, a nuclear force might seem the only deterrent impressive enough to keep the USSR from going over the brink. Since the latter possibility is more dangerous, especially to U.S. interests, it will be the focus of discussion in this section. Any nuclear force postured against the Soviet Union would be even more capable if used in the South Asian theater.

The Soviet Union could bring pressure to bear on Tehran on land, at the border, or at sea along Iran's Persian Gulf oil lifeline. At present the United States has credible options for countering a limited Soviet attempt to interdict Iran's sea lines of communication. Some Iranians during the shah's reign feared the decline of such protection, in view of the eroding Western base structure (Masirah, Bahrain, Djibouti, "and question-marks hanging over those in the Philippines") that could affect the ability to reinforce the Persian Gulf: "the loss of base rights required for projecting power into the region, the Soviet naval buildup and the military imbalance in the region, could make a Western response to a rapid Soviet incursion costly and less credible, therefore, less effective as a deterrent."[37] A related hypothetical situation could be a conflict between Iran and Iraq in which one devastated the other, provoking—depending on the evolution of relations in this volatile area—Soviet intervention. The risk that the United States would fail to launch counterintervention would be substantial since, first, it would entail the danger of strategic escalation; second, the theater is lower in priority than Europe; and third, the legitimacy of the anti-Soviet side's action, as seen in the West, might be in question at the time. Such situations seem improbable, and it is unlikely that the revolutionary government in Iran perceives contingencies in this way, but any consideration of nuclear war must assume major changes in policy.

On the northern border, past Iranian military deployments were purposely restrained to avoid appearing provocative to the USSR. Under some circumstances, in the view of one Iranian analyst, this posture could lead to a dilemma. "Just suppose" an Iranian separatist "liberation" group rises in a border province, and the USSR either recognizes a provisional government and sends in troops to protect it or simply demands that Iran negotiate with the dissidents and not send its own troops to pacify the area.[38] In this situation possession of nuclear weapons might

37. Chubin, *Iran's Military Security in the 1980s*, pp. 6–7.
38. Conversation with Shahram Chubin, December 10, 1977.

seem useful for bolstering Tehran's ability to call the Soviet bluff—or to deter the real threat in case it was not a bluff—and quell the revolt. Consistent with the logic of "proportional deterrence," the stakes would be much higher for the Soviet Union in this case and the prospective gain too limited to risk the possibility of nuclear conflict. Nuclear capability, indeed, might be seen as a means of dissuading the Russians from initially attempting to exploit the unrest.

An important question is whether an Iranian nuclear force—especially one without survivable ballistic missiles—could credibly threaten the USSR. Soviet air defenses are dense and, though their effectiveness is uncertain, Iran's air force would probably have difficulty penetrating very far. A large majority of Russian military and high-value civilian targets would be immune. But a substantial number of important targets would remain vulnerable. The Baku oil complex—cited in the past by Secretary of Defense James Schlesinger as a possible target for selective U.S. strikes short of total nuclear war—is close to the Iranian border. If a number of F-4s flew low across the Caspian Sea, one or more could surely reach the target. The city of Odessa is less than a thousand miles from the Iranian airfield at Tabriz, and attacking planes overflying Turkey and the Black Sea might avoid all but terminal defenses. Other population concentrations are closer. If a Soviet attack should occur in conjunction with hostilities in Europe (which in Iran's view would make an autonomous Iranian deterrent even more essential, since Western attention and forces would be diverted and concern with escalation control heightened), defense against Iranian aircraft might be weakened if the Soviet Union had diverted interceptors westward.

Thus if Iran does have the potential for a proportional deterrent, the problems of crisis stability and vulnerability to a Soviet counterforce strike assume central importance. Aside from the deployment of missile-launching submarines—which would require long lead times, massive investment, and superior scientific and engineering personnel—there is little Iran could do to reduce vulnerability. All airfields could be destroyed by nuclear missiles with negligible warning time; the six fields in the northern part of the country could probably be rendered inoperable by a surprise conventional attack. With strategic warning Iran might be able to operate on limited airborne alert, keeping one squadron of nuclear-armed planes aloft at all times on a rotating basis. But airborne alert is extremely costly, is hard to coordinate and maintain for any length of time, and severely taxes logistical capacities. It would be difficult even for the impressive forces Iran was developing under the shah, and much more so for the limited and less disciplined forces it is likely to have in the future.

Iran's vulnerability, Soviet strength, challenging operational difficulties in organizing a secure deterrent, the possibility that undertaking a nuclear program would worsen relations with the USSR more than it would enhance Iranian security, and the recent indifference of the Iranian government to military realities all suggest that the attractiveness of a nuclearized defense posture is limited when one considers how such a strategy would be implemented. However, a strategically rational Iran could still see political utility, even against the USSR, in a nuclear defense posture. (Continuing fanaticism could make it attractive against "The Great Satan America" as well.) As Marwah argues, "For possible newcomers [to the nuclear club], both the irrationality and symbolism connected with nuclear weapons have some uses. Newcomers are frequently categorized as immature, hence likely to be irresponsible or unpredictable. Their few nuclear weapons, therefore, carry a value in excess of numbers."[39] In case such a rationale seems utterly reckless, it is relevant that some U.S. strategists—including Secretary of Defense Harold Brown—have placed a high value on the uncertainty factor as a reinforcement of American deterrence. That is, even if countervalue retaliation in response to a counterforce attack by the USSR would be irrational (inviting counterretaliation against U.S. cities by Soviet ICBM reserves), the fact that Soviet leaders could not be sure the United States would not so retaliate dissuades them from risking a first strike.[40]

THERE are innumerable reasons to view prospective Indian, Pakistani, or Iranian nuclear forces as unusable, dangerous, destabilizing, or inappropriate for deterrence. It is a mistake, however, to assume either that these reasons are conclusive or that they will appear as compelling to local strategists as they do to detached American observers interested more in nonproliferation than in the national security of the states at

39. Marwah, "India's Nuclear and Space Programs," p. 114.

40. "The Soviets might—and should—fear that, in response [to a Soviet counterforce attack], we would retaliate with a massive attack on Soviet cities and industry. The alleged 'irrationality' of such a response from a detached perspective would be no consolation in retrospect and would not necessarily be in advance an absolute guarantee that we would not so respond." *Department of Defense Annual Report, Fiscal Year 1979*, p. 63.

issue. There are three principal things to remember. First, many of the logical criticisms of strategic reasoning that can be applied to prospective nuclear forces and doctrines in South and West Asia can also be applied to American and Soviet policies, yet the persistence of deterrence dilemmas has not prevented Americans from continuing to regard nuclear weapons as integral to security. Second, most strategic challenges can be surmounted if the state is willing to sacrifice and search for alternatives; alert and highly motivated strategists can usually design around logical obstacles. Third, the dangers inherent in a nuclear posture of questionable stability or effectiveness will prove dissuasive only if they appear greater than the alternative dangers of nuclear nakedness.

PART THREE

The Middle East

HENRY S. ROWEN

RICHARD BRODY

CHAPTER EIGHT

The Growing Nuclear "Overhang" in the Middle East

IT SEEMS more and more likely that by 1990 several states in the Middle East will have nuclear explosives or be in a position to acquire them quickly. Israel is reported to have them already. Nuclear energy research programs planned in Iraq, Egypt, and Libya are advancing the capacity of these countries to make nuclear explosives, and other Arab states, including Kuwait and Syria, have evinced interest in nuclear projects. Moreover, evolving domestic capacities to move toward nuclear explosives might be greatly helped by direct assistance in certain areas from countries outside the region.

This prospect should be assessed in relation to the principal regional rivalries that have existed for several decades and that seem likely to persist: the enduring conflict between Israel and the Arabs, rivalries among the Arab states, and the competition between the United States and the Soviet Union.[1] The instabilities created by these rivalries make the Middle East not only turbulent—sometimes lethally so—for its inhabitants, but also dangerous for outsiders. It has been observed that the Middle East is as dangerous to bystanders as the Balkans were before

1. This analysis omits the northern tier countries, Turkey and Iran, except insofar as these countries might affect the choices of the others. It also excludes the Maghreb.

1914. A Middle East in which many of the governments, and perhaps nongovernmental groups as well, have access to nuclear explosives would be even more dangerous; what happens there can affect most of the world. Developments in the region, most notably the oil crisis in 1973–74 and sharp increases in oil prices since then, have already affected the rest of the world. Outside powers since World War II, however, have had little combat involvement in the region—the British and French actions against Egypt at Suez in 1956 being the most important exception. Nonetheless, the superpowers, the United States and the Soviet Union, have become involved in a limited way in several conflicts and have had a notable influence on the region, and their role seems unlikely to diminish in the foreseeable future. As for the interests of the West (including Japan), consider only that for many decades it will be dependent on the Middle East for half of its oil supplies.

Of the three sets of rivalries, that between Israel and the Arabs has been the most intense. Although the Egyptian-Israeli peace treaty was a momentous change, Israel's confrontation with the other Arab states continues and the stability of its agreement with Egypt is questionable. All the basic Arab-Israeli differences are unlikely to be resolved soon, and further conflicts seem all too likely.

Relations among many of the Arabs have been and remain competitive, changeable, and often hostile. Pan-Arabism has been too weak to overcome an impressive set of rivalries. A partial list, past and current, includes regimes and factions in Syria versus Iraq, Egypt versus Yemen, Egypt versus Libya, Sudan versus Libya, Christians versus Muslims in Lebanon, Jordan versus Syria, and Saudi Arabia and the Persian Gulf sheikhdoms versus the radical states, especially Iraq and Libya. These rivalries are based not only on differences in political ideology, but are often rooted in cultural differences as well, for instance, between the Bedouin and the Palestinians in Jordan, between the fundamentalists of the Arabian desert and progressives elsewhere, and between the settled and numerous population of Egypt and the smaller populations of other countries. Aspirations for leadership in the Arab world as well as personality conflicts among leaders have heightened these differences.

Instabilities exist inside many of the Arab states as well. Most of the present governments acquired power through the use of force. Some have a history of repeated coups. The propensity to change governments violently at irregular intervals bears importantly on the consequences of the future availability of nuclear explosives in these countries.

The third principal rivalry in the region, that between the United States and the Soviet Union, emerged soon after World War II with Soviet claims against Iran and Turkey in 1946. U.S. interests are dominated by concern for the survival of Israel, access of the West to oil, and prevention of Soviet domination of the area. At times in the past there was heightened perception of a connection between Western security and developments in the Middle East, although awareness of this nexus faded in the 1960s. It has regained its clarity since the 1973–74 oil embargo highlighted the West's dependence on oil from the region, especially in Europe and Japan. In contrast, Soviet interests seem to include neutralizing a potential threat from NATO's southern flank, countering U.S. military power in the region, gaining political influence in the area (especially evident in the radical states), improving access to more remote regions such as Africa and the Indian Ocean, and being able to affect the disposition of the region's oil resources.

Although Europe's influence in the region has receded, it remains crucially dependent on Middle East oil and is still an important source of arms. Moreover, the southern flank members of NATO, Turkey and Greece, would be directly affected by possible extensions of Soviet power in the region and this, in turn, would affect the others. This relationship of Europe to the Middle East may be a major factor in the future.

There are many sources for conflict in this contrasting set of superpower objectives, although not all their objectives are likely to be in opposition. Both the United States and the Soviet Union, for instance, will probably want to avoid direct conflict that could escalate and to avert the spread of nuclear weapons in the area. Nonetheless, great power rivalry has produced confrontations on several occasions, most recently in 1973, and competition—and a potential for conflict—seems likely to be sustained.

Less central has been a fourth rivalry, that between Iran and the Arab states across the Persian Gulf, especially Iraq and, potentially, Saudi Arabia. In the coming decade, this could become more important. Given Iran's current state of flux and internal instability, it is difficult to predict the development of Iranian-Arab relations. Clearly, however, there is little ground for optimism about their stability.

Associated with these various Middle East rivalries and produced in part by the rise in oil revenues after 1973 is the enormous buildup of arms by many of the states in the region. The most modern weapons being developed anywhere are being bought in large quantities: F-15s, MIG-23s, SU-17s and -20s, surface effects ships, SA-6 air defense missiles, and the like. Israel has more medium tanks than France and Britain combined. This buildup of arms has produced a capacity to wage conflict on an extremely intense scale. It also provides the means of delivering weapons from a distance, a prospect that gives one pause when contemplating a future in which many countries in the region may have nuclear weapons.

The diffusion of civilian nuclear technology, together with the great wealth of the oil-producing states, is advancing the capacity of the Arab nations to acquire nuclear weapons technology. But the most important ingredient for such a capacity—a substantial cadre of technically trained people—has been missing. The Arabs have lagged in training physicists, nuclear chemists, chemical engineers, electronic specialists, and those in other disciplines central to the development of nuclear explosives. Technically trained manpower exists principally in Egypt, Iraq, Lebanon, and among the Palestinians (although the nuclear sector is not prominently represented). However, a growing number of people with relevant skills are available in the world market, and civilian nuclear energy programs being negotiated or planned will draw them in.

Israel is, of course, different. Not only does it have extraordinary technical and military talents, but also it has reportedly directed some of this expertise to developing nuclear explosives. The fact that since the early 1960s Israel has had an unsafeguarded reactor capable of producing at least a few kilograms of plutonium a year is consistent with its having a modest nuclear explosive capacity. If it is true that Israel has nuclear weapons, the regional asymmetry cannot be expected to persist indefinitely. Although the Arabs responded slowly to early signals of a developing Israeli nuclear weapons potential, projects to narrow the gap are being started. In any case, the Arabs have their own rivalries to move them in that direction.

The possession of nuclear weapons might have a sobering effect on all those able to order their use, but confidence that they will not be used is hardly warranted. Developing forces that are proof against surprise attack and under tight command and control has required continuing and diligent efforts by the states that now have weapons, and there have been periods when these important attributes have been absent. Such conditions are likely to be much more difficult to meet in the Middle East. Particularly catastrophic would be the use of these weapons against populations; only a few could kill hundreds of thousands.

This poses serious questions for the future role of outside powers. Their actions can be either stabilizing or the opposite. The United States, in particular, by having a strong and visible capacity to intervene in the area can reduce Israel's incentive to depend on nuclear threats for its security. For the United States, as some analysts have proposed, to offer Israel a bare guarantee in exchange for Israel's returning to its pre-1967 borders (without clearly adequate nonnuclear forces to support it) would leave Israel exposed to attack and dependent on a guarantee of low credibility. The probable result would be increased Israeli reliance on a nuclear threat, whose own credibility would lessen with the growth of Arab nuclear strength.

What might be the effect of wide access to nuclear weapons on the other main U.S. regional interests—continued access to oil and averting Soviet dominance? Dependence for much of its energy supplies on a politically unstable region with growing numbers of nuclear-weapons-capable countries will be an increasingly troublesome prospect for the West. Moreover, the incentive for several countries in the region to move closer to nuclear weapons will be affected by their estimate of the future stability of the region and, in particular, their reading of the growing influence—direct and indirect—of the Soviet Union.

CHAPTER NINE

Regional Instabilities

ALTHOUGH the conflict between the Arab states and Israel is the most acute and visible one in the region, it would be a gross oversimplification to ignore others. There have been five sources of instability, rivalry, and conflict: the Arab-Israeli conflict; rivalries between Arab countries; interaction with peripheral powers (such as Iran and Ethiopia); varying relations with the great powers; and internal instabilities. Rivalries between Arab countries have never broken out in full interstate war, and the Arabs' relations with Israel, with the notable recent exception of Egypt, have fluctuated between hostility and open warfare.[1] Nonetheless, each of these sources of instability has implications for moves toward the bomb.

First, they may create incentives for one of the regional countries to acquire nuclear weapons in response to a conventional threat. This is particularly likely where tension is combined with a lack of confidence in the long-run conventional balance or in great power support. This may have already happened in Israel; Iranian-Arab (for instance, Iraqi) tension is a future possibility.

Although the Arabs are unlikely to develop nuclear weapons primarily to deter or to counter other Arabs, should, say, Libya acquire them, its rivals such as Egypt could feel compelled to get them as well. This process can ramify. Through the Iran-Iraq-Saudi Arabia rivalry, a com-

---

1. Egyptian involvement in Yemen was in a civil war but it was on a large scale and included up to 70,000 troops. International Institute for Strategic Studies, *The Military Balance, 1965–1966* (London: IISS, 1965), p. 38.

petitive move toward nuclear weapons could work either from the Arab-Israeli to the Indo-Pakistani rivalry or vice versa.[2]

The third and widest implication of Middle East instabilities is the risk that nuclear weapons, once available, will be used. This is not only because the many conflicts there create opportunities and temptations for threatening use. The risks are heightened because the stable technical relations, near-perfect information, and high rationality usually assumed when analyzing the superpower nuclear balance are likely to be fragile for small, unstable powers in close proximity, particularly in a region also beset by rapid changes in external and internal relations.

A fourth implication may cut the other way—that is to say, against rapid, widespread acquisition of nuclear explosives. For a nuclear weapon program to move ahead, a steady purpose is needed. Instability in a country could delay a program and fear of instability could discourage the start of a program whose payoff would not come for several years. Changing domestic and international relations are especially likely to hinder efforts to develop nuclear weapons if organized in the form of a multinational program.

The Arab-Israeli Conflict[3]

The progress that has been made toward a peace settlement between Egypt and Israel suggests that this most fertile regional source of conflict may be undergoing a lasting change. Nonetheless, the history of the region inclines one to be cautious. The long-term outlook for the peace process is uncertain; that it will be expanded soon to include the other Arab states is dubious. The intensity of the Arab-Israeli conflict and its enduring nature scarcely need emphasis. Some Arabs reject Israel as a state even within its 1949 boundaries; others may accept Israel within those boundaries but reject the post-1967 occupations. Nor is there any

2. See Shahram Chubin's comment in Dieter Braun, "Implications of India's Nuclear Policy for the Region," in Abbas Amirie, ed., *The Persian Gulf and Indian Ocean in International Politics* (Tehran: Institute for International Political and Economic Studies, 1975), p. 218.

3. This discussion is based on Albert Wohlstetter, Henry Rowen, and Richard Brody, "Middle-East Instabilities and Distant Guarantors (and Disturbers) of the Peace: The Arab-Israeli Case," paper prepared for the California Seminar on Arms Control and Foreign Policy, March 6, 1978.

consensus in Israel on necessary boundaries, but many—perhaps most—Israelis appear willing to accept ones more limited than biblical or present dimensions if adequate security measures are provided.

Israel's 1949 boundaries left it with borders exceptionally difficult to defend; for instance, it allowed Arab forces within nine miles of the Mediterranean at the country's narrowest point. This made Israel vulnerable to major surprise attacks, and exposed it to the shelling of settlements from the Golan Heights, guerrilla raids from the West Bank and Gaza, and blockade of the Gulf of Aqaba. The resulting brevity of tactical warning and lack of strategic depth provided the Israelis with a powerful incentive—indeed, a vital need—to be able to mobilize rapidly in response to signals of a possible attack and to attack preemptively. The almost constant background of less than full-scale warfare ensured continuous tension and uncertainty. This in turn left the Arabs to face the prospect that an Israeli attack could be mounted against them with little notice; other motives aside, this was an inducement for them to keep large forces in being. In such a situation, obtaining tactical warning of an impending attack—on both sides—has been extraordinarily difficult and is heightened by the "noise" of the repeated low-level incidents. It has also been heightened by deliberate deception, which, according to Heikal, was employed successfully by the Egyptians in 1973.[4] The Israelis in 1967 used partial demobilization to deceive the Egyptians, with similar success.

The problem of obtaining reliable early warning of attack continues to be made more difficult on the one side by the existence of sizable Arab forces and on the other by the rapid mobilization and deep airstrike capacity of the Israelis. The sudden shifts in Arab relations and the shifts in position between the immediate adversaries and their superpower supporters add to the uncertainties. The net effect (especially for the Israelis) is to increase the incentives to preempt, to strike and make gains fast not only because of the tactical advantage of doing so but also in expectation that the superpowers will intervene and stop the conflict before initial successes or losses can be reversed. To be sure, the Israelis were apparently inhibited from preempting on at least one occasion—at the outset of the 1973 war—by worry about the U.S. reaction. The

4. Mohamed Heikal, *The Road to Ramadan* (Ballantine, 1975).

Egyptians and the Syrians were not so inhibited, and the reaction of the rest of the world showed that they had little reason for concern. As Bernard Lewis has said, "Their action was received with acclaim by the third world and with acquiescence by Europe."[5]

This situation, which closely conforms to the classical definition of instability, is rendered even more worrisome when some potential longer term trends are considered. One is the erosion of Western support for Israel, which stems in part from the reluctance of the United States to risk involvement in foreign conflicts. Also reducing the West's role has been the great increase in the Arab oil producers' economic power and therefore in their political influence.[6] A third trend is the growth of the Soviet capacity to project power beyond its borders. Fourth, in contrast, U.S. access to the eastern Mediterranean and the Persian Gulf has become increasingly difficult. Over the past decade there has been a major shift in relative U.S.-Soviet power projection capacity, a matter that bears directly on the value of American guarantees of the security of Israel, as well as of American support of Saudi Arabia or other friendly regional states. To the extent that these governments interpret these trends as unfavorable to their security, they will feel it necessary to depend more on their own resources, including nuclear ones.

Finally, there is potential long-term growth in Arab strength relative to that of Israel. In the short run Israeli military power relative to that of the Arabs has probably increased since 1973, partly because of the great efforts made by Israel—with U.S. financial and material support—to remedy the shortcomings revealed in the October war and partly through the relative decline of Egyptian strength resulting from the cutoff of Soviet help.[7] But several long-term trends favor the Arabs, including the improved performance of Arab soldiers, the growing technical com-

5. *Priorities for Peace in the Middle East,* Hearings before the Subcommittee on Near Eastern and South Asian Affairs of the Senate Committee on Foreign Relations, 94 Cong. 1 sess. (Government Printing Office, 1975), p. 128.

6. The shift in influence was evident in the May 1978 congressional vote for the sale of F-15s to Saudi Arabia (as part of the tripartite deal including aircraft for Egypt and Israel). Despite intensive lobbying in opposition by supporters of Israel, the package passed.

7. For the case that Israel is strong relative to the Arabs, see Anthony H. Cordesman, "How Much Is Too Much?" *Armed Forces Journal International* (October 1977), pp. 36–37.

petency of the Arab forces, and the expanding ability of the oil-rich states to buy arms and supporting services for themselves and for the confrontation states.

As a result, most Arabs believe that time is on their side, both militarily and politically, and that they can help the inevitable along. This may also make Israel less willing to concede the territory that gives it strategic depth. Currently, although the Israelis have proved willing to give up the Sinai in exchange for a peace settlement with Egypt and the creation of a demilitarized zone in the Sinai, they are reluctant to give up the region deemed most essential to their security, the West Bank. If Israel comes to see itself as unable in the long run either to depend on its own conventional strength or to depend on support from the United States, an overt Gallois type of nuclear policy might seem less bad than the alternatives, despite the risks. Indeed, while out of office, former Foreign Minister Moshe Dayan made statements to this effect.[8]

Various proposals intended to promote stability or a settlement between Israel and the Arabs have been advanced. One kind of proposal would have Israel revert to its 1967 borders in return for only a joint guarantee by the superpowers or at least a guarantee by the United States.[9] But the resulting situation, with Israel deprived of buffer territories, would be one in which warning could be very short indeed, perhaps nonexistent. The ability of outside guarantors to act, and in particular the ability of the United States to act in circumstances of short or nonexistent warning time, would not permit effective responses. Proposals that there be joint U.S.-Soviet guarantees hardly add comfort. The Soviet objectives in the Middle East sketched in the preceding chapter are in sharp conflict with those of the United States. Such divergences mean that U.S. guarantees that are not credible in themselves could not be made so by tying them to a Soviet coguarantee. At worst a joint guarantee might provide an excuse for locating additional Soviet forces in the region, further complicating any U.S. intervention. With Israel limited to shrunken, nearly

---

8. *Jerusalem Post,* November 30, 1976, p. 3 (quoted in U.S. Foreign Broadcast Information Service [FBIS], *Daily Report: Middle East and North Africa,* December 10, 1976, p. N-8), and *Davar* (Tel Aviv), December 31, 1976, p. 15 (quoted in FBIS, *Daily Report: Middle East,* January 4, 1977, p. N-10).

9. Zbigniew Brzezinski, François Duchêne, and Kiichi Saeki, "Peace in an International Framework," *Foreign Policy,* no. 19 (Summer 1975), pp. 3–17. A similar proposal was made by a Brookings study group in which Brzezinski also participated: *Toward Peace in the Middle East* (Brookings Institution, 1975).

indefensible borders and without a locally available U.S. capacity to act effectively (or only at enormous cost), the United States would be under great pressure to interpret events so that it would be unnecessary for it to act. The Israelis have seen such bare international assurances—including those of the United States—fail in the past.[10] Neither the Egyptians nor various other Arabs have welcomed the prospect of a Soviet "guaranteeing" presence in the area.

Some analysts have proposed a remedy in the form of a formal alliance between the United States and Israel.[11] Americans do not take treaty commitments lightly, and such a commitment would be worth a good deal. But under the circumstances, this would be a treaty unlike other principal U.S. ones, not posed primarily for defense against the Soviet Union but against the Arabs. Given the reluctance of the United States to increase external foreign commitments and its growing ties with the Saudis and the Egyptians, together with the perception that, though troublesome, Arab interests are not basically opposed to American ones, such a treaty would receive an uncertain response and be of uncertain value.[12] Moreover, the idea of such a treaty has not been welcomed by the Israelis. A particular problem for a U.S.-Israeli treaty would be how to handle limited actions by the Arabs, a problem that also exists for a "guarantee" solution.

These trends suggest *faute de mieux* that Israel might depend increasingly on nuclear threats for its security. Some both inside and outside Israel have come to regard this as the least bad of the alternatives. While out of power, Moshe Dayan evidently held the view that U.S. support could not be counted on and that an Israeli nuclear capacity was needed as insurance against a possible failure at the conventional level.[13] Others go further and argue that Israel's stance should be made explicitly nu-

10. For example, there were the pledges of the United States, Britain, and France involved in the trilateral declaration and Eisenhower's 1957 pledge to keep the Strait of Tiran open to Israeli shipping. One should also not forget the 1938 Munich settlement, which was to strip Czechoslovakia of its relatively defensible borders and replace them with a "joint guarantee" by Britain, Germany, France, and Italy.

11. Richard H. Ullman, "Alliance with Israel?" *Foreign Policy*, no. 19 (Summer 1975), pp. 18–33.

12. This is similar to the termination of the other U.S. "non anti-Soviet alliance," the mutual defense treaty with Taiwan. For an interesting discussion of the issue relative to Taiwan, see *Wall Street Journal*, August 23, 1977. Relations with South Korea are somewhat mixed.

13. FBIS, *Daily Report: Middle East* (December 10, 1976), p. N-8.

clear. Shlomo Aronson holds that both sides should make political, territorial, and ideological concessions together with "the open and acknowledged presence of nuclear weapons in the region."[14] He assumes that they will be introduced anyway and that the Arabs will seek nuclear guarantees of some kind from the Soviet Union. He holds that Israel cannot keep up in the conventional arms race, that it cannot afford more limited wars, and that in any case the Arabs will acquire a nuclear option. He proposes that Israel stop participating in the conventional arms race and find a functional substitute for the Arab territories. Israel therefore needs a large stockpile of nuclear weapons and "eventual acquisition" of a second-strike capability, though in the interim a reasonable level of conventional armaments will be needed. In the end, he believes, Arab nuclear weapons will exist. He proposes specifically:

—The return of territories captured in 1967 and the demilitarization of contiguous territories to act as a zone of escalation or an alarm system.

—A declaration that the agreed border will be "red lines" defended if necessary by the use of nuclear weapons.[15] These weapons might be used "massively" against targets anywhere in the Arab world.

—A comprehensive, final peace settlement with the participation of all Arab states, including Palestinian groups with standing in the Arab coalition.

—An agreement limiting the level of conventional arms but with no restrictions on nuclear arms.

In short, Israel must exploit its temporary advantage in the nuclear arms race in order to reach an overall settlement now.

Robert Tucker has made a similar proposal. He, too, views the spread of nuclear weapons to all the major countries in the Middle East as both inevitable and stabilizing. It will permit the Israelis to give up the occupied territories, reduce military spending, and become less dependent on

14. Shlomo Aronson, "Nuclearization of the Middle East: A Dovish View," *Jerusalem Quarterly,* no. 2 (Winter 1977), p. 33.

15. Aronson argues that Arab perception of Israel's sensitivity to Arab armies approaching its "core" territory and of the possibility of a nuclear response was responsible for Syria's not pressing its initial advantage in the Golan Heights in 1973. Shlomo Aronson, "Israel's Nuclear Option," ACIS Working Paper 7 (Los Angeles: University of California, Center for Arms Control and International Security, November 1977), pp. 24–34. His analysis gives too little weight to the facts that the advanced Syrian thrust in question was overextended and exposed to a flanking attack, that it was so attacked, and that it suffered heavy losses in retreating.

the United States. Since Tucker would have the Arabs possess nuclear weapons also, this would prevent Israel from acting aggressively as well. These nuclear forces would not be used unless vital or core areas were threatened.[16] A similar view has been put forward by Steven Rosen.[17] Paul Jabber predicts rather than advocates a Middle East future with around four states deploying nuclear weapons by 1990. He sees the prospective dangers of instability as requiring uncharacteristic integration among the Arabs and the prospect of nuclear war as providing "the requisite stimulant for an honorable, negotiated solution" of the Arab-Israeli dispute.[18]

These proposals beg many questions. One concerns the acts that a nuclear force plausibly might be expected to prevent, especially if the Arabs are not precluded, as in Tucker's formulation, from creating a massive nonnuclear threat along the pre-1967 border. This is particularly important in view of the history of less than all-out warfare between the Arabs and Israel (ranging from cross-border raids to blockades to the war of attrition).

Aronson and Tucker simply assume that second-strike forces will be

16. Robert W. Tucker, "Israel and the United States: From Dependence to Nuclear Weapons?" *Commentary*, vol. 60 (November 1975), pp. 29–43.

17. Steven J. Rosen, "Nuclearization and Stability in the Middle East," *Jerusalem Journal of International Relations*, vol. 1 (Spring 1976), pp. 1–32. In a more recent article, "A Stable System of Mutual Nuclear Deterrence in the Arab-Israeli Conflict," *American Political Science Review*, vol. 71 (December 1977), pp. 1367–83, Rosen asserts that he does not see nuclear weapons as a substitute for conventional ones. This later piece pays more attention to the problems of having a secure military force than the earlier one. However, this remains a problem of great difficulty and the development of such a force would be costly and either would have to be an additional defense burden or would detract from nonnuclear forces. Moreover, despite discussion of permissive action links (locking or disabling devices on bombs), his discussion of the vital problem of maintaining secure and responsible command and control is inadequate, particularly since the command and control system itself would be subject to attack. Finally, the role of nuclear weapons is unclear: "an Israeli [nuclear] deterrent capable of hitting five Arab capital cities would be quite sufficient to constitute an 'unacceptable' level of damage" (p. 1373). Unacceptable in relation to what alternative? We are not told. Clearly this matter is closely tied to the conditions under which such a purely suicidal use would be credible. We are told, in a familiar line of argument, that uncertainty about possible use of nuclear weapons is a restraining influence. If true, how this would enhance security in the complex contingencies that seem likely to arise is left unclear.

18. Paul Jabber, "A Nuclear Middle East: Infrastructure, Likely Military Postures, and Prospects for Strategic Stability," ACIS Working Paper 6 (UCLA, Center for Arms Control and International Security, September 1977), p. 39.

feasible. And Tucker considers only an Israeli nuclear attack on Arab population centers, a suicidal act.[19] The willingness of the survivors of the holocaust to live with the ever-present threats is doubtful. It is, of course, the very threat that the advocates of mutual assured destruction see as appropriate for the U.S.-Soviet nuclear relationship—in fact the only stabilizing and moral policy for the superpowers. While it has fatal defects as a policy for the superpowers, at least the distance, measured in several dimensions, between the United States and the Soviet Union is much greater than that between Israel and the Arabs. The intensity and volatility of the Arab-Israeli dispute is also greater.

The advocates of dependence on nuclear weapons, or those who view their emergence calmly, often too easily conclude that there is no serious difficulty in deploying a protected nuclear force capable of surviving an attack. Such analyses as those of Tucker and Aronson underestimate the evolution in the means of attack, and especially in the means of attacking small forces at close range and in restricted areas. Revolutionary developments in guidance technology are making underground silos vulnerable to nuclear attack and, in time, may make them vulnerable to nonnuclear attack as well. Mobile forces are costly to operate and vulnerable to low overpressures spread over large areas from the bursts of nuclear bombs. The superpowers may provide their regional allies with aid in the form of intelligence sensor data (as from satellites). Moreover, in assessing vulnerability it is important to take account of the possibility that the superpowers might directly strike with their own forces as well (say, a Soviet preemptive strike on an Israeli nuclear force in response to an Israeli attack on an ally or to forestall a perceived danger of Israeli nuclear attack on locally deployed Soviet units or the homeland).

The most serious defect of these proposals, however, is that they neglect the problem of assuring prudent and responsible decisions on the part of all those in a position to direct the use of nuclear weapons. There are problems of response to surprise attacks, of response to ambiguous evidence of an attack or to unauthorized acts in the chain of command, and of possible seizure or theft of weapons by nongovernmental groups. The more weapons are dispersed and put on alert to reduce their vulner-

19. Rosen advocated aiming at population only in his 1976 article but amends that in his more recent one. Aronson mentions attacking oil facilities; he neglects to discuss possible targets the Arabs might select in response. "Nuclearization of the Middle East," p. 42.

ability, the worse the problem of unauthorized or mistaken use becomes.[20] Moreover, the construction of a prudent, effective chain of command capable of surviving an attack directed against it is a matter of no small difficulty for the superpowers. It will not be easy in the Middle East with its record of coups and rivalries and its many terrorist groups.

Relations among the Arabs

Arab-Arab relations have been highly unstable, with competition and low-level conflicts paralleling and to varying degrees interacting with the Arab-Israeli one. They have also contributed importantly to Arab arms purchases (the competition with Israel has most directly affected Egypt).[21] This tendency may also be relevant in analyzing the incentives of other Arab states to acquire nuclear weapons.[22]

Safran, writing in 1968, summed up intra-Arab involvements as follows:

1. Egypt at one time or another sent troops into Syria, Iraq, Kuwait, the Sudan, Algeria. Its armed forces have been engaged in hostilities in Yemen since 1962. Its air force has raided Saudi Arabian territory several times. It has attempted to instigate or support revolution in Syria, Lebanon, Iraq, Jordan, Saudi Arabia, and Yemen, not to speak of the western Arab world.

2. Syria has sent troops into Iraq and Jordan on some occasions and has attempted to instigate rebellion in both of them on other occasions.

3. Iraq has sent troops into Jordan, has massed troops to threaten Syria, and has attempted to instigate coups and rebellions there on more than one occasion.

4. Saudi Arabia has sent troops into Jordan a number of times, into

20. This danger can be reduced by sophisticated locks with remotely held codes, if they are available. However, even with them the problem of vulnerability and error in the chain of command remains. Indeed, if control is centralized, it becomes a prime target.

21. For a view that competition among the Arabs has been dominant in arms purchases in many Arab countries, at least in their timing, see Lewis W. Snider, *Arabesque: Untangling the Patterns of Supply of Conventional Arms to Israel and the Arab States and the Implications for United States Policy on Supply of "Lethal" Weapons to Egypt,* Monograph Series in World Affairs, vol. 15 (University of Denver, Colorado Seminary, 1977). This pattern may have changed, though, with the increasing involvement of nonconfrontation states in the Arab-Israeli conflict.

22. *Nucleonics Week,* vol. 19 (February 23, 1978), p. 2, reports Syrian interest in acquiring nuclear technology arising from concern about recent nuclear efforts by other Arab states.

Kuwait once, has supported with money and arms the royalists in Yemen against the Egyptians and the republicans since 1962, and has attempted to instigate rebellion and political assassination at one time or another in Syria, Jordan, and Egypt.

5. Jordan has sent troops into Kuwait, massed troops against Syria, and supported the Yemeni royalists at different times.[23]

There are several strands of conflict among the Arabs, some continuing, some of brief duration. The most basic has been the conservative-radical split, which pits the Western-oriented traditional monarchies and Egypt against the Soviet-backed "radicals" (Libya, Syria, Algeria, South Yemen, and Iraq). However, only a few years ago Libya's Muammar Qaddafi was working against Egypt's involvement with the Soviet Union at a time when Egypt's Arab socialism represented the principal Soviet ideological as well as operating ties in the Middle East.[24] The current cleavage is between Sadat and most other Arab states, which oppose Sadat's initiatives with Israel, with the more moderate and radical states somewhat split on what degree of sanctions should be imposed. At the military level is Egypt's recent skirmish with Libya and the Dhofar-Omani conflict in Oman (in which South Yemen and Iraq aided the revolutionaries, and Iran and Jordan provided the sultan of Oman with troops). Historically, the largest recent conflict between Arabs was the Yemen civil war (1962–68). Saudi Arabia provided the royalists with arms and other support; Egypt supported the republicans with air raids into Saudi Arabia and up to 70,000 troops.[25] More recently, the "Black September" 1970 Jordanian civil war pitted Hussein's army against the Palestinians supported by a limited Syrian invasion.

Within each of the ideological blocs, there has also been tension. Iraq and Libya have fought for leadership of the current anti-Sadat front. In the midst of the radicals' earlier attack on Sadat for the 1975 Sinai II Accord, Syria and Iraq got into a dispute over water rights on the Euphrates. By 1976 Iraq and Syria were maneuvering troops against

23. Nadav Safran, *From War to War: The Arab-Israeli Confrontation, 1948–1967, A Study of the Conflict from the Perspective of Coercion in the Context of Inter-Arab and Big Power Relations* (Pegasus, 1969), p. 58.

24. Heikal, *Road to Ramadan,* pp. 160–61.

25. Egypt also was reported by the International Red Cross to have used poison gas. International Institute for Strategic Studies, *Strategic Survey, 1967* (London: IISS, 1968), p. 38.

each other over the latter's intervention in Lebanon.[26] The 1976 Lebanese civil war also provoked the curious coalitions of the rightist Christian Lebanese, the Syrians, and the Israelis against the Palestinians supported by Iraq and Egypt. Since then, this alignment has changed again.

Earlier there was a long rivalry between radical Nasserists and Baathists as well as the continuing rivalry between the Baathists' Iraqi and Syrian wings. Originally the Baathists in Syria pushed that country's union with Egypt under Nasser in 1958. In consolidating his power there, however, Nasser purged the Baathists. Eventually this and other Nasser reforms (particularly socialist ones) led to a 1962 coup in Syria by a coalition of Baathists and rightists that broke up the United Arab Republic.

These rivalries have several implications. One is that a resolution of the dispute with Israel will surely not eliminate tension in the area. Indeed, substantial reduction of Arab-Israeli differences could make Arab-Arab differences emerge more clearly. Moreover, although these Arab differences contribute to incentives for maintaining a high level of arms in many Arab states, from Israel's perspective the possibility that all of the Arab forces might be brought to bear against it seems all too likely. This has induced Israel not only to make a large conventional arms effort but also to achieve at least the capacity to acquire nuclear weapons quickly. On the other hand, these inter-Arab rivalries may also set strict limits on the possibilities for Arab cooperation on arms efforts in general and nuclear weapons in particular.

Interactions with Peripheral Powers

The two peripheral powers that are most important to international stability in the region are Turkey and Iran. Turkey is pivotal. Aside from its role in NATO vis-à-vis the Warsaw Pact, Turkey sits astride the main sea and air routes from the Soviet Union to the eastern Mediterranean and the Persian Gulf. As long as Turkey is aligned in opposition to the Soviet Union, the Soviet capacity to operate military forces in the region

---

26. R. D. McLaurin, Mohammed Mughisuddin, and Abraham R. Wagner, *Foreign Policy Making in the Middle East: Domestic Influences on Policy in Egypt, Iraq, Israel, and Syria* (Praeger, 1977), pp. 260–61.

is subject to uncertainty.[27] This uncertainty affects the extent to which the Soviet Union can with confidence back allies such as Iraq and Libya or challenge the United States in the area.

Although political interaction between Turkey and the nations to the south of it has been weak, Turkey exerts a strong indirect effect. At the least, Turkish willingness to allow—or inability to prevent—Soviet overflights greatly increases the Soviet capacity to project power into the region. Therefore the estrangement of Turkey from the United States and from the West in general is an ominous development, quite apart from its impact on NATO. A neutral Turkey would greatly increase the potential power of the Soviet Union in the region. And while the most damaging effects of the 1974 Cyprus crisis may be past, the disaffection of Turkey is a continuing problem in which that was just a high point.

Iran also occupies a strategic situation in relation to the Soviet Union, similar to that of Turkey. But Iran not only serves as a "buffer" against the Soviet Union, it is also a source of direct concern to some Arab states, which fear that it may one day try to enforce its claims to regional hegemony—a fear fueled by Iran's massive buildup of modern arms over the past several years. Iran's 1968 occupation of several strategic islands in the Persian Gulf—Abu Musa and the Greater and Lesser Tumbs— was sharply protested by the Arabs. Even the Saudis were apprehensive about Iran's sending troops to support Oman against radical-backed insurgents, as well as about the support it offered Kuwait and other Gulf emirates should they face radical threats. And while the downfall of the shah may have removed the "imperial" element of potential Iranian expansion, members of the new Islamic government have already spoken of renewing Iran's claim to Bahrain.[28]

The Iranians' chief preoccupation in the Arab world has been with Iraq, centering on Iranian support of Kurdish separatists in Iraq and border delineation differences. The major problems were, at least temporarily, settled by an agreement in 1975. However, competition in the buildup of arms continued throughout the shah's reign.

The implications for Iranian-Arab relations of the shah's fall and

27. Soviet forces can and do cross Yugoslavia, as well as other countries, to reach the Middle East and Africa. However, the direct air routes are across Turkey and Iran and the direct sea route is through the Dardanelles.

28. William Branigin, "Foreign Minister Denies Iran Seeks to Export Revolution," *Washington Post,* October 4, 1979.

Khomeini's rise to power are complex. As a leader of the Shiites, who are an oppressed majority in Iraq, Khomeini is likely to find ample grounds for continuing the shah's quarrels with that state. On the other hand, Khomeini has also called for the overthrow of the conservative Gulf emirates, with which the old imperial government tried to build relations. However, for a while Iran's attention will be on dealing with its various internal, regional, and factional conflicts. Thus the main immediate effect in the area of the shah's fall is probably the negative one of freeing Iraq and the Soviet Union from the only local restraint on their military dominance of the Arab part of the Gulf. Similarly, Iraq's ability to project power into any future Arab-Israeli war without fear for its own defenses has greatly increased. This is especially ominous in light of the enormous buildup in Iraqi arms that has taken place since the October 1973 war.

The fact that the Arab-Israeli region has "fuzzy" edges and complicated relations means that nearby countries—Turkey, Iran, Algeria, and others—can affect developments in the region, and vice versa. For example, an Iranian move to acquire nuclear explosives is likely to give its Arab rivals, Iraq and Saudi Arabia, incentives for gaining nuclear weapons. In any case, they may find enough motivation to move toward getting nuclear explosives in their Arab-Israeli and Arab-Arab competition.

The Role of Other Outside Powers

Historically, outside powers have played an active part in the region—most notably Britain and France in the 1956 Sinai campaign. The United States sent marines into Lebanon in 1958, signaled possible intervention in Jordan in 1970, and set up a protected line of communication with Israel through the Mediterranean in 1973. The Soviet Union was directly involved in air-to-air and surface-to-air combat during the war of attrition (1969–70) and has long maintained large numbers of advisers in its client states. A Cuban brigade was stationed on the Golan Heights in 1973–74. Even North Koreans are reported to have fought during the October war.

Outside powers play several roles. First, their arms are critical to the conventional power balance in the area. Israel, which has the most developed domestic weapons industry and is itself an exporter, is nonetheless heavily dependent on the United States for its more sophisticated arms. The Arab states, despite various efforts, are far behind Israel in domestic arms production.

This dependence on continuing outside support is particularly important to incentives for going nuclear because the outsiders are not always dependable. Israel had a bad experience in 1967, when it suddenly found itself abandoned by the French, until then its chief arms supplier. Its victory in the Six-Day War enabled it to outlast the transition to receiving arms from the United States, but the episode must have been unsettling. Both the United States and the Soviet Union have used delays in arms supplies as a tactic for putting pressure on their respective clients. With the increasing dependence of the West on Arab oil and the current isolationist mood in the United States, Israel can hardly regard strong U.S. support as certain to continue. As for the radical Arabs, the USSR's sudden abandonment of Somalia in favor of Ethiopia must cast doubt on Russian reliability. Independent nuclear strength may be seen as a way of reducing dependence although it risks alienating such superpower support as is available.

The October war made it clear that of the outsiders only the two superpowers could be expected to take a major part in an Arab-Israeli conflict. Moreover, they became more directly involved than they had in earlier Arab-Israeli wars. The U.S. call for a worldwide alert is indicative of another important factor about the superpowers' role in the Middle East: it is not confined to serving and trying to influence local clients. The Mediterranean is of great importance to both NATO and Warsaw Pact military interests. Its position is also valuable in providing access to the Indian subcontinent and Africa. The Soviet Union, in particular, has used friendly Arabs for supplying its other clients in those areas (for instance, during the Angolan civil war, the 1971 Indo-Pakistani conflict, and the current fighting in Ethiopia).

These interests of the superpowers reduce the extent to which their actions can be predicted by weighing purely local factors. The superpowers may take actions in the area aimed at objectives elsewhere, as when the Soviet Union diverted arms from Egypt to India. This process can work both ways; for example, the oil embargo and production cuts in 1973–74, which were basically directed at the United States, had a large effect on Europe and Japan. This means that instabilities can be communicated from outside the region into it, and vice versa.

In addition to these sources of uncertainty is the fear of the nonradical

Arab states and Israel that growing Soviet capacity to project power to the region increasingly exposes them to Soviet power. There is evidence that the Carter administration recognizes the need for countervailing action to this Soviet capacity. Secretary of Defense Harold Brown observed that the Soviet Union "has developed a long-range aircraft force and a Navy capable of challenging our maritime interests."[29] To cope with this kind of contingency, he identified the need for a mixture of Marine and light Army divisions, naval and tactical air forces, and strategic mobility forces with the range and payload to minimize dependence on overseas staging and logistical support bases.

To the extent that those in the region who look to the United States for support regard its capacity to project power in their defense as important to their security and believe that capacity is strong, they may be less inclined to rely on nuclear threats.[30] The danger of relying on nuclear weapons as a substitute for nonnuclear ones or for guarantees by a great power (backed up by strength usable in the region) was discussed above for Israel. The principle is a general one; it applies also to Saudi Arabia, Egypt, and other countries that might face serious threats and that might look to the United States for help (although U.S. ineffectiveness against the Soviet invasion of Afghanistan is not an encouraging precedent). Unfortunately, the prospect is that political relations in the region and with outside powers will continue to be unstable indefinitely.

29. Remarks by Secretary of Defense Harold Brown at the Thirty-fourth Annual Dinner of the National Security Industrial Association, Washington, D.C., September 15, 1977.

30. It might seem that, if increases in Soviet power projection capabilities could lead U.S. allies to edge toward nuclear weapons, strengthening U.S. power projection capabilities in response might reassure U.S. friends, but symmetrically give opponents incentives for nuclearization. There is, however, an empirical and theoretical reason not to expect this. First, the United States is generally seen as a power more oriented to the status quo than the Soviet Union; thus U.S. strength would probably be seen as less threatening. Second, the key is not so much whether a superpower increases or decreases its projection capabilities as what effect that has on the perceived balance between the two, either regionally or globally. It is the potential for instabilities arising from an imbalance that could lead nations to the "dangerous security" of nuclear weapons. To the extent that the United States balances the Russian extension of power projection capabilities, such actions will help reassure allies and do little to frighten opponents into risky responses. Maintaining a clear capability to counter possible Soviet moves in ways that are not escalatory or too risky is especially important in the Middle East. With the borders and politics less settled than in Europe, there is a much more fragile "tradition of stability" to hold matters together during the times when the balance is allowed to tip.

Internal Instabilities

Like many third world states, most of the countries in the area have experienced internal instability. As in many traditional societies, the authority of the mostly monarchical post–World War II Arab countries has been subjected to extreme strain by the increasing politicization of the masses. Antimonarchical "radical" coups have taken place in Egypt (1952), Iraq (1958), Yemen (1962), and Libya (1969), with Iran in 1979 as a regional non-Arab case. Attempts have also been made in Jordan and Morocco, and the long-term immunity of the Gulf states from such events is doubtful (both Saudi Arabia and Oman have had particularly unpopular monarchs replaced by other members of the royal family). In Libya and Algeria, radical governments once in place have managed to stay in power; this was not true in Syria and Iraq until recently. As in many authoritarian countries, however, stability is based neither on tradition nor on consent of the masses but largely on the maintenance of a preponderance of force by a small group. Thus there are likely to be substantial succession crises at periodic intervals (such as Sadat's factional fight with the Soviet-backed Ali Sabri group in Egypt after Nasser's death).

Many of these countries are also afflicted with ethnic or factional divisions. The current ruling group in Syria comes from a small religious sect, the Alawites, and maintains an uneasy hold over the majority. Iraq, besides being ruled by a religious minority, also suffered a major revolt by the Kurds. The Palestinians are a problem not only for Israel and Lebanon but also for Jordan.

Heightening these internal instabilities is their exploitation by other countries. Israeli backing of Lebanese rightist Christians is well known, as is the backing of Palestinians against both Israel and Jordan by various Arab states. Nasser used his pan-Arab appeal to the masses throughout the Arab world to put pressure on neighboring governments, particularly Saudi Arabia and other conservatives. In a turn of the tables, Qaddafi's ideological appeal to Egyptians has been of major concern to Sadat.[31] Syria and Iran have both been involved in supporting Kurdish separatists

31. See Abraham S. Becker, Bert Hansen, and Malcolm H. Kerr, *The Economics and Politics of the Middle East* (American Elsevier, 1975), pp. 60–61.

in Iraq, which in turn, along with South Yemen, has supported Dhofar separatists in Oman and Arab separatists in Iran.

Outside powers have also been involved in these internal conflicts. In 1958 British and Americans moved troops into Jordan and Lebanon respectively to forestall a spread of the Iraqi radical revolution. The Russians have been reported as directly involved in suppressing the Kurdish revolt in Iraq—to the extent of running armed combat missions. The Cubans are reported to have played a key role in the triumph of the radical faction in the recent South Yemen coup.[32]

Moreover, groups nominally in power have not always been able to maintain control. In the Arab countries there have been serious instances of lack of coordination. When Syria invaded Jordan during Jordan's 1970 civil war, its armored column was attacked by the Jordanian air force. Syria's air force was much larger than Jordan's, but the Syrian air commander, Hafiz al-Assad, was a political rival of the president, and reportedly for that reason the air force refused to take part in the invasion.[33] Another reported example concerned an Egyptian submarine stationed in Tripoli, Libya. Qaddafi is supposed to have ordered the submarine to sink the British ocean liner *Queen Elizabeth II,* which was on a charter cruise to Israel. Fortunately, after setting out on this mission, the Egyptian submarine's commander radioed Egypt to report Qaddafi's order. The matter worked its way through the naval commander at Alexandria to the armed forces commander-in-chief to Sadat, who ordered the mission called off in time.[34] An example of an Israeli breakdown in command and control was the Israeli attack on the U.S.S. *Liberty* in the 1967 war.

These internal instabilities and errors are of central importance to maintaining control of nuclear weapons that someday may become available. Responsible control means that these weapons be physically protected from terrorists, and that they not be set off by accident or as a result of mistakes in the chain of command. If an attempt were made to overthrow a government, these weapons might become a prize in the contest (along with the presidential palace, the radio station, and the local airport). And threats to use the weapons might be employed in internal uprisings.

32. "Cubans Called Key to Aden Coup," *Washington Star,* June 28, 1978.
33. McLaurin, Mughisuddin, and Wagner, *Foreign Policy Making,* p. 226.
34. Heikal, *Road to Ramadan,* pp. 96–97.

The danger that terrorists might obtain nuclear weapons raises the possibility of nuclear terrorist threats throughout the world, especially in areas that permit relatively free movements of people and goods. One or more of the several Palestinian terrorist groups might undertake to acquire these weapons, although their manufacture by such a group would involve difficult technical tasks and success in stealing them from states that have them seems dubious. However, in the future, both tasks may be easier: the barriers to the theft of plutonium will be lower if this material is widely traded and the barriers to the theft of nuclear weapons are likely to be lower if many more countries have them. Any state that has nuclear weapons may be unable to control them if measures of protection are inadequate, but this seems most likely to occur in states that are internally unstable, of which the Middle East has a fair proportion.

Steps could be taken to reduce this risk. Not only can sophisticated locks be built into nuclear weapons (by a country with access to the appropriate technology), but also disabling devices can effectively destroy the bombs if their use is "unprogrammed." These devices are no solution to the inherently difficult problems of command and control, but they provide some defense against seizure by terrorists. Nonetheless, the prospect that nuclear weapons could come into the possession of those who would employ them in frightening ways cannot be excluded.

Implications of the Conventional Arms Rivalries

With the collection of rivalries described above, it is not surprising that the Middle East has become one of the most heavily armed regions of the world. This has been greatly facilitated by the huge increase in income flowing to the oil-producing nations since 1973. The resulting conventional arms balances and their trends are important for several reasons. The perception of unfavorable trends in these balances may lead to decisions to acquire nuclear explosives; nuclear weapons may be assembled or even used if a conventional war is progressing unfavorably; many weapons are dual purpose (they can be used for nuclear as well as nonnuclear delivery); and the arms balances can change rapidly with transfers of arms or troops from outside the region.

Table 9-1 shows the increase in the major weapons inventories of Israel and selected Arab states from before the 1973 war to 1979. This

Table 9-1. *Major Weapons of Israel and Selected Arab Countries, 1973 and 1979*

Country	Tanks[a]		Armored fighting vehicles[b]		Combat aircraft	
	1973	1979	1973	1979	1973	1979
Israel	1,700	3,050	3,000	4,000	488	576
Egypt	1,880	1,600	2,000	3,000	620	563
Syria	1,170	2,600	1,000	1,600	326	389
Jordan	420	500	670	890	52	73
Subtotal	3,470	4,700	3,670	5,490	998+	1,025
Iraq	990	1,800+	1,300	1,500	224	339
Libya	221	2,000	210+	1,000+	44	201
Saudi Arabia	25	350	200+	600+	70	178
Subtotal	1,236	4,150+	1,710+	3,100+	338	718
Iran	920	1,735	2,000+	1,075+	159	447

Sources: International Institute for Strategic Studies, *The Military Balance, 1973–1974* (London: IISS, 1973), pp. 31–36; IISS, *The Military Balance, 1979–1980* (IISS, 1979), pp. 38–42, 44–45; and IISS, *Strategic Survey, 1974* (IISS, 1975), p. 15.

a. Excluding light tanks.
b. Excluding tanks.

increase is especially notable in light of the losses of the 1973 war, in which, for example, the Syrians and the Egyptians each lost about a thousand tanks and other armored vehicles. As important, though not shown in the table, are the improvements in the quality of these weapons.

On the Israeli side, the buildup reflects several factors: the need felt by Israel for a stronger military position because of the early Arab success in 1973, greater U.S. willingness to supply and to subsidize this buildup, a desire to prepare for political negotiations and make up for territorial concessions, and efforts to achieve the ability to project power at a distance. This last effort was motivated, for example, by the blockade at the entrance of the Red Sea in 1973 and by the wish to be able to reach Arab opponents in nonconfrontation states.[35]

Among the Arabs, the Iraqi increases could be seen as adding to the aggregate Arab strength opposing Israel and as bolstering Iraq's position vis-à-vis Iran, Syria, and Saudi Arabia. Syria had many losses from the war to replace, but it has gone beyond replacement and increased its air

35. For a discussion of arms transfers and arms control in the Middle East, see Yair Evron, *The Role of Arms Control in the Middle East,* Adelphi Paper 138 (London: International Institute for Strategic Studies, 1977).

and tank strength considerably. Libya has received large quantities of Soviet equipment, such as tanks that the Libyans do not know how to operate. This stockpiling of Soviet arms suggests that they might be shipped to the front for use by the confrontation states in a conflict with Israel; another possibility is that they would be manned by Soviet troops who could be flown in quickly.

Egypt's situation has been more difficult. Immediately after the 1973 war it received replacements for many of its lost weapons: aircraft including the new MIG-23, modern T-62 tanks, and air defense missiles. But cooling relations with the Soviet Union have made Egypt turn increasingly for arms to the West, especially to France and the United States.

Large relative changes are also taking place in Saudi Arabia, which in the past has had little capacity to operate modern arms. A long time will probably be needed for it to absorb weapons such as the sixty F-15s the Carter administration offered it as part of a package that also includes weapons for Egypt and Israel.

The implications of trends in the conventional balance for creating nuclear weapon capacities are clearest in the case of Israel, especially if a grand anti-Israel coalition of Arabs should emerge along with an expectation of growing Arab competence and financial strength. The Arabs so far have not seemed interested in nuclear arms as a way of dealing with Israel's historical military superiority, but this attitude may now be changing. In terms of Arab-Arab struggles, conventional force changes are not dominated by a single balance but instead by the frequent shifts in alignments. This seems also to be true of Arab relations with peripheral powers, for example, the Iran-Iraq balance. In all these balances, the tremendous growth in weaponry is both a symptom of and a likely contributor to a sense of insecurity that, along with specific events, might lead one or more nations to move closer to or to acquire nuclear weapons.

CHAPTER TEN

Nuclear Potential
and Possible Contingencies

A NATION's degree of industrial development and its capacity to make nuclear explosives are highly correlated. The two less developed nations that have such explosives, China and India, both received a great deal of help from the Soviet Union and from the United States and Canada, respectively. There is also a large overlap between the technologies of civilian nuclear energy and those useful for military—specifically, explosive—purposes. A civilian program reduces the incremental time and cost of further steps that might be taken toward military uses. It provides training and technology and can, without violation under the present international rules, furnish the explosive materials themselves.[1] Even direct work with metallic plutonium or highly enriched uranium in forms immediately usable in nuclear explosives is permitted under the Treaty on the Non-Proliferation of Nuclear Weapons (NPT) and almost all existing agreements for cooperation.[2]

This overlap of civilian and military applications creates ambiguity in the interpretation of possible moves toward a bomb. Civilian applica-

1. Albert Wohlstetter and others, *Swords from Plowshares: The Military Potential of Civilian Nuclear Energy* (University of Chicago Press, 1979).

2. Although the existing U.S. agreement for cooperation with Egypt specifies that the reprocessing and storage of plutonium from U.S. facilities will take place outside Egypt, neither these agreements for cooperation nor the 1979 U.S. legislation tightening the restrictions on nuclear exports would preclude Egypt from obtaining nuclear explosive materials from other countries.

tions—or rationalizations—provide a kind of cover for military activities. For instance, a plutonium production reactor can be called a research reactor. India so labeled, with Canadian and U.S. acquiescence, its CIRUS reactor, from which it extracted plutonium for its 1974 bomb test. Israel first said that its plant at Dimona was a textile plant and has since described it as a research reactor. The 70-megawatt (thermal) Osiris type of reactor with which France is supplying Iraq is also described as being for research, although as fuel it uses highly enriched uranium, which is also immediately usable in nuclear explosives.[3] Unlike the Dimona reactor, the Iraqi one will be subjected to international safeguards, although this does not necessarily mean that its fuel is "safe."

The implicit subsidy to military nuclear programs from civilian programs is widely perceived as being of great importance in lowering the barriers of cost and time to getting the bomb. However, the additional importance of civilian programs as covers for military programs has been neglected. They clearly are not important for countries such as Britain and France, which have overt weapons programs. But the governments of countries in the Middle East, as elsewhere, have good reason to try to conceal moves toward a bomb or at least to keep such moves ambiguous. In Israel, for instance, an overt nuclear weapons program would spur Arab nuclear efforts, create political difficulties with the United States, and perhaps diminish other outside support. It might also result in increased Soviet arms support for the Arabs, perhaps including support in nuclear technology. Although, as described in the preceding chapter, some analysts believe Israel should rely on an overt bomb program, this view has not prevailed in Israel.

On the Arab side, there are also arguments for covertness and ambiguity. For one thing, the Arabs appear to be a long way from acquiring nuclear weapons. They need to train people and carry out other long lead time activities. Internal and external differences might slow progress. An announced weapons program followed by years of little visible progress would lack credibility. These governments might also fear being subjected to external pressure and sanctions, or at least to more difficulty in buying nuclear technology.

To varying degrees, the advocates of open acquisition of nuclear

---

3. There are reported plans to reduce the enrichment level of this fuel. See footnote 9, below. However, the accuracy of these reports is uncertain.

weapons—Aronson, Jabber, Rosen, and Tucker—see such a policy as promoting stability and a political settlement between Israel and the Arab countries. Domestic political forces in one or more countries might push nuclear weapons programs to the surface. Such was the case in India, the timing of whose nuclear test was in part motivated by the internal difficulties that Indira Gandhi's regime faced in 1974.[4]

In any case, the lead time needed to develop nuclear explosives will shrink as the countries in the region acquire civilian nuclear power. Under the international agreements generally in force, all that governments have to do to have a modest nuclear weapons capability is to undertake some "research" activities that require the use of separated plutonium ("criticality" experiments, for instance) and to develop the nonnuclear components of bombs. The latter task could be carried out under the cover of military research on high explosives ballistics or even basic research on the effects of very high pressures on materials.

Once work was completed on the nonnuclear components of bombs, if metallic plutonium or highly enriched uranium was available through a civilian program, the time required to assemble bombs would amount to only a few days or even hours. All of this could be done without any clear violation of today's international safeguards, which say nothing about access to these bomb materials. However, Israel's reactor, the only one producing explosive material of any consequence known to be in the region, is not even covered under international safeguards. The Dimona reactor provided by France evidently came without restrictions, and informal arrangements for biannual U.S. inspection of Dimona apparently ended in 1969.[5] Israel's nuclear posture may be one that any nation would be permitted under current International Atomic Energy Agency (IAEA) safeguards, meaning that it could legally be within hours of having bombs ready to be used.[6]

4. Roberta Wohlstetter, *'The Bhudda Smiles': Absent-Minded Peaceful Aid and the Indian Bomb,* PH 77-04-370-23, monograph 3, prepared for the U.S. Energy Research and Development Administration (Los Angeles: Pan Heuristics, April 1977), p. 2.

5. Shlomo Aronson, "Israel's Nuclear Option," ACIS Working Paper 7 (Los Angeles: University of California, Center for Arms Control and International Security, November 1977), p. 7.

6. It might, of course, have fissile material in assembled bombs, a step that would strain most interpretations of the nonproliferation treaty and IAEA safeguards.

The Status of Announced Nuclear Plans

The simplest way to acquire nuclear weapons would be to buy them from someone else instead of going through the work of developing them oneself. This is the path that Colonel Qaddafi apparently tried to take when he sent Major Abdel Salem Jalloud, his deputy, to Peking in 1969 to buy a bomb.[7] Jalloud was turned down by Chou En-lai with the admonition that every nation must practice self-reliance.

Today only Israel among the states in the Middle East apparently has access to enough readily fissionable material for nuclear explosives. (The research reactors now in Egypt and Iraq are too small to produce bomb-usable quantities of plutonium.) The Dimona reactor (unless its capacity has been increased) is capable of producing about 8 kilograms of plutonium a year and in the period since start-up in 1963 around 100 kilograms could have been produced, enough for, say, twenty bombs. If left in the spent fuel rods, it would be unavailable for ready use in weapons. If a reprocessing plant had to be built from scratch, the lead time to a bomb would probably be around two years; however, with such a plant already built, the time necessary to reprocess enough fuel to get a bomb's worth of plutonium would probably be several months.[8] With plutonium already separated and nonnuclear components fabricated, bombs would be virtually ready for use.

This asymmetry between Israel and the Arabs is unlikely to last. Several nations in the region have plans for building a nuclear capacity.

Egypt
Research reactor
WWR-C-Cairo; 2 megawatts; 1961; 10 percent enriched uranium.

Power reactors
Two 600-megawatt (electric) reactors have been under negotiation for several years with Westinghouse (with a letter of intent signed for one); this deal has been delayed by lack of congressional approval. There have also been press reports that two 150-megawatt (electric)

---

7. Mohamed Heikal, *The Road to Ramadan* (Ballantine, 1975), pp. 70–71.
8. The IAEA reports that Israel has an unsafeguarded "pilot reprocessing facility"; *IAEA Bulletin*, vol. 19 (October 1977), p. 4.

reactors will be provided by a German-Austrian consortium for installation in Suez. None of these plans seem likely to be implemented in the immediate future.

Iraq
Research reactors
IRT-2000; 2 megawatts (electric); in operation; 10 percent enriched uranium.
Osiris type (under construction by France; also Italian participation); 70 megawatts (electric); 93 percent enriched uranium.[9]

Power reactors
600 megawatts (electric) (apparently under negotiation with France); pressurized water reactor; late 1980s?; 3 percent enriched uranium.

Israel
Research reactors
IRR-1; 5 megawatts (thermal); 1960; 90 percent enriched uranium.
IRR-2; 26 megawatts (thermal); 1964; natural uranium.

Power reactors
None on order. A 950-megawatt (electric) light water reactor has been under negotiation with various supplier states. If unable to import one under conditions it deems acceptable, officials assert Israel may build one of its own design.

Kuwait
Research reactors
None.

Power reactors
None. But interest has been expressed in obtaining four to six 600-megawatt (electric) dual-purpose units by 2000, starting in the late 1980s.

9. There are reports of plans to decrease this to 20 percent. *Nucleonics Week,* vol. 18 (May 5, 1977), pp. 3–4. If 93 percent enriched fuel were used, a single fuel load might be about enough to make a primitive bomb (11.6 kilograms in a fuel load versus a nominal 15 kilograms of highly enriched uranium per bomb; see Wohlstetter and others, *Swords from Plowshares,* p. 26). Italy meanwhile is supplying Iraq with "a sensitive nuclear facility known as a 'hot cell' . . . big enough to obtain enough plutonium to produce a nuclear weapon in about a year's time." Associated with this is a major Italian-Iraqi nuclear training program. Richard Burt, *New York Times,* March 18, 1980.

Libya
  Research reactors
  None.

  Power reactors
  440 megawatts (electric) (negotiated with the USSR)—dual purpose: power and desalinization.
  600 megawatts (electric) (under discussion with France)—pressurized water reactor.

Syria
  Research reactors
  None.

  Power reactors
  None planned. Syria contemplates a feasibility study for a 600-megawatt (electric) nuclear power plant.

These Arab nuclear programs, if implemented, will greatly reduce the time necessary to acquire bombs and provide material for large numbers of them. For instance, a 440-megawatt (electric) pressurized water reactor of the type Libya proposes to acquire would produce about 70 kilograms of plutonium annually. This estimate assumes operation of the reactors for maximum efficiency in the production of electricity. The resulting high burnup plutonium, which contains a substantial proportion of the isotope Pu-240, is nevertheless usable in bombs, a fact which was long treated ambiguously or obscured. Yields in the 1- to 20-kiloton range can be assured. However, if a government wants access to weapons-grade plutonium (which has a higher expected explosive yield and lower variance in yield), it can be made in power reactors by removing some fuel rods that have been irradiated for comparatively short times. This can be done during normally scheduled refueling operations or when unscheduled shutdowns occur. (The joint production of weapons-grade plutonium and electricity is hardly a novel idea; it was adopted years ago by the United States in its N reactor at Hanford, Washington.) Up to a point, the incremental cost of acquiring weapons-grade plutonium would be low.

Access to a reprocessing plant is needed if the plutonium is to be available for weapons. Under the present international rules such plants can be located anywhere. British Nuclear Fuels, Limited, or COGEMA in France will also provide the reprocessing services, although their policies on shipping back plutonium are unclear—so far neither country has stated limitations on countries to which they will ship it. In any case, such facilities might be built by individual Arab nations or they might cooperate in building a pan-Arab one. If Israel has made explosives from spent fuel from its Dimona reactor, it already has such a facility.[10]

There is no publicly available evidence that any of the countries in the region contemplate building isotope separation plants capable of producing highly enriched uranium. Israel, however, is working on laser isotope separation. Success in this field anywhere in the world, if not kept secret, could eventually result in enrichment capacity in the region. However, a less uncertain prospect for the special enrichment technology is the spread of uranium enrichment centrifuges, which are being developed and built in Europe, the United States, and Japan. Compared to traditional diffusion enrichment technology, centrifuge enrichment can be both built efficiently on a smaller scale (meaning lower initial construction costs and lead time) and shifted much more quickly from producing safe low-enriched uranium to bomb-usable highly enriched uranium. On balance, Israel's lead in advanced technologies gives it a potential initial advantage in this field. It should be noted that Pakistan appears to be following the centrifuge route with the participation of a Pakistani who was employed in the Dutch centrifuge effort.

The Economics of Nuclear Power in the Region

The close connection between civilian and military uses of nuclear power makes the economic worth of announced civilian programs a matter of great interest. Although the existence of valid economic applications does not detract from possible military uses that would be advanced as a by-product, the absence of a reasonable economic case makes military utility stand out more clearly.

If economic criteria were decisive, few if any power reactors would be built in this region. For small plants of the scale appropriate to the existing electricity grids, electricity from oil-fueled plants would cost no more

10. See footnote 8, above.

to produce than electricity from nuclear plants.[11] More important, natural gas is abundant in the region. On the same basis as the estimates of nuclear- and oil-fueled electricity, a gas-fired plant at $400 per megawatt (electric), a 70 percent capacity factor, and 15 percent fixed charge rate would produce a kilowatt-hour capital cost of around 10 mills. Using natural gas costs at 50 cents per million BTUs (or thousand cubic feet) would lead to total costs of only 15–17 mills per kilowatt-hour. By contrast, a nuclear plant with cost and operating factors appropriate—or even optimistic—for the region ($1,200 per kilowatt [electric] in 1977 dollars, a 60 percent capacity factor, and 15 percent fixed charge rate in real terms) would produce electricity at a cost per kilowatt-hour of 42 mills, almost three times as expensive as gas-fired electricity.

In short, Middle Eastern countries that have natural gas, especially if it is being wasted, have no economic justification for building nuclear plants. For Egypt, aside from the use of its proven natural gas, much of which is located in the Gulf of Suez, there is the possibility of imports of gas via pipelines from Saudi Arabia. Syria and Jordan might also import natural gas from Saudi Arabia or Iraq. To be sure, these countries have good reason to be concerned about the security of supplies from these sources. But worries about the vulnerability of supplies from other Arab countries should be weighed against the dependency engendered by receiving nuclear supplies from the industrial states (as well as their vulnerability). And not only is using oil to fuel power plants comparable in cost to using nuclear reactors; it is also much easier to scale down to the plant sizes appropriate to the region. Of course, there may be those who, like the shah, see nuclear power as the energy source on which to depend when the oil and gas run out. Given the hydrocarbon resources of the area and any reasonable discount rate, however, heavy dependence on nuclear energy would be a highly costly strategy.[12] (A research and development program aimed at having a nuclear capacity further in the future would not be as vulnerable to this criticism.)

11. For an extensive analysis of the relative costs of nuclear and other means of electricity generation in some similar developing countries, see Zalmay Khalilzad, *Nuclear Power and Economic Development, Seven Cases*, PH 78-04-832-33, prepared as part of Draft Final Report to U.S. Arms Control and Disarmament Agency (Los Angeles: Pan Heuristics, 1978).

12. Iran has discovered the high cost of following a nuclear strategy in a country that has large quantities of natural gas. The new government has canceled the Iranian nuclear program.

More important is the fact that the economics of recycling plutonium and unburned uranium from spent fuel, where the proliferation
danger is greatest, will be even less favorable in this region than in highly
industrialized regions. Even when carried out in countries that have large
nuclear programs where economies of scale in reprocessing might be
attained (for instance, where fifty large reactors might feed a large reprocessing plant), the costs are unfavorable by comparison with the cost
of using fresh uranium fuel. At the level of projected nuclear reactor
programs in the Middle East, recycling would be extremely uneconomic.
And even shipping the spent fuel to France for reprocessing is costly;
COGEMA is reportedly charging the German utilities almost $500 per
kilogram of spent fuel, a rate that makes the recovered plutonium and
uranium considerably more costly than fresh fuel.[13] There is no need
for such reprocessing on waste management grounds either.[14] Whether
these economic arguments would be decisive with governments, many of
which are now extremely rich, is another matter, however.

The U.S.-Egyptian agreement for cooperation states that the plutonium produced in reactors provided under the agreement or derived
from U.S. fuel will be reprocessed, fabricated, and stored outside Egypt.
This provision reflected the then-current belief of the U.S. Atomic Energy
Commission that reprocessing would be economical as well as the concern in Congress and elsewhere that it would be dangerous for Egypt to
have access to separated plutonium or even to the plutonium in spent
fuel. Removal has therefore been stipulated. There is no publicly available evidence that agreements between other supplier nations and Middle Eastern countries contain similar provisions limiting access to nuclear
explosive materials. (However, the Soviet Union requires the return of
spent fuel by Eastern European countries.)

Romanticism about big electricity projects is not new to this region or
confined to nuclear reactors. The Aswan Dam, instead of producing the
2,100 megawatts promised by Nasser's regime, because of irrigation requirements for Egyptian agriculture produces only 1,500 megawatts at
a maximum and sometimes as little as 500 megawatts.

13. *Nuclear Fuel,* vol. 2 (December 26, 1977), p. 5.
14. "Draft Report of Task Force for Review of Nuclear Waste Management,"
U.S. Department of Energy, February 1978. See also "Proof of Evidence of Albert
Wohlstetter on Behalf of Friends of the Earth, Ltd." (California Seminar on Arms
Control and Foreign Policy, September 5–6, 1977), pp. 14–17.

One proposed nuclear project of particular interest in the region is that of using peaceful nuclear explosives to create a canal from the Mediterranean to the Qattara Depression in the northwestern part of Egypt. Water flowing into the Qattara would be used to generate electricity; long-term production would be sustained at a rate determined by evaporation of the water. Such schemes are supposed to be supported by the weapons states in accordance with article V of the Treaty on the Non-Proliferation of Nuclear Weapons, which calls on them to make explosives for peaceful projects available to the nonweapons states. The promotion of peaceful nuclear explosions by some of the weapons states —earlier, mainly the United States and the Soviet Union, and more recently, only the latter—and their legitimation in the NPT as a reasonable and implicitly economic use for nuclear explosives opened a path for states interested in acquiring nuclear weapons to obscure their intent slightly. India exploited this legitimation in its nuclear explosion carried out with what the Indians call their "peace bomb." No economic applications of this peace bomb have yet been described by India; indeed, no economic use of peaceful nuclear explosives has been demonstrated anywhere.

There are many unanswered questions about the Qattara project, including possible seismic effects on Alexandria and other communities and the environmental effects of flooding a large area of Egypt (a point of some interest since there have been some serious and unexpected consequences from the impounding of large amounts of water in Lake Nasser behind the Aswan Dam). It seems unlikely to produce economic benefits commensurate with its costs or with alternative uses of capital. The West Germans began a feasibility study of the idea in 1974. However, little has been heard of it in recent years.

Nuclear Desalting in the Middle East

Nuclear romanticism, of course, did not originate in the Middle East nor, aside from the Qattara project, is it evident in particularly acute forms in that region. Initially it was "made in America," and the U.S. role in promoting desalinization projects in the Middle East provides a splendid illustration of economic and political irrationality.[15]

15. This discussion is based largely on Paul Wolfowitz, "The Consequences of Technological Intervention: Nuclear Desalting Projects in the Middle East," paper prepared for the 1970 annual meeting of the American Political Science Association.

Desalinization is not a matter of historic interest only. Plans for such projects are under way in Libya and Kuwait. These plans may be lineal descendants of earlier American proposals.[16] Under Atoms for Peace and article V of the NPT, the United States was committed to the dissemination of nuclear technology. To this was added Lyndon Johnson's Water for Peace program, which he heralded as providing the only commodity that "can give future generations a chance to escape wholesale misery and wholesale starvation."[17]

The conjunction of the atom and water, both for peace, served several needs felt by various U.S. groups, though less clearly the needs of the potential recipients. Nuclear power comes in large units, but few developing countries could accommodate them in their small power grids and even fewer could afford them; fresh water from special-purpose desalting plants was enormously costly. What could be better, it seemed, than to build dual-purpose nuclear plants to produce the electricity vitally needed for development and the water with which to make the deserts bloom. More was promised. After the 1967 war, former Atomic Energy Commission Chairman Lewis L. Strauss and President Eisenhower suggested that a massive investment in nuclear desalting could advance peace. The Strauss plan envisioned three large nuclear desalting plants to provide water for arid areas of Egypt, Jordan, and Israel. He asserted that the "shortage of water is a fundamental basis of rivalry, hatred and war in the Middle East" and that eliminating this shortage with his plan could supply "the new and dramatic element . . . required to establish a climate in which peace can begin to be negotiated." As for the dangers of advancing the capacity of these countries to acquire nuclear explosives, he merely suggested that the operation of the plants be made the responsibility of the IAEA, which would control reprocessing activities "to ensure that all nuclear material was accounted for."[18]

16. To illustrate the longevity of this family of ideas, recent proposals have been made to build nuclear power reactors in a demilitarized zone in the Sinai. As with earlier schemes, the connection between such a project and peace between the parties is far from clear. Such a proposal was made by Professor Shimon Yiftah, a member of Israel's Atomic Energy Commission. *Jewish Telegraph Daily News Bulletin,* December 5, 1977.

17. Speech delivered to the First International Symposium on Water Desalination, Washington, D.C., October 6, 1965.

18. *Construction of Nuclear Desalting Plants in the Middle East,* Hearings before the Senate Committee on Foreign Relations, 90 Cong. 1 sess. (Government Printing Office, 1967), pp. 58, 60.

The project initially investigated, as a result of a meeting between President Johnson and Israeli Premier Levi Eshkol in 1964, was for a plant producing 100 million gallons a day. (The later Strauss proposal called for larger plants.) In the same year a U.S. team examined the proposal for the similar Borg el-Arab project in Egypt. The 1967 war pushed these projects into the background.

The initial Israeli plant would have cost at least $200 million (in 1965 dollars); the Strauss plan plants at least $1 billion (also in 1965 dollars), probably more than the cost of the Aswan Dam. But they would have provided less than 10 percent as much water as Aswan.

The cost estimates were ludicrous. Strauss used a figure of 22 cents per 1,000 gallons, a figure apparently taken from a proposed large nuclear desalting plant in southern California that later experienced an estimated capital cost increase of 72 percent before being abandoned in 1968. The Kaiser report on the Israeli plant proposed by Johnson and Eshkol estimated costs as low as 28.6 cents per 1,000 gallons, using an average 85 percent capacity factor. Actual experience with nuclear reactors (without desalting plants) has been closer to 60 percent. (These cost estimates were for water at the plant, not water delivered to users— a considerable difference.) The 28.6 cents per 1,000 gallons Kaiser estimated was calculated at an interest rate of 1.6 percent. Wolfowitz estimated water costs of $1 per 1,000 gallons at an 8.4 percent interest rate, close to the rate used by the Israeli government for development projects. This rate is, of course, low for any country and especially for a country in Israel's stage of development. For Egypt an even higher discount rate and water costs would apply. Wolfowitz further observed that the cost of water from existing sources in the Middle East was very much less; an Israeli estimate was 11 to 19 cents per 1,000 gallons, with 11 cents corresponding to the more relevant market price. For Egypt he calculated a cost of no more than 5 cents per 1,000 gallons. In short, there was an estimated ten- to twentyfold disparity in costs between existing sources of water and water obtained by nuclear desalting.

Nonetheless, the large, 440-megawatt (electric) reactor Libya is reported to be getting from the Soviet Union is dual purpose, for electricity production and desalinization.[19] There are probably cheaper sources of water than desalinization in others of these countries besides Egypt

19. *Wall Street Journal,* October 4, 1978.

(Kuwait being a likely exception), and there are certainly cheaper sources of energy available for desalting plants than nuclear energy. Dual-purpose, gas-fired electricity-producing and water-desalinization plants, though probably uneconomic, would certainly be less so than the proposed nuclear plants.

The Shortage of Trained People

Nowhere else in the world is the gap between economic infrastructure, including human capital, and command over financial resources as great as in the Arab countries. It is the consequence of the rapid acquisition of great wealth by developing societies and means that much can be acquired by purchase but far less through internal technical development. This results in the Arabs being able to buy many of the most modern arms but to lag in the ability to use them. The problem is partially met by employing foreign technicians. At the peak in Egypt in 1970–72 there were apparently as many as 15,000 Soviet military and technical personnel. Sizable numbers have also been reported in Syria, Libya, and Iraq. Large numbers of U.S. technicians are active in Saudi Arabia. Despite this technological lag, though, Egyptian and Syrian forces performed more effectively than was expected by Israel or the West in the October 1973 war.

The Arab countries, of course, differ significantly in their capacity to use modern weapons, at least on a large scale. Egypt has a much larger body of indigenous technicians than Saudi Arabia does, for instance. The Arabs also lag in the training of people in the particular fields that are central to developments in nuclear explosives and their use: physics, nuclear chemistry, chemical engineering, and the like. Although comprehensive data are not available, an indication of the interest and degree of preparation in these fields can be derived from the participation of foreign scientists in U.S. AEC research (see table 10-1). The numbers are small for the Arab countries; moreover, it is by no means clear that most of those trained have returned to their countries; they may have found better opportunities in the West. However, with the expansion of nuclear programs in their own countries and with adequate financial incentives, many may return. In any case, it seems likely that much larger numbers of scientists and engineers will be trained in the coming years,

Table 10-1. *Participation of Scientists from Countries Outside the Soviet Bloc in U.S. Atomic Energy Research from 1955 to 1976*

Country	Number of scientists	Country	Number of scientists
Afghanistan	3	*Jordan*	7
Argentina	192	Kenya	2
Australia	164	Korea	195
Austria	179	*Kuwait*	2
Belgium	176	*Lebanon*	31
Bolivia	14	*Libya*	3
Brazil	133	Liechtenstein	2
Burma	14	Luxembourg	6
Cameroon	1	Malaysia	16
Canada	539	Mexico	104
Ceylon	12	Monaco	2
Chile	70	*Morocco*	2
China, Republic of	713	Netherlands	216
Colombia	86	Norway	101
Congo	8	*Pakistan*	120
Costa Rica	11	Panama	14
Cuba	28	Paraguay	11
Cyprus	10	Peru	41
Denmark	96	Philippines	118
Dominican Republic	33	Portugal	26
Ecuador	13	*Saudi Arabia*	3
El Salvador	12	Senegal	1
Ethiopia	7	Sierra Leone	1
Finland	41	Singapore	3
France	471	South Africa	88
Germany	833	South Vietnam	23
Ghana	10	Spain	139
Greece	159	Sweden	180
Guatemala	16	Switzerland	229
Guyana	5	Tanzania	3
Haiti	11	Thailand	70
Honduras	1	Trinidad	6
Hong Kong	59	*Tunisia*	3
Iceland	9	Turkey	108
India	1,104	Uganda	1
Indonesia	34	*United Arab Republic*	103
Iran	73	United Kingdom	1,186
Iraq	24	Uruguay	22
Ireland	32	Venezuela	59
Israel	250	Yugoslavia	106
Italy	693	Zambia	3
Jamaica	15		
Japan	803	Total	10,513

Source: *S. 1439: Export Reorganization Act of 1976*, Hearings before the Joint Committee on Atomic Energy, 94 Cong. 2 sess. (Government Printing Office, 1976), vol. 1, p. 463.

and patriotism, pan-Arabism, the depression in the West's nuclear industry, and new Arab oil wealth may induce many to work at home.

Prospects for an Arab Cooperative Nuclear Program

In the absence of a substantial cadre of people highly trained in the relevant disciplines or of the necessary technical infrastructure in the individual Arab states, some sort of multinational cooperation seems attractive. However, several factors work against a combined effort. Perhaps most important is the instability of relations among the Arab states. They have cooperated intermittently in opposing Israel, but even on this issue their cooperation has been of relatively brief duration and limited effectiveness. The October 1973 war is perhaps the best example of this. Despite unprecedented pan-Arab cooperation during 1973–74, the two Sinai accords had split the moderate and rejectionist camps by 1975. A year later, even the radicals in Syria, Iraq, and the Palestine Liberation Organization were bickering among themselves.

A distinctive characteristic of a complex high-technology program is the years of preparation necessary. Thus more indicative for a cooperative nuclear weapons project than the all-Arab effort in the 1973 war was the Arab armies' inability to work effectively together in peacetime to develop coordinated doctrines and command procedures.

Another factor may be the expectation of limited immediate return from joint efforts. As an early twentieth century Egyptian politician reacted to the whole pan-Arab movement, "zero plus zero equals zero."[20] While this is an exaggeration of a prospective Arab nuclear capability, it is not totally without application. The problem is not only one of not having enough money, population, or even highly educated people. Rather it is a lack anywhere in the Arab world of a strong technical foundation of trained personnel, major research institutions, and substantial experience with nuclear technology. This leaves them at a disadvantage regardless of how they combine their assets. Of course, these countries are beginning to build such a nuclear foundation, and a group could develop it more easily and quickly perhaps than any individual Arab state. The point is, however, that at the starting point, how much

20. Nadav Safran, *From War to War: The Arab-Israeli Confrontation, 1948–1967, A Study of the Conflict from the Perspective of Coercion in the Context of Inter-Arab and Big Power Relations* (Pegasus, 1969), p. 63.

is to be gained by joining their present modest competencies may be questioned.

A third obstacle is that there are costs in doing things jointly. British and French experience with the Concorde, U.S. and West German experience with the MBT-70 tank program, and recent NATO experience in joint production of F-16 fighters show how multinational programs can add to costs. Moreover, unless the Arabs prove to be mutually trusting, the nuclear facilities are unlikely to be concentrated in one country. In the World War II cooperation on the atom bomb, Britain and Canada, partners of the United States in the Manhattan project, were excluded from some aspects; in 1946 Britain was cut off from the technology and facilities it had helped develop without having itself gotten any weapons out of it. More recently, Britain and France each insisted on assembling Concordes, at great cost. A similar dispersion of facilities among several Arab states would mean either duplication (cutting down sharply on the advantages of a combined program) or mutual dependence that would be vulnerable to dropouts or denials. Despite those prospective problems, some sort of cooperative arrangement might provide several advantages and perhaps some of the pitfalls could be avoided.

One asset of some of the Arab nations with small technological skills is the large amount of liquid capital (in two senses) in the oil-rich states. These states have in the past shown themselves willing to financially support the military efforts of their more technologically and militarily capable fellow Arab states, principally Egypt, Syria, and Jordan (as well as the Palestinians). Moreover, even if the money cannot easily flow from those rich in funds to those rich in skills, the skilled people can go to the money. There has been a stream of trained personnel into the oil-rich states—often those who received their training in the military programs of the confrontation states. The flow of Palestinians is notable in this regard. One of the most highly educated Arab groups, the Palestinians provide much of the technical infrastructure for the Gulf coast Arabs. Another example is the role of Egyptians in Libya. Despite the ups and downs in relations between the two states, Libya has continued to operate its economy with large numbers of Egyptian technicians.[21]

Another possibility would be cooperation among a smaller group such

21. A hint of this is given by the background of a Mr. Elmeshad reported murdered in Paris—he was a French-trained Egyptian nuclear scientist working for Iraq. *New York Times,* June 18, 1980.

as Egypt, Saudi Arabia, and other conservative states. The Persian Gulf Arabs have surplus capital and Egypt has a large share of the technological capability of the Arab world. Perhaps as important, this coalition has existed, in effect, since 1973, with the oil-producing states supplying funds for Egyptian military efforts. More directly analogous to nuclear cooperation and showing its pitfalls were efforts to set up joint facilities for the production of conventional weapons in Egypt. The Arab Organization for Industrialization, as it was called, always produced more plans than tangible accomplishments. Contracts were recently signed for factories to produce antitank missiles, helicopters, and jeeps.[22] More ambitious intentions for equipment manufacturing were reportedly in the works. Recently Saudi Arabia announced plans for the building of a "missile city." However, Gulf Arab financial support of Egyptian industry has collapsed as a result of the divisions caused by Sadat's peace moves.

A possible development would be industrial cooperation extended to include nuclear activities: research, fabrication of fuel rods, storage of spent fuel, or, in time, reprocessing or enrichment. If this pattern were to emerge, there might be no overt Arab cooperation in making weapons, only in making nuclear explosive materials. The final stages of development and construction might be left to the individual states.[23]

An Arab nuclear program might also involve scientists and technicians trained in any of the several programs offered by the major nuclear supplier states—both in the Arab countries themselves and in the supplier states. U.S. programs alone have trained Middle Eastern students from Israel, Egypt, Iran, Iraq, Jordan, Kuwait, Lebanon, Libya, Morocco, Saudi Arabia, Tunisia, and Turkey (see table 10-1). Foreign technicians could also be directly involved, at least in the openly civilian part of the

22. *Aviation Week and Space Technology* (May 15, 1978), pp. 14–16.

23. It has been proposed that the parts of the nuclear fuel cycle (such as enrichment and reprocessing facilities) most easily converted to the production of readily fissionable nuclear explosive materials be located in fuel centers in weapons states, with only nonexplosive materials being distributed widely. This nonproliferation proposal would be defeated if the centers shipped out materials such as mixed oxide (plutonium and uranium) fuel and highly enriched uranium, which were immediately usable in explosives or with a little reworking could be so used. Proposals that such centers be located in "politically stable" states instead of weapons states face the difficulty that, while the distinction between the states with weapons and those without has received wide acceptance, the politically "stable" and "nonstable" distinction has not won such endorsement and is unlikely to.

programs. Foreign aid might be available for obtaining fissionable material from which the Arabs themselves could fashion weapons. Most directly this could mean shipping either highly enriched uranium or plutonium to the Arabs. The Osiris type of research reactor, with which the French are supplying Iraq, has been mentioned, and both Britain and France are negotiating contracts involving the export of plutonium to other countries. Outsiders also might supply Arab countries with their own plants for making either separated plutonium from spent fuel or, eventually, enriched uranium.

It should be noted that in all likelihood any substantial future aid from the major supplier states to the Arabs will be under safeguards to discourage their use in nuclear explosives—probably under IAEA supervision (though the French in an earlier time helped Israel build its unsafeguarded Dimona reactor). Several factors would affect a country's perception of the costs of violating safeguards agreements; these include the urgency of its security needs at the time, the sanctions it is likely to face, and the time necessary to develop the weapon after the violation. The likelihood of sanctions being imposed as a result of an Arab violation of nuclear safeguards must be considered in the light of the prospect of sanctions imposed on the oil supply by the Arabs. Perhaps relevant are the lengths to which the United States went to avoid calling the Indian use of U.S. materials in their bomb program a violation of American bilateral safeguard agreements. Canada, in contrast, blew the whistle on India.[24]

Possible Third World Nuclear Suppliers

With the continued spread of nuclear technology, an increasing number of countries besides the ones that have weapons have developed substantial nuclear capability. This enables these nuclear-capable states to export their nuclear expertise. The most important example of this is West Germany, which has become a leading exporter of reactors and plans to export reprocessing and enrichment facilities to Brazil. Also, some countries in the third world, though not commercially competitive with the industrial states, could greatly aid an Arab nuclear program. Some are already doing so. Any state with a reactor, including Egypt

24. Wohlstetter, *'The Bhudda Smiles,'* p. 123.

Table 10-2. *Third World Nuclear Export Capabilities*[a]

Country	Bomb design	Enrichment services	Enrichment technology	Reprocessing services	Reprocessing technology	Reactors
India	C	...	...	C	C	C
Pakistan	...	P	P	P[b]	P[b]	...
Argentina	...	...	...	...	...	(C)[c]
Brazil	...	(P)	...	(P)	...	...
South Africa	...	C	C	...	...	...
Israel	?[d]	?[d]	?[d]	C	C	...

a. C = current; P = planned; ( ) = safeguarded (not legally exportable without the nuclear supplier state's permission).

b. The French-Pakistani contract for building the reprocessing plant was canceled after the bulk of the blueprints, though not several components, were transferred. The project's current status is unclear.

c. Argentina has signed an agreement to build a small research reactor for Peru. *Nuclear News*, vol. 20 (Mid-April 1977), p. 90B. See also *Nucleonics Week*, vol. 19 (May 11, 1978), p. 11.

d. A document recently released by the CIA reports: "We believe that Israel has produced nuclear weapons" and that Israel has conducted "ambiguous" efforts in enrichment. *Prospects for Further Proliferation of Nuclear Weapons*, DCI-N10-1945-74, September 4, 1974.

and Iraq, can be a minimal exporter, for example, by providing training in reactor operations or by supplying unreprocessed plutonium. The third world states shown in table 10-2, however, have a much greater capability.

Pakistan is the most probable source of such aid because of the political and religious ties between the Arabs and the Pakistanis. India may also hope to gain from selling certain nuclear technologies to oil-rich Arabs. Both Pakistan and India have already begun to assist Arab nuclear programs.

Pakistan currently provides training. Pakistanis emigrated to Iran to join that country's nuclear program, and an Arab nuclear program would be likely to attract similar or greater participation—especially since many Pakistanis are already in the Gulf Arab states as both civilian and military technical personnel.

Pakistan's special importance as a potential helper to Arab nuclear programs derives from its persistent effort to become capable of producing nuclear material that can be used in weapons. Its first effort was an attempt to buy a plutonium-reprocessing plant from the French. At the urging of the United States the French canceled this deal in 1978, though reportedly the Pakistanis intend to try to complete it. More recently it was revealed that Pakistan is covertly developing a centrifuge uranium-enrichment capability. Apparently a Pakistani once employed in the Anglo-Dutch-German centrifuge consortium directed purchases of components for, and now heads, the Pakistani centrifuge program. Before these purchases were stopped (which, notably, was several months after they were discovered by the British), sufficient equipment may have been bought for a significant enrichment capability. Some press reports state that bomb quantities of highly enriched uranium may be produced within three to five years.[25]

Although under Pakistan's old agreement with France to purchase a reprocessing facility the plant would have been under safeguards, they contained a major hole: the Pakistanis were free to export plutonium or even the design of the reprocessing plant to anyone—so long as that plutonium or a new plant was safeguarded.[26] The indigenous Pakistani development of enrichment or reprocessing now contemplated would be, of course, subject to no safeguards.

Moreover, the Arabs apparently have been involved in Pakistan's atomic efforts. Whether their involvement extended to Pakistan's enrichment effort, currently its main line of development, it was widely reported that they offered funding of the planned French-supplied reprocessing plant. These reports came immediately after France's initial effort to brake the reprocessing plant deal by holding up export credit guarantees.[27] Arab support reportedly followed attempts by Pakistani President Ali Bhutto to convince the Arabs of the danger they faced from a unilateral Israeli nuclear capability: "The Arabs would be unable to get nuclear know-how from the U.S., Bhutto successfully argued, but given the funds Pakistan could supply it. As a result, the UAE [United Arab Emirates] financed a small fuel reprocessing plant capable of producing plutonium—which is now the bone of contention."[28] Bhutto commented that his objectives in seeking a "full nuclear capability" were not limited to Pakistan's narrow interests. "We know that Israel and South Africa have full nuclear capability. The Christian, Jewish and Hindu

25. Don Oberdorfer, "Pakistan: The Quest for Atomic Bomb," *Washington Post,* August 27, 1979.

26. "The Text of the Safeguards Agreement of 18 March 1976 Between the Agency, France and Pakistan," *IAEA Information Circular,* no. 239 (June 22, 1976), p. 5, article 11.

27. *Nucleonics Week,* vol. 18 (June 9, 1977), pp. 2–3; and ibid. (June 16, 1977), p. 5.

28. Salamat Ali, "Zia's Search for Parity," *Far East Economic Review* (January 6, 1978), p. 43.

civilisations have this capability. The Communist powers also possess it. Only the Islamic civilisation was without it, but that position was about to change."[29]

Pakistan has an economic incentive to aid an Arab weapons program: it is among the world's poorest countries and depends on receiving oil at a subsidized price. Another motive is Pakistan's competition with India. In trying to obtain Arab political support, Pakistan might provide nuclear aid on pan-Islamic grounds. It should be recognized, however, that Pakistan's dominant motive for seeking nuclear weapons is probably concern about its national security in relation to India. And the Arabs may also be an important source of conventional arms in exchange (a process that has already begun).[30] If India should move ahead with an expanded nuclear weapons program, a combined Arab-Pakistani nuclear weapons effort (adding Arab money and diplomatic strength to Pakistani skills and facilities) might seem mutually beneficial.

India is also currently training Arab nuclear technicians. India is in perhaps the best position of any third world nuclear supplier to aid an Arab program. It has proven ability to separate plutonium, build nuclear devices, and build reactors. Thus India could give the Arabs anything, from their own nuclear infrastructure to completed weapons, with little constraint from existing safeguard arrangements.

While less likely than Pakistani support, Indian support of an Arab nuclear program has a basis as well. For example, during the Indo-Pakistani war, military supplies were flown from Egypt to India. India has also been helping to train the Iraqi air force and overhaul Egypt's naval craft. To be sure, much of the mutual aid developed out of these three states' one-time joint involvement as Soviet allies—a condition no longer true, at least temporarily, for Egypt.

India, like Pakistan, may have an economic incentive. India, too, is quite poor, and offers to buy nuclear technology, perhaps free of safeguards, might be very attractive. As with Pakistan, a flow of trained nuclear technicians is probable if the Arabs offer high pay. Indian competition with Pakistan as well as India's aspiration to be leader of the third world might also be motives. This would be analogous to the 1955

29. *Financial Times* (London), October 5, 1978.
30. *Defense and Foreign Affairs Handbook, 1975–76* (Washington, D.C.: Copley and Associates), reported the deployment of Kuwaiti fighters to Pakistan. During the 1971 Indo-Pakistani war, Saudi Arabia provided Pakistan with arms and funds.

Soviet move to gain influence in the Middle East by massively breaking the tripartite group's limits on arms transfers to the area—probably with similarly destabilizing results. On the other hand, India has several cross-cutting motives that would make its helping an Arab bomb program less likely. The Indians may fear that helping the Arabs will eventually redound to Pakistan's benefit. Moreover, any moves by India to aid another state's nuclear weapons program, particularly more overt and direct ones, are likely to anger and provoke substantial pressure from the great powers.

Other third world states that will be in a position to aid an Arab nuclear program are Argentina, Brazil, and South Africa. As time goes on, this list is likely to grow longer. Argentina, Brazil, and South Africa all have a much less direct interest in what goes on in the Middle East than either India or Pakistan does. The economic motive may apply, of course, at both the national and subnational levels. One of these nations might elect to support a "civilian Arab program" as a way of evading possible constraints by the suppliers. Or there might be more direct support for an Arab military nuclear effort.

Argentina already deals with India on nuclear matters and Argentinians (including the former president of the Argentine Atomic Energy Commission) were involved in Iran's nuclear program.[31] Among third world nuclear-capable states, only Argentina has announced plans for substantial nuclear export by signing an agreement to build a research reactor for Peru.

Brazil's agreement with Germany would inhibit Brazilian aid to an Arab program. However, the maintenance of safeguards is a matter of will, not capability, and the options of Germany and the world for restraining a change in Brazilian policy would be limited once the full fuel cycle was in place. Unlike Argentina, Brazil will be able to produce highly enriched uranium. Brazil is already developing a nuclear technology supply relationship with Iraq—the Arab state that currently seems to be most actively pursuing the nuclear option.[32] The exact extent and limits of this cooperation are not clear, but since Brazil is receiving technical support from West Germany on reprocessing and enrichment

31. Zalmay Khalilzad, *Iran: The Nuclear Option*, report prepared for the U.S. Energy Research and Development Administration (Los Angeles: Pan Heuristics, 1977), p. 9.
32. "Brazil, Iraq Sign Nuclear Pact," *Baltimore Sun*, January 8, 1980.

technologies, it hardly bodes well and is particularly ominous in light of a Brazilian-Iraqi exchange of arms for oil.[33]

South Africa's enrichment technology gives it the ability to aid others by building enrichment plants for them, by providing highly enriched (weapons grade) uranium, or by providing the low enriched uranium for power reactors. While low enriched uranium cannot be used directly to make weapons, a cutoff of low enriched fuel is one of the sanctions with which the nuclear powers have threatened would-be acquirers of nuclear explosives. South Africa's ties to Israel make its helping the Arabs unlikely. This cooperation is not only based on the similarities of their positions of isolation, but may also be influenced by the existence of the influential South African Jewish community. Nevertheless, a future South African–conservative Arab alliance is not impossible, although there would have to be major changes for South Africa to be a source of nuclear technology for the Arabs.

NPT Status

Although several countries in the region have signed and ratified the nonproliferation treaty, many have not, including some of the most important ones. The following table shows the current status:

Country	Signed	Ratified
Algeria	No	No
Egypt	Yes	No
Iran	Yes	Yes
Iraq	Yes	Yes
Israel	No	No
Jordan	Yes	Yes
Lebanon	Yes	Yes
Libya	Yes	Yes
Morocco	Yes	Yes
Saudi Arabia	No	No
Sudan	Yes	Yes
Syria	Yes	Yes (with disclaimer)
Tunisia	Yes	Yes
Yemen, North	Yes	No
Yemen, South	Yes	No

33. "Brazil Cutting U.S. Influence," *New York Times,* January 17, 1980.

Israel's justification for not signing or ratifying the treaty is, officially, that it fears insufficient protection from Arab violation and, unofficially, that it needs to keep its options open. Israeli spokesmen have said that Israel will not be the first to introduce nuclear weapons into the Middle East but also that it will not be the second. The NPT, which provides for only ninety days' notification of withdrawal, could be seen as interfering with Israel's flexibility. Adherence to the treaty would mean accepting IAEA inspection of its currently unsafeguarded nuclear facilities.

Among the confrontation Arab states, only Jordan and Lebanon have adhered to the treaty without reservation; Syria has done so but with a disclaimer,[34] and Egypt has not completed ratification on grounds of Israeli nonadherence. Two militant Arab states, Libya and Iraq, have both signed and ratified the treaty. Saudi Arabia—generally regarded as moderate—has done neither.

Objectives, Types, and Costs of Possible Nuclear Forces

Possible nuclear weapons programs could have several broad objectives, although they might shift with time and changing circumstances. These objectives are mixed and might include the following:

—To prevent the nation from being overrun; this is the basic Israeli concern.

—More loosely, to discourage a major attack. For the Israelis particularly, to discourage one that threatened their pre-1967 borders. The Arab countries might see nuclear weapons as preventing major Israeli attacks and, especially, capture of their capitals.

—To discourage the use of nuclear weapons by adversaries; also to deter the use of chemical or biological agents.

—To get "more punch for the pound." This argument is attractive to some Israelis who believe either that Israel is disadvantaged in the long run in the nonnuclear competition or that nuclearization would relieve Israel of an excessive defense burden.[35] (Perhaps the "more punch for the pound" argument could win adherents to the Egyptian pound.)

---

34. That their signing the treaty did not mean that they recognized all the other signatories. This is a fairly common device in multilateral treaties—presumably directed in this case against the possibility that Israel might later sign also. It would not affect Syrian responsibilities under the treaty.

35. Aronson, "Israel's Nuclear Option," pp. 30–32.

—To reduce dependence on support from outsiders (such as Israel's dependence on the United States and Iraq's and Syria's dependence on the Soviet Union).

—To use the threat of developing nuclear weapons to elicit conventional arms from suppliers; for instance, by Israel from the United States. Used as an explicit bargaining tactic, this is risky for it might provoke a hostile reaction. On the other hand, the inherent logic of a situation might be that if a regional ally was weak at the nonnuclear level it would have to rely on its nuclear option willy-nilly.[36]

As goals favoring restraint or at least discretion, to be avoided are the following:

—Stimulating opponents to develop nuclear forces themselves or to invest more heavily in them. This is a principal reason that Israel is not more explicit about having a nuclear force and not conducting nuclear tests. Such restraint could also be the result of concern about the reaction of allies.

—Coercing adversaries.

The urgency with which these objectives are pursued is a function of the state of tension between adversaries. For example, if the current treaty between Egypt and Israel results in reduced tension, these objectives will recede in importance.

If, however, a nation acquired nuclear weapons, a wide range of specific missions and levels of capabilities might be chosen. First, mere possession of one or a few devices as a threat to enemy cities might be seen as enough—even with a vulnerable delivery capability. Against a nuclear-equipped adversary, this sort of posture could be suicidal and would also produce preemptive instability.

Second, a likely goal would be a somewhat more secure strike force. The lowest level would be a minimal force of weapons (two to ten) with a protected delivery capacity. The requirements for a secure force—particularly a small one—are difficult to meet, and having a protected force can never be assured. The minimal force might be expanded and planned for use against a number of cities, as in the assured destruction doctrine, or against military targets. A capacity to destroy a given frac-

36. "It was feared that excessive pressure on Israel, such as withholding conventional arms, might accelerate Israel's search for a nuclear option." William B. Quandt, *Decade of Decisions: American Policy Toward the Arab-Israeli Conflict, 1967–1976* (University of California Press, 1977), p. 80.

tion of the opponent's population and economy or to prevent or impair recovery after attack might be sought. For instance, the fiscal year 1978 report of the secretary of defense identified several possible missions: attack on military forces and critical industries, and an assured destruction mission. Alternatively, assured retaliation might be sought with a capacity to prevent or retard opponents' military, political, or economic recovery from a nuclear exchange. The planning objectives cited were to aim directly at military forces and critical industries and to slow recovery.[37]

The small, concentrated populations and economies of most of the Middle East countries would require relatively small numbers of *delivered* weapons. But the demands of even a small force that could survive a well-designed and well-executed enemy attack are heavy, especially when the crucial and difficult problem of maintaining responsible and protected command and control is taken into account.

Third, a more ambitious force goal analogous to that of the current nuclear powers would be to add a protected capacity to use nuclear weapons on the battlefield or against targets directly related to combat operations in the rear. Possible forward targets include troop concentrations massed for breakthrough attempts, headquarters, and logistic facilities. Such use might be limited to one's own territory to block invasion or it might be extended to targets located in a "shallow" zone across the border, such as airfields. This case would be similar to the Israeli attacks on Egyptian SAM sites and other facilities beyond the Suez Canal in 1970 (exclusive of the deeper Israeli attacks on the Helwan area). In another variant, use might be extended to war-related targets anywhere in the opponent's territory, including factories for war production. The Israeli attack on the Homs refinery in Syria in 1973 falls into this category.

In all the variants of this third case, the nuclear forces could be designed to satisfy the dual criteria of achieving a given level of target damage while minimizing collateral civilian damage. This would mean emphasizing good targeting data, high accuracy, and yields tailored to the characteristics of targets. An understanding could also be sought on avoiding attack on civilian populations, although how well such an agreement would stand up in the heat of war is uncertain. This case

---

37. *Annual Defense Department Report, FY 1978*, pp. 67–68.

would probably include a protected force held in reserve for possible follow-up missions and to discourage opponents' attacks on one's own population.

These different missions imply different levels of expenditure on nuclear forces and related systems. A small, vulnerable force would not be costly—at least in resources, although other high costs would probably be incurred. These other costs would depend largely on the international reaction. If nuclear weapons were acquired in violation of existing agreements or if acquisition were to set off nuclear weapons efforts, or even an attack, by other regional countries, the costs could be very high.

As noted, under the present rules highly enriched uranium or separated plutonium is available legitimately. With this sort of material, the direct economic cost of having a device amounts to that of designing and building the nonnuclear components. If a program of testing, delivery systems, and basing are excluded, a budget of only a few million dollars a year for several years might be enough. But the posture would be risky.

In contrast, if international rules or practice precluded a country's access to enriched uranium or readily separable plutonium, an investment of about $50 million would be needed.[38] Together with other costs (possibly including those of operating power reactors inefficiently if such reactors were the chosen source of the explosive material), this might mean a direct economic cost of around $10 million a year or more.

The direct economic cost would be far greater with the much more demanding requirements for having protected delivery systems able to penetrate to target. Missiles in silos are vulnerable to accurate attack. The short warning times in the area make it necessary to maintain aircraft on alert, which is costly, prone to launch based on mistaken information, and unlikely to be adequate especially against a sudden missile attack. Submarine-based missiles in quiet electric submarines would be hard to detect, but they are expensive and they are not necessarily invulnerable. Land-mobile missiles are expensive to keep in operation, and their approximate locations may be detectable too; if so, attack with high-yield weapons, able to cover large areas with low overpressures, might destroy them.

A force designed to deliver five weapons on target might necessitate the possession of, say, twenty to thirty delivery vehicles against an adver-

38. Wohlstetter and others, *Swords from Plowshares*, pp. 196ff.

sary with moderate nuclear surprise attack competency (allowing for submarines or ships in port, mobile missiles at bases, bomb-equipped aircraft not on alert, and so forth). Against a more sophisticated adversary, the surviving force may be less; for example, if the attack were made by a great power with advanced sensing and attack capabilities, the surviving force might be zero. In any case, such a force would cost several hundred million dollars a year to build and operate.[39]

By comparison, the dedicated nuclear force of the French, which has eighteen fixed land-based intermediate-range missiles in silos, sixty-four submarine-based missiles, thirty-three Mirage IVA bombers (plus others in reserve, together with tankers, reconnaissance aircraft, and so on), and thirty-two short-range Pluton missiles, apparently costs $3 billion annually.[40]

What do these costs imply for the "more punch for the pound" argument? Defense budgets for Israel and Egypt are currently around $3.5 billion; for Syria, $2 billion; for Jordan, $380 million; for Iraq, $2 billion; and for Saudi Arabia, $14.1 billion.[41] Saudi Arabia is also helping to finance Jordan's and Syria's defense budgets. A very small force with some measure of protection is within the means of most of these countries, but a larger force designed for low vulnerability and wider capability would require the resources of the countries with the larger defense budgets. Moreover, either the defense burden would be higher or the nuclear forces would be built at the expense of nonnuclear ones. In the latter case, the capability to deal with the more likely, lower level contingencies would be reduced. Also, demands on nuclear forces escalate

39. Including provisions for warning systems, communication, local protection of nuclear forces, and personnel to operate on a high alert state, an annual system cost of around $10 million or more per vehicle is a plausible overall benchmark figure for dedicated nuclear delivery systems. When relevant indirect costs are included, this is approximately the U.S. cost per "strategic vehicle." Although its requirements are arguably much greater than those of a small nuclear power, the United States also benefits importantly from economies of scale. By contrast, the French pay an estimated $20 million to $30 million per vehicle dedicated to nuclear delivery (see footnote 40).

40. The numbers of weapons are taken from International Institute for Strategic Studies, *The Military Balance, 1978–1979* (London: IISS, 1978), p. 24, and do not include dual-capable tactical strike craft. Nuclear-related costs for the French are reported to be 14 percent of their $21 billion defense budget. *Los Angeles Times,* September 27, 1979.

41. IISS, *The Military Balance, 1978–1979.*

with changes in opponents' technology and forces. Continuing work—and expense—would be needed to keep the vulnerability of forces low (assuming that this objective had been met initially) and to maintain surveillance, targeting, and command and control.

Does this imply an ever-escalating nuclear arms race in the region? Budgets *are* limited and needs for nonnuclear forces will continue. In the mutual assured destruction view popular in the West, including a variant put forward by French General Pierre Gallois that universal distribution of nuclear weapons would have a generally stabilizing effect, all that is needed is the simple ability to deliver a few bombs—or even only one—on opposing populations.[42] But this theory has fatal defects. If it is rejected, although the capability for attacking cities will remain, tasks relating to military forces and bases and perhaps war-related facilities will dominate. Such a set of tasks is not unbounded since a protected capacity—for example, to block invasion paths with nuclear weapons—might be defined (although this is not easy to do in a region in which invasion routes are not channeled). Nonetheless, the pressure for increasing expenditures on nuclear forces could be powerful: to reduce vulnerability, to increase selectivity (for instance, the dual criteria of being militarily effective while avoiding damage to populations), and to increase the number of weapons deliverable on target.

Nuclear-Relevant Delivery Capabilities

Several nuclear-capable delivery systems exist in the Middle East today. Any nation with civil jet aircraft has this capability—though not necessarily the ability to penetrate reliably to target. Also, Libya, Syria, Iraq, and Egypt have Soviet Scud missiles that can hit all of Israel from currently held Arab territory. (The range for the Scud missile is estimated to be either 50 or 135 miles, depending on the type.) However, nuclear warheads carried by these missiles—or by fighter-bombers—would have to be a good deal lighter than those carried by civil jet aircraft. Syria, Iraq, and Egypt, as well as Algeria, also have various versions of the shorter range nuclear-capable FROG rocket. The Israelis are reported to have developed the Jericho ballistic missile with an esti-

42. Pierre Gallois, *The Balance of Terror: Strategy for the Nuclear Age,* Richard Howard, trans. (Houghton Mifflin, 1961).

mated range of 280 to 300 miles.[43] They are known to have ordered non-nuclear versions of the (dual-purpose nonnuclear or nuclear-armed) Lance missile with a range of 70 miles.

Despite the advantages of mobile missiles in dispersal, concealment, and penetration of active defenses, aircraft have the potential for greater range, can generally carry larger or heavier nuclear weapons (which may be important at an early stage in a weapons program), and, with the technology that has been available for some time to many Middle Eastern countries, are likely to be more accurate. Aircraft are also dual-capable weapons, usable for nonnuclear as well as nuclear delivery. Long-range delivery may be particularly important for the Israelis, who have far to travel before reaching their distant adversaries. Extending Israel's capabilities in this direction are its KC-130H aerial tankers, which can potentially at least double the combat radius of Israeli F-4s, which, without refueling, is up to 600 miles.

Nonnuclear weapons of mass destruction may also play a role in the area. Egypt is reported to have used chemical warfare against the Yemeni royalists during the civil war in Yemen.[44] If Egypt now actually has stockpiles of gas or the capability for making them, its Scuds or aircraft could effectively deliver the gas against populations.[45] Israel, with its greater degree of air control, could probably repay any such damage many times over with either nuclear or chemical weapons. But the threat of Scuds with chemical warheads might seem useful to the Arabs against Israeli exploitation of a nuclear force advantage.

Control of Arab Nuclear Forces

A central factor is the control of nuclear weapons and forces. With the enormous stakes and the uncertain consequences of the use of nuclear weapons, this is a difficult problem for a single government. It is

43. Steven J. Rosen, "A Stable System of Mutual Nuclear Deterrence in the Arab-Israeli Conflict," *American Political Science Review*, vol. 71 (December 1977), p. 1376, n. 64.

44. International Institute for Strategic Studies, *Strategic Survey, 1967* (London: IISS, 1968), p. 38.

45. "Egypt Asserts New Military Strength," *Washington Post*, July 14, 1977.

even more difficult in an alliance, whose members inevitably differ in interests, competency, and vulnerability. Evidence of this is NATO, which has three nuclear powers, each of which has reserved the right to decide on the use of nuclear weapons in accordance with its national interests and constitutional processes. The problem of coordinating the use of nuclear weapons under such circumstances is formidable. The NATO multilateral force proposed in the early 1960s was an ambitious effort to create a nuclear force intended to be more than a set of co-operating national nuclear forces. It failed for several reasons, including the impossibility of defining an acceptable control system. Had the concept been pursued, it seems likely that the force would have been subject to multiple vetoes of its use and would therefore have lacked credibility.

The assumption that the Arabs might, or should, create a single command is, of course, quite inconsistent with the Gallois theory, which holds that each nation must have its own independent power of decision on the use of nuclear weapons. Moreover, given the history of differences among the Arabs, whatever cooperative arrangements might be made would probably not last. Even without such differences, since life or death for millions or tens of millions of people could be at stake, changes in or disintegration of a unified system in a crisis is not unlikely. At least in NATO, one country, the United States, is clearly stronger than the others. (In the Warsaw Pact there is an even more dominant one, the Soviet Union, but its allies are not allowed to have nuclear weapons.) But there is no clear leader of an Arab alliance. Egypt, Iraq, Saudi Arabia, and Syria are all competitive pretenders.

If the Arabs could manage a credibly unified nuclear program, including a unified command, it would have some significance, especially if they were also to achieve growing relative strength in nonnuclear forces. However, a set of separate national forces would be much more likely. The existence of several, perhaps many, decision centers would create several kinds of uncertainties. When might these weapons be used? Against whom and against what targets? Might adversaries, such as the Israelis, preempt? Might the great powers respond with the use of nuclear weapons if those weapons were used against their regional allies? These are difficult questions. They suggest that any of several leaders—or worse, any of a much larger number of people in several chains of command—could act with potentially catastrophic consequences.

Contingencies and Consequences

Predicting future events in highly political matters is close to impossible. Nonetheless, there sometimes is heuristic value in exploring general trends and possible particular developments.

Likely Developments in Nuclear Weapons Capability

It seems unlikely that either Israel or the Arab countries will adopt overt nuclear weapons programs in the next decade. The Arabs are so far from having a weapons capacity that they have little incentive to adopt overt programs; virtually all of what they would need to do in the next several years to move toward weapons could be done under a civilian label. And given the current balance of forces and trends, Israel will probably not switch from its current policy of ambiguity.

This estimate could, of course, be wrong—if, for instance, there were a break in Israeli-U.S. relations or an unexpected increase in Arab power. The latter might occur through large transfers of Soviet arms or even through direct Soviet participation in support of the Arabs (analogous to but going beyond Soviet help to Egypt during the war of attrition in 1969–70). Another possibility could be a major, sustained increase in the coordination of Arab efforts directed against Israel. Or a similar result might be produced by a debilitating series of small wars or a prolonged war of attrition. On the Arab side, early possession of nuclear weapons would probably require direct aid from outsiders, including the supply of readily fissionable material, such as separated plutonium, that might be shipped from the reprocessing plants at Windscale or Cape La Hague. Earlier French help in the construction of Dimona is an example of the importance of outsiders' nuclear transfers into the region.

But in the long run many of these nations seem likely to at least drift closer to having nuclear weapons. The rate of drift would be slowed by progress toward a settlement of the Arab-Israeli dispute, a low Israeli nuclear profile, no major increase in Soviet support of the radical states or direct intervention, and safer international rules for the use of nuclear energy in the region. Without a global or regional agreement limiting access to nuclear explosive materials, several states will be able to obtain readily fissionable material and will probably take steps beyond those required for civilian nuclear energy to shorten the lead time to having weapons. To be sure, if any state wants to do business with countries requiring full-scope safeguards but also wants to work with nuclear materials without safeguards, it would have to undertake covert activities. But since extensive activities can be legally carried out under full-scope safeguards, covert activities may seem unnecessary, and they would become both much more important if the international nuclear rules were tightened and more difficult to conceal without a good "cover."

In all such estimates, it is important to keep in mind the size and character of the nuclear forces at issue. The different levels of nuclear force capability discussed earlier can be related to different objectives and time periods. For example, if Israel actually had nuclear weapons by the late 1960s[46] and continued to work on improving designs and accumulating fissionable material, its capacity by the late 1980s could be well advanced (it could have at least forty nuclear weapons) though limited by the lack of tests—assuming that that lack exists and continues. It might also have thermonuclear weapons, but without testing their reliability would be questionable. By then, Israel could have a variety of means for delivering nuclear weapons, possibly including cruise missiles that could be mounted in vans, on surface ships, in cargo aircraft, or even in submarines.

Such a force would present tough competition for the Arabs' capacity to build a preemptive capability against Israel or, more important, their capacity to build a nuclear force secure against an Israeli attack. The security of such a force might be increased by stationing it far from Israel—in Algeria or eastern Saudi Arabia, for instance—and operating in a mobile mode.

Without substantial help from outsiders, it would be around 1990 before one or several Arab states might begin to obtain nuclear explosives. As such weapons neared fabrication and deployment, they could become prime targets for commando raids and air or missile attack, either before or during a conflict. This too suggests that any future Arab nuclear weapons facilities might prudently be located far from Israel's borders,[47] although the differences between Arab countries make the political prospects for such arrangements doubtful.

46. *New York Times,* March 2, 1978.
47. In this light, note the rumored role of Israel in the mysterious sabotage of a French highly enriched uranium research reactor being constructed for Iraq just before it was shipped. *Facts on File* (April 20, 1979), p. 276.

Possibility of Overt Demonstration, Threat, or Use

Once it becomes possible to make or use weapons quickly, any one of several situations might lead a nation to go over the edge. Some of these situations may even be domestic. For example, as noted above, India's decision to test its "peace bomb" was apparently based in part on domestic political developments.

For overt threats—or conceivably, actual use—the most likely circumstances are a war in which one side threatens a core value of the other. For Israel, this could be its existence; for the Arab countries, existence would not be threatened but Cairo or Damascus might be (although the Israelis have recognized the importance of not advancing too close to these cities in several wars).

Any use of nuclear weapons in such circumstances is likely to be exceptionally risky—though in some cases it may not seem as dangerous as nonuse—but some uses would be even more dangerous than others. Use limited to the battlefield, to block the attacker while avoiding the civilian population of the adversary as well as one's own, would be the least risky. There would be powerful incentives to avoid attacks on the population if both sides had nuclear weapons, although the possibility of such attacks cannot be excluded. The fact that sizable numbers of Arabs live or work in Israeli cities might affect the choice of targets.

In conflicts between Arabs, it is even more difficult to envisage the role of nuclear weapons. Perhaps this kind of contingency should be regarded as analogous to internal instabilities. And despite the events portrayed in a recent best seller, a nuclear conflict involving Iran and Saudi Arabia or any other Arab state is remote.[48] However, if both sides had nuclear weapons, there would always be the danger of the unpredictable or the accidental happening.

The possibility of the great powers being drawn into a nuclear conflict cannot be excluded. While the danger from regional nuclear forces might discourage outside intervention, the fear of spillovers from local nuclear conflicts as well as the intrinsic importance of the Middle East are likely to counter much withdrawal of involvement. Rather, the desire to forestall a regional nuclear conflict could lead to increased superpower efforts to manage crises, thus increasing the potential of their getting

48. Paul Erdman, *The Crash of 79* (Simon and Schuster, 1976).

caught up in them. This might result from their role as guarantors of allies' security in the region: they might be called on to provide a response to a nuclear threat or attack. The military forces of the superpowers might also be the deliberate or inadvertent targets of nuclear attack.[49]

Finally, the reported Soviet movement of nuclear weapons by ship to Alexandria[50] and the Egyptian use of Scud missiles (armed with nonnuclear warheads) against the Israelis occupying Sinai during the 1973 war suggest that future Soviet moves in the region associated with nuclear weapons should not be ruled out.

49. The Israeli attack on the U.S.S. *Liberty* in the 1967 war is an example of an inadvertent attack on the regional forces of a great power.

50. Aronson, "Israel's Nuclear Option," pp. 15–18.

PART FOUR

Brazil and Argentina

WILLIAM H. COURTNEY

CHAPTER ELEVEN

Nuclear Choices
for Friendly Rivals

SOUTH AMERICA is the most peaceful continent in the third world. Its last major conflict, the Chaco war between Bolivia and Paraguay, took place more than four decades ago. The major powers, Brazil and Argentina, have not fought in the same war since they combined forces with Uruguay over a century ago to dismember an aggressive Paraguay, nor have they ever fought against each other. Although political and economic rivalry exists on the continent, the level of military tension is low. This is in keeping with South America's traditions of infrequent interstate conflict and peaceful settlement of disputes. Internal security generally preoccupies South American leaders more than the threat of external attack.

Still, there are potential sources of regional conflict. Among them are the Argentine-Chilean dispute over the Beagle Channel and Chilean-Peruvian-Bolivian tension over contested territory and Bolivian access to the sea. Were fighting to break out in either case, its duration and scope might be limited. Potential belligerents may lack the wherewithal, the allies, and the motives to engage in sustained conflict in foreign territory or at sea. Moreover, regional nations and the United States would act quickly to seek a cessation of fighting. Mediation by the Organization of American States or others might offer a face-saving way to avert further conflict, at least temporarily. Even if conflict were brief, however, heightened regional tension might persist for years. Unlike Argentina, Brazil has no serious territorial disputes with its neighbors. Nevertheless Brazil and

241

Argentina have experienced sharp political differences (now reduced) over the exploitation of shared natural resources in the region.

Nuclear weapons proliferation could upset the relatively benign security environment in the southern cone. Unlike potential nuclear rivals elsewhere in the third world, Argentina and Brazil have at present no motive to fight a conventional war. But the acquisition of nuclear weapons would transform these countries' current rivalry—largely political, economic, and cultural—into military rivalry. The tragic irony is that such acquisition would inevitably lead to new uncertainty about each other's military intentions and capabilities (such as the capacity to launch a disabling nuclear first strike). Hence even if relations between Argentina and Brazil were friendly and improving (as they are), the acquisition of nuclear weapons could undercut political accommodation and give rise to military tension where almost none previously existed.

Argentina and Brazil therefore have strong interests in averting a nuclear face-off. But development needs and consequent energy demands, mutual rivalry, ambition for regional influence and international prestige, a steadfast desire to keep nuclear options open in part because of uncertainty about each other's nuclear plans and reluctance to acquiesce in perceived international discrimination, have all raised the question of whether the two nations will take timely steps to avert the proliferation of nuclear weapons.

Brazil and Argentina now face a choice. They can continue nuclear policies that have in the past led to uncertainty and suspicion about national nuclear activities and intentions. Or they can pursue cooperative and confidence-building policies designed to allay suspicion and reduce uncertainty. The choice is mainly theirs. They and their neighbors have fundamental security interests at stake. Outside powers have less at stake. Brazil and Argentina themselves have the power either to assure or to risk those interests.

Nuclear Programs

Brazil's civil nuclear program is relatively new and ambitious, although high costs and revised projections for energy demand have spurred Brazil to scale down its plans. Argentina, which has South America's only operating power reactor, has more experience with nuclear technology but less ambitious plans than Brazil for nuclear power generation. What is most important for the question of nuclear proliferation is that both nations aspire to develop independent full nuclear fuel cycles.

The Brazilian Program

Until 1975 Brazil's nuclear experience was limited to experimenting with research reactors and initiating construction of a turnkey Westinghouse light water power reactor, Angra I (due to start operating in 1980). On June 27, 1975, however, Brazil formally signaled that it had decided on a massive new commitment to nuclear energy and nuclear technology. On that date it signed an agreement with West Germany providing for (1) the construction of up to eight light water power reactors, each with a capacity of 1,200 megawatts; (2) the transfer of technology and equipment to Brazil for uranium enrichment, fuel fabrication, and spent fuel reprocessing, and the establishment of a reactor production industry in Brazil; and (3) cooperation in uranium prospecting, extraction, and processing. The administration of President Ernesto Geisel estimated the total cost of the program to be $10 billion. In return for its investment, Brazil hoped to be producing 10,000 megawatts of nuclear power by 1990, to complement a hydroelectric capacity of 60,000 megawatts.[1] It also hoped to develop a viable reactor construction and engineering industry to service domestic and foreign markets.

From a proliferation standpoint, two parts of the Brazilian–West German program are of special interest: uranium enrichment and spent fuel reprocessing. The enrichment program became controversial in Brazil as soon as it was announced, though not for proliferation reasons. Brazil purchased rights to develop and use the Becker aerodynamic jet-nozzle process in association with two German firms, Steag and Interatom. The joint venture was to build a semicommercial plant capable of producing up to 250 tons of separative work units a year. According to the Brazilian government, the facility would have the capacity to provide fuel for two 1,200-megawatt reactors. In purchasing the Becker technology, the Brazilians were aware that its high consumption of electricity had to be lowered

1. Government of the Federative Republic of Brazil, *The Brazilian Nuclear Program* (Brasilia, 1977), p. 10.

if it was to become competitive internationally with other methods of enriching uranium.[2]

Two factors probably alleviated any doubt the Geisel administration may have had about committing Brazil to such a commercially risky technology. First, the German partners in the joint venture were participating on an equity basis.[3] Second, and probably most important, Brazil had nowhere else to turn for enrichment technology. Gaseous diffusion and gas centrifuge technologies were unavailable for sale to Brazil. Nations with access to them had classified them as state secrets. Also, West Germany could not have released gas centrifuge technology to Brazil without the consent of its partners in Urenco, the United Kingdom and the Netherlands. By comparison, the jet-nozzle process held two advantages for Brazil: West Germany had exclusive access to it and the technology was unclassified. But one of these advantages signaled a disadvantage: the Becker process had never been classified because it was considered unpromising.

Despite the deficiencies of the process, Brazil seemed happy to get it and optimistic about its prospects. President Nogueira Batista of Nuclebras predicted that a follow-on commercial-sized facility would supply fuel for all of Brazil's reactors as well as for export. Also, Brazil "would become a co-owner of a vanguard technology with rights to royalties from worldwide sales."[4] Brazil never made public the cost of buying into the Becker process.

The reprocessing plant was to be a less strenuous and risky undertaking. Two West German firms were to help Brazil build a pilot-scale facility. Later, if Brazil decided to construct a full-sized plant, there might be an opportunity for joint-venture participation by German companies. In justifying Brazil's investment in this "particularly sensitive" technology, Nogueira Batista cited the "great scope" of technology transfer to Brazil and, perhaps with an eye to allaying Argentine concern about Brazil's

2. Paulo Nogueira Batista, president of Nuclebras, *Testimony Before the Commission on Mines and Energy,* Federal Senate of Brazil, October 9, 1975; reproduced in Virgilio Tavora, ed., *Acordo Sobre Cooperaçao no Campo dos Usos Pacificos da Energia Nuclear, Assinado Entre a Republica Federativa do Brasil e a Republica Federal da Alemanha,* vol. 1 (Federal Senate of Brazil, undated), p. 296.

3. Ibid.

4. Ibid.

motivation, the "substantially lower" costs of reprocessing in the light water fuel cycle than in the heavy water cycle.[5]

In the years since the signing of the West German agreement Brazil's optimism about its nuclear future has steadily given way to realism. Start-up for Angra I was delayed for several years. Unstable geological conditions at the Angra dos Reis site forced Brazil to consider locating its third reactor elsewhere and to make expensive alterations in the civil engineering for Angra II, the first German reactor.[6]

Brazil's reactor construction industry is already experiencing idle capacity; few domestic and no foreign orders have yet been received. Reflecting a nationalistic import-substitution approach, Brazil's decision to develop such a large industry may have been premature.

In late 1978 Nogueira Batista predicted that the total cost of Brazil's nuclear program with West Germany (including eight power reactors) would reach $15 billion, though critics asserted that it would cost twice that amount. Nogueira Batista also foresaw that by 1990 the investment cost of Brazil's 10,000 megawatts of nuclear electricity-generating capacity would average $1,200 a kilowatt in 1978 dollars. The president of the electric company that will operate some of the reactors countered, however, that Angra I costs would reach $1,400 a kilowatt and Angra II costs, $1,700 a kilowatt.[7]

Brazil's rising costs, while disappointing, may not be too far out of line with the experiences of other developing nations. One study indicates that building nuclear power plants in developing nations costs considerably more than in industrial countries. Reasons for the difference include the cost of expensive infrastructure, the limited size of programs, and high training and labor costs.[8] All these factors are relevant to Brazil, although the limited size problem will ease as Brazil expands its nuclear program.

Less is known about the enrichment and reprocessing plants. A Nuclebras official predicted at the end of 1978 that the enrichment plant would begin operations in 1983–84, rather than in 1981 as planned. The re-

---

5. Ibid., p. 297.
6. *Nucleonics Week,* vol. 19 (November 2, 1978), pp. 11–12.
7. Ibid., p. 13.
8. Onkar Marwah, "Factors in the Assessment of the Economics of Nuclear Plant Construction, Power Generation, and Related Facilities in LDCs" (Harvard University, Center for Science and International Affairs, no date).

processing plant is still scheduled to commence operations in 1984.[9] Its capacity is not publicly known nor is the extent, if any, of West German equity participation in it.

Brazil has accepted safeguards on all technology, equipment, and materials transferred in the Brazilian–West German agreement or used in facilities built under that agreement, and a storage regime controlled by the International Atomic Energy Agency for plutonium produced by the reprocessing of reactor fuel furnished by Urenco. Both of these commitments constitute precedents of worldwide importance and contribute to the nonproliferation environment in South America.

The safeguards on transferred technology require that any nuclear facility constructed or operated in Brazil during the twenty years after the conclusion of the safeguards agreement be safeguarded if it is based on physical or chemical processes similar to those transferred under the Brazilian–West German agreement.[10] These so-called replication safeguards effectively preclude Brazil from building any significant reprocessing or enrichment plants on its own without safeguards until near the end of the century. While these are not full-scope safeguards, they may have a nearly equivalent effect on Brazil's ability to undertake any nuclear weapons program during the time involved. For example, a different enrichment process may be the only route open to Brazil if it seeks to build unsafeguarded sensitive facilities without breaking IAEA–West German–Brazilian safeguards.

The outlook for Brazil's nuclear program is more uncertain than it was in 1975. Domestic criticism of the costs of the program may have given the Figueiredo administration pause. The minister of mines and energy has indicated that the government might postpone installation of the last four of the eight German reactors if energy demand is insufficient.[11] This decision will apparently hinge on Brazil's economic conditions as well as on prices and supplies of alternative sources of energy. A congressional investigation of the nuclear program, concern voiced by environmentalists, press stories about disappointment with West German technology transfer and technical problems, and the high costs of the nuclear program have all made the public in Brazil more skeptical of the program than it was

9. *Nucleonics Week,* vol. 19 (December 21, 1978), p. 12.
10. *Nucleonics Week,* vol. 20 (February 8, 1979), p. 11.
11. *Nuclear Engineering International* (November 1979), p. 3.

during the national euphoria following the signing of the agreement with West Germany.

Brazil may develop increasing doubts about its nuclear ambitions. For an emerging nation with high opportunity costs for capital and technological resources, Brazil is making an expensive bet that the enrichment process in which it is investing will not be outmoded by the time its plant is built. Since research on other enrichment technologies is proceeding rapidly and the jet-nozzle process has never been competitive, Brazil has bet against heavy odds. Combining the development of an independent full nuclear fuel cycle with a power reactor construction industry is risky even for large advanced countries such as West Germany. But such an effort by a nation that cannot hope to match the technological prowess of its major nuclear competitors for many decades is riskier still.

The Argentine Program

Argentina has a well-established nuclear program with a staff of highly trained personnel. It operates five research reactors and, since 1974, a heavy water power reactor, Atucha I, located near Buenos Aires. Atucha I has a generating capacity of 360 megawatts. A second heavy water reactor, a Canadian CANDU design, is in the advanced stages of construction at Embalse de Rio Tercero, near Cordoba. It will add 600 megawatts of capacity after it begins operations, now set for 1980. The construction of Embalse has been plagued with technical problems, delays, and large cost overruns.[12]

In early 1979 the Argentine government approved the installation of four more heavy water reactors, each with a capacity of 600–700 megawatts, and the construction of a plant to produce heavy water. The reactors are to start up between 1987 and 1997. Rear Admiral Carlos Castro Madero, president of Argentina's National Atomic Energy Commission (CNEA), estimated that the new program will require a $4.2 billion investment over a twenty-year period.[13]

In late 1979 the Argentine government awarded the contract for the first of the new power reactors to the West German consortium Kraftwerk

12. U.S. Foreign Broadcast Information Service (FBIS), *Daily Report: Latin America* (January 19, 1979), p. B3.
13. Ibid., p. B4.

Union, which built Atucha I. The award followed an intense competition between Atomic Energy of Canada Limited and Kraftwerk Union. The president of the Canadian firm had been optimistic. Commenting earlier in the year on Argentina's impending decision on who would build Atucha II, he said: "While the Germans have built one [heavy water power] plant, we have built 31; therefore it seems clear to me what the Argentines will decide."[14]

Some Argentines may have shared these sentiments because they believed that the CANDU technology could be more easily assimilated by Argentine industry than the German pressure-vessel heavy water reactor technology could be. The Canadians also had other advantages in the Atucha II competition: they submitted the lower bid (30 percent lower than Kraftwerk Union's, according to Madero), and they pledged to have a greater share of local content in their project.[15]

Nevertheless, Kraftwerk Union won the contract. The Argentines had been disappointed with Canadian performance on the Embalse project. Second, according to Madero, Argentina wanted to maintain competition among potential suppliers of heavy water reactors.[16] Third, safeguards may have been a factor: although at the start of the bidding competition the Germans and the Canadians had agreed not to compete on the basis of safeguards requirements, the Germans apparently made lesser demands. Canada reacted strongly and bitterly; *Der Spiegel* blamed West Germany for resorting to "shabby competition."[17] Faced with mounting criticism, West Germany may have made a belated attempt to stiffen safeguards. Visiting Buenos Aires in early 1980, the West German foreign minister said he would raise the question of Argentina's position on safeguards.[18]

At the same time that Argentina announced the Atucha II contract it also selected a Swiss firm, Sulzer, to build a $300 million demonstration plant for the production of heavy water. The plant, which is to produce 250 tons of heavy water a year, will serve as a successor to a small pilot

14. *Nucleonics Week,* vol. 20 (February 1, 1979), p. 13.
15. *Nuclear Engineering International* (November 1979), p. 3.
16. *Nuclear Engineering International* (January 1980), p. 10; *Nucleonics Week,* vol. 20 (February 1, 1979), pp. 12–13; "The Fight about the Water Plant," *Der Spiegel,* November 19, 1979, translated in FBIS, *Worldwide Report: Nuclear Development and Nonproliferation* (December 10, 1979), pp. 18–21.
17. Noticias Argentinas, March 19, 1980, translated in FBIS, *Worldwide Report* (April 15, 1980), p. 12.
18. *Nucleonics Week,* vol. 21 (February 22, 1980), p. 6.

plant that Argentina is building on its own and expects to have operating in 1981. In the competition to build the demonstration plant, Atomic Energy of Canada was the big loser. Securing technology for the production of heavy water is a top priority in the Argentine nuclear program. Such technology could eventually allow Argentina to be independent of foreign sources of heavy water for its power reactors and to export heavy water to other nations, including purchasers of Argentine reactors.

Argentina has succeeded in obtaining the Swiss technology without agreeing to full-scope safeguards but without objecting to safeguards on the imported technology, the heavy water produced by it, reactors that use the heavy water, or the products of these reactors. Canada's insistence on full-scope safeguards may have doomed its chances of winning the contract from the start. As Admiral Madero reportedly put it in commenting on the Canadian offer to build both the Atucha II reactor and the heavy water plant, to have accepted such a bid would have "affected Argentina's capacity to develop an independent program with a minimum of possibilities of outside interference."[19]

As a member of the London nuclear suppliers' group, Switzerland has promised to abide by the group's guidelines for nuclear transfers of items on an unspecified "trigger list." The guidelines stipulate that for facilities for reprocessing, enrichment, or heavy water production exporters must require that "IAEA safeguards apply to any facilities of the same type (that is, if the design, construction or operating processes are based on the same or similar physical or chemical processes, as defined in the trigger list) constructed during an agreed upon period in the recipient country."[20] Assuming that Switzerland requires replication safeguards, Argentina would be unable to close an unsafeguarded nuclear fuel cycle by copying Swiss heavy water technology. There is a question, however, whether these safeguards would apply to any small heavy water production facilities that Argentina might design or build before the construction of the Swiss plant.

Argentine reprocessing plans are unclear. In October 1978 Admiral Madero reportedly said that Argentina planned to build an experimental reprocessing plant at the Ezeiza nuclear research center near Buenos Aires. (An earlier laboratory reprocessing facility at Ezeiza was allegedly dismantled in the early 1970s.) He added that the plant would be safe-guarded by virtue of reprocessing safeguarded fuel.[21] In November 1978 a CNEA spokeswoman said that the CNEA was building the facility with its own technology and hence it would not be subject to international safeguards. Curiously, she added that Argentina has no apparent reason for separating plutonium since it uses heavy water reactors.[22] At present, however, Argentine reprocessing plans are not clearly defined. Argentina would run a special safety risk by locating a facility at Ezeiza, which is adjacent to the Buenos Aires international airport.

Restrictions on press and political freedoms in Argentina have made it difficult to measure public attitudes toward that country's nuclear pro-grams. A so-called opposition group of the Peronist party, however, has reportedly criticized the Sulzer contract, arguing that similar heavy water plants built by the company in India and France had malfunctioned (in India, exploded) and that the plant envisioned for Argentina was far larger than these plants or any plant in Switzerland. The Peronist com-muniqué also criticized Kraftwerk Union for allegedly seeking to establish a West German nuclear monopoly in South America, to be controlled from Brazil.[23]

National Goals and Foreign Policy

Argentina and Brazil view their nuclear programs as contributing to several national goals—development, independence, regional influence, and a greater role in the international system. (Another goal may be a hedge against uncertainty about each other's military and nuclear weapons intentions.)

Brazil and Argentina attach high priority to national development, but their experiences have differed sharply. By 1930 Argentina was widely considered a developed nation; since then it has experienced periods of political decay and economic instability that have stunted development. It is now considered a less developed nation. Brazil, by comparison, has

21. Milton R. Benjamin, "Argentina on Threshold of Nuclear Reprocessing," *Washington Post,* October 16, 1978.
22. "CNEA Official Gives Details of Reprocessing Plans," *O Globo,* November 7, 1978, translated in FBIS, *Daily Report: Latin America* (November 8, 1978), p. B2.
23. Noticias Argentinas, October 19, 1979, translated in FBIS, *Worldwide Report* (November 21, 1979), p. 13.

Table 11-1. *Growth in Argentina and Brazil*

Item	Argentina	Brazil
Population (millions)		
Mid-1977	26	116
2000 (projected)	33	200
Gross national product		
1977 (billions of U.S. dollars)	45	158
Per capita, 1977 (U.S. dollars)	1,730	1,360
Average annual growth rate		
per capita, 1960–77 (percent)	2.7	4.9

Source: World Bank, *World Development Report, 1979* (August 1979), annex, various tables.

always been a less developed nation, but its economic dynamism promises to lift it out of this status by the end of the century. Although Brazil has suffered less political turmoil than Argentina, both countries have experienced military intervention in civil affairs and are now ruled by military regimes.

Several differences in national development and dynamism are illustrated in table 11-1. With a population well over four times that of Argentina, Brazil is projected to have 200 million people by the end of the century. Between 1977 and 2000 it will add 84 million to its population; Argentina will add only 7 million. Disparities in economic dynamism are also pronounced. Brazil's gross national product is over three times the size of Argentina's. Between 1960 and 1977 Brazil's per capita gross national product grew nearly twice as fast as Argentina's, this in spite of Brazil's much higher rate of population growth. Because of Argentina's earlier advantage, however, it had a higher per capita gross national product in 1977 than Brazil did. In sum, population and economic trends make Brazil one of the most dynamic countries in the third world but put Argentina in a much less dynamic class.

Independence is a traditional goal of Argentine foreign policy and a newer goal for Brazil. Beginning in the nineteenth century, Argentina "led Latin America in devising a web of treaties to restrain the United States and enshrine the principles of non-intervention and sovereign equality of states."[24] In 1943 a pro-fascist government was installed in Argentina, but in January 1945 it declared war on Germany, mainly to avoid exclu-

24. Edward S. Milenky, *Argentina's Foreign Policies* (Westview Press, 1978), p. 10.

sion from the United Nations. The election of Juan Perón to the presidency in 1946 led to a reinforcement of Argentina's independent posture. He introduced into Argentine foreign policy the concept of the "third position," allegedly equidistant between U.S. and Soviet imperialism. It was an international reflection of "Peronism's third road for development: autonomous, anti-imperialist national development and social justice for the masses."[25] Under the present military regime Argentina has taken a more anticommunist line but without sacrificing the country's essential posture of independence, which has been reinforced by Western reluctance to establish closer political ties until human rights practices in Argentina improve.

Especially in the twentieth century, Brazil and the United States have enjoyed close ties, fostered by economic complementarity, shared strategic aims, and Brazil's desire to offset natural affinities among the Spanish-speaking nations of South America. In the late 1950s and early 1960s a number of factors, particularly rising nationalism and the growth of leftist political strength, led Brazil to move toward a more independent position in world affairs and to oppose U.S. "imperialism." The military takeover in 1964 brought to power soldiers who were pro-Western and staunchly opposed to communism.[26] Starting in the early 1970s, however, the military regimes countenanced a steady move toward a more independent foreign policy, guided by principles of "responsible pragmatism," "no automatic alignments," and "ecumenism."

The 1975 nuclear agreement symbolized Brazil's pursuit of a "European option," a Brazilian concept that implies lessening dependence on the United States and increasing ties with Europe. Brazil also sought to "diversify" its foreign contacts and project its dynamism into the third world. It has given special emphasis to Africa, so important to its own cultural traditions. Nevertheless, Brazilians have conflicting views on what should be the "third world–first world" balance in Brazilian foreign policy. They are confident that their country, even if it stumbles occasionally, is on its way to realizing the dream of *grandeza*—greatness with independence—but they are ambivalent about moving toward industrial country status, even though their economy is now the largest in the third world. They fear this would cost Brazil its privileges as a developing na-

---

25. Ibid., p. 13.
26. Riordan Roett, *Brazil: Politics in a Patrimonial Society* (Praeger, 1978), p. 159.

tion (such as trade preferences, access to World Bank resources, and political protection afforded by association with the third world) and would require it to join the West in assuming international responsibilities for which Brazil, with its present state of development and political system, is still unprepared.

The traditional focal point of Argentine and Brazilian diplomatic energies has been the western hemisphere. In addition to opposing intervention, the main tenets of Argentine foreign policy through the years have been hegemonical aspirations in the Plate River basin, the construction of a special relationship with other Spanish-speaking states of Latin America, and the avoidance of multilateral alliances and other security arrangements.[27] Hence Argentina saw the United States as a rival for influence in Latin America and resisted U.S. initiatives dating back over a century to build a Pan-American movement. Brazil, by comparison, has historically supported Pan-American efforts and viewed the United States as a counterweight to Argentina's influence.

Since the 1930s economic dynamism and an absence of territorial disputes with its neighbors have enabled Brazil to erode Argentine influence. Brazil has made strong efforts with all its neighbors—especially its longtime friend, Chile—to forge new economic, transportation, and communications links. Being realistic, however, Brazil has not sought regional hegemony. It realizes that such aspirations are incompatible with its neighbors' nationalism and traditional skepticism toward Brazilian ambitions. Brazil prefers to maintain good relations with its neighbors but not to exercise regional political leadership. Along with Argentina, Brazil opposes the formation of regional blocs or alliances.

In consonance with the rise of third world power, Brazil and Argentina see greater roles for themselves in the international system. Argentina realizes that its gains can be only measured until its economic and political difficulties abate. Brazil, however, sees itself as standing on the threshold of a new era of Brazilian power and influence. Its expanded and diversified economic ties with the world are the bedrock of its influence in and beyond the western hemisphere. Although for years it has played a major role in international forums with a major technical context (such as the law of the sea conference, the General Agreement on Tariffs and

27. Arthur P. Whitaker, *The United States and Argentina* (Harvard University Press, 1954), pp. 86–87.

Trade, and the IAEA), Brazil has moved more cautiously to increase its profile on broader political issues.

These national goals—development, independence, regional influence, greater international roles—are all affected by the nuclear programs of Argentina and Brazil. They increase and diversify national sources of energy and bring technologies that contribute to development, although the high costs and risks of nuclear power, especially large uranium enrichment and heavy water production projects, raise questions of net costs and benefits. Because nuclear technology is so sophisticated and the dissemination of certain technologies has been so restricted, their acquisition by the two countries is a major boost to national prestige. For Argentina it is a strong point that compensates for other weaknesses in national power and image. For Brazil nuclear programs are both an instrument and a sign of rapidly growing national power. For both nations their nuclear programs are symbols, if not always realities, of greater national independence.

These goals and the contribution that nuclear programs make to them have shaped the nuclear diplomacy of both nations. That diplomacy has been reflected in dealings with their nuclear suppliers, in stances on safeguards, the Treaty on the Non-Proliferation of Nuclear Weapons, and the Treaty of Tlatelolco, and in diplomacy with each other.

The NPT

Brazil and Argentina have opposed the NPT since its inception. As a member of the United Nations Eighteen-Nation Disarmament Committee, which considered the question of a nonproliferation treaty from 1965 to 1968, Brazil urged that a treaty take into account the security of non-nuclear states; joined with eight nonaligned members of the UN committee to urge that nonproliferation measures be linked to arms control by the nuclear powers; combined with India to object to the treaty's ban on peaceful nuclear explosions by nonnuclear weapons states, to propose that safeguards be compulsory for all parties on a nondiscriminatory and universal basis, and to criticize the draft treaty as one-sided and discriminatory and as not providing the balance of mutual responsibilities and obligations called for in a 1965 General Assembly resolution. Brazil also sought a legal commitment to specific disarmament measures to be taken by the nuclear powers, with part of the savings to be achieved by disarmament to go to the developing nations; favored deleting from the withdrawal clause of the treaty the requirement that a withdrawing nation submit a statement explaining its reasons; and along with Rumania and India faulted the draft treaty for failing to halt vertical proliferation by nuclear weapons powers.[28]

On June 21, 1968, the General Assembly adopted a resolution commending the NPT. Argentina and Brazil abstained from the vote. In the years since, Brazil and Argentina have given no indication that they will adhere to the NPT.[29]

The Treaty of Tlatelolco

On November 3, 1962, only days after the end of the Cuban missile crisis, Brazil proposed in the United Nations the creation of a Latin American nuclear-free zone. The impetus behind the proposal was not only to forestall a similar crisis in the future but also to prevent a nuclear arms race on the continent.

Visionary though it was, the idea caught on. On April 29, 1963, the presidents of Bolivia, Brazil, Chile, Ecuador, and Mexico proclaimed that their governments were willing to sign a multilateral Latin American agreement not "to manufacture, store, or test nuclear weapons or devices for launching nuclear weapons."[30] Several weeks later, eleven Latin American nations proposed a resolution in the General Assembly expressing the hope that negotiations for such an agreement would start and seeking the cooperation of all countries, "especially the nuclear Powers." The resolution passed, 91–0, with 15 abstentions.[31]

After two and a half years of negotiations, the Latin American republics, under forceful and effective Mexican leadership, produced a draft agreement of the Treaty for the Prohibition of Nuclear Weapons in Latin America, known as the Treaty of Tlatelolco. The treaty was opened for signature on February 14, 1967. To date, all the Latin American republics except Cuba have signed it. Of the twenty-three signatories, every nation but Argentina has ratified it. During the United Nations Special

28. William Epstein, *The Last Chance: Nuclear Proliferation and Arms Control* (Free Press, 1976), pp. 137, 66, 73–78.
29. Ibid., pp. 83–84.
30. Ibid., pp. 117, 56.
31. UN Doc. A/5515 (November 27, 1963), pp. 14–15.

Session on Disarmament in 1977 and a later visit to Buenos Aires by U.S. Secretary of State Cyrus Vance, Argentina pledged to ratify the treaty, but it has not yet done so. All the ratifying nations except Brazil and Chile have also waived certain requirements so that the treaty could enter into force for them immediately. Once the treaty enters into force for a country, it is obliged to negotiate a full-scope safeguard agreement with the IAEA.

The main pledges made by the parties to the Tlatelolco treaty are to "prohibit and prevent in their respective territories" the "testing, use, manufacture, production, or acquisition" of nuclear weapons, and "the receipt, storage, installation, deployment, or any form of possession of any nuclear weapons, directly or indirectly"; and "to refrain from engaging in, encouraging or authorizing, directly or indirectly, or in any way participating in the testing, use, manufacture, production, possession or control of any nuclear weapons."[32] The treaty also established a supervisory body (OPANAL, Agency for the Prohibition of Nuclear Weapons in Latin America) and provided for regular IAEA safeguards inspections, as well as for special inspections when violations are suspected.

The Treaty of Tlatelolco imposes restraints on extracontinental powers. Additional Protocol I stipulates that nations which are internationally responsible for territories in Latin America pledge to apply the treaty to those territories. The United Kingdom and the Netherlands have ratified Additional Protocol I, and France and the United States have promised to ratify it. In 1978 President Carter signed it, but the Senate still has not ratified it.

In Additional Protocol II, all nuclear weapons states pledge to respect the nuclear-free status of the Latin American zone. All five of these states —China, France, Great Britain, the United States, and the Soviet Union— have ratified it.

The main weakness of the Tlatelolco treaty, from a nonproliferation point of view, relates to peaceful nuclear explosions. Article 18 states that parties "may carry out explosions of nuclear devices for peaceful purposes —including explosions which involve devices similar to those used in nuclear weapons—or collaborate with third parties for the same purpose," so long as this does not contravene other parts of the treaty. Articles 1 and 5 combined preclude parties from detonating or acquiring a nuclear

32. The Tlatelolco treaty does not deal with the question of restricting nuclear weapons launchers (such as strategic missiles), a feature included in the five-nation declaration of April 1963. Epstein, *Last Chance,* pp. 299–315.

weapon, defined as any device that is "capable of releasing nuclear energy in an uncontrolled manner and which has a group of characteristics that are appropriate for use for warlike purposes."[33]

To the extent that the characteristics of peaceful nuclear explosives and nuclear weapons are similar, there is a contradiction between article 18 and articles 1 and 5. Arguing that these characteristics are similar, the United States, when it signed Additional Protocol II, stated that it interpreted the treaty as precluding peaceful nuclear explosives. Mexico and a number of other countries have supported this interpretation. Argentina and Brazil, which had made strong efforts in the negotiation of the treaty for the retention of the parties' right to carry out peaceful nuclear explosions, disputed this interpretation when they, respectively, signed and ratified the treaty.

Since it is unlikely that either Argentina or Brazil will ratify the NPT, the Tlatelolco treaty may represent the best multilateral diplomatic instrument for reducing the threat of nuclear weapons proliferation in South America. This is because Argentina (assuming it carries out its pledge to ratify Tlatelolco) and Brazil (and Chile) will be required by the treaty to agree to full-scope IAEA safeguards once all eligible nations ratify the treaty or its protocols, as the case may be. Every IAEA full-scope agreement concluded to date has precluded peaceful nuclear explosives. Assuming the IAEA maintains this policy, Cuban ratification of the treaty would generate an international legal obligation for Argentina and Brazil to forgo an option that their national policies have sought to keep open. They would be reluctant to evade this obligation.

The USSR, which has supported most international nonproliferation efforts, is aware that Cuban ratification could become a linchpin for the full entry into force of the Tlatelolco treaty. Cuba's intentions remain unclear. In 1978 Cuba's foreign minister claimed that U.S. abandonment of its Guantanamo naval base was a precondition for Cuban ratification. If so, Tlatelolco's prospects may not be bright.

Bilateral Nuclear Diplomacy

Brazil and Argentina have begun to take steps to establish mutual confidence about nuclear intentions and thus reduce long-term strategic uncertainty in the southern cone. In May 1980, during a historic visit to Buenos Aires by the Brazilian president, the two nations concluded a large

33. Ibid., pp. 301, 302, 308, 309.

number of agreements, including some in the nuclear field, and established
a mechanism for future consultations between foreign ministers.[34] The
scope of the nuclear agreements included research and development on
experimental and power reactors, exchanges of nuclear materials, and
uranium research, prospecting, and processing, including the manufacture
of ziracloy and fuel elements.[35] Doubtless Argentina hopes to provide
Brazil with fuel elements made from ziracloy tubing produced in Argentina. Brazil, for its part, would like to supply reactor components and
reactor engineering services. Since Argentina and Brazil have chosen
different types of reactors for power generation, however, there are limits
on the development of industrial cooperation in the nuclear field.

Although the presidents stressed the recent improvement in relations,
Argentine-Brazilian relations have for decades alternated between warm
and cool. The two countries have not yet established a durable foundation
for close political cooperation. The rhetoric of recent years on the Itaipu
dam issue made both nations wary. Argentina's behavior toward Chile on
the Beagle Channel dispute caused anxiety among Brazilians. Finally,
Brazil is acutely aware that it has ratified the Tlatelolco treaty and Argentina has delayed this step.

Although Argentina and Brazil have differing perspectives on nuclear
policy, areas of mutual interest do exist. The conclusion of the nuclear
cooperation agreements demonstrated this. The two countries could also
venture into other areas of collaboration. These might include mutual
reassurances on national nuclear programs and intentions, cooperation in
planning defenses against international criticism, coordination to oppose
restrictions by nuclear suppliers on technology transfers, and consultation
on policies in the IAEA. Whether these areas of possible cooperation are
being explored is unknown, but it is clear that opportunities exist for
cooperation that could both help and hurt the prospects for averting nuclear weapons proliferation.

Energy Policy

Brazil and Argentina need energy for national development. With
nuclear power they can both expand and diversify their sources of energy.

34. Telam (official Argentine news service), May 17, 1980, translated in FBIS,
Daily Report: Latin America (May 19, 1980), pp. B3–B4.
35. Ibid., pp. B7–B8.

Because diversification of sources reduces risks, it is worth payment of an incremental premium. Nevertheless, Argentina and Brazil are not in the same boat. For example, while Argentina has been nearly self-sufficient in petroleum, Brazil imports more than three-fourths of its consumption. Also, Argentina's economy and hence its demand for energy have expanded less rapidly than Brazil's. Nevertheless, despite their differing situations both countries attach high priority to producing more energy.

Well endowed with energy resources, Argentina has substantial deposits of coal, oil, natural gas, and uranium, although petroleum reserves known today could be exhausted by the end of the century. Argentina also has a large, underdeveloped hydroelectric capacity. Argentina's consumption of energy, however, is not proportional to its endowments: in 1976 crude oil and natural gas constituted 25 percent of domestic energy reserves and 85 percent of primary energy consumed, whereas hydroelectric energy made up 60 percent of domestic energy reserves and only 4 percent of the consumption of primary energy.[36]

To bring energy consumption patterns into better alignment with resource endowments, Argentina is building new hydroelectric projects (the largest of which is Yacyretá, being undertaken jointly with Paraguay), emphasizing nuclear power, and seeking to expand coal production. It is also encouraging some substitution of natural gas for oil (to take advantage of gas reserves in Tierra del Fuego), boosting oil and gas exploration, and promoting the substitution of coal for oil in the generation of electricity. Of all these steps, the government regards the Yacyretá project as the "backbone" of its least-cost solution for power expansion and the "critical step" in its strategy to use domestic energy resources more fully and effectively. The Argentine energy program is also seeking to overcome past difficulties, such as inefficiency in the state-owned petroleum exploration company and a fragmented structure in the electric power industry that allegedly led to decisions to overinvest in national electricity-generating capacity in 1980–84.[37]

By comparison with Argentina, Brazil is poorly endowed with easily exploitable energy resources and its energy needs are staggering. The Brazilian energy program seeks to meet energy challenges with a three-point strategy: (1) energy conservation and rationalization of energy

36. Argentine Ministry of Economy, Secretariat of Energy, *The Argentine Energy Sector: Highlights of the National Plan of Energy* (Buenos Aires, 1978), pp. 1–4.

37. Ibid., pp. 2–4.

use; (2) substitution for imported energy (petroleum, metallurgical coal) of energy produced at home, with an emphasis on renewable sources when technically and economically attractive; and (3) increase of domestic energy reserves and development of sources of energy that are used poorly or not at all at present.[38]

Energy substitution efforts focus on substituting alcohol, steam from coal, and electrical energy for petroleum products, and on adopting steel-making processes that can use Brazilian coal in place of imported metallurgical coal. Programs to expand domestic sources of energy supply concentrate on the following areas: intensified petroleum exploration, especially on the continental shelf, by the state-owned oil company and foreign companies; exploitation of hydroelectric power (such as the continuing construction of Itaipu, the world's largest hydroelectric installation); implementation of the nuclear power program, including intensive uranium prospecting; and other programs involving coal, shale oil, waterfalls, biomass, and solar energy.[39] Brazil's energy programs have been hurt by widely publicized inefficiencies in its state-owned oil company, by nationalistically motivated delays in allowing foreign companies to explore for oil under "risk contracts," and by the high costs of alternative energy sources.

Trends in Argentine and Brazilian consumption of primary energy are shown in table 11-2. Crude oil and natural gas were the most important energy sources for Argentina in 1976, and they will supply most of the increase in demand through 1985. For Brazil crude oil and hydroelectric power were the preponderant sources of energy consumed in 1977. They will remain so through 1985, at which time electric power from Itaipu and other sources will have sharply increased the role of hydroelectric power, making it nearly as important as crude oil.

In both countries nuclear power is expected to make little contribution by 1985: 2.6 percent of primary energy consumption in Argentina and 2.1 percent in Brazil. Delays in the construction of nuclear reactors in both countries will make these percentages lower still. Beyond 1985 the relative role of nuclear power may well increase, especially if technology (such as long-distance electric power transmission) does not permit

38. Government of the Federative Republic of Brazil, Ministry of Mines and Energy, *National Energy Balance* (Brasilia, 1978), p. 7.
39. Ibid., pp. 7–8.

Table 11-2. *Energy Consumption in Argentina and Brazil, Selected Years*
Millions of metric tons of oil equivalent

Source of energy	Argentina		Brazil	
	1976	1985[a]	1977	1985[a]
Crude oil	23.2	31.0[b]	43.1	58.5
Hydroelectric	1.5	5.7	27.0	57.8
Natural gas	11.5	18.3	0.5	1.2
Coal	1.0	2.6	4.1	10.0
Nuclear	0.6	1.6	0	3.5
Other	1.9	1.5	28.6	36.0
Total	39.7	60.7	103.3	167.0

Sources: Argentine Ministry of Economy, Secretariat of Energy, *The Argentine Energy Sector: Highlights of the National Plan of Energy* (Buenos Aires, 1978), p. 6; Government of the Federative Republic of Brazil, Ministry of Mines and Energy, *National Energy Balance* (Brasilia, 1978), pp. 12, 14.
a. All figures include imports as well as domestic production except where noted otherwise. Projections for 1985 assume average annual growth rates of gross domestic product equal to 5.5 percent for Argentina and 7.0 percent for Brazil.
b. Projections of imports of petroleum products (other than liquid gas), which totaled 0.6 million metric tons of oil equivalent in 1976, were not available.

Argentina and Brazil to exploit hydroelectric potential situated farther away from population centers than the power now being harnessed.

National Security Policy

The national security policies of Argentina and Brazil are conditioned by several factors. Internal sources of insecurity outweigh external sources. Brazil and Argentina are out of the path of East-West military rivalry, which gives them a greater opportunity to influence their regional security environment. Conflict in the region has been infrequent. The main disagreement between Argentina and Brazil involves the construction of the Itaipu hydroelectric complex by Brazil and Paraguay on the Parana River. At present there are no potential sources of military conflict between Brazil and its neighbors. Argentina, however, has forced a confrontation with Chile over the Beagle Channel. It strongly opposes British control of the Falkland Islands (Islas Malvinas). Argentina has also staked a claim to a wedge of Antarctica that is not widely recognized. Thus far, none of these sources of tension have erupted in conflict, although war with Chile

may have been only narrowly averted in late 1978 during bilateral negotiations on the Beagle Channel question.[40]

The Treaty of Rio de Janeiro

Since World War I the "new concept of international collective security
based on the principle of universality of interest" has been given tangible
expression on a global scale in the League of Nations and the United
Nations and on a regional scale in "the classical example of all regional
arrangements: the inter-American system."[41] The formal instrument underlying this system is the Inter-American Treaty of Reciprocal Assistance, or the Treaty of Rio de Janeiro, negotiated in 1947.[42]

The treaty includes all the Latin American republics, although the
United States sought for a time to bar Argentina from the treaty negotiations because of its former Nazi ties and its Peronist leadership. The
United States finally relented on the eve of the negotiations, enabling
Argentina to participate in its first major inter-American event since the
partial quarantine of World War II. Pressure by American states (including Brazil) and escalating East-West tension led the United States to
withdraw its objections and give priority to concluding the hemispheric
defense pact. Once admitted to the negotiations, Argentina resumed its
traditional role of rival to the United States in hemispheric forums.[43]

The central feature of the Rio treaty is that an attack on one American
state is considered an attack on all (a principle later embodied in the
North Atlantic treaty).[44] In the event of an attack, parties to the treaty
undertake to assist the defender in meeting the attack, "in the exercise
of the inherent right of individual or collective self-defense recognized by

40. "Latin America's Territorial Disputes Endanger Peace," *Washington Post,*
October 30, 1979.

41. J. Lloyd Mecham, *The United States and Inter-American Security, 1889–
1960* (University of Texas Press for the Institute of Latin American Studies, 1961),
pp. 1, 3.

42. See the documents in *Department of State Bulletin,* August 17, 1947, pp.
324–26; August 24, 1947, p. 367; August 31, 1947, pp. 414–15; September 14, 1947,
pp. 498–505; "Text of the Treaty and the Final Act," September 21, 1947, pp. 565–
75; December 14, 1947, pp. 1188–91; December 22, 1975, pp. 903–04; August 8,
1977, p. 191; and June 1978, p. 59.

43. Harold F. Peterson, *Argentina and the United States, 1810–1960* (State University of New York, 1964), pp. 466–67.

44. Dean Acheson, *Present at the Creation* (Norton, 1969), p. 280.

article 51 of the Charter of the United Nations." The Rio treaty also allows individual parties to the treaty, upon request by the state or states directly attacked, to take "immediate measures" of assistance pending a determination by the consultative organ established by the treaty (now the Organization of American States) on what collective action is to be taken.[45] As a U.S. official put it, these provisions convert "the right of individual and collective self-defense, as recognized in the United Nations Charter, into an obligation under this treaty."[46]

The Rio treaty makes provision for dealing with conflicts between contracting parties. In such eventualities, the parties "meeting in consultation shall call upon the contending States to suspend hostilities and restore matters to the *status quo ante bellum*" and shall take all other measures necessary to reestablish or maintain peace and to resolve the conflict by peaceful means.[47]

A unique feature of the Rio treaty is its establishment of collective sanctions. The Organization of American States (OAS) may agree on measures including "one or more of the following: recall of chiefs of diplomatic missions; breaking of consular relations; partial or complete interruption of economic relations or of rail, sea, air, postal, telegraphic, telephonic, and radiotelephonic or radiotelegraphic communications; and use of armed force."[48] Other "advanced and significant" provisions of the treaty stipulate that a two-thirds vote of the parties shall be sufficient to make decisions and that decisions taken on collective sanctions shall be binding on all parties except that no party "shall be required to use armed force without its consent."[49]

The Rio treaty is relevant in several ways to the challenges posed by the potential or actual spread of nuclear weapons. The American republics could rely on the treaty as justification for expressing their views about the consequences for hemispheric security of Argentine and Brazilian actions that raised the risks of nuclear proliferation. Were a regional crisis

45. *Department of State Bulletin* (September 21, 1947), pp. 565, article 3. Article 51 of the United Nations Charter stipulates that nothing in the charter "shall impair the inherent right of individual or collective self-defense if an armed attack occurs against a Member of the United Nations" until the Security Council has acted.

46. In a letter of December 1, 1947, from Robert A. Lovett to President Truman, reprinted in *Department of State Bulletin* (December 14, 1947), p. 1190.

47. *Department of State Bulletin* (September 21, 1947), p. 566, article 7.

48. Ibid., article 8.

49. Ibid., articles 17, 20.

involving a nuclear-armed Argentina or Brazil to develop, the American states could consult as provided for by the treaty, and could use the treaty as an instrument to justify and implement conciliation or mediation and to call for peaceful settlement of the dispute. Were these steps to fail, the parties to the treaty could invoke the sanctions envisioned by the treaty and request that the United States and other states deploy forces to deter conflict and protect threatened or attacked states.

Defense Policies

In 1906 Brazil contracted with British shipyards for the construction of three new battleships. A few months later Argentina reacted with a shipbuilding program of its own. Argentina had seen in Brazil's action a challenge to its naval supremacy in the region and had become worried about "the frequent public demonstrations of close friendship" between the United States and Brazil.[50]

Since that time several features of Argentine and Brazilian national security policies have persisted: concern about the regional military balance, competition for regional influence, the importance of naval power, and Brazil's close ties with the United States. To illustrate the latter point, Brazil sent an expeditionary force to Italy in World War II and, when the United States needed support for its Dominican Republic operation in 1965, sent forces and supplied the nominal commander for the overall effort.

It is difficult to gain a full understanding of Argentine and Brazilian defense policies toward external threats, particularly from each other. Political and military leaders in both countries view the question of external threats as sensitive and are generally unwilling to discuss it publicly. The current level of military rivalry between the two countries is low, and it is felt that public debate about it could lead only to embarrassment and inaccurate perceptions. Moreover, in recent decades Brazil and Argentina have been more preoccupied with perceived internal threats to national security than with external threats.

Concern with internal security in these nations has led to profound changes in the military's role in governmental and political affairs and in

---

50. Peterson, *Argentina and the United States,* pp. 291–93.

military doctrine.[51] In Brazil the changing military role in social and economic activities since 1964 has led to a "new political and economic model of authoritarian development."[52] It remains to be seen whether the current military rule in Argentina will have a comparable impact.

The military's role in politics in both Brazil and Argentina reflects changes in military doctrine that were accentuated after Castro's takeover of Cuba. Writing in 1959, Brazil's leading military strategist said, "Latin America now faces threats more real than at any other time, threats which could result in insurrection," aimed at implanting "a government favorable to the Communist ideology and constituting a grave and urgent danger to the unity and the security of the Americas and the Western world."[53] American policy encouraged such perceptions of threat: by 1961 U.S. military assistance programs in Latin America "were largely devoted to exporting doctrines concerned with the military's role in counterinsurgency, civic action and nation building."[54] This emphasis took hold so strongly in Brazil that in 1966 the curriculum of the army's General Staff School contained 222 hours on internal security, 129 on irregular warfare, and only 24 on conventional warfare.[55]

The relationship between internal and external security in Brazil was summarized by President Castelo Branco in a 1967 address at Brazil's influential Superior War College (Escola Superior de Guerra). He observed that the doctrine taught at the school, "Development and Security," was "today already integrated in its essence in the new Brazilian constitution and in modern laws." Castelo Branco described "national security" as more encompassing than the "traditional concept of national defense," which "places more emphasis on the military aspects of security and hence

51. Two of the best studies of civil-military relations are Alfred Stepan, *The Military in Politics: Changing Patterns in Brazil* (Princeton University Press, 1971); and Robert A. Potash, *The Army and Politics in Argentina, 1928–1945: Yrigoyen to Perón* (Stanford University Press, 1969).

52. Alfred Stepan, "The New Professionalism of Internal Warfare and Military Role Expansion," in Alfred Stepan, ed., *Authoritarian Brazil: Origins, Policies, and Future* (Yale University Press, 1973), p. 47.

53. Golbery do Couto e Silva, *Geopolítica do Brasil* (Rio de Janeiro: Livraria José Olympio Editora, 1967), pp. 198–99 (from material written in 1959), as quoted in Stepan, "New Professionalism," p. 56. See also Golbery do Couto e Silva, *Planejamento Estratégico* (Rio de Janeiro: Biblioteca do Exército Editora, 1955).

54. Stepan, "New Professionalism," p. 50.

55. Ibid., p. 57.

the problems of external aggression." National security, on the other hand, includes "the global defense of institutions, including psychological aspects, [and] the preservation of development and internal political stability." Also, "the concept of security much more explicitly than [the concept of] defense takes the line that internal aggression, embodied in ideological infiltration and subversion and even in guerrilla movements," is a more probable form of conflict than external aggression.[56]

In the years since Castelo Branco uttered these words, some Brazilian and Argentine security priorities have changed and some have not. The military rulers of both nations, especially Argentina, are still preoccupied with internal security. The dominant position of army leadership in both countries reflects this priority. Nevertheless, their regimes broke the back of terrorism—Brazil in the early 1970s and Argentina in the late 1970s. Whether these victories over terrorism are permanent, however, is another question. Since the mid-1970s the Brazilian military have countenanced gradual movement toward a limited political opening, although they have reasserted authority at times when they felt they were losing control of the process. No prospects for political liberalization are yet in sight for Argentina.

Lessened threats of internal subversion and terrorism have enabled the military regimes in Brazil and Argentina to devote greater attention to problems of external security, including the defense of territorial waters and adjacent economic zones. For Brazil this has meant new diplomatic initiatives and modernization of its military power. In the late 1970s Brazil succeeded in persuading its neighbors in the Amazon region to conclude an agreement (the Amazon Pact) that provides a political foundation for improving economic cooperation and physical integration in the region. To the south Brazil has concluded new economic arrangements with Bolivia, Paraguay, and Uruguay.

Brazil has also sought to allay Argentine concern about the downstream effects of the Itaipu dam. Brazil's diplomacy on this issue has been inconsistent, however, keeping alive Argentine anxiety about the ultimate effects of the Itaipu project. Neither country, despite heated rhetoric, has seriously threatened military action to resolve the problem.

Argentina has focused its external security policies on preparing for the Beagle Channel confrontation with Chile and on modernizing its

56. Quoted in Carlos de Meira Mattos, *Brasil: Geopolítica e Destino* (Rio de Janeiro: Livraria José Olympio Editora, 1975), pp. 61–62.

military forces. After the Queen of England's 1977 arbitration award to Chile of sovereignty over the Picton, Lennox, and Nueva islands, Argentina began a major arms-buying spree. In 1978 the Argentine armed forces mobilized and augmented deployments in the south of the country. This buildup failed to persuade Chile to make the concessions Argentina wanted (probably cession of Chilean sovereignty over parts or all of those islands so that Argentina could expand its maritime boundaries, giving it control of a larger area of the ocean and its resources). In late 1978 Argentine-Chilean tension reached a peak of intensity when military action was forestalled by papal willingness to mediate the dispute. If this mediation were to falter, however, military tension could again erupt. Military conflict between Argentina and Chile would pose a serious threat to regional security, one that would sharply escalate if Peru decided to exploit Chile's difficulties by launching an attack against northern Chile to satisfy century-old irredentist claims. Such a conflict could not leave Brazil unscathed, and probably not uninvolved.

On occasion Argentines have floated the idea of creating a South Atlantic Treaty Organization with Brazil and South Africa. Brazil has shown no interest in the idea. While Brazil wants to play a greater naval role in the South Atlantic, it wants to do so on its own terms, with its top priority being the defense of adjacent waters of the Atlantic. Brazil has concentrated on improving its ties with black Africa; any military association with South Africa would jeopardize these efforts. Brazil would not trust Argentina to avoid seeking to use such an alliance to intimidate its friend Chile and to contain Brazil's freedom of action and expanding regional influence. Finally, Brazil has traditionally been wary of regional blocs, fearing they might be used to isolate it on important issues.

Military Spending, Force Levels, and Arms Production

By third world standards Brazil and Argentina do not maintain large military establishments. They did not, however, escape the wave of force modernization in the third world that began in the 1960s. They have modernized their military power in three ways: increased defense spending, imports of sophisticated major equipment (mostly from traditional suppliers in Europe), and expanded domestic arms production.

Statistics on Brazilian and Argentine military spending and force levels are shown in table 11-3. In 1978 Brazil's military spending, slightly over

Table 11-3. *Military Spending and Force Levels, Argentina and Brazil,*
Selected Years

Item	Argentina	Brazil
Military spending		
1978 (billions of U.S. dollars)	1.7	2.1
Average annual rate of increase of real		
spending, 1968–77 (percent)	3.8	1.9
As percentage of gross national product, 1977	2.0	1.0
Total armed forces	132,900	281,000
Major military equipment		
Combat aircraft (navy and air force)	244	142
Tanks	220	595
Major naval combatants[a]	16	27

Sources: International Institute for Strategic Studies, *The Military Balance, 1979–1980* (London: IISS, 1980), pp. 75–78; U.S. Arms Control and Disarmament Agency, *World Military Expenditures and Arms Transfers, 1968–1977* (Government Printing Office, 1979), pp. 33, 35. The IISS cautions that rapid inflation makes data on defense expenditures and gross national product for Argentina unreliable.
a. Aircraft carriers, submarines ,cruisers, destroyers, frigates.

$2 billion, exceeded that of Argentina, even though from 1968 to 1977 Argentine spending increased twice as rapidly in real terms as Brazil's. In 1977 Argentina spent 2 percent of its gross national product on defense, twice what Brazil spent (Brazil's percentages were higher in the recent past), but only about half the rate of spending by developing countries as a whole. In number of personnel, Brazil's armed forces are over twice as large as Argentina's. This disparity reflects Argentina's traditional policy of spending more to equip, train, and support its soldiers than Brazil has.

The military balance between Argentina and Brazil is hard to estimate. Neither country's armed forces have been tested on a large scale in modern conventional combat, but the armies of both nations have trained extensively in internal defense (counterinsurgency), cutting down on the amount of time available for training in conventional warfare. Financial constraints have also inhibited training. Performance in combat would depend on many factors besides size and proper training of the armed forces. These include the nature and location of conflict, the strategies employed, the amount of surprise achieved, leadership, and logistical capabilities.

Another important factor is the stock of military equipment on hand at the start of conflict. On this score, Brazil might have an advantage on the ground and at sea, and Argentina in the air. The Brazilian army has over twice the personnel and nearly three times as many tanks as the Argentine army. The Brazilian navy has more major naval combatants than its Argentine counterpart, including larger numbers of modern ships and ships equipped with surface-to-surface and surface-to-air missiles. Argentina has on order nine new major naval combatants, and Brazil is planning to build new ones in its own shipyards with foreign assistance. These new procurements could alter comparative naval strength. Argentina has twelve squadrons of combat aircraft (excluding counterinsurgency squadrons and including one naval air squadron); Brazil has only three squadrons. Argentina's air arm is optimized for ground attack and bombing roles; Brazil's is more oriented to air defense.

Except for the most sophisticated items of major combat equipment, Brazil and Argentina are producing increasing amounts of their arms needs at home. Brazil's ambitious plan to build destroyers and submarines in its own shipyards is a prominent example. This venture will doubtless prove to be very expensive. Brazil is producing armored personnel carriers for its own army and for export. It is also making an Italian-licensed jet fighter-trainer, the Xavante, as well as propeller-driven patrol aircraft.

Argentina has a longer tradition than Brazil of major arms production, but it does not make the diversified array of equipment that Brazil produces. Argentina makes a light tank (based on West German technology), a propeller-driven counterinsurgency aircraft (the Pucara), and a variety of light arms. Argentina's shipyards build fast-attack patrol boats, and they have assembled not only foreign submarines but also modern frigates using substantial foreign technology and components. Like Brazil, Argentina exports arms, mostly to other third world nations.

Nuclear Weapons Policy

If there is one subject that leaders in Argentina and Brazil have been less willing to comment on publicly than the issue of military rivalry, it is the question of the advantages and disadvantages of acquiring nuclear weapons. The official policy of both nations has been that they do not seek to acquire such weapons.

Citing the "undeniable risks" of proliferation, especially the "more serious and immediate danger of uninterrupted vertical proliferation,"

Argentina has declared its "opposition to nuclear arms as such wherever they may exist and whoever may possess them."[57] Brazil stresses that it "is a party to a Treaty [of Tlatelolco] which prohibits the manufacture or possession of nuclear weapons," and while the treaty is not yet in force for Brazil, it "has committed itself . . . not to perform any act which defeats the objectives of the Treaty" so long as other signatories do likewise.[58]

There is no reason to believe that the current defense policies of Argentina and Brazil are in any way inconsistent with these pledges. No credible assertions have been publicly made that either nation is engaged or plans to engage in a nuclear weapons program. Moreover, at least one Brazilian leader has pointed out the low utility of nuclear weapons for dealing with Brazil's main security challenges. Former President Castelo Branco stated that the capacity of the United States and the USSR to inflict "unacceptable damage" on each other helped "rehabilitate" conventional arms, "the only type adequate" for "wars of liberation or revolutionary wars, insurrection, counter-insurrection, and even guerrilla movements."[59]

Nuclear Options for the Future

The future nuclear choices of Brazil and Argentina can be grouped into four broad options: (1) *using* nuclear technology in electric power programs and for other civilian, nonexplosive purposes; (2) *supplying* other nations with nuclear technology; (3) developing *peaceful nuclear explosives;* and (4) *deploying nuclear weapons* with their armed forces.

Option 1: Nuclear User

Brazil and Argentina are well down the road in pursuit of option 1. Between them the two countries hope to have more than a dozen power reactors in operation before the century is out. They are making costly investments to acquire independent large-scale nuclear fuel cycles. Both countries are using nuclear technology for a variety of other purposes

57. Vice Admiral Oscar A. Montes, Minister of Foreign Affairs of the Argentine Republic, "Statement Delivered at the 10th Special Session of the United Nations General Assembly Devoted to Disarmament" (New York: Permanent Mission of Argentina to the United Nations, May 26, 1978), p. 7.

58. *Brazilian Nuclear Program*, pp. 21–22.

59. Quoted in Meira Mattos, *Brasil*, p. 63.

(such as research and health care). Finally, Brazil is attempting to establish a viable industry for the construction of light water power reactors.

Argentina and Brazil may scale down some of their nuclear plans, or at least take a cautious approach to new investments. Their reasons for doing so may include high costs, the obsolescence of certain technologies, environmental factors, and the attitudes toward nuclear programs of new governments.

Nevertheless, Brazil and Argentina are highly likely to retain commitments to absorbing nuclear technology. The political and technological benefits and the value of diversifying energy sources make these commitments worthwhile. Moreover, investments in nuclear technology today will put Brazil and Argentina in a better position to take advantage of future cost-reducing breakthroughs and, if ever necessary, to undertake nuclear weapons programs.

If Argentina and Brazil are interested solely in option 1, their hesitancy to accede to de jure full-scope safeguards and thereby forgo peaceful explosives may eventually diminish. For example, Argentina could be expected to ratify the Tlatelolco treaty, as Brazil has done. For reasons of prestige, sovereignty, and perhaps strategic uncertainty, however, the two nations might remain reluctant to agree to further restrictions, especially if foreign pressure were perceived as seeking to force concessions.

Option 2: Nuclear Supplier

Besides being nuclear users, Argentina and Brazil seem intent on becoming nuclear suppliers. This would boost their international prestige and influence, particularly in Latin America and the third world.

In pursuing the supplier option, Argentina is off to a head start. Having trained nuclear talent for three decades, it has exported significant numbers of nuclear technicians. Argentines have participated in nuclear programs in, for example, Brazil and Iran. Starting over a decade ago, Argentina began concluding nuclear cooperation agreements with Paraguay (1969), Peru (1969, 1977), Bolivia (1971), Colombia (1972), Rumania (1972), Uruguay (1979), Venezuela (1979), and South Korea (1980).[60]

60. Noticias Argentinas, February 12, 1980, translated in FBIS, *Worldwide Report* (March 10, 1980), p. 6; Agence France Presse (September 17, 1979), trans-

The program concluded in 1977 with Peru, a nation traditionally closer to Argentina than to Brazil, is the most prominent. Argentina has supplied Peru with a zero-power training reactor, for which Peru is acquiring fuel from the United States through Argentina. The Argentine-Peruvian agreement also calls for the transfer to Peru of a low-power (10-megawatt) reactor for the production of radioisotopes. This reactor will be similar to one that the Argentines have operated at Ezeiza for over a decade. In addition to supplying research reactors, Argentina will provide equipment for medical and agronomical use, for the treatment of uranium ores, and for uranium prospecting, and civil engineering structures for a nuclear complex.[61] The Argentine-Peruvian program is in many respects a model comprehensive agreement for nuclear cooperation between two third world nations that have different levels of experience in the nuclear field.

With the conclusion of the 1975 agreement with West Germany, Brazil took steps to become simultaneously a major supplier and user. In 1979 Brazil cashed in on its supplier potential by signing a wide-ranging agreement for nuclear cooperation with Iraq, one of its major oil suppliers. The nuclear agreement is an important symbol of the close mutual relationship the two countries have nurtured to reinforce and stabilize the oil connection. Iraq, on its part, may view Brazil's attitude toward the Arab-Israeli dispute as an aspect of the relationship. In early 1980 a high Iraqi official declared that Brazil's support in the United Nations for a resolution condemning Zionism as a form of racism "opened the doors of the Arab countries to Brazil and represented a milestone in Brazilian relations with these countries."[62]

The Brazilian-Iraqi agreement, unlike the Argentine-Peruvian accord, does not involve the transfer of research reactors (which Brazil may not yet be capable of exporting). It does, however, include the following areas of cooperation: uranium prospecting, supply of fuel (lightly enriched uranium for use in Iraqi nuclear reactors), reactor safety, use of the

---

lated in FBIS, *Worldwide Report* (October 10, 1979), p. 6; Latin (news service), August 8, 1979, translated in FBIS, *Worldwide Report* (September 14, 1979), pp. 46–47.

61. "Nuclear Assistance," *Clarin,* June 14, 1979, translated in FBIS, *Worldwide Report* (August 14, 1979), p. 42.

62. *O Estado de São Paulo* (January 20, 1980), p. 8, translated in FBIS, *Worldwide Report* (March 4, 1980), p. 3.

international nuclear information system of the IAEA, exchange of visits, and the conduct of scientific experiments and personnel training. Doubtless at Brazilian insistence and in accordance with restrictions in the 1975 Brazilian–West German agreement, the Brazilian-Iraqi accord stipulates that no "sensitive" materials or technology, including highly enriched uranium and reprocessing technology, will be transferred.[63]

Brazil has an interest in undertaking similar types of cooperation with other countries, but its most ambitious hope is to become an exporter of major power reactor components, and even complete reactors, to the rest of Latin America and elsewhere. Since Brazil cannot expect to compete internationally in reactor construction on a sustained basis with such giants as Westinghouse and Kraftwerk Union—in a field in which experience, innovation, and proven reliability count for a great deal—it should consider a more realistic approach—to attempt to establish itself as an international subcontractor for selected components and services used by large reactor builders. This would allow it to proceed step by step in competing in the international market, finding and developing comparative advantages in ways that best use its technological and financial resources. In retrospect, a major Brazilian mistake in negotiating the 1975 agreement with West Germany was its failure to bargain with Kraftwerk Union for assured subcontracting roles in the consortium's international reactor construction business.

Option 3: Nuclear Explosives

Argentina and Brazil have stoutly maintained their "right" to exercise a peaceful nuclear explosives option.[64] But the credibility of the peaceful explosives rationale is not what it once was. Despite early hopes, the U.S. peaceful nuclear explosive program never passed the experimental stage. The problems in using peaceful explosives were found to be considerable: "the dangers of long-lived radioactivity (and the potential difficulty of marketing even slightly radioactive products); the extreme difficulty of controlling the technical results from such large explosions; and the possibility of seismic shock waves that could damage buildings and other

---

63. "Text of Agreement," *O Estado de São Paulo* (January 25, 1980), translated in FBIS, *Worldwide Report* (March 4, 1980), pp. 5–6.

64. A recent example was a statement by Admiral Castro Madero, reported in Noticias Argentinas (May 12, 1980), translated in FBIS, *Daily Report: Latin America* (May 19, 1980), p. B2.

installations many miles away."[65] To be "clean," such explosions must be thermonuclear (that is, fusion-fission), but there are limits on how much the fission component of a thermonuclear explosion can be reduced. Also, the fusion part of the explosion produces some radioactivity itself.[66]

If Argentina and Brazil were to exercise the peaceful explosives option, they would arouse regional and international suspicion that they had done so for military reasons. Even without testing, an effort to develop nuclear explosives might not escape notice. With warning, hemispheric and other nations would bring strong diplomatic pressure to bear.

There are other reasons to believe that the costs and benefits of explosives testing would be greater for Argentina and Brazil than they were for India in 1974. The security environment in the southern cone is more tranquil than in South Asia. Nonproliferation diplomacy now has more international momentum than it did in 1974. And the economic rationale for nuclear explosives is becoming less and less persuasive.

On the other hand, the effects on Argentina and Brazil of detonating explosives might not be completely adverse, at least after a period of years following a detonation. For years both countries have aggressively maintained their right to detonate peaceful devices at little political cost in the region (although an actual test could dramatically change regional attitudes). Foreign nations have economic and other tangible interests in Brazil and Argentina; these interests will continue whether or not a test takes place.

Option 4: Nuclear Weapons

A fourth option is to develop and deploy nuclear weapons. The concept of "medium power nuclear forces" has been defined as "the ability of the country possessing the force to be able to threaten, in a second-strike mode, major strategic targets of at least one of the two superpowers."[67] Although this is more than Brazil and Argentina could achieve in the next decade or two, a lesser force might be within reach.

Such a capability may be termed a "small nuclear force," one that can

65. U.S. Arms Control and Disarmament Agency, *The American Experience with Peaceful Nuclear Explosives* (Government Printing Office, 1978), p. 6.

66. Ibid., p. 3.

67. Geoffrey Kemp, "Medium Power Nuclear Forces: Some Strategic Considerations," in Geoffrey Kemp, Robert L. Pfaltzgraff, Jr., and Uri Ra'anan, eds., *The Superpowers in a Multinuclear World* (Heath, 1974), pp. 145–46.

launch a credible first strike against a regional power but cannot expect to threaten a second strike against strategic targets of either superpower. There is a lot of leeway in this definition, which does not specify the numbers or types of weapons or delivery systems. A small nuclear force would, however, be capable enough to make its owner reasonably confident of maintaining regional finite deterrence (that is, a force capable of "surviving" a nuclear strike by another regional power with a small nuclear force and inflicting heavy damage in retaliation).[68] Even with only small nuclear forces, Argentina and Brazil would acquire a strategic military potential that they could not hope to achieve with conventional weaponry or expect Rio treaty allies to furnish on their behalf.

By the late 1980s Argentina and Brazil might have acquired the capacity to deploy, if they so chose, small nuclear forces. But both nations would have to overcome several obstacles. The largest hurdle would be obtaining the necessary explosive materials, highly enriched uranium or plutonium. Since Brazil is enjoined not to replicate technologies received under the Brazilian–West German agreement, it would probably have to break safeguards to acquire material for weapons. If its enrichment plant did not produce highly enriched uranium, Brazil would have to rely on plutonium produced in its reprocessing plant. It could not divert sufficient plutonium to equip a small nuclear force without timely detection by safeguards inspectors. The only way Brazil could produce unsafeguarded weapons-grade materials would be to develop its own sensitive technologies unrelated to the technologies furnished by West Germany. This may not be beyond its capacity in the late 1980s.

Having greater experience with nuclear technology, including heavy water production and reprocessing, Argentina might find it easier to acquire weapons-grade material (plutonium). Even though constrained by the safeguards against replication applied to the Sulzer heavy water plant, Argentina might be able to build a small, totally independent, unsafeguarded heavy water production plant, reactor, and reprocessing plant. The heavy water plant could not of course use Sulzer technology.

To deploy small nuclear forces Argentina and Brazil would also have to adapt or acquire new delivery systems, devise survivable basing modes, and develop reliable and secure command, control, and communications systems linking national command authorities to the nuclear forces.

68. Jerome H. Kahan, *Security in the Nuclear Age: Developing U.S. Strategic Arms Policy* (Brookings Institution, 1975), pp. 33–34.

At present, neither Argentina nor Brazil has a good delivery system although both could adapt aircraft in their current inventories for this purpose. Argentina could carry nuclear weapons in its aging British Canberra bombers or on its U.S. A-4 Skyhawk fighter-bombers, and Brazil on its Mirage III interceptors. If Brazil and Argentina were to decide to make the large investments and take the strategic risks required to deploy small nuclear forces, they almost certainly would purchase new, more capable delivery systems. A good choice would be the Jaguar International, the export version of the Anglo-French Jaguar, which France and Great Britain have used in nuclear roles. India recently made a large purchase of Jaguar Internationals. Whichever modern aircraft Argentina and Brazil chose, they would have only moderate difficulty in converting them for nuclear roles. Export versions of modern fighter-bombers have some computer-assisted bomb delivery capabilities and onboard computers that could be programmed for nuclear missions. Although export models would not contain nuclear wiring and delivery hardware, Brazil and Argentina could reconfigure the aircraft with simple but reliable nuclear safing, arming, fusing, and firing mechanisms.

Both countries would find it difficult to meet the size and weight constraints of external bomb carriage on fighter-bombers. But with moderate effort and possibly nuclear testing, they might be able to build suitable, aerodynamically styled bombs within the weight constraints of modern fighter-bombers.

Establishing a survivable basing mode would also be a large task for Argentina and Brazil. Both could deploy their nuclear fighter-bombers in hardened shelters at a number of dispersed airfields. Aircraft could be rotated frequently to other airfields, and techniques of concealment and deception could be used to further increase survivability. A limited number of nuclear fighter-bombers could remain on quick reaction alert. Brazil and Argentina could invest in air defense systems (including air-combat fighters, ground and airborne radar and control systems, and surface-to-air missiles) to protect nuclear fighter-bombers and their bases. Because most strategic targets in Argentina of possible interest to Brazil are located relatively close to Brazilian territory while most Brazilian targets are far from Argentina, Brazil would have a geographical advantage in devising its basing mode. It would also have a larger area over which to disperse its nuclear forces.

Since both Argentina and Brazil have competent and disciplined military forces, they would face no insurmountable obstacles in putting into place adequate command structures for decisionmaking on nuclear employment. The instabilities inherent in military regimes, however, would weaken these structures and heighten the risk of nuclear "accidents." The secure communications and control equipment needed probably could be purchased abroad, and procedures could be developed and practiced.

Argentina's large pool of skilled scientific manpower might give it an advantage in performing certain tasks (such as weapons development necessary to develop an effective small nuclear force). In time, Brazil could reduce this advantage by producing increased numbers of skilled personnel.

If Argentina and Brazil chose to build small nuclear forces, to what uses would they be put? Probably both nations would view their forces primarily as strategic deterrents. Neither has any motive for launching a strategic offensive against the other or for using nuclear weapons in tactical roles (such as to blunt enemy armored assaults in strategic corridors). Hence both countries could be expected to place great stress on enhancing stable deterrence. To do this they could invest in survivable basing modes and penetrative delivery systems. They could also try to acquire better reconnaissance capabilities to provide earlier warning and monitor enemy deployments, but satellite reconnaissance systems are many years away. This would put a premium on pursuing confidence-building measures (such as political accommodation in disputes and prior notification of military exercises) and cooperative measures to make reconnaissance easier (such as permitting frequent and flexible mutual inspections of military and nuclear facilities). Nuclear arms control negotiations between the two countries would therefore seem an attractive option.

Conclusions

The regional security environments of Argentina and Brazil seem enviably benign. Nevertheless, their nuclear choices are not predetermined. Many factors will influence these choices. For one, the acquisition by either nation of nuclear weapons would put strong pressure on the other to do likewise. Neither nation would look forward with confidence to a future in which the other could use nuclear weapons as an instrument of coercive diplomacy, to say nothing of strategic warfare. A second development could also distort nuclear choices: a major military conflict between Argentina and Chile over the Beagle Channel dispute. Such an event could prolong military tension in the southern cone, reduce Chilean deterrent power against a Peruvian attack from the north, lead to new Brazilian perception of Argentina as a militarily aggressive nation, and persuade Argentine leaders that their country's security required the development of nuclear weapons.

If either of these contingencies were to occur, nuclear weapons proliferation by both nations would be a real risk. If they do not occur, however, the future nuclear choices of Argentina and Brazil may depend in great part on the advantages and disadvantages of each option that are already apparent.

Brazil and Argentina are strongly committed to using nuclear energy and technology. This is unlikely to change. The desire of both to expand and diversify energy sources, assert national independence, and master nuclear technology is so strong that nuclear power programs will continue even if they are slowed by rising costs or technical and environmental problems. The desire of both to gain independent fuel cycles is also strong. They may well retain major programs for this purpose—uranium enrichment, reprocessing, and heavy water production—even if they cost much more than importing the final products. But Brazil's enthusiasm for the jet-nozzle enrichment process may fade, and commercial-scale reprocessing may prove to have more costs than benefits. Argentina and Brazil are almost sure to continue nuclear research for a variety of peaceful applications, including medical and assorted industrial uses.

Supplying nuclear equipment, technology, and services is also an option that Argentina and Brazil will probably continue to pursue. For both countries nuclear cooperation with Latin American countries and a few nations outside the region has already proved to be a useful instrument of foreign policy. Compared with the size of their domestic nuclear programs, however, external programs of cooperation are small. Brazil's reactor production and engineering enterprises are unlikely to win many large foreign contracts unless they are heavily subsidized. If Brazil is to realize its hope of becoming a major nuclear exporter, these companies must specialize, enabling them to exploit comparative advantages in acquiring an international subcontracting role for the major nuclear suppliers.

Neither country is likely to find the peaceful nuclear explosives option economically or environmentally alluring. The research experience of the United States does not lead to optimism about the utility of such explosives anywhere in the world. Pursuit of this option by Argentina or Brazil, however, could give rise to mutual misunderstandings and misperceptions about each other's intentions. This risk would not be worth running in the current security environment in South America unless the nation taking the risk saw the peaceful explosives option as a precautionary staging area, from which it could reevaluate the security interests and reactions of rivals before deciding whether to deploy nuclear weapons.

Unless contingencies having sharply destabilizing effects on regional security environments materialize, the incentives for Argentina and Brazil to deploy nuclear weapons will be low. But if such weapons are deployed, the incentives for bilateral nuclear arms control will be high.

Whatever nuclear choices Brazil and Argentina make, the two countries probably will continue to try to keep their nuclear options open. Their fierce opposition to the NPT, reluctance to bring the Tlatelolco treaty into force for themselves, refusal to agree to de jure full-scope safeguards, and insistence on the right (even under the Tlatelolco treaty) to conduct peaceful nuclear explosions are all signs that both nations remain committed to preserving political and strategic flexibility.

Such policies are not without risk, however. Mutual strategic flexibility implies mutual strategic uncertainty. The historic May 1980 meeting of the presidents of Argentina and Brazil offered some reassurance about national intentions, including nuclear intentions. But close political cooperation between the two nations on matters of strategic consequence does not enjoy a long or recent tradition. The task for Brazil and Argentina is to create such a tradition.

PART FIVE

South Africa

RICHARD K. BETTS

A Diplomatic Bomb? South Africa's Nuclear Potential

A NATION'S decision to manufacture nuclear weapons depends on its incentives, capabilities, and disincentives. For two reasons South Africa should not be a threat to the cause of nonproliferation. First, it has few plausible military uses for nuclear weapons. Second, the government in Pretoria has something to lose—by alienating what little Western support it still has and inviting diplomatic and economic retaliation—if it acquires a bomb. At present, in short, incentives are negligible and disincentives substantial.

Four other considerations, however, suggest there is great reason for concern. First, disincentives exist, but they are declining. As the apartheid regime becomes increasingly isolated and supportive European and American involvement in the country (including nuclear cooperation) erodes, South Africa has progressively less to lose by provocative behavior. It is an agonizing dilemma that as trends become more favorable for the black African cause they may become less favorable for nonproliferation. Second, capabilities are no barrier to a nuclear decision; with a highly developed nuclear establishment, including unsafeguarded uranium enrichment facilities, Pretoria could build a bomb any time it wishes to. Third, because these capabilities are sufficient, it does not matter if analysts in

Washington or other capitals perceive few rational incentives and many disincentives for a South African weapons program; the only determining factors are the calculations and perceptions of South African authorities. If they see the issue differently, they may build a bomb. According to public reports, the Soviet and American governments were sure that South Africa planned to test a nuclear device in the Kalahari Desert in the summer of 1977, a course from which it was dissuaded only by heavy pressure. Preventing such action in the future could require more strenuous threats or inducements. Fourth, and most obvious, circumstantial evidence indicates that a nuclear detonation may have occurred in the South Atlantic on September 22, 1979, and South Africa is the prime suspect. Even more obviously than Israel, South Africa has at least a "bomb in the basement"—a card it might try to play in the rough-and-tumble of international bargaining, a prospective "nuclear *laager*"[1]—and at worst it has, like India, entered the nuclear club already.

South African Nuclear Capabilities

There are no longer any illusions about whether Pretoria can easily build a bomb. When asked in a 1976 interview if South Africa's defenses include a nuclear capability, Prime Minister John Vorster replied pointedly, "We are only interested in the peaceful applications of nuclear power. But we can enrich uranium, and we have the capability. And we did not sign the nuclear-nonproliferation treaty."[2] This statement attracted widespread attention and comment. Tanzania's leader Julius Nyerere noted, in predicting the ultimate victory of black nationalists in South Africa, that they would be the first African leaders with nuclear weapons.[3] While capability is undisputed, it is useful to outline its specific nature and limits, to deduce where leverage—both by and against

1. The phrase is from Ronald W. Walters, "U.S. Policy and Nuclear Proliferation in South Africa," in Western Massachusetts Association of Concerned African Scholars, *U.S. Military Involvement in Southern Africa* (Boston: South End Press, 1978), p. 177. The *laager* refers to the old defensive encampments of Afrikaner pioneers and is used metaphorically like the Israeli "Masada complex."
2. Quoted in *Newsweek* (May 17, 1976), p. 53.
3. John F. Burns, "South Africa's Secret Atom Plant Suspected of Working on a Bomb," *New York Times*, April 30, 1977.

South Africa—exists. The remaining dependence of the country's nuclear program on external sources may furnish one of the few openings for directing influence against proliferation, but uranium and enrichment resources also give the regime some potential influence with energy-hungry nations.

The South African Atomic Energy Board (AEB) was established in 1949, the first uranium plant was opened at Krugersdorp in 1952, a research and development program began in 1957 at the Nuclear Physics Research Unit of the University of Witwatersrand, and the country's first research reactor—called Safari-I, with a capacity of 20 megawatts, and supplied by the United States—began operating at Pelindaba in 1965. There are a second working, zero-energy research reactor, called Pelunduna Zero, entirely designed and built indigenously, and two French-supplied 922-megawatt light water power reactors planned to become operational at Koeberg in 1982 and 1983. As of 1978 nuclear generating capacity was projected to be 1,844 megawatts by 1985, 3,844 megawatts by 1990, and 11,844 megawatts by the end of the century.[4] A pilot plant for uranium enrichment with a capacity of 40,000 separative work units (SWUs) was completed in 1975.[5]

The economic rationales advanced for moving toward nuclear generation of energy are considerable but do not seem entirely consistent. South Africa has a high rate of energy consumption because of its energy-intensive mining and metallurgical industries, but the country has massive coal resources, which can be extracted profitably (in part because of low wages in the mines). Development of nuclear power generation is justified by some as necessary to conserve coal for conversion into liquid fuel, since oil is the one critical energy resource South Africa lacks. (The country is also potentially more vulnerable to an ideologically inspired oil embargo, as the decision by Iran—previously the source of 80 to 90 per-

4. John J. Stobbs, Judith B. Fox, and James H. Allen, *International Data Collection and Analysis*, vol. 4, EN-77-C-01-5072, prepared for U.S. Department of Energy (Atlanta: Nuclear Assurance Corporation, 1978), pp. SOUTH AFRICA-8, -9, -29; J. E. Spence, "The Republic of South Africa: Proliferation and the Politics of 'Outward Movement,' " in Robert M. Lawrence and Joel Larus, eds., *Nuclear Proliferation: Phase II* (University Press of Kansas for the National Security Education Program, 1974), pp. 214–15; R. L. M. Patil, "South Africa's Nuclear Situation," *Africa Quarterly* (New Delhi), vol. 8 (April–June 1968), p. 46.

5. Robert I. Rotberg, *Suffer the Future: Policy Choices in Southern Africa* (Harvard University Press, 1980), p. 152.

cent of the country's petroleum—to cut off supply demonstrated.)[6] Yet because of its abundant coal South Africa uses much less oil (as a proportion of total energy generation) than other countries of its size, sales of coal abroad help the balance of payments, and hence the government plans to export substantial amounts of coal. Nuclear power becomes more economically attractive, in turn, as coal prices rise. The combination of uranium and coal resources are cited happily by some South Africans as enabling the country to become a net exporter of energy.[7] Thus nuclear power is justified alternately by the need to conserve coal for domestic use and the need to export it (although nuclear power is also justified by the desire not to construct expensive facilities for transmitting power over the 1,000-mile distance from the Transvaal coalfields to the Cape). Probably either the country will not place a high priority on expanding nuclear

6. Two SASOL plants (the acronym is derived from the Afrikaans for South African Coal, Oil, and Gas Corporations) have been developed for gasification and liquefaction of coal. South African estimates of the proportion of the country's petroleum needs these plants will provide when their expansion is complete in the early 1980s range between 30 and 47 percent. Some British economists' estimates are lower (26 to 30 percent with three complete plants). See "Fuel Crisis: And Now for Sasol 2½," *Financial Mail* (Johannesburg), February 23, 1979; Caryle Murphy, "To Cope with Embargoes, S. Africa Converts Coal Into Oil," *Washington Post,* April 27, 1979; and Carel Birkby, "Oil from Coal," in *South Africa—the Free World's Treasure House* (Sandton, S.A.: Broadside Publishers, 1977), p. 102. This process is an inefficient way to produce fuel because it requires vast amounts of energy itself. There is a certain irreducible need for oil, however, that cannot be satisfied by other energy substitutes. Oil price rises have made the SASOL process less economically unattractive, and the threat of an oil embargo adds to incentives for it. Even if it is exceptionally expensive, the rationale is that "strategically, and in the light of long-term development, it is a must." Birkby, "Oil from Coal," pp. 104, 106. See also "Oil Supplies: Crunch Could Come Soon," *Financial Mail,* February 9, 1979; and Jan C. Hoogendoorn, "Gas from Coal for Synthesis of Hydrocarbons" (Communication 960), paper prepared for the 112th IGE Annual General Meeting, London, May 1975. The government's sensitivity to the oil situation after Iran's cutoff is reflected by the bill in parliament in 1979 to outlaw news reporting on South Africa's sources of supply and shipping, which coincided with allegations of a scheme to have oil laundered through Dominica. David Taylor, "Oily Intrigue . . . Bungled Invasion," *New African* (July 1979), pp. 10, 13.

7. See P. E. Rousseau, "Energy," *South Africa International* (Johannesburg), vol. 9 (July 1978), pp. 26, 28; "Does South Africa Have the Bomb?" *New African* (October 1977), p. 971; Chester Crocker, "South Africa: Strategic Perspectives and Capabilities," paper prepared for the Institute for Foreign Policy Analysis collection for the U.S. Navy, *U.S. Maritime Interests in the South Atlantic* (February 1977), pp. 22–23.

power generation if cost pressure or other constraints arise in the future or (more likely) its reasons for maintaining a commitment to nuclear power are not purely economic (for instance, national pride in being on the leading edge of modern science and technology or desire to maintain the nuclear military option).

In any case, two significant factors make South Africa's commercial nuclear plans important to the outside world: the country's large share of global noncommunist uranium reserves, and its emerging capability to enrich uranium. (The only substantial lack in the fuel cycle is fuel fabrication facilities, and this could be overcome fairly easily if necessary.) Past estimates of South African uranium resources have ranged as high as 25 percent of noncommunist reserves (all now agree this figure is too high); the rest are concentrated in the United States, Canada, Australia, and Niger. Some South Africans see their country's large share as a significant source of potential international economic leverage, given the energy crisis.[8] Uranium output averaged 13 to 14 percent of noncommunist production in the mid-1970s and increased greatly (to over 23 percent in 1977) as demand and prices rose and domestic debate curtailed Australian exports. The South African Nuclear Fuels Corporation had earlier announced plans to double production to about 6,000 tons by 1980,[9] but this figure was substantially exceeded even by 1977 (6,700 tons estimated).

There has been some criticism from Europeans opposed to large purchases of South African natural uranium. In 1978 there was a controversy in the European Parliament over the European Community's growing dependence on supplies from Pretoria caused by restrictions imposed by Canada and Australia. Socialist members were opposed to supporting the apartheid economy with large orders.[10] Half a year later, nevertheless, Belgium contracted to buy more South African uranium specifically to diversify sources of supply. Unlike Canada and Australia, Pretoria im-

8. See Zdenek Červenka and Barbara Rogers, *The Nuclear Axis: Secret Collaboration Between West Germany and South Africa* (Times Books, 1978), pp. 153–54.
9. Crocker, "South Africa," p. 23. The 1977 percentage is calculated from estimated data in *Uranium: Resources, Production, and Demand,* joint report by the OECD Nuclear Energy Agency and the IAEA (Paris: Organization for Economic Cooperation and Development, December 1977), p. 23.
10. "European Parliament Worried Over Dependence on South African Uranium," *Nuclear Engineering International* (July 1978), p. 11.

posed no conditions beyond those required by Euratom and the International Atomic Energy Agency.[11] On balance there seems to be no evidence that the anti-apartheid movement is about to infringe significantly on South African uranium sales.

How significant the country's market power will be, though, is uncertain. Data of the IAEA and the Organization for Economic Cooperation and Development for 1979 projected South Africa's and Namibia's combined share of reasonably assured uranium resources outside the Soviet bloc and China to be about 20 percent at forward costs of less than $80 per kilogram. At forward costs of between $80 and $130 a kilogram, the combined share is only about 22 percent. If Namibia is excluded, South Africa's shares decline to 13 and 19 percent, respectively. South Africa's share of attainable uranium production capabilities in the world outside the USSR and China is projected to decline to about 13 percent by 1990 if Namibia is still included, and less than 9 percent if it is not. If Namibia gains independence under a genuinely autonomous government, Pretoria's leverage in the international uranium market will be less impressive than many observers now believe.[12]

Enrichment capability is the central aspect of South Africa's potential for acquiring weapons. Combined with possession of all the natural uranium any weapons program could require, it makes relatively inconsequential the scale of the country's power generation capacity. Suppliers' restrictions on aid in the development of power reactors or reprocessing facilities might constrain a weapons program by limiting the accumulation and separability of plutonium, but plutonium is not necessary for the South African option. (The spent fuel from the Koeberg reactors, according to French Foreign Minister Louis de Guiringaud, is to be sent to France for reprocessing and the plutonium would not be returned to South Africa.[13]) The salient factor is that Pretoria has its own indigenously developed enrichment process, which would be the most direct and logical source of fissionable material. Government secrecy prevents sure knowledge of whether the process is capable of weapons-grade enrich-

11. "Synatom to Use S. African Uranium," *Nuclear Engineering International* (February 1979), p. 7.

12. *Uranium: Resources, Production, and Demand*, pp. 18, 23.

13. Jim Hoagland, "Paris Warns South Africa on A-Testing," *Washington Post*, August 23, 1977.

ment, but there is no public evidence to contradict South African statements that it is.

The South African process, touted in 1970 as new and "unique," is called "high-performance stationary-walled centrifuge" and is similar to the West German Becker jet-nozzle concept.[14] The government had too ambitious hopes for what this development would provide. A. J. A. Roux, chairman of the AEB, estimated that the country could earn $300 million a year by exporting enriched rather than raw uranium. Several years ago it planned to be able to meet 14 percent of the world need for enriched uranium by 1980, even though there was only a pilot plant at Valindaba.[15] These hopes proved unrealistic, but plans were made for a commercial enrichment facility (built mostly with indigenous materials and by South African firms) with an annual capacity of 5 million SWUs starting in 1986; and in 1977 there were claims of technical improvements and increased economic efficiency in the process and the Uranium Enrichment Corporation solicited contracts for enrichment from other countries. There were also unconfirmed reports that new contracts for exported uranium contained stipulations for enrichment in South Africa.[16]

Commercial enrichment goals were soon reduced drastically. The 5,000 tons of SWU capacity planned was extraordinarily large and there was no certainty that enough domestic uranium would be available to feed it. There was also a large escalation of cost estimates, a local recession, and difficulty in raising capital for the project. The United States refused to sell special components and encouraged other suppliers to refuse as well. The government decided simply to expand the pilot plant, for a

14. Central Intelligence Agency, "Nuclear Energy," ER 77-10468 (CIA, August 1977), p. 17. Červenka and Rogers, in *Nuclear Axis*, present a not entirely convincing amount of circumstantial evidence that the Germans colluded with South Africa in the latter's enrichment development. Whether or not this is true has little bearing on future prospects for proliferation by Pretoria.

15. P. Boskma, "Uranium Enrichment Proliferation of Nuclear Weapons," in Bhupendra Jasani, ed., *Nuclear Proliferation Problems* (MIT Press for the Stockholm International Peace Research Institute, 1974), p. 105; "South Africa Is Calm Amid Nuclear Furor," *New York Times*, August 28, 1977.

16. *Resource Development in South Africa and U.S. Policy*, Hearings before the Subcommittee on International Resources, Food, and Energy of the House Committee on International Relations, 94 Cong. 2 sess. (Government Printing Office, 1976), p. 61; *Nucleonics Week*, vol. 18 (May 5, 1977), p. 9; *Nucleonics Week*, vol. 19 (January 5, 1978), p. 12; Stobbs, Fox, and Allen, *International Data Collection and Analysis*, vol. 4, p. SOUTH AFRICA-23.

capacity that was more modest but at least enough to meet the fuel reload requirements of the reactors at Koeberg.[17] American estimates for an International Nuclear Fuel Cycle Evaluation working group state that this facility will provide 256 tons of SWUs by 1983 and note South African suggestions that further expansion of capacity for export is being held open as an option.[18] Even if South African hopes of becoming a major international supplier of enrichment services are disappointed, however, there is no physical barrier to indigenous production of substantial amounts of fissionable bomb-making material. If the pilot plant were to be dedicated to weapons, it could turn out enough material for up to twenty bombs a year. By dedicating only the excess from the expansion of the pilot plant, rather than full capacity, about twelve bombs a year could be produced.[19]

Strategic Incentives and Military Options

South Africa does have some economic and political incentives for achieving full fuel-cycle capabilities. While underdeveloped countries like India seek technical autonomy as a matter of principle, to achieve equality and break the pattern of dependence on old colonial powers that are viewed as exploiting economic relationships for uneven gain, South Africa seeks autonomy as a matter of pragmatism, to reduce its vulnerability to decisions by other powers to cut off the technical relationship. This rationale for independence might mitigate the threatening implications of the regime's nuclear capabilities.[20] There are, however, indicators of other grounds for concern.

17. "Unenriched, But Rich," *The Economist* (February 25, 1978), p. 79; Červenka and Rogers, *Nuclear Axis,* pp. 186–87; Rotberg, *Suffer the Future,* p. 152. The decision was partly motivated by the desire to have enrichment capacity on line in time for the start-up of the Koeberg reactors since South Africa can no longer rely on the willingness of other states to supply enriched uranium. The larger plant could not have been finished in time. Robert S. Jaster, *South Africa's Narrowing Security Options,* Adelphi Paper 159 (London: International Institute for Strategic Studies, 1980), p. 46.

18. "Uranium Enrichment Present Position," paper prepared by the United States of America for Working Group 3–Supply Assurances, International Nuclear Fuel Cycle Evaluation Program (March 24, 1978), pp. 4–5.

19. Rotberg, *Suffer the Future,* pp. 152–53.

20. For an analysis that stresses weaknesses, see Pauline H. Baker, "South Africa's Strategic Vulnerabilities: The 'Citadel Assumption' Reconsidered," *African Studies Review,* vol. 20 (September 1977), pp. 89–99.

Like Israel, South Africa's official position renounces acquisition of nuclear weapons under current circumstances but presents a calculated ambiguity and a series of subtly conflicting indications about what its policy might be if conditions change. Pretoria has refused to sign the Treaty on the Non-Proliferation of Nuclear Weapons (NPT) but justifies this entirely on economic grounds—that external safeguards could jeopardize the security of its enrichment technology or, if extended in coverage, its gold-production industry (most uranium extraction in South Africa is done in tandem with gold mining).

As early as the inauguration of the country's first research reactor in 1965, however, Prime Minister Hendrik F. Verwoerd referred explicitly to the government's "duty" to "consider" the military uses of nuclear material. Chairman Roux of the AEB quickly discounted this and consistently downplayed suggestions of official interest in nuclear arms. In February 1965 the AEB said production of one nuclear weapon would cost as much as one-quarter of the defense budget. Such an estimate was transparently excessive; indeed one board member, Andries Visser, promoted the idea of a bomb and said, "Money is no problem." (It is certainly no problem now. The Central Intelligence Agency reported a South African defense budget of $2.3 billion for the fiscal year ending in March 1979. At this rate the country could spend $100 million a year on a nuclear weapons program, exclusive of the required elements already funded by other allocations—such as aircraft procurement—by diverting less than 5 percent of conventional military expenditures.) In December 1968 General H. J. Martin, chief of staff of the army, noted that the country was prepared to manufacture nuclear arms and connected this with missile-development programs under way; Minister of Defense Pieter W. Botha (now prime minister) denied this.[21] In 1972 the AEB's annual report admitted it was considering peaceful nuclear explosions, although this was not mentioned in subsequent reports.[22]

The government in Pretoria obviously perceives a serious threat to its security and little prospect for any external help in reducing the threat. As the last regime on earth constitutionally based on blatant and comprehensive racial discrimination, it has many local adversaries and few

21. Spence, "Republic of South Africa," p. 215. On the defense budget, see Central Intelligence Agency, *National Basic Intelligence Factbook* (GPO, July 1979), p. 181.
22. Rotberg, *Suffer the Future*, p. 155, n. 25.

friends in the international community. In military terms, though, it is hard for any strategist to devise a usable role for a nuclear force. The country's conventional military power is overwhelming compared to that of antagonistic neighboring states. In the 1970s, despite supplier restraints, nearly a third of the arms imported into sub-Saharan Africa went to South Africa, and by 1976 South Africa's defense expenditures constituted a third of the expenditures of all of Africa except Egypt.[23] Nuclear explosions offer no conceivable tactical advantages in dealing with internal and unconventional military opponents.

After the Sharpeville massacre, formation of the Organization of African Unity, and the 1963 United Nations arms embargo, South Africa undertook a massive defense buildup. Military expenditures grew sixteenfold between 1960 and 1975, with particularly sharp and consistent increases after 1972. In 1977, according to the government's own figures, defense spending rose 21.3 percent, to constitute 18 percent of the total budget; by 1980 the defense budget was even higher in absolute terms (though declining as a percentage of total government expenditures) and represented only 5 percent of gross domestic product.[24]

Despite these figures, there is no severe strain on the South African economy. Even at recently high levels, they are not markedly greater as a percentage of gross national product than current American defense budgets. So Pretoria's conventional military establishment remains even more expansible; another massive increase of even a quarter or a third would hardly boost the effort above the GNP-allocation level of U.S. defense spending in the late 1950s and early 1960s. And the current size of South Africa's military establishment dwarfs its regional competitors: in 1977 the government doubled the term of conscription to two years, and there have been major increases in white reserve forces. By 1979 the armed forces had 63,250 active personnel and a full mobilization strength of 404,500 (the total is lower if only active reserves are counted). Despite the limitations placed on arms sales by foreign suppliers, the military's equipment is substantial and sophisticated. The navy, for example, has

23. Chester A. Crocker, "Current and Projected Military Balances in Southern Africa," in Richard E. Bissell and Chester A. Crocker, eds., *South Africa into the 1980s* (Westview Press, 1979), p. 71.

24. Edouard Bustin, "South Africa's Foreign Policy Alternatives and Deterrence Needs," in Onkar Marwah and Ann Schulz, eds., *Nuclear Proliferation and the Near-Nuclear Countries* (Ballinger, 1975), pp. 207, 212, 213; "South Africa Increases Outlays for Defense," *New York Times,* March 31, 1977; CIA, *National Basic Intelligence Factbook* (July 1979), p. 181.

three submarines, and the air force has 416 combat aircraft (more than Italy or Canada, over six times as many as bordering black African adversaries Angola and Mozambique together, and still over a third more than the combined total for those two countries and Nigeria, Tanzania, Zambia, and Zaire, which suggests what the "balance" in the air would be even if several major African states transferred their assets to front-line combatants). The South African total includes two light bomber squadrons of Canberras and Buccaneers, several fighter squadrons of Mirages, four helicopter squadrons, and a number of reconnaissance squadrons.[25]

One major problem is the United Nations arms embargo, imposed as voluntary in 1963 and made mandatory in 1977. But this has not been airtight by any means. Even Britain's Labour government moderated the embargo in the 1960s, continuing to supply spare parts for weapons sold previously if the weapons were not applicable to enforcing apartheid. This prevented the grounding of South Africa's jets.[26] France continued to sell South Africa arms for many years, and much material from other countries seems to have found its way there through "laundering" in third countries or by clandestine routes.[27] Moreover, the international restrictions stimulated the development of the domestic arms industry, which has made the country self-sufficient in many types of conventional weaponry.

The embargo, however, is tighter than in the past. The Nixon administration, following the notorious National Security Study Memorandum 39 (on southern Africa), applied generous standards to cases of "gray area" sales—materials for civilian purposes that could be applied to military forces. The Carter administration suspended such sales (for instance, spare parts for C-130 cargo planes),[28] as well as sales of police equipment and "nonlethal" items such as uniforms. And when Defense Min-

25. International Institute for Strategic Studies, *The Military Balance, 1979–1980* (London: IISS, 1979), pp. 23, 28, 49, 52, 54–55. Two analysts working separately, Sean Gervasi and General Sir Walter Walker, concluded that South Africa's forces are larger, perhaps double the IISS figures on many kinds of equipment. See Barry Cohen, "The Question Mark Over South African Arms," *New African* (October 1977), p. 972; "South Africa's New Muscle," *To the Point,* November 3, 1978.

26. John Stanley and Maurice Pearton, *The International Trade in Arms* (Praeger for the International Institute for Strategic Studies, 1972), p. 174.

27. For example, see David C. Martin and John Walcott, "Smuggling Arms to South Africa," *Washington Post,* August 5, 1979.

28. Mohamed A. El-Khawas and Barry Cohen, eds., *The Kissinger Study of Southern Africa: National Security Study Memorandum 39* (Lawrence Hill, 1976), pp. 36, 107. See also William H. Lewis, "U.S. Arms Embargo Against South Africa," *Department of State Bulletin* (September 5, 1977), pp. 320–22.

ister Botha said France would not renege on contracts for ships and sub-marines, the French responded by confining the corvette *Good Hope* (already paid for and with a crew standing by) to port. Israel, which had previously agreed to sell patrol boats with Gabriel missiles, also an-nounced it would observe the stricter embargo. The French, however, admitted that the South Africans have had enough experience with the licensed manufacture of Mirage planes, Panhard armored cars, and Crotale missiles to make them themselves[29] and did not forbid delivery of the goods that were in the pipeline before the strengthening of the em-bargo.

Because of South Africa's geographic position and the weakness of black African states, there is realistically no conventional threat that Pre-toria could not handle easily. African states today have minimal air power and airlift, lack bases within reach of important areas in South Africa, and face language and political problems that make an integrated African alliance command structure infeasible.[30] The only nation with the eco-nomic resources to develop an impressive military force if it chooses to is Nigeria, which is far away. Deployable Cuban forces would increase the danger but would not decisively challenge the South African edge—espe-cially if the results of Cuban-South African engagement in Angola in 1975 are indicative of the relative capabilities of the forces.[31] The principal threat South Africa faces is internal revolution and guerrilla warfare, perhaps supported by bordering states. A leap of imagination is required to see how even small and discriminate tactical nuclear weapons could seem applicable to this threat. A nuclear force would have no plausible targets. At best, the bomb could hypothetically be used to blackmail either Angola or Mozambique into sealing its borders and interning guerrillas,

29. Bob Atkinson, "UN Arms Embargo—Will It Really Bite?" *New African* (January 1978), p. 85. This article noted rumors "that Pretoria was ready to lean heavily on the French to get the warships and submarines, and would go so far as to cancel . . . [the] contract for [the Koeberg nuclear power stations] . . . if the French didn't deliver." This is a minor example (if the deal were for reprocessing or en-richment facilities, it would be a major one) of the potential dilemma for non-proliferationists in situations where weapons-applicable nuclear capabilities might be constrained at the price of offsetting and distasteful favors. See Richard K. Betts, "Paranoids, Pygmies, Pariahs, and Nonproliferation," *Foreign Policy*, no. 26 (Spring 1977), pp. 179–83.

30. William Gutteridge, "Southern Africa: A Study in Conflict," in David Carlton and Carlo Schaerf, eds., *The Dynamics of the Arms Race* (Wiley, 1975), p. 236.

31. See Kenneth L. Adelman, "The Strategy of Defiance: South Africa," *Com-parative Strategy*, vol. 1 (1978), pp. 37–38.

by threatening to destroy Luanda, Maputo, or Cuban cantonments. This strategy would obviously be incalculably reckless and could not conceivably seem preferable to using conventional military power unless white control was crumbling. In the latter instance a bomb might be detonated for demonstrative purposes, perhaps over the Kalahari Desert, to shock the enemy, deter further action, and persuade the enemy to withdraw.[32]

There is one remote contingency for which a nuclear force for deterrence or use as a last resort might seem militarily applicable. The Soviet naval presence in the Indian Ocean, as well as support for Angola and Mozambique, make the eventuality of Soviet intervention more plausible to authorities in South Africa than it may appear to others. To determine whether nuclear weapons would be useful for dealing with this contingency depends on making some assumptions about future desperation: (1) Soviet development of massive long-range power projection forces; (2) direct Soviet intervention with large forces on behalf of elements fighting the apartheid regime; (3) refusal of Western nations to become involved. Nuclear weapons could conceivably be useful against massed naval forces or bases in neighboring countries. Pretoria might rationalize the credibility of such an option by the fact that Afrikaner society would be fighting against its own extinction, that Soviet nuclear preemption would be constrained by the prospect of numerous black African casualties, and that the Soviet gains from intervention would not be worth even the risk of facing nuclear combat. This sort of South African capability would be a proportional deterrent, a tactical *force de frappe:* tactical to the Soviet Union, strategic to South Africa. (Use against a Soviet naval blockade is another possibility, though even less likely since nuclear weapons would be harder to employ effectively against submarines.) One might argue that even with the Soviet Union Pretoria has more to lose than to gain from nuclear status, since it would propel the country onto the Soviet targeting list. But South African military analysts have long speculated that this has happened anyway because Western access to South Africa's ports would require the USSR to interdict them in a general war.[33] All things considered, the purely military rationales for a South African nuclear force are not nonexistent, but they are negligible

---

32. Kenneth L. Adelman and Albion W. Knight, "Can South Africa Go Nuclear?" *Orbis,* vol. 23 (Fall 1979), p. 643.

33. Captain Deon Fourie, "Is South Africa a Soviet Nuclear Target?" *Kommando* (Pretoria), vol. 15 (June 1964), pp. 21–22.

and are not imminent. Purely military motives, however, are not necessarily the only ones that could impel a decision to build the bomb.

Diplomatic Uses of the Nuclear Option

The South African regime has tried energetically to alleviate its diplomatic isolation. The "outward" policy of détente in the early 1970s began to make some headway with states such as Zambia, Liberia, Senegal, and Ivory Coast but was aborted by the collapse of the Portuguese empire and ensuing events in Angola. South Africa has tried particularly to convince Western nations that it would be a valuable partner in the global struggle against communism. This effort had modest success at best in the decades after World War II and has had almost none in recent years. (Press reports based on revelations of former South African officials claim that the government engaged in a sub-rosa campaign of bribery and propaganda purveyed through front organizations to curry favor with Western officials and improve the regime's image. There appears to be little evidence that such "Pretoriagate" operations were effective.)

The main argument white South Africans have used to promote ties with the West—and one of the few arguments to attract any substantial support outside of reactionary circles in the United States—is that the country is geostrategically vital because of its mineral resources and the sea-lanes around the Cape of Good Hope, along which oil supplies critical to Europe and America travel. A hostile regime in South Africa, this argument maintains, could cut these lines of communication and choke off energy supplies, and a friendly regime offers naval bases that would be critical in a global war. Former Commander in Chief, Pacific, Admiral John McCain, for instance, has said, "We absolutely need access to South African naval facilities at Simonstown and Durban." British apologists for Pretoria also cited the United Kingdom's need to offset the phaseout of aircraft carriers with land-based air capabilities in South Africa.[34] The British did secure naval base rights in the country (which they had had

34. McCain quoted in Bustin, "South Africa's Foreign Policy Alternatives," p. 219. For examples of pro-South African briefs based on strategic necessity, see Captain Jacques A. Rondeau, USAF, "Apartheid: Shadow Over South Africa," *United States Naval Institute Proceedings,* vol. 102 (September 1976), pp. 18–27; and A. T. Culwick, "Southern Africa: A Strategic View," *Strategic Review,* vol. 2 (Summer 1974), pp. 30–37.

unofficially since the early nineteenth century) through the Simonstown agreements of 1955, but these agreements were terminated twenty years later. Strategic arguments retain some currency in conservative circles in the United States, but they no longer influence policy in any major Western capitals. According to rumor, feelers were extended toward Brazil and Argentina to establish some sort of South Atlantic Treaty Organization, but there have been no indications that anything has come of this. To many today, long-term strategic interest dictates staying on the good side of black African nationalists. If maintaining military capabilities in the area is vital, they should be independent rather than requiring South African cooperation.

Western support for South Africa has declined steadily. In the past France was a "reliable" arms supplier when other states were observing the embargo, but President Valéry Giscard d'Estaing has backed away from this policy in recent years. He announced that France would prohibit sales and deliveries of military equipment, and during the summer 1977 crisis over the prospective South African nuclear test, Paris issued declarations that it would ship no more spare parts for arms already delivered and would terminate trade if the explosion occurred.[35] In 1976 French Secretary of State for Foreign Affairs Pierre Christian Tattinger also said his government would sell no more reactors after the Koeberg stations are completed (although France contracted one of the biggest deals for purchasing natural uranium from Pretoria, with deliveries to begin in 1980).[36]

One alternative frequently mentioned is a closer, more symbiotic relationship with other international outcasts, a consortium of pariahs.[37] Links between Pretoria, Tel Aviv, and Taipei tightened in the 1970s, with emphasis on scientific and technical cooperation. In 1976 there was speculation that South Africa had agreed covertly to supply Israel with uranium.[38]

35. David B. Ottaway, "The Embargo: Arms Ban Too Late to Hurt S. Africa," *Washington Post*, October 28, 1977; "France Would Sever Trade Ties," *New York Times*, August 24, 1977.

36. Lloyd Shearer, "Intelligence Report," *Washington Post*, March 5, 1978.

37. See Betts, "Paranoids, Pygmies, Pariahs, and Nonproliferation," pp. 166–67, 173.

38. Terence Smith, "Israeli-South African Ties Stir Criticism," *New York Times*, April 18, 1976; "South Africa and Taiwan Re-establishing Full Ties," *New York Times*, April 27, 1976; "Israelis and South Africa Strengthen Scientific Ties," *New York Times*, June 1, 1976; William E. Farrell, "South Africa Link to Israel Grows," *New York Times*, August 18, 1976.

Some Washington observers guessed that the suspected test in the Kalahari Desert in 1977 was to be of an Israeli bomb rather than of a South African device, and that the possible explosion in 1979 was an Israeli bomb. Such rumors prove nothing but suggest that possibilities for collusion have become less implausible. There have even been allegations of cooperation with the most recent entrant into the pariah club; the South West Africa People's Organization (SWAPO) claimed five hundred Chilean mercenaries were fighting with South African regulars in Namibia.[39]

Israel, Taiwan, and South Africa all have highly developed nuclear capabilities as well as severe security problems. Taiwan in particular may be drawn toward Pretoria (the two regimes established diplomatic relations in April 1976), since it wishes to keep some distance from Israel in deference to oil suppliers, like Saudi Arabia, that are less morally outraged by South Africa than by Israel. (This may be one reason Taipei decided not to buy Kfir fighters even after the United States withdrew its objections and refused to sell F-4s.) Also, access to South African enrichment facilities may become an increasingly valued hedge for Taiwan, in case Western suppliers embargo fuel charges for the island's reactors. This consideration points to another bargaining chip that Pretoria may have in the future: the threat of unsafeguarded sales of enriched or natural uranium.[40]

Alliances with outcasts, however, are not a sufficient solution for South Africa's rulers. First, other pariahs are likely to bolt from the arrangement or at least retract some favors whenever they foresee benefits in alleviating their isolation from the diplomatic mainstream. Israel, for instance, agreed to observe the UN arms embargo when that issue became prominent as a result of a 1977 General Assembly resolution. The most dependable pariah allies are those that need the most help themselves (such as Taiwan) and thus have the least to offer. Second, even a staunchly united front of "outlaw" states would not add to the conventional military security of any of them. Geographic separation prohibits much mutual aid in time of war. The greatest efficacy of a pariah coalition would probably be in nuclear cooperation. Here, however, South Africa has more to give

---

39. Adelman, "Strategy of Defiance," p. 49.

40. George Quester, *The Politics of Nuclear Proliferation* (Johns Hopkins University Press, 1973), p. 203.

than to gain—it can supply natural uranium and enrichment but has little need for the reprocessing technology or technical expertise Israel or Taiwan could provide. In short, South Africa is insecure and isolated, and its problems cannot be solved by mutual back-scratching of countries in similar straits. Incentives or disincentives for nuclear weapons, at least, will not be measurably affected.

South Africa thus finds itself in a position where it must minimize the alienation of Western states but continue to intimidate potential black African military opponents, and it faces trends that are adverse to both aims. Would overt nuclear weapon development help or hinder Pretoria's diplomatic battle? The answers are easier to guess at the extremes of nuclear options than in the middle.

At the least provocative end of the spectrum of possibilities—the untested, unassembled, but designed and nearly ready "bomb in the basement"—the balance of political benefits against costs is probably favorable. Since it is not overt, such capability does not invite retaliation or pressure, and can be denied if it does, and the suspicions of other states may yield most of the deterrent effects a more visible capability would offer. At the other extreme—a small but serious, deployed nuclear force, perhaps fifty to a hundred small warheads deliverable by aircraft or missiles—the dangers appear to outweigh the gains. Such a force or threats to use it "could well crystallize the sort of collective international reaction which Pretoria has been attempting to prevent for years through its 'outward' policy."[41] A nuclear force could provoke African countries to seek greater Soviet presence and assistance rather than less, perhaps including friendship treaties that would implicitly offer the protection of an extended deterrent against South African nuclear coercion. This would also help legitimate and encourage expansion of Soviet naval operations in the Indian Ocean.[42] The strategic threats South Africa should fear most would thus be aggravated rather than alleviated.

The intermediate option of demonstrating weapon capability by a test but refraining from development of a nuclear force—à la India—is more difficult to evaluate. One rationale might simply be psychological: either to remind neighboring African countries of their scientific and technical

41. Bustin, "South Africa's Foreign Policy Alternatives," p. 222.
42. P. R. Chari, "South Africa's Nuclear Option," *India International Centre Quarterly,* vol. 3 (October 1976), p. 231.

underdevelopment and inability to indigenously develop a counter to this form of apartheid's muscle[43] or to remind the great powers that white South Africa is an independent power, to be taken seriously. If the event in the South Atlantic was indeed a South African test, it may have been designed to accomplish such purposes while retaining the value of ambiguity in policy and avoiding the diplomatic effects of overt South African accession to nuclear status.

An admitted test would cause more severe problems with the nations Pretoria wishes to court. It would infuriate American authorities (who can afford to soft pedal the issue on grounds of suspended judgment as long as Pretoria denies the act) and jeopardize nuclear cooperation agreements (although the South Africans might calculate that the furor would blow over and give way to more favorable and attentive consideration, in a way like what happened after the 1974 Indian test). All things considered, it seems that "whatever bargaining advantage Pretoria might be able to spin off from the exercise of its nuclear options could be derived more effectively . . . from publicizing its capacity to 'go nuclear'—which is highly credible—rather than from the threat of subsequently using such weapons —which is demonstrably less credible."[44] But if the covert bomb or proto-weapon status is logically preferable for South African policymakers, why did they apparently plan to detonate a device on land in 1977, and why would they proceed with a test at sea in 1979 that could be attributed to them?

The Test That Wasn't, the Test That May Have Been

In August 1977 it was reported that Soviet satellites detected a tower and facilities in the Kalahari Desert that demonstrated South African preparations for testing a nuclear device, and these observations were confirmed by American reconnaissance. The two superpowers, France, Britain, and West Germany launched a diplomatic offensive to prevent the detonation. The government in Pretoria denied adamantly that any such

43. Ibid., p. 230. Chari quotes Mozambique's leader Samora Machel as professing to be unimpressed by prospective South African nuclear capability but nevertheless obviously very aware of it: "There is no bomb that can crush the people's power, and this was proved in Vietnam, Cambodia, and elsewhere. We are not worried about the bombs."
44. Bustin, "South Africa's Foreign Policy Alternatives," pp. 223–24.

explosion was planned and maintained that the Soviet Union had trumped up the charge to coincide with a United Nations conference on apartheid in Nigeria.[45] No public explanation was forthcoming, however, about what the Kalahari facilities were for if not a nuclear test. Nor were the facilities dismantled in the month following the flap, although reconnaissance reportedly revealed that they were gone by spring 1978.[46]

President Carter announced in late August that South Africa had assured the United States it would not develop or test nuclear weapons in the future.[47] Prime Minister Vorster, however, said in October, "I am not aware of any promise that I gave to President Carter," and denounced American and Soviet "meddling."[48] The U.S. government quickly countered by revealing a letter from Vorster to Carter which said "that South Africa did not have, nor did it intend to develop, a nuclear explosive device for any purpose, peaceful or otherwise . . . and that there would not be any nuclear testing of any kind in South Africa."[49] The second statement sounds unconditional, but the first specified only a current intention, not a permanent promise. In any case, the letter did not constitute a legal agreement, and Vorster's own words suggest that the South Africans did not view themselves as irrevocably bound by the assurance. He reserved the option, depending on future circumstances. This could be seen as normal prudence, a reservation that hedges only against unlikely dire conditions, or as a more substantial warning that the threat is a valued option.

This apparent near-test incident is puzzling, and its implications for preventing South African proliferation could be seen as either encouraging or ominous. It is difficult to see what the South African government believed it would gain by a detectable test. In 1977 the Vorster cabinet was smarting under the Carter administration's vigorous rhetorical opposition to apartheid, support of progressive forces in southern Africa, and the

45. Graham Hovey, "South Africa Tells U.S. It Doesn't Plan Any Nuclear Testing," *New York Times,* August 24, 1977.

46. Henry S. Bradsher, "South Africa and the Bomb," *Washington Star,* September 19, 1977; Rotberg, *Suffer the Future,* p. 155.

47. Murray Marder, "Carter Says South Africa Has Pledged It Will Not Develop Nuclear Explosives," *Washington Post,* August 24, 1977.

48. Quoted in Warren Brown, "No Pledge on A-Arms, Vorster Says," *Washington Post,* October 24, 1977.

49. Quoted in Edward Walsh, "Vorster Pledge on A-Testing Made Public by White House," *Washington Post,* October 26, 1977.

high profile of Andrew Young in the formulation of America's Africa policy. Pretoria's détente policy of the earlier part of the decade, which involved conciliatory demarches toward moderate black African governments, had foundered in the Angola imbroglio of 1975. In these circumstances a nuclear shock may have seemed the appropriate counter to mounting pressure, a way of highlighting Afrikaner power and determination, a demonstration that apartheid is here to stay and that the world must deal gingerly with Pretoria.

In view of the meager and tenuous support for the regime in the West, however, one would think that this move would have been reserved for a moment of desperation or crisis that had not yet arrived, since it would probably accelerate the erosion of Western tolerance and energize external pressure rather than enervate it. And this is just what the evidence of test preparations did. It prompted Soviet-American cooperation against the apartheid regime, a development that Vorster and his colleagues could not have desired. Thus either the South African claims that no test was planned were true or the country's leaders calculated that an explosion would yield more benefits than costs.

Alternatively, the Vorster government might have faked the incident or taken advantage of an intelligence mistake by the great powers. The former possibility could have been an attempt to jolt the West and show it that Pretoria had to be taken seriously, without bearing the costs that would have come from following through. The second possibility would be consistent with rumors in South Africa that the tower and buildings spotted by reconnaissance were merely part of a mining operation. If so, Vorster's failure to explain clearly what the disputed facilities were might mean the government had decided to take advantage of the great powers' mistake and exploit their fright by not discrediting the evidence.

The strong global reaction in 1977 suggested at first that South African authorities miscalculated, learned their lesson, and would avoid nuclear provocation. It also showed, however, that the world cares a great deal about preventing the development of South African nuclear arms, and it thus emphasized the value of the nuclear threat as diplomatic leverage, an option to be forgone only for reciprocal favors. The desired reciprocity might simply be maintenance of the status quo; no nuclear mischief so long as there is no vigorous coercion of Pretoria by the United States or the USSR. In this sense Western alarm at the prospect of a test in 1977 showed white South Africans how much potential influence they have in the nuclear threat.[50] Most of the leverage at that time, of course, was on the other side, since severe Western displeasure or sanctions were to be avoided. The point at which the threat could become most credible is the point at which South Africa had little left to lose in the area of external support or tolerance, the point at which sanctions had already been applied to their practical limits.

The 1977 imbroglio, however, was not the end of the controversy and confusion over Pretoria's nuclear intentions. Two years later an American Vela satellite detected what appeared to be a small nuclear explosion—between two and four kilotons in yield—in the South Atlantic in the vicinity of the Cape of Good Hope. The government in Pretoria denied any knowledge of the event. In Washington a scientific investigation by a panel of experts was mounted under the auspices of the White House Office of Science and Technology Policy. Press accounts indicate that the panel considered numerous alternative explanations of what the flashes monitored by the satellite could have been, such as bizarre atmospheric phenomena or "superbolts" of lightning, and arrived at an uncertain verdict.[51]

Officials who doubted that the event was a South African nuclear detonation cited the fact that there were no confirming data, as there should have been, from complementary sensors such as aircraft searching for radioactive debris in the area.[52] Those who leaned in the other direction argued that the blast was so small that the fallout could easily have escaped detection, and they pointed out that the Vela satellite had monitored identical visual signatures forty-one times before and that each of those times the event was known to be a nuclear explosion. Moreover, a South African naval task force was conducting a naval exercise at the time

50. One South African foreign policy analyst claimed at a conference I attended in late 1977 that there had been virtually no interest in or consideration of the nuclear option among the white South African elite before the August controversy but voluble and extensive discussion of it afterward.

51. Richard Burt, "U.S. Is Unable to Confirm A-Blast," *New York Times,* January 24, 1980.

52. Faint pulses were picked up by U.S. underwater sensors but were not reported to be definitive signals. Ambiguous indications that debris had wafted to New Zealand and been monitored there were later dismissed. John J. Fialka, "Underwater Sensors Felt Blast Near S. Africa," *Washington Star,* November 2, 1979; "Data Suggesting Bomb Test in Southern Region Revised," *New York Times,* November 27, 1979. Later accounts said that the White House group's final report doubted the occurrence, but the Defense Intelligence Agency insisted the detonation had happened. Walter S. Mossberg, "Mystery Explosion Off South Africa Still Fuels Dispute," *Wall Street Journal,* July 16, 1980.

and place of the flash, and an investigation of who had undertaken a National Technical Information Service computer search of literature on seismic detection of nuclear explosions revealed that South African military attachés had done so.[53]

In one sense the uncertainty over whether Pretoria did test a bomb is not important. Objectively it would prove nothing new about the country's capability, since it has long been obvious that political will rather than technical prowess is the only questionable variable in South Africa's nuclear policy. (It should be noted, though, that the extremely small yield of the explosion, if that is what it was, does indicate that technical capability is either somewhat better or somewhat worse than might have been predicted for an inaugural test. Two to four kilotons would represent either a "fizzle" of a normal first-generation weapon or, at the opposite extreme of competence, a highly sophisticated "trigger" device.) Publicity concerning the September 1979 event may have made more leaders around the world aware of South Africa's nuclear potential, but Pretoria's denial of testing means that the government is not moving boldly to capitalize on its capability. The next critical steps—overt development and deployment of nuclear weapons—remain to be taken.

Some believe that there are motives short of impending doom that could prompt an open bomb-building decision. One suggested by a South African expatriate is that it would provide a morale boost, a pep pill for a white South African public beginning to feel abused and betrayed by the West and insulted by presumptuous black states to the north. This is a sort of "nuclear Geritol" rationale. Another is that the government might reckon that unveiling nuclear arms would change the stakes for the West in who controls South Africa, would make American authorities rethink indifference to the long-term prospect of a takeover by black radicals, and would remove Western pressure at least by complicating the situation—a sort of "nuclear monkey wrench" rationale.

Both these propositions would be reinforced to the extent that the rest of my analysis overestimates Western influence on the Pretoria government or how much value it places on Western support. Prime Minister

53. Thomas O'Toole and Milton Benjamin, "Officials Hotly Debate Whether African Event Was Atom Blast," *Washington Post,* January 17, 1980; Thomas O'Toole, "New Light Cast on Sky-Flash Mystery," *Washington Post,* January 1, 1980; Thomas O'Toole, "Fallout Studied to Confirm Blast Near S. Africa," *Washington Post,* November 14, 1979.

Botha took a tough line in mid-1979 with the expulsion of American military attachés for spying; this may exemplify a feeling that gaining substantial Western support is hopeless. And earlier, in August 1977, Prime Minister Vorster attacked foreign double standards on nuclear matters by saying that if pressures "do not stop, the time will arrive when South Africa will have no option—small as it is—but to say to the world: 'So far and no further. Do your damnedest if you wish.' "[54] Whether or not either proposition is plausible, both could complement the more drastic scenarios of white desperation. Moreover, authorities in Pretoria might reason that a threat to use the bomb in dire straits could prompt the United States (or even the Soviet Union) to ensure that deterioration of South Africa's security never reached such a point.

Under conditions that appear politically apocalyptic to the white regime—such as the imminent end of white control and the apartheid system—the option of an admitted test or even deployment of a small nuclear force would probably be exercised. In this sense the likelihood of an overt South African bomb may be a long-term threat more than an immediate one. But if the moral and political aim of most of the rest of the world—genuine majority rule in South Africa—comes close to being realized, the nuclear threat will too. The hope is that over the long term South African whites can be coaxed into accepting the peaceful transformation of their society toward the elimination of apartheid (in which case the nuclear option would then become an issue for the new black leaders, who might or might not be disinclined to implement it), but there is scant evidence to indicate that this is likely. Unfortunately, it is more probable either that the white regime will endure and, at best, desist from nuclear weapon deployment as a matter of prudence or that a bloody solution to the apartheid problem will begin to unfold at some point and manipulation of the nuclear threat will be one stratagem—aimed at encouraging Western intervention and deterring Soviet and African intervention—used by Afrikaners to hold off the wave of the future.

54. Quoted in "South Africa: Atomic Explosion Prevented," *Africa Research Bulletin,* Political, Social, and Cultural Series, vol. 14 (September 15, 1977), p. 4546.

PART SIX

U.S. Policy Choices

RICHARD K. BETTS

WILLIAM H. COURTNEY

HENRY S. ROWEN *and* RICHARD BRODY

JOSEPH A. YAGER

CHAPTER THIRTEEN

Northeast Asia

NONE of the noncommunist countries of Northeast Asia possess nuclear weapons. All of them have adhered to the Treaty on the Non-Proliferation of Nuclear Weapons. And there are good reasons to believe that the present and likely future interests of these countries will not be served by their acquiring nuclear weapons.

This comforting conclusion is not necessarily the end of the matter, however. The leaders of the Northeast Asian countries may not evaluate the complex considerations involved in setting nuclear policy in the same way as has been done in this study. Moreover, in an international crisis, fear or national pride might distort judgment and bring about a decision in favor of nuclear weapons that could not be justified by an objective evaluation of the national interest.

U.S. nonproliferation policy in Northeast Asia, as elsewhere, is essentially an effort to influence probabilities. The United States must try to create or maintain conditions in which the incentives to acquire nuclear weapons are weak. And by inhibiting the development of near-nuclear weapons capabilities, the United States may reduce the risk that one of the nonnuclear weapons states will suddenly and unexpectedly cross the line.

Japan

Japan has no reason at present to consider the acquisition of nuclear weapons seriously. It depends on the alliance with the United States to deter or defeat all but the most limited threats to its security. Only if Japan were to decide that it must increasingly look after its own defense might the acquisition of nuclear weapons become an active issue. Even then, it would probably decide that nuclear weapons were not in its best interest. But it would be better for U.S. nonproliferation policy if Japan did not have to face the issue.

In principle, a U.S. defense policy that maintains the vitality of the U.S.-Japan alliance will effectively support U.S. nonproliferation policy. Japan would then have no need to provide for its own defense or even to consider the acquisition of nuclear weapons. Applying this principle, however, requires more than preserving the formal legal validity of the U.S.-Japan mutual defense treaty. The security relationship must evolve with changing circumstances if it is to continue to be the cornerstone of Japanese defense policy. It must become more of a partnership, with closer consultation and more joint planning. Then the credibility of the U.S. security commitment is more likely to be maintained and the attractions of a more autonomous Japanese defense policy minimized.

Specific developments that might move Japan away from this close security relationship must be avoided. The United States must conduct its global and regional defense policy so as to sustain Japan's belief that U.S. commitments are reliable and that the alliance with the United States does not endanger Japan.

A weakening of the U.S. strategic deterrent of the Soviet Union could make Japan seek safety in neutrality. (Although it would probably be lightly armed at first, the question of acquiring nuclear weapons would eventually arise.) U.S. support of China in its dispute with the Soviet Union might also make the Japanese conclude that the U.S. alliance was dangerous and should be gradually loosened. Somewhat the same reaction might result from U.S. use of Japanese bases in a new war in Korea, particularly if the Japanese were uncertain about which side started the war. On the other hand, if the United States failed to assist South Korea in repelling a clear-cut North Korean attack, the Japanese would question the value of U.S. security commitments.

Should the United States lose its ability to counter Soviet naval and air power in the western Pacific, Japan might reassess the value of the U.S. security connection and adopt an increasingly autonomous defense policy. A similar drift in Japanese defense policy could be set off, or reinforced, by sharp disagreements with the United States over defense issues, such as the use of bases in Japan in defense of South Korea.

In broad terms, what the United States should do if it wishes to avoid undermining U.S.-Japanese security ties is clear. The United States is already taking many of the necessary actions and will probably continue to do so without any special reference to their effects on Japanese defense policy.

Presumably the United States will seek to maintain the credibility of its strategic deterrent of the Soviet Union, and concern about Japanese defense policy is unlikely to affect U.S. strategic deployments. The United States is also likely to keep strong conventional naval and air forces in the western Pacific to protect its interests and support its commitments in that area. The desire to prevent Japan from taking a more independent course could, however, affect the details of the U.S. military posture in the western Pacific and the way in which any changes in that posture were executed.

Present U.S. deployments in the western Pacific seem more than adequate to support a continued close U.S.-Japanese security relationship. In fact, some reduction in force levels may be justifiable in response to changed conditions and to meet more pressing needs in other parts of the world. If some U.S. forces are shifted to other areas, care must be taken not to undermine the credibility of the U.S. security commitment. The problem is largely one of style and timing.

Basing U.S. deployments in the western Pacific on joint U.S.-Japanese plans and increasing the complementarity of U.S. and Japanese deployments should be taken as guiding principles. Major changes in U.S. deployments should be made only after consultation with the Japanese authorities. For example, if the need to maintain two carrier task forces in the western Pacific was questioned (as it might well be), the United States should not decide the issue unilaterally and then merely inform the Japanese, but should try to arrive at an agreed-upon position. The United States should also be prepared to consult with the Japanese, if they wished it, on their own defense plans. A gradual increase in Japanese antisubmarine warfare and air defense capabilities should be encouraged.

The U.S. reaction to new Soviet deployments to the general area of Japan is also important. For instance, when the Soviet Union assigned the aircraft carrier *Minsk* to its Far Eastern fleet, the U.S. explanation that this was of limited significance may have prevented an excessive Japanese reaction.[1] However, some changes in Soviet deployments are so clearly related to the Sino-Soviet dispute that they create no problem for Japan.[2]

It should not be difficult for the United States to avoid alarming Japan about the possibility of being drawn into a dangerous military confrontation with the Soviet Union on the side of China. The United States would gain little but expense and trouble by backing China militarily against the Soviet Union. But Japan must be convinced that U.S. policy is based on full awareness of that fact.

Substantial sales of U.S. arms to the PRC could not easily be explained to the Japanese as no more than an effort to exert political pressure on the Soviet Union in support of U.S. objectives in other areas. The Japanese are all too ready to see the beginning of a shift in the U.S. alliance from Japan to China and might overreact by revising downward their assessment of the long-term viability of the security relationship with the United States.

One final point should be made about the possible effect of U.S. defense policy on Japan's policy toward nuclear weapons. If the U.S. security commitment became less credible, Japan might pursue an increasingly autonomous defense policy. But the adoption of such a policy would make the maintenance of a security commitment inconsistent with U.S. nonproliferation goals.

A major obstacle to Japan's acquiring nuclear weapons would be the fear that Soviet intervention would not allow Japan the time needed to develop the only kind of nuclear force that would make sense for it—a fleet of nuclear-powered submarines carrying missiles with nuclear warheads. This fear would be greatly reduced if Japan were still protected by the U.S. nuclear umbrella. At some point, it might therefore become necessary for the United States to make a difficult choice between tacitly acquiescing in Japan's becoming a nuclear weapons state and informing it that the U.S. security commitment would be withdrawn if Japan acquired nuclear weapons.

1. *Yomiuri,* August 13 and 14, 1979 (translated in American Embassy, Tokyo, "Daily Summary of Japanese Press," August 17 and 21, 1979).

2. The deployment of "somewhat less than 100 operational SS-20 launchers" to the Soviet Far East falls into this category. (This deployment is reported in General David C. Jones, *United States Military Posture for FY 1980* [Government Printing Office, 1979], p. 49.) Unlike the Western European reaction to a similar deployment of these IRBMs in Europe, there has been little or no reaction in Japan.

The Republic of Korea

If the people and government of the Republic of Korea had complete confidence that there would be no new attack from the North, they would have little or no interest in acquiring nuclear weapons. To the extent that U.S. defense policy builds South Korean confidence in the stability of the peace, it supports U.S. nonproliferation policy.

Belief that war will not come can be equated to belief in the effective deterrence of North Korea. It therefore varies with perceptions of the relative strengths of the opposing forces on the Korean peninsula and with judgments about the reliability of the U.S. security commitment. Confidence (like deterrence) is a subjective phenomenon; in attempting to build it, style as well as substance is important. While the U.S. security commitment expressed in the Mutual Defense Treaty of 1954 is basic to South Korean confidence, this formal commitment is not enough. More tangible evidence of the U.S. readiness to honor its commitment is required. Deployments of U.S. forces have a psychological importance disproportionate to their weight in the military balance.

The decision to withdraw the U.S. Army Second Division over a period of five years shook South Korean confidence to a degree that is difficult for outsiders to understand.[3] One of the consequences of the decision was an upsurge of interest in nuclear weapons to compensate for what was perceived as a weakening of the deterrent against a North Korean attack. The decision to defer the withdrawal of the Second Division has presumably helped restore South Korean confidence and reduce interest in nuclear weapons. However, in the aftermath of the assassination of President Park in October 1979, the withdrawal of ground combat troops, or even the announcement of their withdrawal at some definite future date, could have unfortunate psychological and political effects. Fear that North Korea would exploit instability in the South would increase, and the ability of the United States to act as a stabilizing force would be weakened.

The withdrawal of other U.S. military forces from South Korea in the next few years could also have negative consequences for U.S. nonproliferation goals. The same may be said of any substantial failure to provide

3. This estimate of South Korean reactions to the original decision to withdraw the Second Division is based in part on conversations in Seoul in November 1977, July 1978, and January 1979.

the arms and other military items needed to carry out the ROK's force improvement plan.[4] The equivalent of a U.S. Air Force wing should remain in Korea indefinitely to remedy the disparity between the sizes of the South Korean and North Korean air forces. Specialized U.S. army units should remain until Koreans can assume their functions. The reported reassessment of North Korean ground force strength by U.S. intelligence has increased the importance of carrying out the force improvement plan.[5]

The tactical nuclear weapons held by U.S. forces in South Korea pose a special problem. Although it is most unlikely that these weapons would be used, North Korea could not be sure, and South Koreans perceive them as an important part of the deterrent. Removing all of the U.S. nuclear weapons in the next few years could be a heavy blow to South Koreans' confidence. If other units or weapons systems were withdrawn, they might think: a part of the total deterrent is being taken away. What can take its place? Perhaps nuclear weapons are the answer. But if nuclear weapons were withdrawn, the sequence of thought would be more straightforward: the United States is weakening the deterrent by removing its nuclear weapons. Why not remedy this loss by building nuclear weapons of our own?

Some U.S. nuclear weapons should remain in Korea until it is reasonably certain that their presence is not needed to deter a North Korean attack. If withdrawal of the Second Division is resumed, the nuclear weapons held by U.S. Army units could gradually be removed. In that event, at least some of the nuclear weapons with U.S. Air Force units should remain.

The Republic of China

The leaders of the Republic of China on Taiwan could see three advantages in possessing nuclear weapons: deterrence of an attack by Com-

---

4. This is not primarily a matter of military assistance but rather one of authorizing ROK purchases and financing them with foreign military sales credits. Most of the special compensation package of about $800 million worth of equipment will be withheld until withdrawals of ground combat forces are actually resumed.

5. This reassessment has not been made public, but its general nature was leaked to the press. See *Army Times*, January 8, 1979, p. 1, and *New York Times*, June 12, 1979. The data on North Korean ground forces in table 3-1 are consistent with press reports of the reassessment.

munist China, reduced domestic fears about the future of the island, and increased international credibility of the ROC. These possible advantages must be weighed against the risks of invoking severe U.S. sanctions and precipitating, rather than deterring, a PRC attack. Until recently, the balance of advantages and risks, as seen by Taiwan's leaders, was against the acquisition of nuclear weapons.[6] The still unanswered question is whether this will continue to be the case now that U.S. diplomatic recognition has been transferred from Taipei to Peking.

As long as the U.S.-ROC mutual defense treaty was in effect—and was not under the shadow of imminent termination—the ROC had every reason to believe that the PRC was adequately deterred. The administration in Washington may believe that, even without the treaty, a sufficient level of deterrence can be achieved by asserting a continued interest in a peaceful solution to the Taiwan problem and by increasing Peking's economic and political stake in good relations with the United States. Taipei, however, is unlikely to share this view. More than half a century of bitter rivalry has made it highly suspicious of Peking's intentions. Moreover, relying on improved U.S.-PRC ties for its own security is distasteful to the ROC and carries ominous implications for its ability to survive as a separate political entity.

The declaration of Congress that an attack on Taiwan would be a matter of "grave concern" to the United States may have temporarily reassured the ROC. But the reluctant acceptance of this declaration by the executive branch makes its long-run efficacy doubtful.[7] The ROC is more likely to be influenced by the way in which the United States carries out the declared intention to sell it defensive arms after the termination of the mutual defense treaty.

The loss of U.S. recognition may also have enhanced the political value of nuclear weapons to the ROC, both domestically and internationally. The ability of the United States to counter these unwanted consequences of its own action is limited. The people of Taiwan feel considerable uneasiness about the future, which their leaders might be tempted to assuage with a nuclear weapons program. Declarations of continued U.S. concern

6. What these leaders may have thought about the desirability of a near-nuclear-weapons capability is less clear.

7. Taiwan was no doubt impressed that the executive branch proceeded to normalize relations with Peking in disregard of a joint congressional resolution requesting prior consultation.

for the security of Taiwan may be of some help in calming popular fears, but they cannot come close to making up for the termination of the mutual defense treaty. A prolonged cessation of threatening words and actions by Peking would be more effective. The United States may be able to influence Peking in this direction but cannot hope to control its policy on the Taiwan issue.

The loss of international status suffered by the ROC when the United States withdrew its diplomatic recognition may be viewed in Taipei as a more serious problem than the state of public morale. Certainly, the most troublesome aspect of the action was the U.S. insistence that there could be no official relations between Taipei and Washington after the United States had opened an embassy in Peking.[8] This position plus the unqualified U.S. recognition of the People's Republic of China as "the sole legal Government of China"[9] placed Taiwan in an anomalous position. Its claim to any kind of international legal personality rested on the thin foundation of recognition by a few states, most of them minor.[10]

The United States can do little in the near term to rescue the ROC from the political limbo that threatens to engulf it. In any event, an unstated assumption of U.S. policy is that the ROC will one day disappear as the consequence of Taiwan's reunification with the mainland. The only faint lease on life granted the ROC by the United States is implied in the proclaimed U.S. expectation that "the Taiwan issue will be settled peacefully by the Chinese themselves."[11] But over a period of years, the United States might, if it wished, help the ROC to check the erosion in its international position. The scope and content of unofficial U.S. relations with Taiwan could be made sufficiently important to indicate clearly that the United States regarded the new status quo as more or less permanent. By its actions, the United States might in effect help create on Taiwan a new kind of international entity: a political unit entitled to security in a de-

8. The ROC had hoped that it could maintain an official liaison office in Washington and that the United States would make similar arrangements in Taipei.

9. "East Asia: U.S. Normalizes Relations with the People's Republic of China," *Department of State Bulletin* (January 1979), p. 25. The Shanghai communiqué of 1972 merely declared, "The United States acknowledges that all Chinese on either side of the Taiwan Strait maintain that there is but one China and that Taiwan is part of China. The United States Government does not challenge that position." "Text of Joint Communique, Issued at Shanghai, February 27," *Department of State Bulletin* (March 20, 1972), pp. 437–38.

10. The most notable exceptions are Saudi Arabia and the Republic of Korea.

11. *Department of State Bulletin* (January 1979), p. 26.

fined territory and competent to conduct nondiplomatic relations with other parts of the world. The United States could not move too rapidly in this direction however, or make explicit declarations about the significance of its actions without damaging its relations with Peking.

Because of the limited ability of the United States to weaken Taiwan's incentives to acquire nuclear weapons, it must do what it can to reinforce the risks involved in such a step. Here, too, there are problems and constraints.

Somewhat paradoxically, the ROC might view the improvement in U.S.-PRC relations as reducing the risk of a preemptive PRC attack but increasing the risk of severe U.S. sanctions. The PRC would be reluctant to jeopardize its valuable U.S. connection by precipitating a crisis with Taiwan. The United States would be anxious to prove to the PRC that it had not conspired with the ROC in its nuclear weapons program. Moreover, the United States would not be restrained (as it would be in a similar situation in Korea) by fear of making an early communist attack more likely. In fact, by moving strongly to force the ROC to give up nuclear weapons, the United States would make military action by the PRC unnecessary.

The Korean and Chinese situations differ in two fundamental respects. First, the United States no longer has to worry about maintaining the credibility of a formal security commitment to Taiwan, but it is still committed to the security of South Korea. Second, the United States relies in large part on good relations with the PRC to keep the peace in the area of Taiwan; in Korea, peace is maintained by deterring a North Korean attack.

The sanctions readily available to the United States are substantial. For example, suspension of shipments of nuclear fuel at present would in one or two years shut down two large power plants that represent more than a sixth of total electrical generating capacity. Suspending shipments of nuclear reactor components would block completion of four more plants that represent a total investment of between $3 billion and $4 billion. Similar actions a few years from now would have a more severe effect on generating capacity, although the number of construction projects affected might be smaller.

Suspension of sales of military equipment, especially parts for equipment already held by the ROC armed forces, would gradually degrade the readiness of those forces and block efforts to modernize them. This action would not seriously affect the security of Taiwan for some time, but its psychological impact on the armed forces and on the public would be strong and immediate.

The actual use of sanctions would be highly undesirable. This country could take no satisfaction in damaging a society with which it has strong sentimental and economic ties. The United States should therefore make it clear that these and, if necessary, other sanctions would be applied if Taiwan abandoned its present policy and developed nuclear weapons. If there is no misunderstanding on this score, the need to apply sanctions will probably never arise.

The Near-Nuclear Problem

The United States must be concerned about preventing not only the spread of nuclear weapons to the noncommunist areas of Northeast Asia, but also the development of near-nuclear-weapons capabilities there. Advances in civil nuclear energy programs inevitably strengthen technical abilities relevant to military programs. In Northeast Asia, this is most clearly demonstrated in Japan. If Japan carries out its well-developed plans to acquire a full nuclear fuel cycle, it will also gain the ability to produce plutonium and highly enriched uranium in substantial quantities. It is already operating a pilot reprocessing plant that extracts plutonium from spent fuel.

The problem with Japan, however, is not that its civil nuclear energy program will bring it closer to a weapons capability. Japan's reluctance to arm itself with nuclear weapons is so strong that such a development is unlikely. The problem rather is that Japan could set an undesirable precedent for other countries whose commitment not to acquire nuclear weapons may be more fragile. There is some danger that Japan (and other advanced industrialized nonnuclear weapons states) will build sensitive fuel cycle facilities—specifically, national reprocessing and enrichment plants—before the international community has made institutional and other arrangements to prevent their misuse.

This problem goes beyond Japan and Northeast Asia. The point to be made here is that, while the United States must avoid giving Japan any reason to reconsider its policy against nuclear weapons, that is not enough. It is also important to work with Japan to create new international arrangements under which civil nuclear energy can continue to develop without increasing the risk of the further spread of nuclear weapons.[12]

In moving toward such arrangements, Japan may have to modify some of its present plans. For example, the recycling of plutonium in light water reactors may have to be abandoned. Building a commercial-scale reprocessing plant and an enrichment plant may have to be deferred and possibly carried out under multinational auspices.

The United States could use its considerable legal and commercial leverage to force Japan to modify its civil nuclear energy program. But since Japan's help is needed in constructing the new arrangements, this leverage should be used in a restrained manner, if at all. Moreover, a sharp confrontation with Japan on nuclear energy policy could damage U.S.-Japanese relations in other fields, possibly including defense. The U.S.-Japanese alliance rests on a mutuality of interests. The alliance is weakened if one partner rides roughshod over an important interest of the other, such as Japan's interest in providing for its future energy needs.

The nuclear energy programs of the Republic of Korea and the Republic of China do not yet raise the same kinds of problems as the more advanced Japanese program. Neither country plans to develop a full nuclear fuel cycle on a national basis; nor could a good economic case for doing so be made for many years. Nevertheless, both countries have shown some interest in the reprocessing of spent fuel, although apparently the United States retains enough leverage with both to prevent their developing independent national reprocessing facilities indefinitely. However, a purely negative U.S. approach to the subject of reprocessing will seem increasingly onerous and unreasonable to Seoul and Taipei.

Reprocessing is seen by both the ROK and the ROC as the preferred approach to the management of spent fuel. Officials of the Korea Electric Company and the Taiwan Power Company are already expressing concern about what is to be done with spent fuel in ten or fifteen years, when the storage capacity of pools at nuclear power plants has been used up. Interest in recycling plutonium will grow in both countries as advanced industrialized nations deploy new kinds of reactors that use plutonium as fuel.

The United States must not appear to be preventing the ROK and the ROC from solving their spent fuel problem or to be trying to hold them

12. How this might be done is the subject of a forthcoming Brookings study on new forms of international cooperation in nuclear energy.

at their present level of nuclear technology. It should therefore take the lead in arranging for the retrievable storage of spent fuel under multinational auspices. The possibility of reprocessing such spent fuel—again under multinational auspices—should be left open. Whether to go ahead with reprocessing would depend on economic need and on the establishment of adequate safeguards, including a new international system for the control of plutonium.[13]

Regional Problems

U.S. policy—especially defense policy—toward any one of the three noncommunist countries of Northeast Asia can have important effects on the other two. For example, the termination of the U.S. mutual defense treaty with Taiwan could lead Japanese and South Koreans to question the reliability of similar U.S. commitments to them, with the result that interest in nuclear weapons could be increased in Japan and South Korea, at least marginally, as well as in Taiwan. Stronger and more direct interactions in the region might occur if one of the three countries were to acquire nuclear weapons. These potential interactions increase the importance of choosing the right policies toward each of the three countries.

If Japan were to become a nuclear power, the people and government of the Republic of Korea would be alarmed even while recognizing that the Japanese capability had been created to deter the Soviet Union. Koreans have not forgotten the oppressive Japanese occupation of their country during the first part of this century and might fear that a militarily strong Japan would once more seek to rule Korea. This fear would be intensified by the realization that a nuclear-armed Japan would no longer be restrained by its alliance with the United States.

The ROK could react to a Japanese nuclear weapons capability by developing its own nuclear weapons, although this course of action would probably be rejected as too difficult and too risky. A nominal nuclear weapons capability—which is all that South Korea could create with its present technology and economic development—would scarcely be the answer to the sophisticated Polaris-like system that Japan would presum-

13. Precisely what arrangements might be made for multinational storage and reprocessing of spent fuel and for the control of plutonium is a subject that lies outside the scope of this study. It will be considered in the previously mentioned forthcoming Brookings study.

ably have created. Moreover, developing nuclear weapons would expose the ROK to the dangers that were described in chapter 3,[14] making it more likely to look to the United States for protection against Japan, as well as against the communist powers. A formal request to this effect could complicate U.S. relations with Tokyo, which might already have been strained by Japan's becoming a nuclear weapons state.

Japan's acquisition of nuclear weapons would affect Taiwan much less than South Korea. Taipei would have little fear of Japanese aggression and might actually welcome the resurgence of Japanese military power as a counterbalance to both China and the Soviet Union. It would therefore probably see no need to create a nuclear weapons capability to deter Japan. But if the United States had not strongly opposed Japan's acquisition of nuclear weapons, Taipei might revise downward its estimate of the costs of taking a similar step.

Japan would be severely shaken by the appearance of a South Korean nuclear weapons capability. Creation of a limited counterbalancing capability would be seriously considered but would probably be rejected because of fear of the Soviet reaction and desire not to damage relations with the United States. Japan is likely to rely on the United States to restrain the ROK in any future crisis between Tokyo and Seoul.

Taiwan would worry about the possible consequences of a South Korean nuclear weapons capability but not about the capability itself. It would be particularly disturbed if Seoul's acquisition of nuclear weapons led to a war that could spread to its own area and if the United States did not give the ROK effective support in resisting a North Korean attack. And Taiwan would be strongly influenced by the precedent set by Seoul. If the ROK developed a nuclear weapons capability without getting into serious difficulties, the ROC might be encouraged to do the same, despite the differences in the two countries' situations. The strength and nature of the U.S. reaction to the South Korean action would be examined carefully as an indication of what the United States would do if Taiwan also decided to acquire nuclear weapons.

Seoul's reactions to the appearance of a nuclear weapons capability on

14. These dangers would be especially great in the hypothetical case under discussion. Japan's assumed adoption of an autonomous defense policy could have resulted from a decline in the U.S. military presence in Northeast Asia, which would make the ROK unsure of effective U.S. support in resisting a preemptive North Korean attack.

Taiwan would be similar to those of Taipei in the reverse situation. Again, the response of the United States would be examined with particular care.

Japan would be only mildly disturbed by the ROC's acquisition of nuclear weapons unless it led to war or to the development of nuclear weapons by the ROK. Taiwan is much farther than South Korea from the main Japanese islands, but the chief reason for anticipating a milder Japanese reaction to a ROC nuclear weapons capability than to a ROK one is psychological. The Japanese respect the Chinese but do not fear them. Their attitude toward Koreans is roughly the opposite.

The United States and Northeast Asia

The United States should avoid creating incentives for Japan to adopt a more autonomous defense policy. This means that the United States must demonstrate that it is a reliable ally and that the alliance will not draw Japan into dangerous situations.

The United States must seek to reinforce South Korean confidence in the stability of peace on the peninsula. The decision to withdraw the Second Division shook that confidence for a time, and the deferral of the withdrawal presumably helped restore it. Any future withdrawals of U.S. forces should be handled with great care. Some U.S. tactical weapons should be left in Korea.

Taiwan's incentives to acquire nuclear weapons may have been increased by the normalization of U.S. relations with Peking. The United States should do what it can within the constraints imposed by its new relations with Peking to persuade the ROC that nuclear weapons are not needed to deter an attack by Communist China.

The United States should continue to discourage the construction of national reprocessing and enrichment facilities. Such facilities should be built only when the economic case for them is clear and subject to adequate safeguards.

The failure of U.S. nonproliferation policy in any one of the three noncommunist countries could potentially interfere with the achievement of nonproliferation goals in the others. In particular, U.S. reaction to the acquisition of nuclear weapons by any one of these countries would be studied closely by the others to gauge how the United States might respond if they made a similar decision.

CHAPTER FOURTEEN

India, Pakistan, and Iran

AMERICAN nonproliferation policy in South Asia has little to show. India has detonated a nuclear explosive, Pakistan may soon do so, and Iran presents no immediate danger because it currently lacks interest in the matter, not because of anything the United States has done to discourage it. The problem is that American policy has been dominated by a desire to control the local diffusion of sensitive technology and by unwillingness to take strong initiatives to weaken strategic incentives for nuclear weapons. This tendency changed briefly during a flurry of anxiety after the Soviet invasion of Afghanistan, but Washington soon pulled back from ambitious plans to bolster Pakistan's defenses. The United States appears to take South Asian security concerns seriously only when they become a central element in global conflict between the superpowers. As a result U.S. policy strikes the targets as not only erratic and undependable, but also arrogant and offensive, applying double standards, seeking to take but not give, and threatening illegal action (abrogation of fuel supply contracts with India).

U.S. leaders in the late 1970s gambled too heavily on unrealistic hopes (that Indian leaders would accept full-scope safeguards out of the goodness of their hearts and that Pakistani leaders would accept economic arguments as sufficient reason to dispense with reprocessing or enrichment), mistakenly saw progress in equivocation (such as believing that Prime Minister Morarji Desai's conditional statements against peaceful nuclear explosions were a promise), and found themselves hobbled by the inflexibility of U.S. laws (principally, the Nuclear Non-Proliferation Act of 1978). For nonproliferation policy to be more realistic and effective, it must deal with local incentives for nuclear weapons and offer much more in exchange for local cooperation in limiting capabilities. More active measures and involvement may be impractical. But the following discussion will at least suggest the limits to what the United States can hope to do to prevent proliferation in the region.

Almost all the effective measures the United States might undertake have some economic, political, diplomatic, or military cost. Controlling *options* to manufacture nuclear weapons—by constraining capabilities —requires offering countries benefits to compensate for the perceived need, fulfilling it in a way that limits their possession of fissile material, or threatening them with sanctions or loss of benefits that are more important to them than autonomy in fuel supply. India, in any case, is not likely to turn back its own clock by dismantling its reprocessing plants. Controlling *decisions* on whether or not to exercise the weapons option (if the countries involved have the capability) similarly requires either offering inducements or disincentives that make a nonweapons status more attractive or resolving the conflicts that lead to the desire for a nuclear force. The only costless alternatives are moral exhortation (whose effect is likely to be limited as long as the great powers themselves depend on nuclear weapons) or reliance on safeguards agreements and the hope that the nuclear candidates will continue to see no need for weapons (in which case there is no proliferation problem anyway). All things considered, the outlook for American policies designed to discourage proliferation in India, Pakistan, or Iran is bleak. Animosity or distrust reduce the chances that these countries will respond favorably to small inducements or threats, and gestures on a scale impressive enough to sway their decisions are gestures too ambitious for most U.S. policymakers to contemplate. But because this region is now one of the most dangerous in the world, in terms of potential nuclear proliferation, it is worthwhile to examine the options in detail even if they are not promising.

Controlling Access to Fissionable Material

There are two general ways to try to reduce the easy availability of fissionable material: multilateral control over facilities that produce such material, and not constructing such facilities at all.

In October 1977 the United States made a conditional offer to store spent fuel for countries that use American-supplied fuel, in part to induce them to forgo plutonium reprocessing.[1] (This is not a cost-free option since it would draw criticism from American environmentalists and anti-nuclear lobbies.) India shows no interest in abandoning either the investment it has already made in plutonium separation or plans for the breeder reactor program, nor has Pakistan given up its quest for a reprocessing plant. If a joint Indian-Pakistani reprocessing facility could be established, this might help reduce tension and suspicion between the two countries and promote the peace-enhancing tendencies toward cooperation that some theorists believe flow from economic interdependence. In view of the political situation, however, this is a fanciful notion. How could it operate so as to be satisfactory to both parties as well as "safe" from a nonproliferation perspective? How would it compensate for Pakistan's abandonment of its desire for at least one indigenous separation plant as long as India did not dismantle its own plant?

In the case of Iran, the shah never indicated an unequivocal willingness to dispense with the use of plutonium in Iran's energy program. During Secretary of State Henry Kissinger's visit to Tehran in August 1976 the shah linked lack of interest in weapons to access to nonnational sources of plutonium: "It would really be silly if masses of countries will be in possession of two or three silly little bombs. So, we are agreeable, if a reprocessing plant is needed in this region, to have it on a multinational basis."[2] This followed Kissinger's proposal at the United Nations in October 1975 that multinational reprocessing centers be established. It also followed Iranian overtures to the United States, West Germany, and France for acquisition of reprocessing technology and discussions with the United States on joint ownership (with some industrialized Western country) of any reprocessing facility built in Iran. At the time of the Kissinger visit U.S. officials reportedly hoped that a regional facility for Iran and Pakistan might induce the latter to cancel its deal with France.[3] The drastic cuts in Iran's nuclear power plans and the brakes the Khomeini forces applied to modernization may eliminate the problem by making reprocessing

1. Remarks of the President at the Plenary Session of the International Nuclear Fuel Cycle Evaluation, White House press release, October 19, 1977.
2. Quoted in William Branigin, "Iran Eyes Regional Reprocessing," *Washington Post*, August 14, 1976.
3. *Nucleonics Week*, vol. 17 (May 27, 1976), p. 6, and ibid. (August 19, 1976), p. 8.

unattractive to authorities in Tehran. If they did become interested in it, ties with the Islamic regime in Islamabad might make such a joint facility a desirable alternative. The close ties between Pakistan and Iran, however, were attenuated after the shah's ouster.

Promoting multinational centers is inconsistent with the recent American drive to defer the resort to plutonium for energy-generating purposes. But the multinational or regional reprocessing option poses other problems as well. Creation of such centers would further disperse knowledge and experience with technology that could eventually widen the base for indigenous reprocessing ventures. The potential danger in this can be surely averted only if the technicians involved remain perpetually under the control of the suppliers. In that case, however, one could argue that reprocessing might as well be done in the supplier countries, under contract, rather than regionally.

Another problem is what happens to separated plutonium after it comes out of the multinational facility. Even if it is legally owned by the supplier of the original fuel, assuming the supplier is not one of the proliferation-prone countries in question, this is crucial only if it is not returned to the countries from whose reactors the spent fuel came. If these countries do not want the separated plutonium and if the United States will accept the wastes, there is no obvious need for the multinational facility in the first place. If they are to get the plutonium back and are allowed to stockpile it, little is gained for nonproliferation purposes beyond what stringent safeguards on domestic reprocessing would provide. In fact, it is unclear what significant constraints on weapons options would be imposed by regional reprocessing that would be more reliable than having the plutonium separated in the supplier nations and rationed to the customers, one or two fuel charges at a time.

Only Pakistan has tried to acquire a domestic capacity for uranium enrichment. Potential weapons programs of India or Iran are likely to rely on plutonium for fissile material. If the United States could control access to plutonium or enriched uranium and, in India's case, U-233 from thorium, it could control access to weapons. The most effective control would be total prevention of enrichment or the separation or purchase of fissile plutonium. Less certain or preclusive would be stringent safeguards against diversion or stockpiling of reprocessed fuel. Neither course seems promising in South and West Asia.

Unless the United States succeeds in convincing the countries involved that there is scant economic justification for energy-related use of plutonium, the costs of attempting to prevent access to it are primarily diplomatic and political—the resentment of those countries against great power discrimination, condescension, or coercion. A continued lobbying effort to "prove" the diseconomies of plutonium recycling (and the unimportance of fuel autonomy) cannot hurt U.S. strategy except to the extent that it angers the targets, but as long as it is not successful, demanding that the countries not obtain any plutonium, especially if they were to agree to accept safeguards, might seem invidious. The targets may simply infer that the United States does not trust them to observe legal agreements not to divert the material for military purposes. As one Pakistani engineer reportedly argued, "We ourselves have enough technology for dirty reprocessing . . . for a bomb and nothing else . . . [willingness to] spend a lot of money for a good plant . . . [should] strengthen the impression that our intentions are not bad."[4] In these terms, forgoing sovereign prerogatives can seem not so much a gesture of mutually beneficial cooperation as a unilateral surrender under duress. Moreover, the outcome of the International Nuclear Fuel Cycle Evaluation did not yield the consensus against reprocessing that the United States had hoped for.

A target country may share the U.S. perception that the spread of plutonium is dangerous and see disadvantages to itself in having such facilities within its borders. In this case, dispensing with plutonium could be a cooperative choice. The shah was inclined to take this view, and his successors' indifference may have the same effect as his prudence. And if Pakistani leaders were to ponder their own country's internal instability or the possibility of a "nuclear coup d'état,"[5] they might have second thoughts. A coercive approach may still be worthwhile, but if not sugarcoated with offsetting inducements, such pressure can be counterproductive.

Indignation over U.S. pressure rigidifies the desire for autonomy, and successfully preventing the importation of sensitive technology covered by safeguards may motivate the deprived nations to construct facilities on their own, which may be bound by no safeguards. Revelation of its enrichment plans should make it harder for Pakistan to obtain the necessary equipment abroad that it was buying under cover of nonnuclear industrial

4. *Nucleonics Week* (May 27, 1976), p. 5.
5. See Lewis A. Dunn, "Military Politics, Nuclear Proliferation, and the 'Nuclear Coup d'Etat,' " *Journal of Strategic Studies*, vol. 1 (May 1978), pp. 31–50.

requirements; similar problems impede the independent development of reprocessing. But motives remain. There were indications that some opposed to Zulfikar Ali Bhutto, such as Asghar Khan, did not see the acquisition of the separation plant as crucial and might have been willing to get along without it had the United States not so loudly turned the issue into a test of Pakistani national sovereignty.[6] The International Atomic Energy Agency safeguards that were to have been imposed on the plant supplied by France included any domestic copies. Nuclear defense options aside, Pakistan's vulnerability to India increases its incentives to retain external diplomatic support for the nation's legitimacy and integrity and to maximize the possibility that a conflict with India would quickly become international. This gives leaders in Islamabad good reason not to breach international legal obligations (safeguards) lightly. Western leverage would have been stronger if the French contract had been fulfilled than it will be if Pakistan builds its own plant without incurring legal commitments that would have to be abrogated in order to deploy nuclear weapons. Pakistan may be able to do this by bearing the higher financial costs, delays, and inefficiencies of getting along without help from foreign experts. The president of Saint-Gobain Techniques Nouvelles said in June 1977 that France had already delivered "about 95 percent of all plans" and blueprints for the plant. "The remaining 5 percent is without significance," he added and indicated that Pakistan could construct the facility based on the plans in hand. Construction of the plant reportedly began the following month.[7] (Pakistani sources, however, said France had not delivered any plant components to Pakistan since 1976.[8]) In any case, it would be nearly impossible to prevent the construction of a small plant, which would also be more relevant to weapons than energy purposes.

If the United States succeeds in preventing the construction of a national reprocessing plant but not the plans to use plutonium for fuel, capabilities will still not be under control. If countries can have spent fuel reprocessed abroad and the plutonium returned—especially if they stockpile it rather than reburning each load as it comes back—they have the same option to divert plutonium for weapons that they would have with a plant of their own. As Victor Gilinsky of the Nuclear Regulatory Com-

6. See Shirin Tahir-Kheli, "Pakistan's Nuclear Option and U.S. Policy," *Orbis*, vol. 22 (Summer 1978), p. 368.

7. *Nucleonics Week*, vol. 18 (June 9, 1977), p. 2, and ibid. (July 14, 1977), p. 9.

8. *Nucleonics Week*, vol. 19 (August 10, 1978), p. 10.

mission put it, "What's the point of our policy of not exporting reprocessing plants, but condoning the export of fuel for reprocessing?"[9] Thus it is necessary to provide reasons not to rely on plutonium for energy generation. One means toward this end is the assurance of adequate uranium fuel supplies.

Controlling Fuel Supplies

India, Pakistan, and Iran all depend to varying degrees on external sources for nuclear fuel. Light water reactors require the importation of low enriched uranium. Pakistan and India have some dependency, though not a great deal, since they plan to emphasize heavy water reactors, which use natural uranium. India needs enriched fuel only for its light water reactors at Tarapur. Any plan to constrict the supply of natural uranium for its other CANDU reactors, however, is impractical since the Uranium Corporation of India stockpiled a ten-year fuel supply in the late 1970s.[10] The United States, as the primary supplier of enriched fuel, might be able to exploit these dependencies slightly, using assurances of supply to compel accommodation with nonproliferation policy, although other, non-American sources of supply are growing. Pressure could best be used by withholding fuel or by continuing to make supply conditional on agreement not to separate plutonium from the fuel once it was spent. Senators Abraham A. Ribicoff and John H. Glenn long favored the withholding strategy, and this pressure is effectively embodied in the Nuclear Non-Proliferation Act of 1978.

Using fuel assurances as leverage, however, could be difficult at best and counterproductive at worst. U.S. dominance in fuel enrichment will wane in coming years as European and Soviet sources become more widely available. Moreover, even if he wants to, the president will find it difficult to wield fuel supply as a tool of U.S. policy; Congress and the Nuclear Regulatory Commission (NRC) are deeply involved in setting the standards for fuel exports. The legislation tying authorization for ex-

9. Quoted in "Tarapur Hearing Covers a Wide Spectrum: Intent, Needs, Policies —You Name It," *Weekly Energy Report,* vol. 4 (July 26, 1976), p. 9.

10. Nuclear Assurance Corporation, *International Data Collection and Analysis,* vol. 1, prepared for U.S. Department of Energy, EN-77-C-01-5072 (Atlanta: NAC, December 1977), p. 202.

ports to acceptance of full-scope safeguards limits executive discretion. Although it provides for presidential waiver of the conditions if enforcing them would "be seriously prejudicial to . . . nonproliferation objectives, or otherwise jeopardize the common defense,"[11] the legislation attempts, in effect, to limit flexibility so as to compel accommodation. It is unlikely the president would be cavalier in his use of the waiver power. U.S. domestic or bureaucratic politics intervene in export decisions in other ways as well. In 1977 the State Department had to go to an appellate court to overturn a stay on exporting low enriched fuel to India. The stay had been granted to the National Resources Defense Council and the Union of Concerned Scientists.[12] The U.S. nuclear industry is one domestic political counterweight to such pressure, but it has been on the defensive, especially since the reactor accident at the Three Mile Island plant in Pennsylvania. Other potential impediments to expeditious supply are exemplified by President Carter's executive order in the fall of 1979 requiring that environmental impact in the customer country be considered before U.S. decisions on nuclear exports are made.[13]

Finally, any attempt to manipulate fuel supplies to compel customer countries to adopt policies consistent with U.S. goals may simply aggravate incentives for nuclear autarky; taking advantage of a vulnerability spurs efforts by the target to eliminate the vulnerability (for instance, reinforcing India's commitment to breeder reactors to assure fuel independence). Making "assurances" conditional emphasizes the lack of assurance. A strategy designed to maximize the perceived reliability of the United States as a fuel supplier is inconsistent with a strategy to manipulate fuel supplies. In any event, other options give customers leverage with suppliers. In the past India responded to Canadian attempts to enforce new safeguards on fuel elements by implicitly threatening to accept Soviet offers of assistance. Canada and the United States then relaxed safeguards on heavy water. In a later instance India asked for technical data for fuel fabrication, which Canada provided to prevent inferior indigenously produced elements from harming the reactor and to prevent India from carrying out its threat to use French and Belgian supplies covered by less stringent safeguards. Agreements of the London nuclear suppliers' group may

11. 92 Stat. 134.
12. *Nucleonics Week,* vol. 18 (July 14, 1977), p. 8.
13. Joanne Omang, "A-Panel Allows Reactor Export to Philippines," *Washington Post,* May 7, 1980.

reduce importers' ability to play one supplier against another, but some freedom of maneuver will probably remain. Bizarre though it may sound, if Pakistan is able to complete its own enrichment plant, it could sell fuel to India. This might make the operation seem more innocent, and India would have an incentive both to compensate for the loss of American fuel and to tie up as much as possible of the Pakistani enrichment capacity, which otherwise could be devoted to turning out bombs.

U.S. fuel supply has been most at issue with India. In 1976 NRC hearings, Deputy Assistant Secretary of State Myron B. Kratzer argued against cutting off supplies to retaliate for the 1974 explosion because such a move would weaken U.S. credibility as a reliable supplier. As a compromise, he accepted the idea of threatening a stoppage after another explosion if there "was a clear affirmation that this was the only reason for which fuel would be cut off."[14] In April 1977 Desai informed the Indian parliament that he had told the United States that any delay in the supply of enriched fuel would hurt the operation of the Tarapur power station and thus hurt the energy supply in western India, and that delays contravened the obligations of the United States under the intergovernmental contract on fuel supply (which mandated U.S. shipments for Tarapur for thirty years). He also hinted that India might "improvise" fuel (perhaps a mixed oxide) for Tarapur if faced with a cutoff. Scientists subsequently worked hard to develop such a substitute. In May 1979 the chairman of the Indian Atomic Energy Commission, H. N. Sethna, predicted it would be available within three years and would finally end Indian dependence on foreign sources.[15]

The Carter administration decided against "an explicitly punitive approach to India," and the State Department said it would recommend licensing fuel exports if India agreed to talks on nuclear policy in general.[16] One problem was U.S. insistence that India not reprocess the fuel it receives for Tarapur.[17] Yet despite President Carter's discomfort at Desai's unwillingness to accept full-scope safeguards, he announced that not only would the United States ship fuel to Tarapur, but it would also supply

14. *Nucleonics Week,* vol. 17 (July 22, 1976), pp. 5–6.

15. *Nucleonics Week,* vol. 18 (April 28, 1977), pp. 8–9; "India," *Nuclear Engineering International* (February 1978), p. 9; U.S. Foreign Broadcast Information Service (FBIS), *Daily Report: Middle East and North Africa* (May 18, 1979), p. S1.

16. *Nucleonics Week,* vol. 18 (June 2, 1977), p. 5.

17. Ibid. (June 23, 1977), p. 6.

American heavy water to make up for India's losses from an accident in its Baroda heavy water production plant.[18]

Soon the Tarapur resupply issue heated up again. The Nuclear Regulatory Commission split 2–2 on the application (without presidential involvement this would constitute rejection), and President Carter decided to approve the shipment on the grounds that India was engaged in good faith negotiations over the cooperation agreement and that rejection of the export would undermine them. Joseph Nye, deputy to the under secretary of state for security assistance, science, and technology, testified that securing Indian acceptance of full-scope safeguards was "a significant possibility."[19] Commissioners Peter Bradford and Victor Gilinsky, who opposed permitting the export, were less sanguine, maintaining that India's conditions for agreement (comprehensive test ban, no additions to U.S. or Soviet nuclear stockpiles, and plans for reductions leading eventually to superpower disarmament) "are formidable, and meeting them is, in any case, not entirely within U.S. control."[20] Opponents of the export feared that, if the United States abrogated the original terms of the cooperation agreement at the end of the grace period, India would not capitulate but would instead respond by reprocessing the accumulated spent fuel from the Tarapur reactors, and that the shipment would simply add to India's fissionable plutonium.

The U.S. government maintains that the cooperation agreement leaves open the right to change the terms for export, since it specifies contracts must conform to U.S. laws, and that American refusal to export fuel because of India's unwillingness to accede to the requirements of the Nuclear Non-Proliferation Act does not relieve New Delhi of its responsibilities under the agreement.[21] Indian leaders have not accepted this interpretation. Prime Minister Desai argued that the U.S.-Indian cooperation agreement could not unilaterally be violated by the United States and noted that "it provides that nothing contained in the relevant article [requiring consultation on modification of the agreement if American laws change] shall affect the obligation of the U.S. government to sell all of our

18. "Text of Address by President Carter before the Indian Parliament in New Delhi," *New York Times,* January 3, 1978; "India," p. 9.
19. *Nuclear Fuel Export to India,* Hearing before the Senate Committee on Foreign Relations, 95 Cong. 2 sess. (Government Printing Office, 1978), p. 344.
20. Ibid., p. 75.
21. Victor Gilinsky, "U.S.-India Nuclear Relations," transcript of remarks before the India Council of Washington, D.C., February 5, 1980.

requirement of enriched uranium. . . . refusal to supply such requirements would be a breach of the agreement."[22] A breach, he said, would free India "to adopt any course we like to safeguard our own interest."[23] One Indian analyst presented his country's legal case thus:

Article 60 of the Vienna Convention on the Law of Treaties provides that a bilateral treaty may be terminated or suspended . . . should a material breach in its terms be committed by the other party. Further, Article 27 . . . expressly prohibits a party to a Treaty from invoking the provisions of its internal laws as an excuse for failure to perform treaty obligations. The U.S. insistence on seeking additional undertakings to supply enriched uranium, under threat to abrogate the TAPS [Tarapur atomic power station] agreement, is legally untenable.[24]

The Indian stand was obviously to threaten to take possession of spent fuel if the United States voided the 1963 cooperation agreement and to establish that it would not be bound to feed the Tarapur reactors with only American fuel as the 1963 agreement specified. In the summer of 1978 rumors of an informal offer from the Soviet Union to enrich uranium for India surfaced.[25]

In June the Senate Foreign Relations Committee sent President Carter a letter stating that Congress was unlikely to accept another waiver at the end of the eighteen-month grace period.[26] At the end of 1978 administration sources revealed that India had agreed to set up a joint committee of scientists to assess how India might apply comprehensive safeguards to its facilities. The recommendations of this committee, however, were not to be binding;[27] furthermore, the committee was scuttled as disagreements arose over operation. In March 1979 Desai told parliament that India was

22. Quoted in Government of India, *Foreign Affairs Record,* vol. 24 (April 1978), p. 169.

23. Quoted in "Desai Attacks U.S. Nuclear Fuel Ban," *New York Times,* April 25, 1978. India also faced a logistical problem that would be solved by reprocessing: storage space for spent fuel at Tarapur was being exhausted. FBIS, *Daily Report: Middle East and North Africa* (May 1, 1979), p. S6.

24. P. R. Chari, "An Indian Reaction to U.S. Nonproliferation Policy," *International Security,* vol. 3 (Fall 1978), p. 59.

25. *Nucleonics Week,* vol. 19 (July 20, 1978), p. 3; Paul F. Power, "The Indo-American Nuclear Controversy," *Asian Survey,* vol. 19 (June 1979), p. 591.

26. *Nucleonics Week,* vol. 19 (June 22, 1978), p. 7.

27. "India Agrees to Air Ways of Monitoring Use of Nuclear Fuel," *Washington Post,* December 13, 1978; "India and U.S. to Set Up Safeguards Panel," *Nuclear Engineering International* (January 1979), p. 8.

prepared for the termination of U.S. fuel supplies for Tarapur.[28] Two weeks later the NRC voted 3–2 to export the next Tarapur fuel charge. The rationale was still the same—continuing negotiations. In April, however, visiting Minister of External Affairs Atal Bihari Vajpayee was intransigent. When President Carter explained that his hands were tied by the Non-Proliferation Act, Vajpayee parried by suggesting that the act be amended to permit the United States to meet its contractual obligations. He later told parliament, "I made it quite clear to them that India would *never* accept a safeguards system which would be discriminatory."[29]

American fuel supply policy has been worse than ineffective; it has become counterproductive. Pressure pushed New Delhi toward experimenting with uranium enrichment, the one important element of nuclear technology in which India had not previously been interested. Moreover, Prime Minister Gandhi linked this development with the weapons option when she told parliament, "While we do not have all that we would like to have in the defense sphere, we are trying to strengthen ourselves. So far as enrichment is concerned . . . we want to be ready."[30] By mid-1980 India seemed to have triumphed in the protracted struggle with Washington over fuel supply for Tarapur. In grappling with the challenge of Soviet advances in the region, President Carter decided to avoid further exacerbation of Indo-American relations. Despite reports of the enrichment experiments, despite New Delhi's refusal to accept full-scope safeguards, and despite Indira Gandhi's announcement that she would not rule out nuclear explosive tests in the future, President Carter overruled the Nuclear Regulatory Commission in June 1980 and approved the export of a two-year supply of fuel for Tarapur.[31] At the time of this writing, Congress is still deliberating about whether it should overrule the president or allow the shipment to proceed.

Pakistan had planned to install heavy water reactors, which use natural uranium, reducing dependency on enriched uranium. More recently, Pakistan indicated that it would build light water reactors. A suspicious

28. "India Says It Is Ready for Cutoff in U.S. Uranium," *New York Times,* March 8, 1979.

29. FBIS, *Daily Report: Middle East and North Africa* (May 1, 1979), p. S5. Vajpayee quoted in Government of India, *Foreign Affairs Record,* vol. 25 (April 1979), p. 98.

30. *Nucleonics Week,* vol. 21 (April 10, 1980), p. 12.

31. Richard Burt, "Carter to Approve India's Atom Fuel," *New York Times,* June 19, 1980.

interpretation would be that the interest in LWRs was a rationalization for enrichment plans rather than a cause. If development of a weapons option is indeed the primary reason for the Kahuta project, it is not surprising that schemes to allay fears about access to fuel, such as an international fuel bank, have not excited Pakistan's interest.[32] Pakistan has been vulnerable because it lacks fuel fabrication facilities. Canada canceled its nuclear co-operation agreement—including fuel supply—after unsuccessful negotiations to ensure that spent fuel from the KANUPP reactor would not be reprocessed in the French-supplied separation plant. But although this presented severe problems for keeping KANUPP in operation, Pakistan did not capitulate.[33] For Pakistan, any U.S. attempt to compel it to cancel its reprocessing and enrichment plans by limiting its fuel supplies would emphasize the advantages of autonomy that reprocessing and enrichment would provide. Indeed, the Pakistan Atomic Energy Commission cited the termination of Canadian assistance as justification for moving more decisively toward such full-cycle capabilities.[34]

The Iranians' plans to use LWRs and their willingness to do without indigenous reprocessing or enrichment facilities does not mean they have always been unconcerned about assured access to fuel. In 1976, when the United States proposed a multinational reprocessing center, there was some uneasy mumbling about the potential danger of being victimized by "a Western nuclear OPEC." In negotiations with West Germany over contracts with Kraftwerk Union, Iran accepted conditions giving Germany the right to veto Iranian contracts to have spent fuel reprocessed in Eastern Europe or a third world country. But this agreement left open the option to have plutonium separated in a Western facility. Under these conditions the United States cannot "control" the use of fuel except through multilateral cooperation with other suppliers. This is one reason for the delay in negotiations on the sale of U.S. reactors in 1976 and 1977 (and for the fear of U.S. industry that sales might be lost to European vendors). The main reason, which is directly related, was Iranian anxiety about an assured supply of enriched uranium. One report said:

The Iranians have thought up a great many hypothetical situations on which they want assurances that the fuel supply will not be cut. . . . Many of these are

32. Tahir-Kheli, "Pakistan's Nuclear Option," p. 373.

33. Robert Trumbull, "Pakistanis Resist a Role for Canada at Nuclear Facility," New York Times, February 26, 1976.

34. Nucleonics Week, vol. 20 (October 4, 1979), p. 12.

very unlikely to come about. . . . One sticking point arose when the Iranians demanded assurances that once a contract was made with a U.S. company to supply a reactor or with Erda [Energy Research and Development Agency] for enrichment, the necessary export licenses would be issued. "Our side was unable to give that kind of assurance because it's the function of the Nuclear Regulatory Commission to issue export licenses on the basis of evidence presented at the time of the sale, making sure the deals are sound and do not go against the U.S. interest," the negotiator said.[35]

After that, the shah reportedly agreed to purchase six to eight American reactors on terms that accorded with pending U.S. legislation.[36] This decision was eased by Iran's ventures in non-American sources of fuel. It invested heavily in European enrichment facilities—Eurodif and Coredif—and there were unconfirmed reports of its participation in South African plans for uranium enrichment. The Iranian revolution made most of the concern about nuclear fuel supply meaningless. But it also washed away part of the solution as revolutionary authorities sought to unload the country's shares in Eurodif and Coredif. Moreover, a post-shah government interested in at least some nuclear generating capacity is even more likely to oppose dependence on an external "nuclear OPEC."[37]

Only a cartel of enrichment suppliers could hope to exert decisive leverage a decade from now. And if India and Pakistan relied primarily on HWRs that are not vulnerable to fuel cutoffs, even that hypothetical concert would probably not be decisive in determining national policies in South and West Asia. The relevance of enriched fuel supply to nonproliferation can best be exploited—if it can be at all—not by unsuccessful attempts to manipulate it (increasing incentives for autonomy), but by eliminating any hint of manipulation and any doubts about fuel availability. There are various proposals for how to do this: Bertrand Goldschmidt sees a healthy free market and competition among suppliers as the best way to alleviate fears of vulnerability among customers;[38] others suggest an international fuel bank; another alternative is providing large

35. *Nucleonics Week,* vol. 17 (August 19, 1976), p. 9.

36. Edward Walsh, "Carter Will Meet Sadat to Discuss Talks on Mideast," *Washington Post,* January 1, 1978.

37. *Nucleonics Week,* vol. 16 (October 2, 1975), p. 1; Fern Racine Gold and Melvin A. Conant, *Access to Oil—The United States Relationships with Saudi Arabia and Iran,* Report to the Senate Committee on Energy and Natural Resources, 95 Cong. 1 sess. (GPO, 1977), p. 82.

38. Bertrand Goldschmidt, "A Historical Survey of Nonproliferation Policies," *International Security,* vol. 2 (Summer 1977), pp. 86–87.

enough stockpiles of fuel to run reactors for as long as necessary to build indigenous reprocessing or enrichment plants. Related to assurances of enriched fuel, assurances of the availability of adequate natural uranium would reinforce the U.S. campaign against plutonium reprocessing.

India now has all the weapons-applicable capabilities, Pakistan is trying to acquire the essential ones as soon as possible, and Iran has the economic resources to get them if it were interested in doing so. For the United States to prevent nuclear weapons acquisition in the region by physically controlling available capabilities would require not only leverage but varying degrees of extreme ingenuity or attractive economic incentives as well. In the 1950s, when restricting the diffusion of nuclear technology was more feasible, American policy encouraged it (Atoms for Peace), but in the 1970s, when U.S. policy encouraged restriction, this became less feasible. The principal remaining problem is that, without compensating inducements, energetic attempts to keep sophisticated nuclear techniques out of the hands of developing nations risks aggravating their desire to acquire and secure them. Moves in this direction could be seen at 1977 conferences in New Delhi and Shiraz and the 1978 Belgrade meeting of nonaligned nations. At New Delhi, Yugoslavia (which was indignant at U.S. moves to hamper its autonomous control over the Westinghouse-built Krsko reactor) proposed a scheme for nuclear "early emancipation" of nonaligned countries based on a pooling of resources, finances, and expertise. At Shiraz there was much discussion of the danger that new U.S. policies presaged a "nuclear OPEC" of supplier states aimed against the third world.[39] The resentment, suspicion, stubborn resistance, and envisioned countertactics represented by the Yugoslav position were revealed in impassioned comments, worth quoting at length, attributed to an unnamed senior government official:

We did not give in to the Nazis or to Stalin, and at very great cost. Why should we give our sovereignty up to the Americans now?

. . . [U.S. officials] keep urging us to understand and accept the new, unacceptable controls, saying they . . . can't be selective in their export policy. But the point is they have been and are being very selective [South Africa, Israel].

. . . And are we supposed to be so understanding that we give up our sovereignty in the name of this punitive selectivity?

. . . The Pakistani experience is very instructive. They say that after the contract was signed, the Canadians turned around and demanded embarrassingly tighter controls. Eventually the Pakistanis agreed, and then the Canadians came

39. *Nucleonics Week,* vol. 18 (April 28, 1977), p. 5.

back with even more unacceptable demands. The Pakistanis walked away from
the whole deal. And their impression was that had they agreed the second time
it would have only meant another escalation. It all makes you stop and think
about motives and intentions.

Carter's policy is not basically military, it is economic. It aims to hamstring
small countries and keep the bigger ones in line.

. . . [Regarding pooled self-help by the nonaligned:] In a way we'd have to
start from scratch, but not completely from scratch. We have a couple of things
going for us . . . uranium in Gabon, Nigeria, Congo, Argentina . . . groundwork
in knowhow in India, which has 100,000 people working in various phases of
nuclear technology today. Egypt, Yugoslavia and Libya are now building [test
reactors] with the Soviets. Computer technology is no secret today to Egypt,
India, Yugoslavia. And the capital could be found in maybe Kuwait, Saudi
Arabia, Libya, Iraq. . . . All the essential elements are there. . . . It'd mean a
10–15 year delay but that is better than what the Americans are offering now.
. . . Until the U.S. understands that the world no longer hangs by their elections,
nor by the current lineup in the Kremlin for that matter, it seems it will be
unavoidable.[40]

Such rhetoric may be hyperbolic or unrealistic. (It is interesting,
though, that sources in Karachi in June 1977 reported that Saudi Arabia
would cover the costs of Pakistan's reprocessing plant with a loan, after
which Pakistan might train Saudis in the nuclear field.[41]) But it suggests
at least the potential challenges to a countercapability nonproliferation
strategy. Similar rhetoric was voiced again in Belgrade when fifteen countries discussed increased nuclear cooperation. Dealing with some of the
security incentives for nuclear weapons, therefore, might not necessarily
be less effective or ultimately more difficult than stunting the growth of
capabilities. In one sense, motives are more determining anyway, since
diffusion of nuclear knowledge has gone as far as it has. If a nation's
incentives are high enough to make the sacrifices and investments necessary, it can eventually attain weapons capability no matter what the great
powers do short of armed intervention. And if incentives are low enough,
the capability will not matter, since there will be no reason to exercise it.

Diplomatic Solutions

Aside from the incentive to gain prestige, there should be some cor-
relation between a rise in security and a decline in the need for nuclear

40. Quoted in ibid., pp. 5–7.
41. *Nucleonics Week*, vol. 18 (June 16, 1977), p. 5.

weapons. Security would be enhanced if the level of tension was reduced or the issues underlying hostilities were resolved. Reduction of tension, however, cannot automatically be assumed to yield reductions in defense efforts. Despite U.S.-Soviet détente and SALT I, both nations continued to expand and modernize their nuclear forces. Nixon, Ford, and Carter explicitly tied the durability of détente to continued maintenance of high military force levels and strong and credible deterrence by the West. (And the deterioration of détente at the end of the 1970s can be viewed by potential proliferators as evidence of the danger of relying on diplomatic solutions to security problems.) To the extent that a détente is reinforced by a stable balance of power, rather than replacing it, such a development may be hard to engineer in South or West Asia, where major imbalances are a large part of the problem.

In 1976 India and China upgraded their diplomatic relations with an exchange of ambassadors. After Indira Gandhi's defeat, the new government in New Delhi moved toward more complete nonalignment, cooling the warm relationship that had developed with the USSR. In August 1977 Vajpayee announced that the government would welcome negotiations with Peking on the border issue, emphasized again that India recognized China's sovereignty over Tibet and would not allow Tibetan refugees to engage in political activities, and noted the normalization of diplomatic relations and improvement of trade ties and scientific-cultural exchanges with China. The following year Desai suggested that India could accept the border status quo but sought to have the issue discussed. He said, "All depends on China. But we are determined not to go to war on that issue."[42] In February 1978 Chinese Vice Premier Teng Hsiao-ping said China was anxious for "closer" relations with India. Coincidentally, however, in what could be interpreted as supportive of Pakistan, he said that all South Asian countries, "big and small, should treat each other equally and co-exist peacefully."[43] Since then disagreements over Cambodia and Vietnam have marred Sino-Indian relations. Thus the trend appears only modestly favorable for calming the antagonism most likely to encourage Indian deployment of a nuclear force, and is not necessarily coupled with resolution of Indo-Pakistani differences. Indeed, if the PRC were to reduce its traditional support of Pakistan, the increased sense of isolation or aban-

42. Quoted in David Binder, "India Ready to Drop China Border Claims," *New York Times,* June 12, 1978.
43. "Teng Calls for Closer Ties with India," *Washington Post,* February 5, 1978.

donment in Islamabad could intensify desire in that capital for a deployed nuclear deterrent.

Indo-Pakistani relations have not deteriorated—and in some ways have improved—since the July 1972 Simla agreement between Prime Ministers Gandhi and Bhutto, in which both agreed to respect the cease-fire line of December 1971 and renounced the use of force as a means of altering it. Although still demanding that Pakistan accept the imbalance of power on the subcontinent, India has reasons for seeking improved relations—to calm its own Muslim population and to avoid weakening ties with other Muslim (especially Arab) states.[44] Pakistan has been cautiously receptive. The near-resolution of the Baluchistan problem in 1975 alleviated Islamabad's fear of domestic fragmentation and the temptation that might be to India (although the Soviet invasion of Afghanistan resurrected fears of Baluchi unrest). By mid-1976 the two countries had renewed diplomatic relations, Pakistan had recognized Bangladesh, and feelers for détente with India had been extended.[45] Early in 1978 the new Pakistani government served as host for talks in Rawalpindi between Vajpayee and General Zia ul-Haq and his foreign minister. "There are only two problems between our two countries," Zia announced enthusiastically. "No. 1 —Kashmir. No. 2—the misconceptions we have of one another. Solve those and we can go as far as we like."[46]

There is probably little the United States can do to change the two nations' "misconceptions" of each other. The communications between the two are certainly civil enough to obviate the need for shuttle-diplomacy mediation comparable to that in the Middle East in recent times. The United States could encourage India to make concessions in the interest of peace, particularly on the Kashmir issue, perhaps emphasizing India's predominance as a reason for generosity—a sort of appeal to *pouvoir oblige.* It is doubtful, however, that such entreaties would be more effective than the New Delhi leadership's own calculations of costs and benefits. At present, although the tension over Kashmir has declined, there are no in-

44. G. S. Bhargava, *India's Security in the 1980s,* Adelphi Paper 125 (London: International Institute for Strategic Studies, 1976), p. 5.

45. See William Borders's *New York Times* stories: "Turn in India's Foreign Policy," April 21, 1976; "Pakistani Aides Hopeful on New Talks with India," May 10, 1976; and "Pakistan, India Agree to Renew Diplomatic Ties," May 15, 1976.

46. Quoted in Simon Winchester, "India, Pakistan Open Talks in Friendly Atmosphere," *Washington Post,* February 7, 1978.

dications that the parties involved foresee a solution to it. Pakistan demands self-determination for the Muslim territory, but India refuses to recognize this principle as a criterion for settlement, fearing it might legitimate secessionist movements in some of India's states. Giving up its foothold in the territory would weaken India's strategic position against China as well as Pakistan: "if India gave up the Vale of Kashmir, through which its troops must pass to reach the Chinese frontier, it would be impossible to defend Ladakh. India would be unwilling to be dependent on transit rights for its troops, even if guaranteed, particularly in view of Pakistan's cooperation with Communist China in recent years."[47] The limits to détente were suggested in early 1979 by India's rejection of Pakistan's proposal for a regional collective security system based on balanced military strength, a code of conduct, and agreement not to build nuclear weapons.[48]

Short of tangible aid or new commitments, which could also aggravate tension, the ability of the United States to make a unique contribution to fostering détente on the subcontinent appears very limited. In one sense the stabilization of the PRC-India-Pakistan triangle (probably more at Pakistan's expense than that of the others) might best be enhanced by Sino-Soviet rapprochement. But the United States would find this undesirable because of its wider implications—a case of conflict between America's regional nonproliferation interests and global strategic interests. Such a development would also do little to reduce Pakistan's insecurity—while moderating the Soviet threat, it would release Indian forces for the Pakistan front—and hence its nuclear incentives, or to reassure Iran about its susceptibility to direct Soviet pressure.

The United States can also continue to support the creation of a nuclear-weapon-free zone, although the lack of response to the Carter initiative in this direction in spring 1979 does not lead one to expect much from such proposals.[49] Pakistan has been the most energetic proponent of a South Asian nuclear-weapon-free zone, having proposed that it be

47. William J. Barnds, *India, Pakistan, and the Great Powers* (Praeger for the Council on Foreign Relations, 1967), p. 314.

48. "India Rejects Pak Security Plan," *Indian & Foreign Review*, vol. 17 (March 1, 1979), p. 9.

49. "U.S. Seeks Atom-Arms Ban in Indian-Pakistani Zone," *International Herald Tribune*, May 28, 1979.

placed on the agenda of the United Nations General Assembly in 1974.[50] That same year the General Assembly passed a resolution sponsored by Iran for a Middle East nuclear-free zone. Neither proposal, however, resulted in a treaty. This is largely because India, though supporting a nuclear-free zone in principle, refuses to accept it on the terms normally proposed. One Indian objection is that a nuclear-free zone cannot be restricted to South Asia because that area cannot be segregated from the rest of Eurasia (which includes most of the nuclear weapons states).[51] India naturally worries about the exclusion of China and the possibility that Pakistan might test a bomb outside the region (for instance, in Saudi Arabia).[52]

In any case, India's conditions preclude any meaningful nuclear-free zone short of worldwide disarmament. But there is another argument, posed by Ram Dhan of the Indian delegation to the United Nations in 1977: "India, practically, was a nuclear-weapon-free zone because of its categorical declarations that it would not make nuclear weapons."[53] (A treaty, of course, would be more likely than a declaration to survive a change of government.) Finally, it is not clear that even if a nuclear-weapon-free zone were established in South Asia—or in the Middle East to include Iran—it would yield any greater benefits or security than the NPT, unless withdrawal from a nuclear-free zone were made more difficult than withdrawal (allowed on ninety days' notice) from the NPT. Neither sort of treaty obligation would prevent attainment of a nuclear option in the form of an untested stock of bomb components. A nuclear-weapon-free zone would be useful as a symbol and a legal constraint on changing intentions, but not as a constraint on threshold capability. Nor would it eliminate incentives for nuclear weapons as deterrents to aggression with conventional forces. The same inadequacy limits the significance of pledges by the nuclear powers—such as President Carter's

50. See the statement by the Pakistani representative in U.S. Arms Control and Disarmament Agency, *Documents on Disarmament, 1974* (GPO, 1976), pp. 648–55; and Kathleen Teltsch, "Pakistan Urging Atom-Free Zone," *New York Times,* October 29, 1974.

51. Rikhi Jaipal, "The Indian Nuclear Explosion," *International Security,* vol. 1 (Spring 1977), p. 49.

52. See "India Reacts to U.S. Pressure," *Nuclear Engineering International* (June 1979), p. 27.

53. "India Named Co-chairman of Fuel Evaluation Group," *Indian & Foreign Review,* vol. 15 (November 1, 1977), p. 10.

qualified pledge in June 1978—not to use nuclear weapons against non-nuclear states.[54]

If the imbalance of power in South Asia could be modified by alliances or aid agreements in the region or with other middle-power states, incentives might be curtailed at little direct cost to the United States. Washington could even rhetorically accept India's assertion of regional predominance. Earlier it seemed that the most obvious alliance possibility of this sort (beyond the Pakistan-China alliance that already exists but has never solved Pakistan's defense problems) would be a strengthening of ties between Tehran and Islamabad. To the extent that Iran functioned as a surrogate for the United States in guaranteeing its neighbor's security, Pakistan's anxieties could be reduced without provoking direct Indian hostility to American policy. On their own, Iran and Pakistan drew closer after the 1971 war. The shah said in 1972 that he would regard an attack on Pakistan as an attack on Iran. Further dismemberment of Pakistan was viewed as risking a communist or radical foothold on the Indian Ocean at Karachi—and a potential threat to oil transit routes.[55] Iran held joint maneuvers with Pakistan in the early 1970s. While such joint interests remain, there is no evidence they will be activated in the post-shah era. Further threatening moves by Soviet forces, however, could impel the revolutionary government in that direction.

Even if it were feasible, it would be dangerous to make a Tehran-Islamabad military linkage more ironclad or explicit; this might increase Indo-Iranian tension. And both New Delhi and Tehran potentially have other interests, as the post-shah regime's devotion to economic backwardness declines, in maintaining amity. Under the shah Iran was one of India's major trading partners, and the two countries entered into a number of cooperative economic ventures. Economic interdependence does not in itself prevent conflict, as World War I showed, but it does provide incentives for caution in undertaking other initiatives that could disrupt relations. At least one Indian military analyst saw the 1974 economic cooperation agreement with Tehran as heading off the solidification of an Iranian-

54. Carter's pledge excepted cases of attacks on U.S. territory or forces by states allied to nuclear powers. Bernard Gwertzman, "U.S. Assures Nonnuclear States," *New York Times,* June 13, 1978.

55. Alvin J. Cottrell and James E. Dougherty, *Iran's Quest for Security: Arms Transfers and the Nuclear Option* (Institute for Foreign Policy Analysis, 1977), p. 33; R. D. M. Furlong, "Iran: A Power to Be Reckoned With," *International Defense Review,* vol. 16 (December 1973), p. 722.

Pakistani axis, feared earlier.[56] The warming of Indo-Iranian ties was also recognized in Pakistan, though skeptics there saw it—wishfully but accurately—as temporary.[57] To the Pakistanis, then, Iran's insularity is a mixed blessing.

Pakistan has alternatives to Iran for reinforcement of its security. One hypothetical form of support is intensified Pan-Islamic pressure on India to leave Pakistan alone. The ultimate form of this help could be an implied threat of a selective Organization of Arab Petroleum Exporting Countries oil embargo against India in the event of war, in which an Islamic government in Tehran might now be induced to join. Aside from the fact that this option is speculative, the United States, in view of its stand on embargoes against the West, could hardly encourage it. Moreover, to be useful as a deterrent the threat would have to be clear to New Delhi, and this would simply fuel India's desire for nuclear autarky and hence for more plutonium production and breeder reactors. Pakistan's movement toward diplomatic integration with the Islamic world, however, has been significant. Rumors that Libya was financing the enrichment plant, hoping to gain access to nuclear weapons, were vehemently denied by the Zia government. However, the government has indulged in considerable anti-Zionist rhetoric and loud declarations of solidarity with other Islamic states.

Limited assistance for Pakistan's military forces is not only more plausible, but has already occurred. The interaction is symbiotic. Islamabad has received financial aid from members of OPEC and has mutual defense agreements with the United Arab Emirates and other emirates (Qatar, Bahrain) of the Persian Gulf. Pakistanis fly Abu Dhabi's force of Mirages, and Abu Dhabi says that those aircraft would be at Pakistan's disposal in an emergency.[58] There has been some consideration of linking Pakistan's assets of skilled manpower and professional military training

56. Brigadier Rathy Sawhny (Ret.), "Strategic Implications of the Indo-Iran Agreement," *Vikrant: Asia's Defence Journal,* vol. 4 (May 1974), pp. 7–9.

57. See Mehrunnisa Ali, "The Changing Pattern of India-Iran Relations," *Pakistan Horizon,* vol. 28, no. 4 (1975), pp. 53–66. An eminent Indian diplomat, on the other hand, had earlier emphasized India's natural and historical strategic interest in defense cooperation with the Persian empire dating back to the British experience and the beginning of the nineteenth century. K. M. Pannikar, *Problems of Indian Defence* (Bombay: Asia Publishing House, 1960), p. 23.

58. Zalmay Khalilzad, "Pakistan: The Making of a Nuclear Power," *Asian Survey,* vol. 16 (June 1976), p. 591.

more systematically with the capital resources of the Middle East to create an Islamic industry in arms.[59] This kind of assistance, however, could only cushion or chip away at Pakistan's military inferiority; it could not fully redress it. And Arab support for Pakistan constricted in the late 1970s,[60] although it revived as a result of the U.S. opposition to the enrichment plant. But Pakistan is close to bankruptcy, and the Saudis cannot keep the whole economy afloat.

Offsetting Inducements

If insecurity motivates the desire for nuclear weapons, greater security may reduce it. Rather than companion evils, nuclear proliferation and conventional arms proliferation may be alternative evils. If the preference for nuclear weapons is limited, it might be further reduced by the offer of other benefits, outside of security assistance, in exchange for a decision not to acquire the weapons. By the same token a threat to curtail or withhold such benefits could be a "stick" to prompt the same decision.

This relationship of incentives and disincentives is not a simple equation, however. Enhancing one of the nations' military capabilities for defense might alarm one of the others, which would see offensive implications in the change. Increasing national power could also whet the desire for prestige, and this could make nuclear weapons attractive for assertive rather than defensive purposes. Also, some components of increases in military assets, such as high-performance aircraft, could be used as delivery systems for a nuclear capability. Nonmilitary economic aid has more than one edge as well. If it was made explicitly reciprocal for abstaining from acquiring a nuclear force, such aid could encourage countries to use the nuclear threat to extort more and better concessions from the United States. Even if there were no such cynical motives, an agreement based on aid-for-abstention might be hard to institute. Past American assistance has obviously not been large enough to create an irresistible incentive to cooperate, and it is unrealistic to think that the United States would consider raising the ante high enough to do so. When the Soviet invasion of Afghanistan prompted Washington to make an offer of $400 million—

59. Stephen P. Cohen, "Security in South Asia," *Asian Survey,* vol. 15 (March 1975), p. 213.
60. Tahir-Kheli, "Pakistan's Nuclear Option," pp. 369–70.

probably the most generous figure possible under present circumstances—
Zia dismissed it as "peanuts." Past attempts at "linkage" of concessions
across issue areas have not proved notably effective; many U.S. attempts
to use foreign aid to influence the policies of client governments have
failed. Nevertheless, some logical connections exist between offsetting inducements and willingness to do without nuclear weapons. The applicability, costs, and benefits of such options vary in each case.

Past Pakistani policy explicitly linked lack of interest in nuclear weapons to adequacy of conventional defenses. After the 1974 Indian detonation Bhutto noted that Pakistan's nuclear weapons policy was continu-
ously reviewed and depended on U.S. readiness to supply adequate conventional weapons: "If we are satisfied with our security requirements in
conventional armaments we would not hazard our economic future and
promote an economic and social upheaval by diverting resources for a
nuclear program."[61] The conditional nature was made more ominously
explicit, however, when Bhutto said that if enough conventional weapons
were not supplied Pakistan "must concentrate all its energy on acquiring
a nuclear capability. If Pakistan is not able to acquire weapons which can
act as a deterrent, it must forego spending on conventional weapons and
make a jump forward."[62] The post-Bhutto government sought to obtain
advanced aircraft from the United States in the late 1970s, but American
reluctance, coupled with heavy pressure against plans to purchase the
reprocessing plant from France, provoked anger and distrust in Islamabad. The clandestine enrichment venture and coolness toward American
offers of assistance to counter Soviet forces on the western border suggest either that Pakistan has given up on the possibility of getting enough
aid from the United States to compensate for the lack of a nuclear deterrent or that it wants a nuclear option no matter what the price.

The problem is not that the United States has refused to aid Pakistan
militarily, but that efforts to do so have been so feeble and inconsistent

61. Khalilzad, "Pakistan: The Making of a Nuclear Power," pp. 590–91. Bhutto
quoted in Lewis A. Dunn, "India, Pakistan, Iran . . . : A Nuclear Proliferation
Chain?" in William H. Overholt, ed., *Asia's Nuclear Future* (Westview Press, 1977),
p. 205.
62. Quoted in Charles K. Ebinger, "U.S. Nuclear Non-proliferation Policy: The
Pakistan Controversy," *Fletcher Forum*, vol. 3 (Summer 1979), pp. 8–9. "If conventional arms are not supplied to Pakistan under treaty obligations," Bhutto said,
". . . the country may be forced into a military nuclear programme." Quoted in
Dilip Mukerjee, "India's Nuclear Test and Pakistan," *India Quarterly*, vol. 30
(October–December 1974), p. 265.

that they offer a country so thoroughly insecure scant reason to rely on such an aid relationship or at least to abandon options for other means. In 1975 the United States ended the arms embargo against India and Pakistan imposed during the war ten years earlier, but the dispensation was in principle limited to defensive weapons. In the following year the United States sold Pakistan $100 million worth of military supplies— mainly antitank missiles, trucks, and ammunition. When in late 1976 the Department of Defense approved the much more important sale of 110 A-7 aircraft, the State Department was reportedly ready to clear the sale if Pakistan agreed to cancel its purchase of the reprocessing plant from France.[63] Probably because Islamabad resisted the condition, the final decision was left to the incoming Carter administration, which ultimately decided against selling the A-7s, primarily because of their range (which made them offensive weapons). After revelation of the enrichment project, the United States offered to sell 50 F-5Es.[64] Pakistan, however, was not thrilled by this offer of a modest number of modest aircraft, particularly since India was purchasing modern deep-strike aircraft in Europe.

Before 1965 Pakistan had received fifteen times as much military aid as India from the United States.[65] This aid was for anticommunist purposes, not defense against India; Pakistan was a Southeast Asia Treaty Organization ally. The embargo imposed in 1965 was modified slightly in 1966 to permit both Pakistan and India to buy "non-lethal end items," in 1967 to permit the sale of spare parts for equipment already provided, and in 1970 as a one-time exception to allow Pakistan to purchase armored personnel carriers. (The value of all types of U.S. military assistance to South Asian countries declined from an annual average of $99 million in the 1950–65 period to less than $16 million in 1966–75. In fiscal 1965 South Asia's share of worldwide American military assistance was 5.5 percent; ten years later it was only 0.06 percent.)[66] Pakistan suffered more than India from the U.S. embargo—which was evenhanded in principle

63. William Borders, "Pakistan Wonders Whether Ties to U.S. Will Erode under Carter," *New York Times,* December 26, 1976; Leslie H. Gelb, "Spread of Nuclear Weapons and U.S. Sales," *New York Times,* August 11, 1976.

64. Richard Burt, "Pakistan Is Offered a Choice on A-Arms," *New York Times,* April 17, 1979.

65. Lorne J. Kavic, "Force Posture: India and Pakistan," in Frank B. Horton III, Anthony C. Rogerson, and Edward L. Warner III, eds., *Comparative Defense Policy* (Johns Hopkins University Press, 1974), p. 379.

66. Archer K. Blood, "Detente and South Asia," *Parameters,* vol. 5, no. 1 (1975), p. 38.

Table 14-1. *Deliveries of Military Equipment to Pakistan and India*
by Various Countries, 1961–71

Millions of dollars

Supplier	1961–65	1966–71	1961–71
To Pakistan			
United States[a]	229	71	300
France	13	107	120
China	10	193	203
Belgium	0	17	17
West Germany	7	24	31
Italy	0	20	20
Turkey	17	13	30
USSR	0	22	22
Other	4	26	30
Total	280	493	773
To India			
USSR	266	821	1,087
United Kingdom	100	190	290
Czechoslovakia	0	80	80
United States[a]	99	27	126
France	20	16	36
Yugoslavia	7	13	20
Bulgaria	0	12	12
West Germany	7	4	11
Poland	0	20	20
Japan	10	0	10
Other	25	45	70
Total	534	1,228	1,762

Source: *The United States and South Asia*, Committee Print, Report of the Subcommittee on the Near East and South Asia of the House Committee on Foreign Affairs, 93 Cong. 1 sess. (Government Printing Office, 1973), p. 27.
a. Figures for U.S. fiscal years.

—because India was able to obtain significant quantities of arms from the Soviet Union and has a sizable arms industry of its own. India's advantage is further highlighted when total amounts of military equipment from external suppliers during the period in which India and Pakistan fought two wars are considered (see table 14-1). From 1966 to 1971 the USSR delivered $821 million in arms and equipment to India, and the PRC supplied Pakistan with $193 million; from 1965 to 1970 U.S. "non-lethal" sales to both amounted to $70 million.[67] Even without an embargo,

67. Table 14-1, above; and Richard C. Thornton, "South Asia: Imbalance on the Subcontinent," *Orbis*, vol. 19 (Fall 1975), p. 866.

the vulnerability caused by dependence remains, because suppliers can cripple a client country's forces by withholding spare parts, other maintenance support, or resupply in response to attrition. Turkey's problems with the United States after the 1974 invasion of Cyprus and Egypt's after breaking with the USSR are striking examples. Not surprisingly, Pakistan, like other third world countries, has moved to maximize indigenous sources of military hardware. Of seven categories of military production, Pakistan engaged in only one in 1965, but in five by 1975.[68]

Another source of support for Pakistan is China. The two countries have had a special relationship for more than two decades, although it cooled briefly in the 1950s when Islamabad aligned itself with Washington. In 1955–76 Pakistan was the only country outside Africa to have an appreciable number of military personnel (375) trained in the PRC.[69] After the 1971 partition, Bhutto visited Peking and had $100 million in Chinese loans converted to grants; and in May 1972 China sent 60 MIG-19s, 100 T-54 and T-59 tanks, and other weapons as part of a $300 million economic and military aid agreement. In the mid-1970s Pakistan was the recipient of the largest amount of Chinese military assistance to a noncommunist state.[70] But Peking's capacity to help Pakistan cannot match the resources, in quantity and quality, with which Moscow can provide New Delhi.

Direct American military assistance remains an option (although Washington has bruised Pakistani feelings so thoroughly since the mid-1970s that the relationship may be impossible to repair). Arms aid that could be construed as purely defensive would have the fewest drawbacks. This criterion would be hard to reconcile with either of the major types of equipment—high-performance aircraft and armor—that provide the backbone of a modern military force. Because of the short distances between both antagonists' targets, even F-5s for Pakistan could have offensive implications for India,[71] and tanks are certainly offensive weapons.

68. International Institute for Strategic Studies, *Strategic Survey, 1976* (London: IISS, 1977), p. 22.

69. U.S. Central Intelligence Agency, *Communist Aid to the Less Developed Countries of the Free World, 1976,* ER 77-10296 (CIA, 1977), p. 6.

70. Ebinger, "U.S. Nuclear Non-proliferation Policy," p. 9.

71. At least as early as 1974 the State Department publicly mentioned a policy "not to proliferate a strategic nuclear delivery capability." Paul C. Warnke with Edward C. Luck, "American Arms Transfers: Policy and Process in the Executive Branch," in Andrew J. Pierre, ed., *Arms Transfers and American Foreign Policy*

Small, self-propelled antitank weapons platforms, however, might more readily be considered reasonable aid, and air defense weapons—even a sophisticated surface-to-air missile system—would be especially relevant. Such a system could be a hedge against a weak, bomber-mounted Indian nuclear attack as well as against conventional strikes. Precision-guided munitions for both antiarmor and antiaircraft purposes are another possibility. Although the defensive, as opposed to the offensive, character of precision-guided munitions has been overstated,[72] they might be a form of assistance that would help Pakistan most while alarming India least. But nuclear options could still remain attractive because precision-guided munitions are sensitive to weather and vulnerable to countermeasures; "nuclear weapons could appear to provide a greater certainty of objective denial."[73]

In any case, arms aid is no simple solution to Islamabad's nuclear incentives. Pakistani leaders, judging from the A-7 dispute and the enrichment controversy, have demonstrated no interest in a nonnuclear quo for an American arms sales quid. Moreover, to substantially reduce Pakistan's security motives for a nuclear deterrent, military assistance would have to be massive. In view of Pakistan's limited resources, this suggests that, in addition to a permissive policy on sales, U.S. *grant* aid would have to be reinvigorated, and to an extent far beyond the $400 million offered early in 1980. The critical obstacle to such a strategy, however, is that U.S. military aid to Pakistan presents the same problem as aid to the PRC— the danger of damaging triangular relationships and provoking more powerful and more important countries (the USSR in the latter case, and India in the former).

(New York University Press, 1979), p. 207. This may have reinforced the decision not to sell A-7s to Pakistan, but between contiguous antagonists with modest air defense systems aircraft of almost any range and capability could deliver nuclear weapons.

72. See Richard Burt's analysis in *New Weapons Technology: Debate and Directions,* Adelphi Paper 126 (London: International Institute for Strategic Studies, 1976), especially pp. 12–16.

73. Lewis A. Dunn, Herman Kahn, and others, *Trends in Nuclear Proliferation, 1975–1995: Projections, Problems, and Policy Options,* HI-2336/3-RR, prepared for U.S. Arms Control and Disarmament Agency (Croton-on-Hudson: Hudson Institute, 1976), p. 96. See also Richard Burt, "Nuclear Proliferation and the Spread of New Conventional Weapons Technology," *International Security,* vol. 1 (Winter 1977), pp. 119–39; and Burt, *Nuclear Proliferation and Conventional Arms Transfers: The Missing Link,* Discussion Paper 76 (Santa Monica: California Seminar on Arms Control and Foreign Policy, September 1977).

Military assistance would not be a useful way to turn India away from a nuclear force. Conventional weakness does not drive Indian interest in a nuclear option; Peking's nuclear capability does. India has also striven, with much success, to minimize the external dependence of its military establishment. Nehru pushed domestic arms production as early as 1956, and the trend toward self-sufficiency was accelerated after the 1965 American embargo.[74] Since that time India has obtained most of its external support from the USSR. Under Desai it moved to curtail that dependence (witness initiatives to buy British Harriers for the navy and to manufacture submarines in collaboration with West Germany, France, the Netherlands, or Sweden), but when Indira Gandhi returned to power, New Delhi concluded a $1.6 billion arms deal with Moscow.[75]

If American arms supplies are to be a means of restraining proliferation in South Asia, they will have to go to Pakistan—the more vulnerable country—in much greater quantities than to India. But in any case military assistance is likely to inflame proliferation incentives as well as quench them because enhancing one side's security will frighten the other.[76] And it is difficult to conceive at this time—in the midst of the hostage crisis—how the United States can do anything positive to affect Iranian views of the nuclear question. Unless resolution of the hostage situation coincides with heavy Soviet pressure on Tehran, renewal of the U.S.-Iran military relationship appears fanciful.

A potential lever in nonproliferation policy would be nonmilitary assistance, as a form of offsetting compensation for the disadvantages of forgoing nuclear weapons. Pakistan's economic weakness compounds its fear of and sense of inferiority to India. To be effective, such assistance would have to be tacitly but clearly linked to the recipient's nuclear policy. If the connection were explicit, it might be best to keep it secret or unpublicized,

74. Barrie Morrison and Donald M. Page, "India's Option: The Nuclear Route to Achieve Goal as World Power," *International Perspectives* (July–August 1974), p. 27; Stockholm International Peace Research Institute, *The Arms Trade with the Third World* (New York: Humanities Press, 1971), pp. 741–58.

75. Mohan Ram, "India Looking to Britain, France for Warplanes," *Christian Science Monitor,* January 18, 1978; Dusko Doder, "Soviets and India Set $1.6 Billion Arms Agreement," *Washington Post,* May 29, 1980.

76. The nonproliferation rationale for the Ford administration's consideration of selling A-7s to Pakistan was somewhat vitiated by its simultaneous consideration of selling A-4s to India. The A-4s could fly from India's carrier; by supporting projection capabilities in this way, they would also constitute a sale of patently offensive weapons. George C. Wilson, "U.S. Moves to Sell Jets to India," *Washington Post,* December 9, 1976.

both to make it easier for the recipient to save face and not appear to be "selling out" sovereign national prerogatives and to avoid tempting other nations to try threats of proliferation to extract money and favors from the United States. This sort of U.S. strategy, which in a pejorative sense may be seen as bribery, could be a tricky and dangerous approach to discouraging proliferation, but it is worth exploring.

A form of aid most logically linked to the proliferation issue is nuclear technical assistance. In exchange for abandoning, curtailing, or accepting additional restraints or safeguards on national reprocessing or enrichment facilities, as the Non-Proliferation Act requires, the United States could significantly increase its supply of technical nuclear advice and equipment, uranium fuel, fuel fabrication technology, and so forth that could not be applied to weapons (perhaps even with subsidies if agreement to non-proliferation was deemed worth the price). This would appeal least to India with its advanced nuclear development and commitment to autonomy. The other form of linked nonmilitary assistance would be increased economic aid, which would not solve security problems (except by freeing a comparable amount of domestic product for defense expenditures) but could still have a positive effect on the recipient's estimate of the national costs and benefits of pursuing a nuclear force. Unless undertaken on a huge scale, comparable to the Marshall Plan, this would probably be effective only with states whose interest in nuclear weapons was marginal. In this sense, the option would probably be more relevant to India than to Pakistan. For instance, even increased direct U.S. aid to India could scarcely exceed that country's debt service payments on American loans from the 1960s. Canceling these debts or some portion of them might be one carrot to offer for cooperative Indian policies on nuclear issues. But India's adamant resistance to U.S. demands suggests little reason to hope it could be bought off. Nor would lavish economic aid tied to nonproliferation be applicable to Iran, since it would be politically unthinkable to subsidize a country that has acted so savagely against the United States and is itself so potentially rich.

The obverse of this strategy would be to terminate aid—military sales and assistance as well as economic aid—to uncooperative countries; this approach has already been tried. After the 1974 explosion Britain and Japan reduced aid to India, and the U.S. House Foreign Affairs Committee cut $25 million from the American aid authorization. Congress also attached a rider restricting aid to India to the International Development

Agency replenishment bill, but since the United States lacked a majority on the IDA board, it was unable to push this through.[77] In 1976 the Symington amendment to the foreign aid authorization bill barred American assistance to countries that import or export reprocessing or enrichment facilities without accepting full-scope safeguards, with allowance for a presidential waiver if an aid cutoff seemed likely to damage vital U.S. interests and the president stated that he had been assured that the recipient would not build nuclear weapons or help other countries to do so.[78]

Such rigorous restrictions embodied in law, rather than simply in executive policy, suggest that a strategy of orchestrating economic or military aid for nonproliferation on a case-by-case basis could lead to controversy, public hearings, and widely publicized debate, making the strategy counterproductive if it embarrassed the recipient by highlighting an agreement to capitulate to U.S. demands on reprocessing. An interesting question is whether such congressional attempts to legislate linkage in the nuclear proliferation area are likely to fare better than other attempts such as the Jackson-Vanik amendment, which tied U.S. trade policy to Soviet emigration policy.

Pakistan has severe financial problems, which implies that aid should have yielded leverage there if anywhere. Since amounts of U.S. aid are small, leverage is limited. The Symington amendment put more than $144 million in development and food assistance at risk,[79] yet there was no receptivity to U.S. nonproliferation demands. The aid canceled by the United States in 1979 amounted to less than $100 million. Pakistan does have other sources. It has received substantial military help from China, though not much economically; it has even received $650 million in Soviet aid.[80] Saudi Arabia offered $1.1 billion in 1976, of which about half was earmarked for military modernization.[81]

Nevertheless, it was probably counterproductive to terminate military sales and economic aid to Pakistan, the country that may be the linchpin

77. Archer K. Blood, "Nuclear Proliferation and the Indian Explosion," *Parameters,* vol. 5, no. 1 (1975), pp. 48–49.

78. *Nucleonics Week,* vol. 17 (June 24, 1976), p. 7.

79. Kenneth J. Freed, "U.S. Warns Bhutto About N-Fuel Plant," *Boston Globe,* August 9, 1976.

80. Central Intelligence Agency, *Communist Aid to the Less Developed Countries,* p. 31.

81. Wilson, "Pakistan Bomber Purchase Cleared by Defense Dept."

of the proliferation problem in the region since nuclear weapons deployment there could prompt similar decisions by leaders in Iran and India,
who might otherwise refrain. First, it touched off an emotional response
emphasizing that sovereignty would not be sold. In a speech Zia emphasized that Muslims were unafraid, would not be pressured economically into surrender, and would rather starve than tarnish national honor.[82]
Second, Islamabad may simply switch completely to non-American arms
suppliers. Rather than accept inferior F-5s when the United States refused
to sell A-7s, Pakistani officials explored the possibility of purchasing
Mirages from France.[83] Third, the termination could—especially if other
sources proved insufficient—reinforce a view that nuclear weapons were
needed to compensate for hopeless conventional inferiority to India. The
more generous offer of U.S. aid early in 1980 did little to overcome the
problems because the previous controversies had made Islamabad skeptical of American constancy.

The essential weaknesses in the strategies discussed are: (1) controlling
fuel supplies is probably infeasible and attempts to control them in order
to exert leverage make the problem worse by confirming the view that
autonomy is necessary; (2) military and economic assistance at levels that
are at all practical will not be sufficient to neutralize interest in a nuclear
weapons option, and aid substantial enough to do so is unrealistic. The
latter point emphasizes the fundamental problem that nonproliferationists
often ignore: the United States has many other interests—or reasons for
noninvolvement—that in practice will take precedence over proliferation
concerns.

Direct Involvement

Financial aid or provision of military equipment are indirect means of
influencing incentives. Direct involvement in the regional strategic interaction might yield greater influence. The only nations with the physical
capacity to determine the balance of power in South and West Asia are the
two superpowers, the United States and the Soviet Union. (China can
strongly affect the balance, but not to the same degree.) Before Soviet

82. FBIS, *Daily Report: Middle East and North Africa* (April 23, 1979), p. S5.
83. Don Oberdorfer, "Arms Sales to Pakistan Urged to Stave Off A-Bomb
There," *Washington Post,* August 6, 1979.

forces struck Afghanistan the advisability of becoming more involved in the region was questionable because of the ramifications for a number of interests besides nonproliferation. And since the invasion the reason for U.S. involvement has grown dramatically, but this reason—a new campaign for containment—has made proliferation a secondary concern.

The form of involvement most perceptibly relevant to regional nuclear incentives would be a nuclear umbrella to protect local states against nuclear attack by any of the others. Such protection could be selective (covering the most vulnerable and proliferation-prone of the countries) or general (threatening retaliation against whichever one initiated nuclear aggression). It could also be a unilateral American commitment or—and this now seems hopelessly idealistic—a joint Soviet-American declaration.[84]

India became concerned about nuclear guarantees after China's first nuclear test in October 1964. The immediate reaction in New Delhi was that a direct guarantee was unnecessary because any Chinese attack would inevitably lead the United States, Great Britain, and the USSR to act on India's behalf. After a debate and secret session of the All-India Congress Committee, parliament and the Congress party endorsed Prime Minister Lal Bahadur Shastri's decision against an Indian nuclear weapons program. Soon, however, the leadership began to explore ways of making the expectation of intervention more certain, while preserving the country's nonalignment, by encouraging the great powers to offer a multilateral guarantee. "It is for the nuclear powers," Shastri said, "to consider how to maintain peace in the world."[85]

The American response to Shastri's suggestion was restrained. U.S. officials considered President Johnson's pledge of October 18, 1964, to support any country threatened by the PRC's test sufficient, and believed a country seeking more specific assurance should approach Washington directly. India struggled through the spring of 1965 to secure a guarantee sponsored by the United Nations. While Shastri visited Moscow, China made its second test, but no Soviet guarantee was forthcoming. In Sep-

84. For a provocative though not convincing exploration of similar possibilities, see Alton Frye, "How to Ban the Bomb: Sell It," *New York Times Magazine,* January 11, 1976. For counterarguments, see Richard K. Betts, "Paranoids, Pygmies, Pariahs, and Nonproliferation," *Foreign Policy,* no. 26 (Spring 1977), pp. 175–76.

85. A. G. Noorani, "India's Quest for a Nuclear Guarantee," *Asian Survey,* vol. 7 (July 1967), p. 491.

tember war broke out with Pakistan, China threatened New Delhi, and sentiment rose in India for national nuclear weapons. In fall 1965 B. K. Nehru, the Indian ambassador to the United States, said that India, if it "does deny itself the position of an independent nuclear capability, must call upon the international community to defend itself against a nuclear attack." He noted that Western opposition to proliferation was not matched by offers for compensatory protection: "It is all very well to ask a person not to defend himself, but then somebody else has got to take on that defense."[86]

In 1967 progress was made toward a UN guarantee, but Foreign Minister M. C. Chagla rejected the proposal, saying that "before the Security Council even called a meeting we might be destroyed."[87] Prime Minister Gandhi sent her personal envoy L. K. Jha to Moscow and Washington in quest of a bond as automatic and ironclad as those of NATO and the Warsaw Pact. The United States appeared ready to offer a guarantee under UN auspices, to be reinforced by a congressional resolution, but not one that was unilateral and formally ratified. The Soviet position was ambiguous. As Quester wrote:

The joint U.S.–U.S.S.R.–U.K. statement suggesting immediate recourse to the processes of the U.N. Security Council. . . . served similarly to convince many Indians that great power guarantees were somewhat deceptive. Security Council action could indeed be vetoed. . . . Recourse to the Security Council in the event of aggression was called for in any event by the terms of the U.N. charter; now the superpowers were suggesting that it would come only on behalf of non-nuclear signers of the NPT—a shrinkage of guarantees, perhaps, rather than an extension.[88]

So India's search was largely fruitless. In the late 1960s Desai said, "I do not believe in nuclear weapons or nuclear umbrella of any sort. If, however, I were to make a choice, I would rather have my own nuclear weapons than to seek the nuclear umbrella of any outside Power. To ask for such umbrella would merely make us dependent on others."[89]

In the mid-1960s Bhutto, then foreign minister, said Pakistan opposed

86. Ibid., p. 495.
87. Ibid., p. 498.
88. George Quester, *The Politics of Nuclear Proliferation* (Johns Hopkins University Press, 1973), pp. 64–65. Since Quester wrote, the PRC—whose aggressive potential provoked India's quest for guarantee—has acquired veto power by its accession to China's seat on the Security Council.
89. Quoted in Basant Chatterjee, *The Mind of Morarji Desai* (Bombay: Orient Longmans, 1969), pp. 90–91.

a nuclear guarantee.[90] This was not surprising in view of Pakistan's alignment with China. By the mid-1970s, however, New Delhi's and Islamabad's positions had flip-flopped. This is not surprising either, since by then India had demonstrated its own capability to build nuclear weapons. After the Indian test Bhutto, as prime minister, asked the UN Security Council's permanent members to guarantee the protection of nonnuclear nations against nuclear attacks or threats, but his request "met with even less success than India's a decade ago."[91] This history suggests that if the United States and the Soviet Union were unwilling to give strong and credible nuclear guarantees in the 1960s, it is far from certain that either would be less unwilling to do so in the 1980s. But this sidesteps the question of what U.S. policy *should* be. If nonproliferation was its first priority, American foreign policy could favor such a commitment if it could be handled in a way that would not prompt a nuclear weapons program by one of the local states in response to the external support given to another and that would not cause severe problems with the Soviet Union or China. A unilateral nuclear guarantee would increase the risk of the United States' being sucked into dangerous situations, with the potential for escalation, that it might otherwise avoid. In short, this means of opposing local proliferation could be more dangerous to the United States than the proliferation itself. A joint guarantee with the Soviet Union would reduce the U.S. risks. However, not only is U.S.-Soviet cooperation in the region implausible now that the superpowers are vigorously competing militarily, but it is hard to see how the operational details could be spelled out enough to make it credible without raising problems of secrecy, joint planning, and inflexibility. Moreover, it would probably wreck Sino-American relations.

While a nuclear guarantee would be a means of providing an impressive commitment without deploying resources and forces in the region, its gravity and probable infeasibility make the alternative of injecting conventional military power and commitment to enforce regional security at least as thinkable. This alternative is more relevant to Pakistan anyway, since that country needs added security less against Indian nuclear coercion than against conventional attack. Indeed, a nuclear guarantee unaccompanied by a conventional guarantee would leave India free to smash Pakistan, because Pakistan would know that a nuclear defense would only

90. Noorani, "India's Quest," p. 501.
91. A. G. Noorani, "Search for New Relationships in the Indian Subcontinent," *The World Today,* vol. 31 (June 1975), pp. 246–47.

invite retaliation by India's guarantor. Conventional involvement is logically more appropriate for nonproliferation.

In theory, direct conventional military involvement could be protective (alliance), punitive (intervention), or cooperatively hegemonic (U.S.-Soviet condominium to enforce the status quo). Until the end of the 1970s none of these hypothetical alternatives were realistic for the United States because it perceived few interests in South Asia apart from nonproliferation, and nonproliferation was not considered important enough to require massive military commitments and political entanglement. Since the Russian thrust southward in December 1979 U.S. priorities have changed and major new American military commitments are unfolding, but the level of insecurity in the area has risen so that even these greater commitments may not be sufficient to weaken incentives for nuclear weapons. American offers of assistance to Pakistan have been designed to protect the country against Soviet incursions, not to increase its security against the old enemy, India. And in current circumstances greater U.S. involvement will not reduce the appeal of nuclear weapons to Iran; if Iranian leaders give the matter any thought, they may find that the U.S. presence makes the nuclear option even more attractive.

Pakistan is the country in the region that would have the most to gain from an American alliance guarantee, but it has been disappointed several times. The retrenchment of American commitments under the Nixon doctrine in the early 1970s did nothing to increase the credibility of more recent offers of support; Pakistani leaders suspect the initiatives spawned by the Afghanistan crisis may be temporary. One other problem is that none of the existing U.S. security treaties are ironclad, in the sense that they automatically and irrevocably commit the United States to combat on allies' behalf. Even before the War Powers Resolution, all had an escape clause based on the American requirement to make such decisions through constitutional processes.[92] Thus even if Pakistan valued an American guarantee, the severity of the threats that the country faces suggests that it would not rely on the guarantee to the exclusion of independent means of enhancing deterrence—means such as nuclear weap-

---

92. See Michael J. Glennon, memorandum for the Senate Committee on Foreign Relations, " 'Non-Automaticity' of U.S. Mutual Security Treaties," in *War Powers Resolution,* Hearings before the Senate Committee on Foreign Relations, 95 Cong. 1 sess. (GPO, 1977), pp. 352–53.

ons. Part of the credibility problem is that states in the region already had alliance ties that did not eliminate their anxieties.

Iran joined the Baghdad Pact, which became the Central Treaty Organization. CENTO, with Pakistan (the United States was not an official member), was designated a "forward defense area" by the United States in the mid-1950s and entered a bilateral defense agreement with the United States in 1959 after rejecting a Soviet proposal for a treaty of friendship and nonaggression. In 1962, though, the shah refused to allow the stationing of American nuclear missiles in Iran and soon began an initiative for détente with the USSR, which led to a 1967 arms deal for $110 million in "nonsensitive" equipment—armored personnel carriers, logistics vehicles, and antiaircraft weapons.[93] Interviews with the shah indicated that the "pivotal point" in his decision to expand Iran's external role was the failure of the CENTO powers (which were American clients) to aid Pakistan in the 1965 war.[94] (This happened again in 1971.) At one point the shah said Iran's bilateral pact with the United States "was not an automatic defense pledge,"[95] but on his November 1977 visit to Washington he stated strongly in an interview that the 1959 agreement signed by Eisenhower did commit the United States to defend Iran.[96] This uncertainty or uneasiness implied that the shah's nuclear incentives would have been dampened if the U.S. commitment to Iran had been made clearer and more forceful and fanned if the reverse had occurred. But as with arms transfers, the best apparent way for the United States to seek to limit Iranian nuclear incentives at that time was not to undertake some new departure in policy, but rather to continue and solidify its current commitments. Secretary of the Air Force John C. Stetson said in April 1978 that the United States had a "tacit obligation" to support Iranian forces against a Soviet attack. The mildness of this declaration ("tacit" is far from ironclad) was probably not reassuring to the shah, yet other American officials reacted to Stetson's remarks by stressing that they were only his personal views and that the United States was not automatically committed to de-

93. Furlong, "Iran: A Power to Be Reckoned With," p. 725.
94. Alvin J. Cottrell, "The Foreign Policy of the Shah," *Strategic Review,* vol. 3 (Fall 1975), p. 32.
95. Quoted in Furlong, "Iran," p. 725.
96. James Yuenger and James O. Jackson, "U.S. Obligated to the Defense of Iran: Shah," *Chicago Tribune,* November 13, 1977.

fense of Iran.[97] All of this ambiguity and its disadvantages seem irrelevant since the United States and Iran became bitter antagonists, but it illustrates the tenuousness of external guarantees as a security solution even under the best of diplomatic circumstances. The likely impetus for an Iranian nuclear weapons program (aside from Pakistan's acquiring one) would be renewed anxiety about Soviet aggressiveness.

Pakistan tried to secure outside supporters in the early 1950s—first the British Commonwealth, then the Muslim world, finally the United States. Washington wanted an alliance between Pakistan and Turkey. A 1954 agreement to that effect was followed by a Pakistani-U.S. Mutual Defense Assistance Agreement.[98] In 1959 the two countries signed a Bilateral Agreement of Cooperation, which hinted at a security guarantee: the "Government of the United States of America regards as vital to its national interest and to world peace, the preservation of the independence and integrity of Pakistan." Article 1 provided that in case of aggression the United States, following its constitutional procedures, "will take such appropriate action, including the use of its armed forces, as may be mutually agreed upon . . . in order to assist the Government of Pakistan at its request."[99]

The problem with these 1950s commitments was that, for the United States, they were aimed against the PRC and the USSR though Pakistan's principal concern was India. At the Manila Conference on the SEATO treaty (which Pakistan joined), the Pakistani delegate insisted that the term "aggression" should be broadly interpreted to cover all types, not only communist, but the United States "appended an 'Understanding' to the treaty that it viewed the aggression referred to in it as Communist aggression."[100] By 1977 Bhutto had already begun to turn toward the USSR, in large part because of American pressure to give up the reprocessing plant. After Bhutto's ouster Pakistani diplomats complained that membership in CENTO "does them no good if the United States will not give them large amounts of arms under it, and only makes them appear suspect

97. George C. Wilson, "U.S. Has 'Tacit Obligation' to Aid Iran, AF Head Says," *Washington Post,* April 21, 1978.

98. Khurshid Hasan, "U.S.-Pakistan Relations," in Latif Ahmed Sherwani and others, *Foreign Policy of Pakistan: An Analysis* (Karachi: Allies Book Corp., 1964), pp. 51–52.

99. Quoted in ibid., pp. 53–54.

100. Ibid., p. 53.

among other third-world nations that are genuinely nonaligned."[101] In March 1979 the country withdrew from CENTO. In the late 1970s the Soviet Union reportedly tried to capitalize on Pakistani disappointment in U.S. support, saying that "the Soviets were giving aid to India because India was a friend of the USSR while the U.S. had let down her closest ally in Asia (Pakistan). We support our friends, even when they are wrong; your friends let you down, even when you are right."[102] Subsequent events in Afghanistan increased the Soviet threat to Pakistan but did not invalidate the argument about the danger of relying on the United States. Thus Pakistan has been left in a sense with the worst of both worlds. The U.S. government was not even willing to replace the 1959 executive agreements on defense with a formal treaty. Faced with such equivocation, Pakistani leaders felt that they had more to lose than to gain from accepting the American embrace since it would threaten the country's newly formed links with the nonaligned nations and the Islamic world.[103]

Spoiling Sino-Pakistani relations was of course also in India's interest. In October 1959 Indian sources gave Pakistan a copy of a Chinese map showing a northern area of the country as PRC territory. Pakistan and China, however, reached a formal agreement on their borders, much to Pakistan's benefit, half a year before the 1962 Sino-Indian border war. Relations between Pakistan and China warmed thereafter, were complicated temporarily by Ayub Khan's moving closer to Moscow to get Soviet arms in the middle and late 1960s, but improved again with President Nixon's initiative toward the PRC.[104] But China proved hardly more helpful or willing to intervene on Pakistan's behalf in 1965 or 1971 than the United

101. William Borders, "Pakistan Worried by Possibility of 'Soviet' Afghanistan on Border," *New York Times,* May 20, 1978.

102. Zalmay Khalilzad and others, *Regional Rivalries and Nuclear Responses,* vol. 1: *Competition and Conflict in the Arabian Sea and the Prospects for Nuclear Proliferation,* DNA 001-77-C-0052, prepared for the Director, U.S. Defense Nuclear Agency (Los Angeles: Pan Heuristics, 1978), p. 62.

103. John M. Goshko, "U.S. Forging Ahead on Aid to Pakistan," *Washington Post,* January 19, 1980; Dusko Doder, "Pakistan Uninterested in U.S. Aid Offer," *Washington Post,* March 6, 1980.

104. Qutubuddin Aziz, "Relations between Pakistan and the People's Republic of China," in Sherwani and others, *Foreign Policy of Pakistan,* pp. 85, 88–89, 90–93; G. W. Choudhury, "Dismemberment of Pakistan, 1971: Its International Implications," *Orbis,* vol. 18 (Spring 1974), p. 186.

States. Alliances as flexible as these are insufficient to wash away nuclear
security incentives in Islamabad.

More credibly reliable guarantees—and hence ones more likely to
weaken motives for nuclear weapons—that would not be counterproductive are hard to conceive even if the wider diplomatic considerations that
might make them inadvisable are disregarded. If the United States deployed forces to Pakistan, leaders in New Delhi would be infuriated, perhaps to the point of launching their own nuclear weapons program. The
only alternative would be reaffirmation and intensification of the Indo-
Soviet alliance. The 1971 friendship treaty between the two countries was
designed to offset the developing entente between Washington, Peking,
and Islamabad.[105] For most American interests other than nonproliferation, strengthened ties between Moscow and New Delhi are undesirable.
Even if India drifts back toward genuine nonalignment, however, nuclear
weapons can become more attractive; complete deterrent independence
may seem the necessary corollary of complete political independence. One
Indian military man, for example, believed the Indo-Soviet Treaty of
Peace, Friendship, and Cooperation "stipulates nuclear cover."[106] Another Indian commentator argued, "In the absence of an independent nuclear capability, nonalignment would be a farce."[107]

If either alternative—major Soviet presence in India (threatening U.S.
strategic interests) or complete Indian nonalignment (threatening nonproliferation)—is unpalatable to the United States, there are three other
conceivable alternatives. One would be for the United States to ally decisively with India, threatening action against Pakistan if the latter moved
toward a nuclear force—an extreme extension of Carter's tilt toward India that seems to recognize and accept the local imbalance of power. U.S.
Ambassador Robert F. Goheen said in late 1977, "India and Pakistan
really aren't competitors any more. India is clear and away the pre-

105. "Article Nine stipulated that an attack on either party would result in
mutual consultation with a view to eliminating the threat. Each party also agreed
not to aid any nation that was at war with the other signatory. . . . The chief point of
the alliance was to counter the Sino-American-Pakistani grouping and make it possible for India to move against Pakistan with confidence." Thornton, "South Asia,"
p. 867.
106. Wing Commander Maharaj K. Chopra, IAF (Ret.), "India's Strategic Environment," *Military Review*, vol. 53 (June 1973), p. 33.
107. Baldev Raj Nayar, "India Wants Nuclear Sovereignty," *Christian Science
Monitor*, March 17, 1978.

eminent nation on the subcontinent, so that game we played for many years of trying to balance one off against the other—that's a dead game."[108] This alternative is abstractly logical but practically naive. First, the Soviet position in Afghanistan makes U.S. indifference to Pakistan's security implausible. Second, India does not want a military alliance with the United States.[109]

A second possibility would be for the United States to assume the role of balancer, regulator, or guarantor of the security of both antagonists, a role somewhat comparable to the one that emerged in the Middle East in 1977–79 as the Egyptian-Israeli peace process unfolded. At best it would be hard to bring off. It would become mired in uncertainty and disagreement about the respective defensive requirements of the two contending clients and in suspicion and recrimination about how evenhanded U.S. policy really was. One hypothetical solution would be a magisterial commitment of some sort to intervene against whichever of the two countries initiated military action against the other. But this option is no more realistic than the first.

A third hypothetical possibility would be a joint Soviet-American commitment to provide the same balancing regulation, but events since the late 1970s make this ridiculous.

Even before the invasion of Afghanistan a condominium strategy was anathema to American leaders, to the countries that would be subject to it, and to other states—especially China—whose policies figure vitally in U.S. global strategic interests. The attitudes of the targets may be most relevant. Some observers see a contradiction in official Indian rhetoric, which emphasizes the need for nuclear disarmament but also reflects fear of superpower condominium and suspicion of détente.[110] But there is no contradiction because fulfillment of the Indian vision would enhance national independence and power by reducing the military weight and dom-

108. Quoted in William Borders, "India Eagerly Awaits Carter Visit as Sign of Affinity between Large Democracies," *New York Times,* December 23, 1977.

109. Wayne Wilcox argued that Henry Kissinger's clear indications that the U.S. defense perimeter did not include India helped prompt the Indian move to enter into the friendship treaty with the Soviet Union in 1971. *The Emergence of Bangladesh: Problems and Opportunities for a Redefined American Policy in South Asia* (Washington, D.C.: American Enterprise Institute for Public Policy Research, 1973), p. 36. Given Indira Gandhi's general attitude toward the United States, however, this is not convincing.

110. See Ashok Kapur, *India's Nuclear Option: Atomic Diplomacy and Decision Making* (Praeger, 1976), pp. 126ff.

inance of both superpowers. And assuming that nuclear disarmament is unrealistic, avoidance of either dictation or indifference by the superpowers would seem consistent with a nuclear strategy. Subrahmanyam cites President Nixon's explanation for his initiative to Peking: 800 million people with nuclear weapons cannot be ignored.[111] Marwah writes, "A desirable environment for Indian strategic interaction with the great powers is one which simultaneously precludes being ignored or coerced by them. Nuclear weapons deny both of these extremes."[112]

The only absolute way for the United States to try to control nuclear proliferation would be direct intervention. Overt use of force simply to punish or reverse a move by one of the states to build nuclear weapons would be an extreme and unlikely option, and it would actually raise the odds of a nuclear weapon being used in combat for the first time since Nagasaki—and this time against American forces. To use conventional force decisively against a powerful large country such as India would be militarily infeasible. Intervention would be more realistic (though only relatively so) as covert action—for instance, financially supporting antinuclear political factions in one or more of the countries to help block a government decision to build nuclear weapons. (The "happiest" example of such tactics was U.S. aid to Christian Democratic and other anticommunist parties in Europe in the late 1940s; the "saddest," perhaps, were similar ventures in Chile in the 1960s and early 1970s.) The obvious danger in such activity—aside from moral or competing political disincentives—is that, if exposed, it could precipitate rather than restrain a pronuclear decision (and since the early 1970s it has become progressively harder to keep covert operations covert). Another type of covert action would be to sabotage facilities dedicated to a nuclear weapons program. This might be practical against a country such as Pakistan, which will have only a few sensitive facilities and a thin nuclear infrastructure, but would probably have only limited utility or nuisance value against a country with an advanced and developed nuclear establishment, such as India. Exposure here, however, became a problem even before the fact. There were reports in August 1979 that an interagency task force under Gerard

111. K. Subrahmanyam, "India's Nuclear Policy," in Onkar Marwah and Ann Schulz, eds., *Nuclear Proliferation and the Near-Nuclear Countries* (Ballinger, 1975), pp. 128–29.

112. Onkar Marwah, "India's Nuclear and Space Programs: Intent and Policy," *International Security,* vol. 2 (Fall 1977), p. 118.

Smith of the State Department was considering the sabotage option as one among many.[113] Pakistan reacted sharply, putting nuclear facilities on alert and encircling some of them with antiaircraft guns and Crotale missiles.[114] Despite U.S. denials,[115] any sabotage now would probably be assumed to have been directed by Washington or Israel. In any case, this type of measure is for coping with proliferation, not preventing it.[116] And it could be undertaken only so long as the United States had no vital interest in avoiding alienation of the states involved. Since the Indian Ocean–Persian Gulf area has become a third front in a new American containment policy this condition does not hold.

American antiproliferation efforts in South Asia have focused principally on controlling nuclear capabilities. In this sense it might be said that the United States has an ambitious policy to deal with the proliferation of nuclear *technology* but, if this fails, no coherent policy against the proliferation of nuclear *weapons*. Perhaps it cannot be otherwise so long as the United States lacks the capacity to resolve local antagonisms and lacks the will and interest to try to stabilize and control the local balance of power. With Iran, for instance, the best policy may be to avoid mentioning the problem as long as the leadership is unstable, resentful and suspicious, preoccupied with other, nonnuclear concerns, and eager to injure and embarrass the United States in any way possible. But more energetic diplomatic initiatives to reduce Sino-Indian and Indo-Pakistani tension would be as beneficial as demands to forgo modern technology—demands that the targets regard as impertinent paternalism at best and cynical profit protection at worst. Raising the diplomatic profile in local conflict resolution and lowering it toward local technology development might not prevent proliferation but at least would not impel it so fast.

113. "U.S. Said Eying Effort to Slow Pakistan N-Bomb," *Japan Times,* August 14, 1979.

114. "Pakistan to Thwart 'U.S. Sabotage' Against N-Plants," *Daily Yomiuri,* August 15, 1979; "Pakistan N-Bases on Alert," *Korea Times,* August 18, 1979.

115. Don Oberdorfer, "U.S. Denies Covert Plans in Pakistan," *Washington Post,* August 15, 1979.

116. See Richard K. Betts, "Nuclear Proliferation and Regional Rivalry: Speculations on South Asia," *Orbis,* vol. 23 (Spring 1979), pp. 167–84.

CHAPTER FIFTEEN

The Middle East

THERE are, of course, important limitations on the U.S. capacity to influence the nuclear choices made by the countries of the Middle East. The most important is that the Arab-Israeli and Arab-Arab disputes and competition have a life of their own, influenced only marginally by outsiders. But action at the margin can make a difference. One constraint on the United States is the relative growth in Soviet military capacity to project power into the region. Another is the increase in the number of countries able to supply nuclear technology.

Nonetheless, the United States is in a position to exert a fair amount of influence in the region in two ways: through helping to provide it with a greater sense of security, and helping to construct an agreement for the use of nuclear energy that would heighten the barriers of cost and time between legitimate civilian nuclear activities and nuclear explosives capability.

It should seem evident to any thoughtful observer that, if a situation in which many nations in the region have nuclear weapons or are on the verge of having them is to be avoided, it will be through these nations' perceived self-interest. The lead time to having nuclear weapons will shrink for many of them. Technical-military capacities will grow, but self-interest may mean that most of these countries will be able to move to acquire nuclear explosives but will not do so. For outsiders such as the United States, the question is what can be done to help avert a situation in which many countries might have nuclear weapons and even use them, or might at least be in a position to acquire them rapidly.

U.S. security support of several countries in the Middle East—Israel,

Saudi Arabia, Egypt, and Jordan—has two effects: it increases their non-nuclear military capacities and it offers the prospect of U.S. help in a conflict. These may reduce incentives to acquire nuclear weapons.[1] The role of the United States as an intermediary in reducing tension serves a similar function. Also, the position of the United States on nuclear exports has changed: it is no longer trying to transfer this technology to the region. Its efforts, together with those of other supplier nations, seem to be slowing transfers, particularly of the sensitive facilities that are especially useful for weapons programs and not essential or even economic for civilian ones.

Thus possible future U.S. policies to discourage proliferation in the area fall into two categories. The first involves direct efforts to change the rules under which nuclear technology is exploited so as to make it more difficult for states to obtain nuclear weapons. The second, which is arguably more important, involves U.S. security policies designed to reduce regional nations' incentives to seek nuclear weapons in the first place.

Helping to Change the Rules on Access to Nuclear Explosives

The present situation, in which Israel is believed to have nuclear weapons and the Arab countries quite evidently do not, is unlikely to persist for long unless the politics of the region change. It is therefore a matter of some urgency to explore the prospects. One objective could be to persuade the countries that it is strongly in their interest to agree not to have nuclear explosives or nuclear materials that are quickly convertible to use in explosives.

There are two large obstacles to the realization of such a goal even if a clear perception of a strong common interest in avoiding potential disaster emerges. One is the belief that Israel now has nuclear weapons. Those familiar with the problem of achieving total nuclear disarmament between the great powers will recognize the problem here: with the possibilities

1. Some caution is necessary when increasing a nation's nonnuclear defense capacity also greatly lessens the cost to it of developing a nuclear defense system (where weapons are dual capable). In this regard, the U.S. decision to withhold Pershing ballistic missiles from Israel is of note since they would do Israel little good in a conventional role but are a capable system for nuclear warhead delivery.

for concealment, how could there be confidence in an agreement to eliminate existing nuclear weapons? The Arabs can reasonably maintain that they have no nuclear weapons because they obviously have no facilities for producing them. The Israelis, however, have the facilities and are reported to have bombs, and there is no way of ensuring that they would not retain them even if a nuclear-weapon-free zone were to be created.

One way to address the problem is to propose that each country give an accounting of the nuclear explosive materials to which it has had access. For Israel, this would mean an accounting of at least the plutonium produced by Dimona. Appropriate disposition of it outside the region could then be made. Similarly, to cover future nuclear activities, the Osiris type of reactor with which Iraq is being supplied by France might be converted to 20 percent enriched uranium, and power reactors slated to be built in the region could have their spent fuel removed to safe repositories outside the Middle East. There is also the broader problem of verifying that there are no covert sensitive facilities in states believed to have no weapons. These problems are difficult, but the fact that there are few such facilities in the region now is an advantage.

The other large obstacle is the importance Israel might attach to having nuclear weapons for a last-ditch defense of its core territories. Why, it might be asked, should a weapon reserved for the ultimate protection of the country be given up for the possibility, perhaps considered tenuous, that adversaries could be persuaded to forgo such weapons? There is no easy answer to this question. But there is a great difference between the short-term situation, in which Israel seems to have a regional nuclear monopoly, and the long-term one, in which it will not. Furthermore, the conditions for averting direct nuclear threats or even use are likely to become increasingly difficult to meet. Realistically, conditions for getting Israel to accede to such an agreement would probably include a general settlement between Israel and the confrontation Arabs as well as the participation of the nonconfrontation Arabs in the nuclear-weapon-free zone.[2]

How stable might a nuclear-free-zone agreement be, especially if nuclear technology became widely accessible? One cannot be sure. Evasion

---

2. Ideally, their participation would be as parties to the nuclear-weapon-free-zone agreement. If that proved impossible, agreement between Israel and its principal opponents might still be possible if there was a provision that actions taken by non-signing Arabs would be grounds for abrogating the treaty as if they were a party to it.

might be attempted but at a risk of detection while weapons were being prepared. Various responses are imaginable, not excluding actions by a great power. Preventive policies by the supplier states would obviously be valuable. At any rate, some time would be allowed for reaction; with present trends, this may not be possible.

In our view, wider access to nuclear explosives carries the prospect of disaster on an enormous scale. That prospect may become more likely in the next several years, perhaps through a regional nuclear conflict elsewhere. If so, despite the formidable obstacles, an agreement limiting access to nuclear explosives may become possible.

Under the present international rules, nations can possess nuclear explosive materials without violating either the NPT-IAEA safeguards or the full-scope safeguards that have recently been adopted by Canada and the United States for their nuclear exports. A basic question about the governments of the Middle East is whether they will perceive a mutual interest in refraining not only from having nuclear weapons but also from coming close to having them.

All, or almost all, of these governments are likely to agree on the importance of keeping nuclear explosives out of the hands of subnational revolutionary groups and terrorists.[3] ("Almost all" because the interest of Muammar Qaddafi of Libya in avoiding this development is far from certain.) But internal instabilities in these countries make it unclear that the governments could succeed. And the United States could not do a great deal to help.

The most obvious step would be special efforts to keep nuclear weapons out of irresponsible hands—politically irresponsible states, states with a major potential for internal instability, and states too small or poor to protect their nuclear systems adequately. Although most of the states in the area fall into one or more of these categories, differences of degree should be recognized. For example, safeguarded sales of low enriched uranium power reactors are probably inevitable in the region eventually, but Libya's planned buy should be viewed with special wariness.[4] This also

3. It is important not to confuse the Palestinian guerrilla forces, which are quite large, have well-developed organizations, and often have effective sovereignty in certain areas, with the much more limited underground urban terrorists more familiar to the industrialized states (for instance, the Symbionese Liberation Army or even the Red Brigade).

4. For reference to this concern at suppliers' group meetings, see *Nuclear News*, vol. 19 (May 1976), p. 83.

emphasizes the point that, merely because some states in the region get nuclear weapons, antiproliferation efforts should not be relaxed. In fact, one of the greatest dangers in the acquisition of nuclear weapons by the "responsible states" is that this will encourage and ease their acquisition by others.

As discussed earlier, devices may be built into nuclear bombs that make them usable only with a proper "key" or that cause them to self-destruct if they are tampered with. The self-destructive type especially could prevent the use of captured weapons by subnational groups that might eventually be able to work their way around a simple locking device. (A locking device is more suitable for the task of preventing spur-of-the-moment unauthorized use by subordinate units.)[5]

If nuclear weapons or materials that can be relatively easily transformed into them (such as highly enriched uranium fuel) are stolen, recapture clearly would be desirable. Although local states are unlikely to transport nuclear weapons by civilian aircraft, aircraft hijackings by Palestinians suggest one way of capturing nuclear weapons. The most notable examples of regional aircraft hijackings were the 1970 hijackings to Palestinian guerrilla-controlled sections of Jordan and the 1976 hijacking to Entebbe. The latter is important in illustrating the possibility that regional terrorist groups might count on aid from a nation outside the region (such as Uganda), as well as in illustrating a successful recapture. Also of interest is that the plane was hijacked from Air France but the rescue was by Israel. Another precedent was the multinational effort involved in the hijacking to Mogadishu, where the rescue was carried out by the West Germans but with British technical aid and with the local cooperation of Somalia. Clearly this is an area where there are broad international common interests, and the United States should be prepared to cooperate. For example, the United States has substantial intelligence and long-distance logistical capabilities (recent multinational operations in Zaire provide an example of such U.S. support). At a higher level of involvement, one can imagine training a group from the Sixth Fleet Marine contingent as a multipurpose, quick-reaction force for the region.

---

5. As noted, depriving local troops of the ability to employ their weapons independently may make the nation vulnerable to first strikes on command and control facilities. Similarly, there is a trade-off between guarding weapons from terrorists in a few well-secured facilities and dispersing them to safeguard them from a preemptive enemy attack.

The last few years have seen major changes in the nuclear export policies of several countries that are large suppliers of nuclear technology and materials. Canada now requires full-scope safeguards as a condition for nuclear exports—that is, countries must agree not to make nuclear explosives and all of their nuclear facilities must be placed under IAEA or equivalent safeguards. A similar requirement was imposed on U.S. exports after mid-1979 (with, however, a presidential exception possible). France and Germany have announced that they will export no more reprocessing plants. The United States has decided not to undertake reprocessing domestically and has urged other countries to follow suit.

Useful as these changes are, countries are still in a position to legitimately acquire nuclear explosive materials ready to convert into weapons without violating even full-scope safeguards. (Full-scope safeguards do not prevent a country from acquiring nuclear explosive materials such as plutonium or highly enriched uranium independently of the country requiring such safeguards, so long as they are subject to inspection.) Recognizing the dangers of widespread distribution of plutonium, the Ford administration decided to defer indefinitely the decision to reprocess spent fuel from light water reactors; this decision was endorsed in the early months of the Carter administration and extended to raise questions about the appropriateness of commercializing the plutonium breeder. Under the proposed U.S. concept, commitment to the recycling of plutonium and the breeder would be deferred while technical alternatives were explored and institutions for helping with these difficult problems were developed. These matters were discussed in the International Nuclear Fuel Cycle Evaluation (INFCE) program.

Among the specifics concerning the Middle East that need to be examined is, first, trying to make it clear that nuclear power in this hydrocarbon-rich corner of the world is poor economics. But it is hard to be confident that better economic analysis will reverse decisions to buy reactors.

Second is to continue to seek limitations on transfers to states that are especially prone to internal instability or that are otherwise poor risks. The sale by France of a large research reactor to Iraq and the sale by the Soviet Union of an electric power plus desalting reactor to Libya are examples of transfers that could fall into this category.

Third, and most important, is to seek agreement that spent fuel will not be reprocessed but will be removed to internationally safeguarded storage centers. The current U.S. policy aims at such international agreements. The agreement for cooperation between the United States and Egypt described earlier is a precedent for a general agreement along these lines, which should include prohibitions not only on national reprocessing but also on shipping spent fuel abroad for reprocessing anywhere and on returning plutonium in any form.

Fourth, although the scale of nuclear power development in the region will be far too small for a long time to support the national or even multinational production of enrichment services, a comprehensive agreement to limit nuclear dangers would deal with this potential path to a bomb.

Helping to Promote Security in the Region

For many of these states, the nuclear option will be seen as a dangerous route to security, as insurance against a time when nothing else seems feasible. Amelioration of their security anxieties through a reduction in tension or a credible U.S. capacity to provide support may thus create a situation in which regional allies and others would be more likely to forgo this course. This is particularly likely if the cost associated with seeking or closely approaching a nuclear weapons capability is increased—for example, through the measures just discussed.

Of the three central competitions, American involvement is highest in the Arab-Israeli conflict. A resolution of Arab-Israeli differences could be a large step toward reducing future nuclear threats. Again, although there are limits to what the United States can do to attain this goal, it can contribute to the military stability of the relationship between the Israelis and the Arabs, which is closely connected with their incentives to seek nuclear weapons.

The substance of the treaty between Israel and Egypt is trading political control over territory for recognition of Israel's legitimacy. An important corollary is that the military threat not increase and perhaps that it be reduced. One way would be to improve strategic warning. Since the Arabs depend on large standing armies, any exercise can quickly turn into a major attack. Moreover, such exercises can be held too frequently for Israel to mobilize against each one. Thus Israel must risk being caught unprepared, as it was in October 1973, which would encourage Arab attack, or itself attack preemptively at the first Arab exercise.[6] If there were significant demobilization of forces (which in practice means more extensive demobilization of the large standing Arab armies), mobilization would furnish earlier signals than at present. Just as giving up occupied territory is a major Israeli concession, substantial demobilization would be a major Arab one. Other measures could include monitoring to detect early signs of mobilization. Sensing technologies might be part of an agreed-upon monitoring system; also, open borders, with extensive internal movement of foreigners, the press, and others permitted, would facilitate reporting. The United States participates in the monitoring station set up as part of the Sinai II agreement; it might also contribute to the monitoring of a more far-reaching agreement. In this light particular attention should be given to maintaining forces trusted by both sides in the Sinai to monitor the treaty.

Tactical warning and more considered response could be helped if forces were separated by wide demilitarized or limited-force zones in the Sinai, measures agreed to by Israel and Egypt. The existence of deeper zones would increase the time between their violation and meeting an opponent's force. Increased time gives the defending party a better chance to mount a defense and reduces the advantage of striking first; it also provides time for choosing appropriate responses to ambiguous signals of attack. Here, too, participation by the United States in monitoring arrangements, and perhaps also a U.S. guarantee of some aspects of the agreements, can be important.

Joint superpower guarantees are sometimes proposed.[7] However, Soviet and American aims are likely to diverge and lead the guarantee system to a crisis or collapse; and Israel, Egypt, Saudi Arabia, and Jordan are unlikely to want Soviet participation. Nonetheless, stability in the area must be underwritten by outside powers—at least against the potential intervention of other outsiders that might disturb the peace. For the West —which means for the United States as the main potential Western

6. For a parallel discussion, see Michael I. Handel, "The Yom Kippur War and the Inevitability of Surprise," *International Studies Quarterly,* vol. 21 (September 1977), pp. 461–502.

7. Zbigniew Brzezinski, François Duchêne, and Kiichi Saeki, "Peace in an International Framework," *Foreign Policy,* no. 19 (Summer 1975), pp. 3–17. For a discussion of superpower guarantees and related arms control measures, see Yair Evron, *The Role of Arms Control in the Middle East,* Adelphi Paper 138 (London: International Institute for Strategic Studies, 1977).

actor—there are two principal concerns: having a capacity to make guarantees credible by being able to apply military force effectively in the region, and limiting Western vulnerability to interruption of oil supplies from the region.

If the United States were inferior to the Soviet Union in its ability to project its military forces, it could still help its regional allies with arms and logistics support and in other ways. As in the case of West Berlin, a locally indefensible place, the threat of a wider conflict might suffice as a deterrent. But there is likely to be little confidence that the United States would actually carry out such a threat. Moreover, the trends are not encouraging. The U.S. capacity to project power into the region is restricted by European allies' denial of bases en route as the Soviet projection capacity increases.

The Carter administration has publicly admitted the importance to the United States and Europe of the Middle East and the Persian Gulf because of the development of this Soviet capacity. Secretary of Defense Harold Brown emphasized how vital it is that the United States maintain its non-NATO interests because of hostile Soviet and local opposition and the possibility of combat simultaneously or subsequently starting in Europe. He also explicitly noted that "commitments (however binding) . . . are not enough for deterrence and defense. We and our Allies must also maintain forces that are modern, ready, and deployed in critical areas."[8] It is important to keep Brown's emphasis on capabilities as well as expressed intentions in mind when considering the call of the "Carter doctrine" for U.S. defense of the Persian Gulf against Soviet attack.

In the interest of developing a stable relationship between Egypt and Israel, it has been suggested that a U.S. presence in a demilitarized zone in the Sinai could be an important part of an agreement. More ambitious proposals than the modest precedent of the U.S. listening post in the current DMZ have been made, including a U.S. naval facility or U.S. use of the air bases now likely to be turned over to Egypt.[9] There would be ob-

8. Remarks by Secretary of Defense Harold Brown at the Thirty-fourth Annual Dinner of the National Security Industrial Association, Washington, D.C., September 15, 1977.

9. S. Fred Singer, "U.S. Base in Sinai Might Be Way to Break Impasse," *Wall Street Journal,* February 2, 1978. Such a presence might provide information on troop movements and an American presence athwart the main route between Israel and Egypt, as well as facilities useful in supporting the reduced U.S. military position in the eastern Mediterranean. It could also increase U.S. capacity to project power into the critical Persian Gulf area.

jections. Anything that smacks of the concession of Egyptian territory to outside powers may be strongly resisted by Egypt. This sensitivity, however, might be lessened by the establishment of a symmetrical basing relationship with Israel, and perhaps some degree of Jordanian or Saudi Arabian involvement as well. U.S. resistance to any expansion of its security obligations would also be a problem, but opposing that is the importance of an Arab-Israeli settlement and U.S. interests in the Persian Gulf. Involvement of Western Europe, which shares many of the United States' interests in the region, might be a useful addition if feasible. Perhaps the Sinai facilities could be used for joint NATO training.

If the West is to exert a useful influence in the region, the other principal need is to avoid the possibility of its being crippled by the cutoff of Arab oil. The capacity of the United States to act in the Middle East free of pressure from Europe and Japan not to do so is dependent on the assurance that they will not be so crippled. The most reliable means of reducing oil vulnerability would be large strategic oil reserves in the United States, Europe, and Japan. These reserves have increased since 1973 in many countries, but in none are they yet large enough to provide much protection. Although several other countries have built stocks for emergencies, the United States has lagged badly in building its strategic petroleum reserve. This and other failures of U.S. energy policy contribute to weakening U.S. influence in the region.

Consideration of a Broader Strategy

The discussion so far has centered on ways of increasing stability between Israel and the Arabs. Important as that rivalry is, the participants have other concerns and hence other reasons to seek nuclear weapons. For the Arabs, differences among them, problems of internal stability, and the growing capacity of the Soviet Union to project power into the region are also absorbing attention. The conservative Arabs have a common interest in not being overthrown by radicals, in limiting the influence of the PLO (including averting a Palestinian state on the West Bank that would stand a good chance of being dominated by radicals supported by the Soviet Union), and in maintaining strength against radical regimes in Iraq, South Yemen, and Libya. In the long run, Iran also may feel the need to align itself once again with the West as a consequence of hostile Soviet-oriented pressure from Afghanistan and Iraq, as well as from the

Soviet Union itself. Iran's seeking American arms to deal with the Kurdish rebellion may have foreshadowed this. However, the unstable internal situation of Iran makes it difficult to predict such matters.

The coups in Afghanistan, Iran, and South Yemen highlight the vulnerability of the Persian Gulf emirates. They are especially vulnerable to the disruptive effects of rapid modernization, including that associated with the introduction of modern weapons. The sudden imposition of an educated elite with high expectations—particularly if it is a military one—on near-feudal societies presents the obvious danger that political evolution will be overtaken by radical revolutions that may be able to retain power, probably aided by the Soviet Union. While this sort of situation is hardly unique to the Middle East, the cost to the West of such developments there would be especially high. The instability is heightened by the Soviet projection of power abroad, as evidenced, for instance, by its practice of overflying the northern tier countries and by its substantial presence in the Horn of Africa.

This set of dangers is of concern not only to the conservative Arab states, but also to the United States and its Western allies, as well as to Israel. Even Iran may come to share this position. But so far, there is little evidence of a perceived common interest in facing these dangers. Divisive elements are visible not only between the Arabs and Israel and between radical and conservative Arabs, but among the conservative Arabs and between Saudi Arabia and Iran as well. At this stage it is by no means clear that the potential community of interest of the conservative Arab states, Iran, Israel, Turkey, and the United States is strong enough to overcome the factors that unite the Arabs against Israel (and therefore to a degree against the United States) or the other regional interests that may be seen as more powerful. However, it is possible that an alignment of interests will become dominant. Such an alignment, which if it comes about will not be independent of U.S. capability and credibility in the area, could lead governments to adopt the steps outlined above and perhaps a political settlement as well.

In any case, the United States and its Western allies face the choice between greater involvement in the area and trying to become decoupled from it. The latter bodes ill for the region and for the West. The former course has its risks as well, but they would probably turn out to be lower.

CHAPTER SIXTEEN

Brazil and Argentina: Strategies for American Diplomacy

AMERICAN nuclear diplomacy in South America has a long tradition and a mixed record.

In the early 1950s the United States signed Atoms for Peace agreements with Argentina and Brazil, and it later furnished Brazil with a research reactor and Argentina with research assistance. In the 1960s the United States supported the Treaty of Tlatelolco, although it delayed ratification of Additional Protocol II of the treaty and still has not ratified Additional Protocol I. It gave greater priority to the Treaty on the Non-Proliferation of Nuclear Weapons, but Argentina and Brazil resisted U.S. efforts to persuade them to adhere to it.

In the late 1960s and early 1970s Argentina and Brazil turned to the United States for equipment to get their nuclear power programs off the ground. Brazil bought its first power reactor from Westinghouse; Argentina bought U.S. heavy water for its initial power reactor.

In the spring of 1975, before the signing of the West German–Brazilian agreement on June 27, the United States attempted to persuade West Germany to prevent the transfer of "sensitive" technologies (uranium enrichment and spent fuel reprocessing) to Brazil and to secure Brazilian acceptance of full-scope safeguards obligations. The United States had no objection to Brazil's being supplied with power reactors and the technology to build them. Some Brazilians did not at first understand this distinction in American policy.

Intensive diplomacy between the United States and West Germany took place in the spring of 1975. By early June it was clear that the United States had failed to stop the transfer of sensitive technologies, although the West Germans required Brazil to submit to "far-reaching" controls on these technologies. Nevertheless, the United States said that it remained concerned about the deal because of its nature and the precedent it set. But American officials showed some ambivalence. For example, Assistant Secretary of State Dixy Lee Ray disclosed that in 1974 the United States had refused to sell fuel cycle technology to Brazil. Dr. Ray added that the Ford administration's reluctance to sell nuclear technology abroad was "self-defeating."[1]

The priority given the Brazilian nuclear issue in American diplomacy with West Germany in the months preceding the signing of the agreement is unclear. West German officials reportedly claimed that, at a May 1975 meeting of the North Atlantic Treaty Organization, President Ford had not raised the matter with West German Chancellor Helmut Schmidt.[2] Days before the signing, Schmidt reportedly stated that he had heard no criticism of the agreement from the United States. Schmidt, like many Brazilians at the time, asserted that the controversy over the agreement had arisen because American nuclear companies had lost the deal.[3] The following day a Department of State spokesman replied indirectly by saying that American concern had been transmitted to West Germany and to Brazil.[4] Later an American official reportedly commented that evidently the United States had decided it "could not afford a major fight with the West Germans just now."[5]

The Brazilian government was stung by American and other interna-

---

1. David Binder, "U.S. Wins Safeguards in German Nuclear Deal with Brazil," *New York Times,* June 4, 1975; Bernard Gwertzman, "Dr. Ray Quits State Department; Critical of Kissinger Policy," *New York Times,* June 21, 1975.
2. Craig R. Whitney, "Bonn Is Pressing Brazilian A-Pact," *New York Times,* June 27, 1975.
3. Associated Press dispatch carried in "Bonn Signing Awaited," *New York Times,* June 27, 1975.
4. "U.S. Expresses Concern," *New York Times,* June 28, 1975.
5. "Brazilians and West Germans Sign $4 Billion Nuclear Pact," *New York Times,* June 28, 1975.

tional criticism of the impending agreement. In early June Brazilian Foreign Minister Azeredo da Silveira, in an apparent effort to quell this criticism, issued a statement that the German program would be restricted to peaceful uses that did not include peaceful nuclear explosions. Emotion ran high in Brazil, and virtually all sectors of Brazilian society, including the opposition political party, closed ranks to support the accord with West Germany. A distinguished Brazilian newspaper, *O Estado de São Paulo,* not only defended the deal but also justified Brazil's acquisition of nuclear weapons as morally just if "other emerging powers have the instrument of intimidation at their disposal." (*O Estado* later backed away from this stand.)[6]

By the end of June Brazil was in a state of nationalistic euphoria. Brazilians realized that they had succeeded in obtaining technology never before transferred on such a scale to a developing nation and had in the process defeated American efforts to keep it from them. In their eyes national sovereignty had triumphed over technological imperialism.

The reaction in the United States to the signing of the agreement was strong. A flurry of editorial commentary in the U.S. press condemned the agreement and the West German role and called for new and tougher international nonproliferation steps.[7] A U.S. senator, in remarks that quickly became infamous in Brazil, castigated West Germany for bringing a nuclear threat to America's "backyard" (in Portuguese, "quintal," a word that roughly equates to barnyard in American usage).[8]

American diplomacy on the transfer of sensitive technologies to Brazil by West Germany was complicated by a misunderstanding. In March 1975 the Bechtel Corporation, an American company, informed the Brazilian government that it could build a uranium enrichment plant in Brazil (although it could not furnish the Brazilians with the technology). Three weeks later, after consultations with the Department of State, Bechtel withdrew the offer.[9] Although Bechtel's initiative may have confused Brazilian officials at first, they were fully aware of American unwillingness to locate such facilities abroad and transfer the classified technology to

6. Marvine Howe, "Brazilians Order Silence on A-Pact," *New York Times,* June 12, 1975.

7. For example, a *New York Times* editorial, June 29, 1979.

8. "Brazilians and West Germans Sign," p. 2.

9. David Burnham, "U.S. Seems to Bar a Nuclear Deal," *New York Times,* December 11, 1975.

foreigners. The Bechtel offer did not distract official Brazilian attention from the West German deal.

American nuclear diplomacy in the first half of 1975 severely strained traditionally close U.S.-Brazilian friendship, already being tested by economic problems, especially Brazil's perception of growing American trade protectionism. In a repeatedly postponed visit to Brasilia in February 1976, Secretary of State Henry Kissinger sought to repair some of the damage. On February 21 Kissinger and Foreign Minister Silveira signed an ambitious memorandum of understanding providing for semiannual political consultations at their level.[10] Many Brazilians interpreted the visit as a formal indication that the United States had finally abandoned its unsuccessful opposition to the nuclear agreement. Almost incredibly, less than a year after the sharpest confrontation in recent memory, neither Kissinger in his public statements in Brazil nor reporters questioning him at a news conference in Brasilia raised the issue of the agreement.[11]

Days after Kissinger left Brasilia, the International Atomic Energy Agency approved a trilateral safeguards agreement with Brazil and West Germany to cover the technology, equipment, and materials involved in the Brazilian–West German accord. Brazilians viewed American concurrence in the decision of the IAEA Board of Governors on the safeguards agreement as yet another indication that U.S. antagonism to the West German agreement had ended.[12] Brazil and West Germany had won.

The wounds in U.S.-Brazilian relations had only begun to heal when Jimmy Carter was elected president. As a candidate Carter had spoken frequently of the need to halt nuclear proliferation and of his concern about the Brazilian–West German agreement. When he took office, he moved quickly. Less than a week after his inauguration, he sent Vice-President Mondale on a European tour. At a news conference in Brussels on January 24, 1977, Mondale announced that stopping the sales of reprocessing plants, such as those to Brazil and Pakistan, would be one of the "central themes" of the Carter administration.[13]

---

10. "Memorandum of Understanding Concerning Consultations on Matters of Mutual Interest," *Department of State Bulletin* (March 15, 1976), pp. 337–38.

11. Kissinger's remarks in Brazil are reprinted in ibid., pp. 322–26, 338–43.

12. IAEA, *The Text of the Safeguards Agreement of 26 February 1976 between the Agency, Brazil and the Federal Republic of Germany*, INFCIRC/237 (May 26, 1976).

13. Bernard Weinraub, "Mondale Pledges U.S. Won't Cut NATO Funds," *New York Times*, January 25, 1977.

At his next stop in Bonn, according to unnamed American and West German officials, Mondale told Chancellor Schmidt that Carter was unalterably opposed to the transfer of the sensitive technologies to Brazil. Schmidt, in what was to become a familiar West German refrain, said publicly that West Germany would fulfill its treaty commitments, including those in the NPT, the Brazilian agreement, and other international agreements. (Schmidt's pledge was consistent with the strict provisions of the safeguards agreement, which satisfied even the nuclear suppliers' guidelines.) Schmidt allowed, however, that "additional contractual obligations" might be assumed (presumably by Brazil). Clearly the issue had become "one of the most divisive" in U.S.–West German relations.[14]

Two weeks later, Deputy Secretary of State-designate Warren Christopher visited Bonn and urged West Germany to defer the transfer to Brazil of technologies for the enrichment and reprocessing plants, at least until regional nuclear fuel cycle centers under international control had been created. The West Germans, according to Carter administration officials, refused to budge from their commitments to Brazil, despite Christopher's offer of an inducement—guaranteed supplies of U.S.-enriched uranium for Brazil's reactors.[15] In early March Deputy Secretary Christopher flew to Brasilia and was given an icy reception. Brazilian press criticism of American policy verged on hysteria. The Brazilian government and the opposition party united in outrage. Probably doomed before it began, Christopher's mission failed. Brazil made no concessions.[16]

After Christopher departed, the Brazilians rejoiced in having successfully called the American bluff twice in two years. They realized, however, that American pressure had not yet ended but would now be applied mainly to West Germany. To be sure its nuclear partner understood the stakes, Brazil made it clear to West Germany that, if it caved in to American demands on the transfer of sensitive technologies, Kraftwerk Union could lose the lucrative reactor construction contracts. Brazil's move was

14. Bernard Weinraub, "Mondale Asks Bonn to Spur Its Economy," *New York Times*, January 26, 1977; Craig R. Whitney, "Schmidt May Modify Rio Atom Pact," *New York Times*, January 27, 1977.

15. David Binder, "Bonn Stands by Sale of Atomic Equipment," *New York Times*, February 12, 1977.

16. Reuters and Agence France Presse dispatches in "Brazil, U.S. at an Impasse on the German Nuclear Deal," *New York Times*, March 3, 1977; "Talks Between U.S. and Brazil on Nuclear Energy End Abruptly," *Washington Post*, March 3, 1977.

smart. West Germany's nuclear construction industry was having serious economic difficulties and desperately needed the Brazilian deal.

Weeks later Brazil canceled a military cooperation pact with the United States. The proximate cause was Brazil's affront at the Department of State's transmission to Congress of a report on human rights in Brazil (one of a series of reports submitted, at the request of Congress, on all countries eligible for U.S. foreign military sales). The military regime was sensitive about international criticism of human rights practices in Brazil; it was also proud of the improvement in these practices since the early 1970s. Nevertheless, Brazil's reaction to the preparation of the report was sufficiently strong to arouse speculation that the main purpose of canceling the military agreement was brinkmanship, a move designed to show Brazilian resolve to resist U.S. pressure on the nuclear agreement.[17]

After the Christopher visit to Brazil, U.S. foreign policy aides conferred intensively with their West German counterparts, and Carter and Schmidt communicated. But, as in 1975, American diplomacy seemed inconsistent. At the end of March 1977 Secretary of State Cyrus Vance met in Bonn with Chancellor Schmidt, but he reportedly gave almost no attention to the Brazilian agreement.[18] A week later the West Germans announced that they had decided to approve export licenses to begin the transfer of enrichment and reprocessing technology to Brazil. The licenses had been held up since Vice-President Mondale's trip to Bonn in January. All major political parties in West Germany backed the decision.[19]

American officials sought to put the best light on the West German decision by indicating that the initial West German exports would be confined to blueprints and other unclassified technical data; hence there was still hope that West Germany could be persuaded to change its mind.[20] It was nonetheless clear that a major political step had been taken. The Carter administration's first diplomatic test on nonproliferation had ended in embarrassment, greater because the administration had sought to maintain such a high profile in its approach. Despite its rhetoric on the Brazilian

17. Jonathan Kandell, "Brazil Bitter at U.S. Effort to Impose Nuclear Curb," *New York Times,* March 28, 1977.

18. "Brazil Remains Source of Friction," *New York Times,* April 1, 1977.

19. Craig R. Whitney, "Bonn to Send Brazil Nuclear Equipment, through U.S. Objects," *New York Times,* April 9, 1977.

20. Ibid.

deal, the Carter administration belatedly realized that other important interests were at stake in U.S.–West German relations (such as reflation of the West German economy, East-West issues, and defense and NATO cooperation). Moreover, the Carter administration lacked international support for its approach.

In both Brazil and West Germany some saw the diplomatic challenges of 1975 and 1977, and the responses to them, in a perspective broader than nuclear diplomacy. A popular view in Brazil was that the Carter administration's attempt to alter the Brazilian agreement was "part of a wider effort aimed at preventing Brazil from achieving its destiny as a great and independent power."[21] The failure of that campaign indicated to Brazilians that the United States was no longer as mighty as it once had been (an attitude to which American frustration in Vietnam had given currency), that the "European option" was real, and that West Germany could be counted on as a reliable future partner. After West Germany scored a success at the May 1977 economic summit in London by maintaining its positions on reflating the domestic economy and continuing to fulfill the Brazilian agreement, a major West German newspaper commented: the notion that West Germany is "an economic giant but a political dwarf is outdated. The London summit marks a turning point."[22]

Since the London summit the Carter administration has taken a more conciliatory approach but has nevertheless reserved the right to express its concern about the Brazilian–West German agreement.[23] In November 1977, on the eve of a trip by Secretary of State Vance to Brazil and other Latin American countries, the administration approved a shipment to Brazil of fuel for the Westinghouse-built reactor Angra I.[24] In a May 1978 visit to Brasilia, President Carter expressed in a low-key way American concern about the nuclear issue and human rights. But he was given a cool reception, doubtless reflecting a Brazilian attitude that had led the foreign minister to declare before the trip that Carter was coming

21. Kandell, "Brazil Bitter."
22. Craig R. Whitney, "Schmidt's Allies and Foes in Bonn Concur on His Success in London," *New York Times,* May 13, 1977.
23. See comments by President Carter at a news conference in Brasilia on March 30, 1978, quoted in *Department of State Bulletin* (May 1978), p. 8.
24. Graham Hovey, "Administration Approves Export of Uranium to Brazil," *New York Times,* November 17, 1977; Juan de Onis, "Vance Asks Brazilians to Restrict Nuclear Programs," *New York Times,* November 23, 1977.

to Brazil on his own initiative and not at the invitation of Brazil.[25] In March 1979 Vice-President Mondale struck a more positive chord: he said U.S. views on the nuclear issue had not changed, but that controversy about the matter had been exaggerated, and there were no serious bilateral issues in the way of "excellent" relations between the two countries.[26]

In dealing with Argentina's nuclear ambitions the Carter administration has perhaps learned from the Brazilian experience that a less confrontational style is politically more realistic. In a November 1977 visit by Secretary of State Vance to Buenos Aires, Argentina declared its intention of ratifying the Tlatelolco treaty and in return the United States offered to enlarge its cooperation with Argentina "to include relevant technology and ways of meeting Argentina's heavy water needs."[27]

In early 1979 West Germany was worried about American reaction to a Kraftwerk Union bid to construct Atucha II if the bid was unaccompanied by a West German condition that Argentina adopt full-scope safeguards. Kraftwerk Union argued, as it did in 1975 on the Brazilian deal, that Argentine business was essential for its survival. Rather than take a public, high-profile position on the matter, the United States used quiet diplomacy to try to persuade West Germany to require full-scope safeguards as a condition for major nuclear cooperation. The United States and Canada also urged West German and Swiss bidders on the commercial-scale heavy water production plant to set such a condition. These efforts were unsuccessful.

American nuclear diplomacy toward Argentina and Brazil is now at a turning point. It failed to persuade European suppliers to require de jure full-scope safeguards as a condition for major nuclear cooperation. It has not convinced Argentina to make good on that nation's stated intention to ratify the Tlatelolco treaty. And finally, it has not prevailed upon Argentina to publicly forswear the construction of an unsafeguarded reprocessing plant. Brazil and Argentina are strong countries, however, as are their European suppliers. Hence the United States should not regard

25. Terrence Smith, "Carter, in Brasilia, Raises Human Rights and A-Weapons Issue," *New York Times,* March 30, 1978; David Vidal, "U.S. Relations with Brazil Have Reached a Low Point," ibid.

26. Charles A. Kraus, "Mondale Shuns Atom Dispute in Visit to Brazil," *Washington Post,* March 23, 1979; Graham Hovey, "Mondale Sees New Brazilian Leaders," *New York Times,* March 23, 1979.

27. "United States, Argentina Issue Joint Communique," *Department of State Bulletin* (December 26, 1977), p. 915.

these weaknesses in the nonproliferation environment in South America as failures of American policy. But this does not mean that there is nothing the United States can do to strengthen the environment.

There are basically four instruments of policy the United States can use in an overall strategy to achieve this purpose: (1) policies of *denial* (such as restrictions on technology transfers); (2) policies of *control* (including safeguards, plutonium storage regimes, and supplier participation in the ownership and operation of sensitive facilities); (3) nuclear *cooperation* (such as access to supplies of U.S. enriched uranium and heavy water); and (4) *defense* policy (such as arms transfers and cooperation with other parties to the Treaty of Rio de Janeiro in the event of a crisis).

Policies of Denial

Policies that seek to deny the transfer of sensitive technologies under safeguards to Brazil and Argentina have no future. This lesson of U.S. diplomacy is now clear. European suppliers may well agree that politically unstable third world nations in high-risk security environments should not receive these technologies even if safeguarded. But most suppliers would not agree to ban transfers of sensitive technologies to all third world nations. Denying transfers of safeguarded sensitive technologies to Argentina and Brazil would be tantamount to such an approach.

The proliferation of unsafeguarded sensitive technologies, however, would be a far more serious threat to the stability of the security environment in the southern cone. Brazil could not build an independent, unsafeguarded reprocessing plant based on the Purex solvent extraction process without violating the "replication" safeguards in the Brazilian–West German agreement. (For this reason, ironically, inclusion of reprocessing in the agreement may lower rather than raise the risk of nuclear weapons proliferation by Brazil.) Argentina will not, however, be constrained by replication safeguards on reprocessing. Thus if it builds its own pilot heavy water production plant before acquiring Sulzer technology, there may be no safeguards obstacles to Argentina's construction of a small unsafeguarded full nuclear fuel cycle.

This risk justifies applying "policies of denial" to foreclose this possibility. There are several ways of proceeding. One is to try to mobilize Latin American opposition to any Argentine attempt to develop such a capability. This can be done bilaterally and through the Organization of American States, but it would have a good prospect for success only if there was evidence that Argentina was seeking to develop the capability to make nuclear weapons.

A second and complementary approach is to undertake to persuade Argentina's main nuclear suppliers (West Germany, Canada, and in the future Switzerland) to adopt a policy of automatically ceasing nuclear cooperation with Argentina if that nation ever begins to develop an unsafeguarded nuclear fuel cycle. In arguing its case with these suppliers, the United States would rely not on altruistic justifications but on the imperatives of specific American security interests in the hemisphere. If the United States could make a sound strategic case, it should have no difficulty in obtaining the cooperation of two of its closest NATO allies, Canada and West Germany.

Policies of Control

If there is no Argentine (or Brazilian) effort to develop an unsafeguarded fuel cycle, the United States should rely mainly on policies of control to achieve its nonproliferation objectives in South America. If such policies are to succeed in any important region, they must succeed in Latin America. The region's record of peaceful settlement of disputes, its legalistic and cooperative traditions, its acceptance of the principle of safeguards, its low propensity for interstate conflict, and the momentum behind the Tlatelolco treaty all support this conclusion. And when the low level of military rivalry between Argentina and Brazil is taken into account, policies of control are likely to be effective, at least so long as there is no major perturbation in the security environment of the southern cone. In fact, there may be no other third world region where policies of control can contribute so much to nonproliferation as in Latin America.

Two instruments of control are most relevant to Brazil and Argentina: IAEA safeguards and the Tlatelolco treaty. Other instruments may become useful in the future, for instance, a comprehensive test ban treaty, new international regimes for establishing multinational fuel centers, and international fuel assurances.

The main issue for American policy toward safeguards is how much confidence to place in their application to sensitive nuclear facilities. Especially since the Indian explosion, some experts argue that safeguards alone fail to constitute adequate protection against the diversion of weapons-usable materials. In a supreme national emergency nations can withdraw from their commitments to safeguards. Therefore, according to this line of argument, not even full-scope safeguards (or safeguards plus adherence to the NPT) are adequate to protect against proliferation, particularly in countries that are prone to political instability or have bitter military rivalries with neighbors.

In a world of sovereign states absolute protection against national behavior is difficult to devise. So it is with proliferation. The question for American policy on safeguards is where to draw the line: for which nations are safeguards "enough" and for which are they not? As Brazil and Argentina see it, the United States has drawn the line between industrial nations and the third world: safeguards are "enough" for Canada, Australia, or West Germany to undertake uranium enrichment on a national basis, even though these nations are not nuclear weapons states. And while the United States has opposed reprocessing in industrial democracies (such as Japan), Argentines and Brazilians believe that it has begun to relent. Argentina and Brazil argue that they are responsible and trustworthy, that they have fulfilled their safeguards commitments to date, and that safeguards should thus be "enough" for them.

Despite strong, genuine American support for safeguards, the United States inevitably risks support for them in Brazil and Argentina when it questions the utility of safeguards in protecting sensitive facilities in third world nations. This is not to say that the United States should not seek to complement safeguards with other protections when they are necessary. It should. But American policymakers need to proceed carefully so as not to undermine Brazilian and Argentine support for safeguards and for future voluntary legal regimes in the nuclear field.

The Tlatelolco treaty, in spite of its latitude on peaceful nuclear explosions, is the most promising instrument for U.S. nonproliferation diplomacy with Argentina and Brazil. President Carter evidently recognized this in 1977 when he signed Additional Protocol I of the treaty, which requires that nuclear weapons states give "no-use" assurances to parties to the treaty and pledge to respect its provisions. For over a decade American presidents had been unwilling to take this step .

There may have been a number of reasons for this reluctance. The United States apparently feared that adherence to Additional Protocol I would limit American flexibility to deploy nuclear weapons in Puerto Rico and other American territories and possessions. It has become embarrassing for the United States to withhold adherence while preaching nonproliferation to others. The West German–Brazilian agreement may have made the United States realize that the proliferation stakes had risen in Latin America and that the treaty was a useful vehicle for gaining Argentine and Brazilian adherence to full-scope safeguards. Moreover, the United States probably realized it had to act if it hoped for Cuban adherence to the treaty. Cuban adherence is important not only because it could activate the entry into full force of the treaty but also because it would represent tacit Cuban acceptance of the 1962 U.S.-Soviet understanding on the introduction into Cuba of "offensive" arms, including nuclear weapons.[28]

Securing Cuban ratification may not be easy. The United States can intervene with the USSR, but Castro may see Cuban adherence as a bargaining chip with which U.S. concessions can be extracted. Nevertheless, the United States should stress to the Soviet Union the priority of Tlatelolco. In dealing with Cuba, Mexico may be more persuasive than the United States. Mexico has incentives for this, including the prestige it would gain were the treaty to enter into full force.

Although the United States may be on uncertain legal ground in interpreting the Tlatelolco treaty as precluding peaceful nuclear explosions, it should make efforts to encourage other parties to the treaty to accept this interpretation. Mexico already does, as do a majority of nations for which the treaty is in effect. When the treaty becomes fully effective, Argentina and Brazil will be forced to give up their rights to peaceful nuclear explosions as they conclude full-scope safeguards agreements with the IAEA.

A word should be said about the view of the U.S. defense establishment toward the Tlatelolco treaty. Over the years the Department of Defense has been concerned almost solely with the implications of the treaty for unimpeded U.S. nuclear weapons transit and transport privileges in Latin America, including overflights and naval ship visits. The treaty does not

---

28. Testimony of Charles A. Meyer, Assistant Secretary of State for Inter-American Affairs, *Additional Protocol II to the Latin American Nuclear Free Zone Treaty,* Hearings before the Senate Committee on Foreign Relations, 91 Cong. 2 sess. and 92 Cong. 1 sess. (Government Printing Office, 1971).

limit these rights. (In the negotiations on the treaty Argentina sought to restrict these rights but failed.) When testifying on the treaty several years ago, a chairman of the Joint Chiefs of Staff stressed this concern but made no effort to acknowledge the contribution of the treaty to nonproliferation or to associate the Chiefs of Staff with this objective.[29]

The question of international legal regimes for storage of weapons-grade materials was highlighted by Brazil's negotiations with Urenco for fuel for two Brazilian power reactors, Angra II and III. The Dutch parliament demanded additional nonproliferation assurances, and eventually received them in an agreement providing for IAEA control over explosives-grade materials produced from spent rods of Urenco-supplied fuel. Some observers feared that this step would amount to tacit acknowledgment of the legitimacy of Brazilian reprocessing. In retrospect, however, the Dutch action seems to have established a useful precedent. U.S. diplomacy should seek to extend it, for instance, to include plutonium separated from fuel elements irradiated in Angra I.

Other legal instruments offer less promise. For at least as long as military regimes remain in power, Brazil and Argentina are unlikely to reverse their positions on the NPT. The United States hopes for a comprehensive test ban, but it should not overestimate the effect on Brazilian or Argentine nuclear policies.

The United States might pursue other policies of control not yet exploited. For one, the United States can try to persuade West Germany to make some marginal changes in its agreement with Brazil—two would make the agreement more consistent with the suppliers' guidelines. Article 8 of the guidelines stipulates that recipient nations should not produce uranium enriched more than 20 percent without the consent of the supplier.[30] It is unclear whether this provision is contained in the West German–Brazilian agreement, but it should be. Article 7 states that, if enrichment or reprocessing technologies are transferred, suppliers should encourage recipients to accept, as an alternative to national plants, the involvement of suppliers or other appropriate multinational participation.[31] The Brazilian enrichment plant is to be a joint venture with West

29. Testimony of Admiral Thomas H. Moorer in ibid., p. 36.
30. Nuclear Suppliers Group, "Guidelines for Nuclear Transfers," *Survival*, vol. 20 (March–April 1978), pp. 85–87.
31. Ibid., p. 86.

Germany, but the reprocessing plant might be controlled solely by Brazil. The United States should attempt to persuade West Germany to partici- pate in the reprocessing plant.

The idea of a multinational fuel cycle center in South America deserves a fair hearing. Admittedly it is a concept that faces obstacles. Brazil and Argentina would be reluctant to participate in any center not located at home. Unlike Brazil, Argentina has no need for enriched uranium (this would change if Argentina switched to light water reactors at some future date). Some nonproliferation enthusiasts are unwilling to trust third world nations as either sites of or technological participants in multina- tional centers. This attitude ignores power realities and the probable lack of international support for such a restrictive approach.

An enlightened and determined U.S. policy toward multinational cen- ters might eventually succeed. Brazil could lose interest in the Becker jet- nozzle enrichment process, Argentina in heavy water production based on current technology, and both nations in large-scale reprocessing. Also, higher costs of power reactor programs than expected may mean that both nations need less fuel and heavy water than they had anticipated, making national production facilities less economical.

It is now too late for the United States to offer current-generation en- richment, heavy water, and reprocessing technology and expect Argentina and Brazil to abandon their national efforts. But in the future an attrac- tive offer of American technology (such as laser or plasma enrichment if they become commercially feasible) for a multinational fuel center, in- cluding Brazil and Argentina as technological and commercial partners, might be persuasive. Such a center could be located on the Brazilian- Argentine border or on the border with Paraguay or Uruguay. The ex- traordinary complexity of the technology might reduce proliferation risks.[32]

U.S. Nuclear Cooperation

Prospects for U.S. cooperation with Argentina and Brazil in the nuclear field are not bright. American unwillingness to sell enrichment and re- processing technologies to Brazil combined with a 1974 misunderstanding

32. "Nonproliferation Effort Seen Enhanced by Laser Isotope Separation Tech- niques," *Nuclear Fuel,* vol. 4 (March 19, 1979), pp. 1–2.

about fuel supply commitments for Angra II and Angra III cost the United States an opportunity to continue to play a major part in Brazil's nuclear program. American reluctance to sell heavy water technology to Argentina limits the role of the United States in Argentina's nuclear program. Nevertheless, the United States continues to ship fuel for Angra I and for Brazilian and Argentine research reactors, and it supplied heavy water for Atucha I.

U.S. Defense Policy

Currently the direct importance of Brazil and Argentina to U.S. security interests is limited. Location and military weaknesses make them of only moderate strategic value to the United States in countering its primary security threat, the Soviet Union and its Warsaw Pact allies. Nationalistic and independent trends in Argentine and Brazilian policies combined with uncertainty and strain in U.S. relations with these countries, especially Argentina, mean that the United States cannot be confident that they would be willing to help it meet these threats.

Still, there are contingencies that would increase the importance of Brazil and Argentina to U.S. security interests. They might include the regular deployment of Soviet naval forces in the South Atlantic, the establishment of a major Soviet military presence in a South American nation, and the proliferation of nuclear weapons in the southern cone.

Of these contingencies, only the first is a near-term threat. At present, a small number of Soviet surface combatants and submarines operate periodically in the central and southern Atlantic Ocean, especially off West Africa and in the Caribbean area. Soviet naval vessels occasionally visit Cuba, but the USSR so far has been unable to establish a naval base in western or southern Africa.

If the Soviet Union's efforts should be successful, in what ways might the United States respond to involve Brazil? It could seek the use of Brazilian or Argentine facilities from which to project U.S. naval and air power. It could also, or alternatively, attempt to involve the growing naval and air capabilities of both nations in certain functions (for example, antisubmarine warfare and demonstrations of force).

Were a significant Soviet naval presence to emerge in the South Atlantic, the United States might counter it with combined forces if possible.

If Brazil and Argentina acquired sophisticated surveillance technologies and equipment, which the United States could provide, each could deploy antisubmarine warfare task forces. When operated in conjunction with modern aerial surveillance platforms (such as P-3s), these task forces would have a potent capability for maritime surveillance and sea defense in the South Atlantic.

Attractive though this may sound from a technical standpoint, the outlook for such operations is uncertain. The lack of a tradition of close U.S.-Argentine military cooperation, strong anti-American sentiment in Argentina, and strain in U.S.-Argentine relations are obstacles to cooperation of this type. Brazil, despite a history of close U.S.-Brazilian military cooperation, might not be interested unless its own strategic interests (such as coastal security, oil imports) were directly threatened and it feared that U.S. (and allied) forces needed help in countering these threats. It would think long and hard about the risks to its security of deploying forces against Soviet naval targets. Brazil's political orientation—to increase its international political independence and prestige, especially in the third world—would reinforce this reluctance. At some future time, however, Brazil might be willing to cooperate with the United States in improving maritime surveillance of Soviet naval activities in the central and southern Atlantic Ocean.

Despite the current limitations on enhancing the American defense posture by improving military cooperation with Brazil and Argentina, the United States cannot foresee all future contingencies, such as how the USSR will use its growing naval power in operations in the central and southern Atlantic Ocean. Moreover, in a U.S.-Soviet conflict, the United States could spare few, if any, naval resources for the South Atlantic. For these reasons, the United States should seek to steadily improve its relations with Argentina and Brazil, especially in military cooperation. Over the long term such an improvement would reassure the two nations that they and the United States have mutual security interests and policies and would restore some degree of American influence in their military establishments. Both these factors could marginally increase American influence in ways that might directly or indirectly affect decisions on nuclear and strategic policies.

The second contingency—the establishment of a major Soviet military presence in South America or of facilities or access privileges to support such a presence—is unlikely. It would require a dramatic political shift by any potential regional host country and a high degree of insensitivity to inevitable strong regional and U.S. opposition. (Although Peru bought Soviet fighter-bombers, it did not give Soviet naval forces basing privileges.) Nevertheless, were such a contingency to materialize, American military cooperation and access to facilities could become urgent.

The third contingency—nuclear weapons proliferation in the region— could directly affect U.S. security interests in two ways: the United States might be called upon by its partners in the Treaty of Rio de Janeiro to provide security assurances and perhaps to deploy force; and U.S. forces, U.S. citizens and their property, and even U.S. territories could face new threats if there should be a nuclear confrontation or accident in South America.

Four instruments of American security policy can be employed to help deal with the potential threat of nuclear weapons proliferation in Argentina and Brazil. They are security assurances, deployments of U.S. forces, arms transfers, and security cooperation. The latter concept encompasses joint exercises (for instance, the annual United International Antisubmarine Warfare [UNITAS] naval exercise), joint contingency planning, and combined operations.

Defense policy is a necessary complement to other instruments of U.S. nonproliferation diplomacy. The more threatening the security environment of the potential proliferator, the greater the responsibility of the United States in assuring the security of that nation; and the closer the potential proliferator to deploying nuclear weapons, the more important defense policy becomes to nonproliferation diplomacy.

The potential role of defense policy in U.S. nonproliferation diplomacy with Argentina and Brazil can be analyzed for three separate contingencies:

—both countries have safeguarded civil nuclear programs and neither has a nuclear weapons program (the present situation);

—one country has a serious nuclear weapons program under way or has begun to deploy nuclear weapons and the other has not;

—both countries have well-developed nuclear weapons programs or have begun to deploy nuclear weapons.

In the first contingency, the role of defense policy is limited. New U.S. security assurances or conventional arms sales are unlikely to make Brazil or Argentina feel more secure. Both nations can purchase whatever sophisticated arms they need from European countries. Improved security cooperation, such as combined naval operations, might achieve common naval objectives but would do little to increase or decrease incentives for acquiring nuclear weapons.

In the second contingency, instruments of U.S. defense policy could play a much greater role. Their purpose would be to demonstrate to the proliferating country that the nonproliferating country had a powerful military ally and to encourage the nonproliferating country not to change its nuclear weapons policy. Were the nonproliferating country to seek new arms, the United States could lower its restrictions on arms sales, especially on air defense equipment. For example, the United States might consider selling F-15 or F-18 aircraft armed with late-generation Side-winder and Sparrow air-to-air missiles. The improved HAWK and Chaparral surface-to-air missiles, radar-directed antiaircraft weapons, and electronic warfare equipment, as well as upgraded intelligence sharing, are also possibilities. The quantities and sophistication of arms transferred to the nonproliferator could increase as the proliferating country came closer to deploying nuclear weapons.

The United States might respond favorably to requests by the nonproliferating country for stronger security assurances than those contained in the Treaty of Rio de Janeiro. New bilateral treaties and, if danger seemed imminent, joint military contingency planning could be undertaken, and Rio treaty sanctions against the proliferating nation might be sought.

Joint planning would presumably involve U.S. commitments to deploy force on behalf of the nonproliferating country were the proliferating country to threaten or launch an unprovoked nuclear attack. Since at present the United States has no major military installations in South America, it might have to rely heavily on U.S. Navy carrier task forces. In an emergency, however, the nonproliferating country would probably offer facilities for forward deployment of U.S. air and sea power. The United States could also airlift radar and antiaircraft equipment for local forces and supply U.S. ground personnel trained in nuclear defense.

Carrying out combined operations with the nonproliferating country before a crisis might have several advantages. It would give the forces of the nonproliferating country and the United States an opportunity to improve the compatibility of their doctrines, their equipment, and their command, control, and communications. If U.S. force deployments were needed in a subsequent crisis, the combined forces could work more efficiently together. For instance, U.S. airborne warning capabilities might be used to guide both U.S. and host country fighters toward hostile aircraft. However, defense cooperation based on nuclear developments in the southern cone would be controversial—and unprecedented—for the United States.

The role of defense policy in U.S. nonproliferation diplomacy declines in the third contingency. If both Argentina and Brazil developed or deployed nuclear weapons, the United States would have no incentive to offer new security ties to either nation, although it might offer command and control and safety technology for nuclear weapons. Should a nuclear conflict between Argentina and Brazil threaten to emerge, the United States might not want to risk its military resources except to evacuate its citizens before the conflict. There would be no domestic support for threatening the use of U.S. forces to deter Argentina and Brazil from attacking each other if both were nuclear-armed.

Third world nuclear war contingencies seem to have received little attention from U.S. policymakers and defense planners. For example, in his fiscal 1981 report, Secretary of Defense Harold Brown did not address the issue of how the United States might respond militarily to a nuclear conflict in the third world. Any evaluation of the role of U.S. defense policy in dealing with proliferation issues concerning Argentina and Brazil is therefore difficult to make until the United States decides how to deal with these issues in other third world areas where nuclear weapons proliferation may be a more immediate threat.

Comparisons with Other Near-Nuclear Countries

As far as the role of defense policy in U.S. nonproliferation diplomacy is concerned, several characteristics set Argentina and Brazil apart from certain other near-nuclear nations in the third world. Since Brazil and Argentina are not in a main area of U.S.-Soviet military rivalry, U.S. nonproliferation diplomacy can be carried forward without the risk of jeopardizing American security interests. With Pakistan and Israel, for example, the United States must carefully balance its nonproliferation interests against other security and political interests. Since the security environments of Brazil and Argentina are relatively benign, U.S. security assurances inherent in the Rio treaty do not require frequent reaffirmation to help avert proliferation. Strong U.S. security assurances are more important to proliferation decisions, for example, in South Korea if they are tangible and repeated often.

Brazil and Argentina are the only potential regional nuclear rivals that are both beneficiaries of U.S. security assurances in treaty form. Using the Rio treaty as a vehicle, the United States in cooperation with other treaty adherents could offer special assurances to parties to the treaty to discourage any decision to proliferate, to protect them from nuclear intimidation or attack, and to marshal their support in putting pressure on Argentina or Brazil not to proliferate. If Argentina or Brazil deployed nuclear weapons, the Rio treaty could become more important to nonproliferation diplomacy in Latin America than the Tlatelolco treaty. But if the Rio treaty was exploited for this purpose prematurely or without the support of regional partners, the United States could debase its value as a mechanism for settling disputes.

Finally, the southern cone is the only major third world area where proliferation would affect the security interests of only one great power, the United States. In Northeast Asia, West and South Asia, and the Middle East, the security interests of the USSR, China, or major European powers would be directly affected. (In southern Africa, the interests of great powers are problematical.) This puts more responsibility on the United States and at the same time makes it harder for this country to gain the support of other great powers for effective nonproliferation policies in the region.

CHAPTER SEVENTEEN

Preventing the Development of South African Nuclear Weapons

SOUTH AFRICA'S leaders will not deploy a nuclear force as long as they believe they have more to lose than to gain by doing so. The United States may be able to affect their calculations marginally by inducements or threats, although the evolution of relations between Pretoria and Washington since President Carter took office gives little reason to believe that South African authorities will be amenable to American influence. (A much more conservative U.S. administration might reverse the trend of mutual alienation but also might be less concerned about the prospect of nuclear proliferation by anticommunist regimes.) Potentially effective measures that the United States could take to dissuade Pretoria from nuclear adventurism are limited by other policy interests and domestic constraints against active and coercive intervention. Threats—tacit or discreet—are more likely to be emphasized than inducements. This was certainly the case in the August 1977 controversy over the alleged plan for a nuclear test. But most measures that are plausible are also feeble. White South Africans may hope that, even if favors cannot be obtained from the United States, passive acceptance of the status quo will be. Although this would not solve their problems, it might prevent them from getting worse. On the assumption that American interest lies in opposing the apartheid system, which is the essence of the regime, there is little the United States can do to reduce South Africa's nuclear weapons incentives by allaying its security anxieties. If the United States should choose an activist role, the most feasible pressure would not be extremely coercive (for example, a threat of forcible intervention) but rather aimed at economic or technological interests. Manipulation of nuclear cooperation is one possibility.

In principle, it would be most desirable for the United States and other countries to exert pressure through internationally coordinated measures. Few multilateral initiatives, however, have as much potential as unilateral ones—particularly U.S. manipulation of nuclear cooperation.

International Controls on South African Nuclear Activities

South African accession to the Treaty on the Non-Proliferation of Nuclear Weapons is desirable, even though it would not be significant for nuclear weapons potential. Although the present ability to build a nuclear device would not be changed, the intention to do so would be constrained. Nations do not blithely violate treaties they have ratified. Adherence to the NPT would raise the political cost of weapon development and would at the least provide a marginal additional incentive to refrain. Ambassador Gerard Smith shuttled between Washington and Pretoria in 1978 in an energetic though vain attempt to secure a signature to the treaty.

The chances of South African ratification are slim. At best, it would be the result of a quid pro quo agreement to maintain American nuclear cooperation. Authorities in Pretoria have justified their refusal to join the NPT, despite their stated intention not to build nuclear weapons, by the need to maintain the security of the secret enrichment process and gold mining operations, security they claim could be compromised by safeguards. Officials say they are worried that, after accession, safeguards might be expanded to cover uranium mining, which is largely coextensive with gold production. South African conditions for ratification, expressed in 1978, were prohibitive: resumption of the supply of highly enriched uranium for Safari-I; sale of low enriched fuel for the new power station; guarantees that the United States would grant export permits for non-sensitive components for the enrichment plant; and U.S. assistance in regaining Pretoria's seat on the International Atomic Energy Agency Board of Governors.[1]

If the South African government believed the country's diplomatic status or international acceptance would be improved by membership in the NPT, its willingness to join would be greater. But there is little to suggest that this would happen. The growing consensus on the regime's illegitimacy would not be reversed, since that consensus is based on apartheid, not nuclear policy. South African leaders understand this quite well and are unlikely to think the regime would be more popular after an NPT gesture. At any rate, recent trends indicate a tendency to reduce rather than increase South Africa's role in international nuclear institutions. The country was expelled from the governing board of the International Atomic Energy Agency in June 1977 (despite votes by Western countries against the expulsion) on grounds that it was illegally exploiting Namibia's uranium resources. Prime Minister John Vorster had announced willingness to discuss South African accession to the NPT, but only if the United States rectified its breach of nuclear cooperation agreements. He used the untrustworthiness of international agreements as an argument against the NPT. He maintained that the treaty's commitments under Article IV to promote the exchange of nuclear information had been "totally ignored" in recent years, that the expulsion from the IAEA board was contrary to the organization's own statutes, and that the United States and other countries had violated bilateral commitments to South Africa.[2] (The United States had long delayed approval for an enriched uranium shipment for Safari-I.) In December 1979 South Africa was barred from participating in the IAEA's general conference in New Delhi; forty-nine nonaligned and communist countries outvoted twenty-four Western industrial countries on the issue of the Pretoria delegation's credentials.[3]

1. J. E. Spence, "The Republic of South Africa: Proliferation and the Politics of 'Outward Movement,' " in Robert M. Lawrence and Joel Larus, eds., *Nuclear Proliferation: Phase II* (University Press of Kansas for the National Security Education Program, 1974), p. 222; Robert S. Jaster, *South Africa's Narrowing Security Options,* Adelphi Paper 159 (London: International Institute for Strategic Studies, 1980), p. 46.

2. Roger Murray, "Why the Atom Authority Kicked South Africa Out," *New African* (October 1977), pp. 970–71; "South Africa: Atomic Explosion Prevented," *Africa Research Bulletin,* Political, Social, and Cultural Series, vol. 14 (September 15, 1977), p. 4546.

3. Michael T. Kaufman, "Nuclear Parley Bars South Africa," *New York Times,* December 6, 1979.

Establishment of an African nuclear-weapon-free zone is only a slightly more reassuring or probable solution than gaining South African adherence to the NPT. There have been many initiatives to create a nuclear-free zone.[4]

—African countries raised the issue in the United Nations in 1960 after France detonated its first bomb in the Sahara.

—The next year in the General Assembly fourteen African countries introduced a nuclear-free-zone resolution aimed principally at keeping the great powers from bringing weapons into the area or testing them there. The USSR supported the move, which passed, but Western countries opposed it because the ban on testing would be uninspected.

—In July 1964 the Organization of African Unity (OAU) summit conference called for regional denuclearization and members offered to make a treaty not to build or obtain nuclear arms.

—The General Assembly in 1965 approved the earlier OAU declaration.

—At the end of 1974 the General Assembly unanimously adopted a resolution reaffirming the earlier resolutions.

—In 1976 the General Assembly adopted a resolution, without formal voting, calling for all nations to refrain from supplying South Africa with any equipment that could "enable" it to build nuclear weapons.

There is still no treaty for a nuclear-weapon-free zone, however, and no evidence that South Africa would sign one. Moreover, the United States has so far opposed the termination of nuclear cooperation on the ground that this would eliminate the chance to use leverage on South Africa and would push it toward autonomy. In any case agreement to a nuclear-free zone, as to the NPT, would merely reflect a South African government decision not to acquire nuclear weapons; it would not determine it. (The only causal efficacy it might have would be in inhibiting decisions by a later government that might reevaluate the desirability of weapon development.)

Adherence to either treaty would also merely suggest intent; it would not limit capability (except insofar as expanding safeguards to cover enrichment facilities would constrain secret development). The only way to accomplish this might be an international embargo on nuclear supplies and assistance, but with South Africa's self-sufficiency in producing fis-

4. These are recorded in William Epstein, "A Nuclear-Weapon-Free Zone in Africa?" Occasional Paper 14 (Muscatine, Iowa: Stanley Foundation, 1977), pp. 10–12, 25–26.

sionable material, even this would not cripple the capability. However, it would mean economic losses and inefficiencies undesirable for the peaceful energy program, and the threat of an embargo would be a significant disincentive so long as the desire for a bomb was only marginal. The prospect of an embargo might do more to prevent a decision to make weapons than carrying out the embargo. As with nuclear weapons themselves, a threat of action is more effective as a deterrent than implementing the action would be if deterrence failed.

Leverage through Nuclear Cooperation: Carrot, Stick, or Boomerang?

Trying to coax South Africa away from proliferation by manipulating nuclear cooperation poses some vexing dilemmas. Many anti-apartheid activists oppose any cooperation because it may enhance South African capabilities; others support maintaining such ties because ending them would reduce American influence on South African policy.

There are few other material inducements or pressures that are both still available and likely to be used against South Africa by the West. Foreign aid, even if countries were willing to give it, is not as vital to South Africa as it would be to a poor country. Military assistance has already been proscribed so cannot be offered to reduce conventional defensive vulnerability; indeed, the point is that most countries do not want to reduce the apartheid regime's insecurity. Economic warfare through some kind of forced disinvestment by Western companies is recommended by some but has little chance of becoming national policy in the United States or Europe. Even if it did, it would probably be aimed at apartheid policy rather than atomic policy, and could thus be counterproductive in the nuclear area by encouraging bomb mischief as a means of counterpressure. The nuclear area, however, is one in which (1) there is a long history of American involvement as well as a high probability of termination; and (2) the linkage of energy policy with weapons policy is clearest and hence potentially most exploitable.

The United States began its nuclear involvement with South Africa soon after the Second World War, largely to ensure provision of enough uranium to build up the American stockpile of atomic bombs. A formal cooperation agreement was made in 1957, subsequently amended in 1962,

1967 (when the program of uranium purchasing ended), and 1974, at which time the term of the agreement was extended to the year 2007.[5] This relationship became very controversial for the first time in 1976 when the State Department approved the sale of two reactors (South Africa subsequently took up a French offer instead) and congressional hearings on the subject brought the issue into prominence. By then the United States had already shipped 228 pounds of weapons-grade uranium to South Africa over the years for use in the Safari-I research reactor, and had just permitted the sale of computers for use in enrichment facilities (such computer transactions were reportedly prohibited later in the year).[6]

In mid-1976 the Congressional Black Caucus and others opposed the application for a license to export enriched uranium for Safari-I. The Ford administration argued that a ban would backfire, encouraging the South Africans to turn their pilot plant from low enrichment toward high enrichment (in order to run the research reactor), thus giving them unsafeguarded weapons-grade uranium.[7] Prominent nonproliferation advocates such as Mason Willrich also testified in this vein in opposing a ban on reactor exports. Since enriched uranium rather than plutonium was the most cost-effective and likely South African route to a bomb, he reasoned, a reactor sale would not increase Pretoria's capability to build a weapon, but barring access to foreign trade and technology might increase its in-

5. *Resource Development in South Africa and U.S. Policy,* Hearings before the Subcommittee on International Resources, Food, and Energy of the House Committee on International Relations, 94 Cong. 2 sess. (Government Printing Office, 1976), p. 58. See also Zdenek Červenka and Barbara Rogers, *The Nuclear Axis: Secret Collaboration Between West Germany and South Africa* (Times Books, 1978), pp. 238ff.; and Abraham A. Ribicoff, "A Market-Sharing Approach to the World Nuclear Sales Problem," *Foreign Affairs,* vol. 54 (July 1976), pp. 764–65.

6. Thomas O'Toole, "S. African Atomic Sales Explained," *Washington Post,* May 28, 1976. Deputy Assistant Secretary of State Myron Kratzer testified these were "small . . . relatively modest, general purpose computers" that South Africa could have obtained from other suppliers; *U.S. Policy Toward Africa,* Hearings before the Senate Committee on Foreign Relations, 94 Cong. 2 sess. (GPO, 1976), p. 292. In late 1976 "US computer subsidiaries in SA had their multiple transaction licenses revoked, only being re-issued when declarations were filed with Washington that those companies would not provide computers or related products . . . for use directly or indirectly for uranium enrichment." "World Digest: South Africa," *Nuclear Engineering International* (August 1977), p. 12.

7. "After India, South African Export Comes Under Fire," *Weekly Energy Report,* vol. 4 (July 26, 1976), p. 7; *U.S. Policy Toward Africa,* Hearings, p. 289.

centive to do so. Moreover, said Willrich, the sale might be used to induce acceptance of full-scope safeguards.[8]

The latter possibility was mooted by Pretoria's decision to buy the reactors from France, but the issue of enriched uranium supply remained alive. Some believed that the upgrading of South Africa's enrichment facilities would not be finished in time to supply its Koeberg reactors and that it would continue to need American supplies in the early 1980s. Press reports indicate vigorous U.S. diplomatic initiatives in 1977 and 1978 to gain South African adherence to the NPT, backed up by the offer of continued enriched fuel supply and technical cooperation if Pretoria agreed and the threat to terminate such assistance if it did not. To maintain the possibility of this kind of reciprocity, the United States opposed moves in the United Nations to ban all nuclear cooperation with South Africa.[9] Ambassador Andrew Young, in a reversal of his position before entering the Carter administration, said that ending cooperation "would only encourage separate development of South Africa's own nuclear potential." He continued:

I think by maintaining some kind of relationship we do have the possibility of influencing them to sign the nuclear nonproliferation treaty and accepting all of the safeguards. . . . If you break the relationship altogether there is no way to monitor and it is almost because you can't trust them that you have to stay close to them.[10]

But it is quite apparent that South Africa has not responded to an American quid pro quo offer, and after the negotiations over Namibia fell apart Washington's NPT initiative was shelved. The Nuclear Non-Proliferation Act of 1978 requires termination of supply (unless the president uses his waiver power, though Congress could overturn a waiver) if Pretoria does not accept full-scope safeguards. Since South African statements have placed exceptional value on the country's internally developed enrichment process, the government seems unlikely to accede to American pressure. This resistance could be fortified by a decision to

8. *U.S. Policy Toward Africa*, Hearings, pp. 235, 258.

9. Richard Burt, "U.S. Tells South Africa to Accept Atomic Curbs or Face Fuel Cutoff," *New York Times*, December 20, 1977; John F. Burns, "South Africans Reported Ready for Nuclear Ban," *New York Times*, June 29, 1978; Milton R. Benjamin, "Arms Ban on S. Africa Remains Stalled in U.N.," *Washington Post*, November 2, 1977.

10. Quoted by Bernard Gwertzman, "Young Bars Refusal to Sell South Africa Atom Reactors Fuels," *New York Times*, October 31, 1977.

accelerate development of the larger enrichment facility or accept curtailment or delay of reactor operations until indigenous enriched uranium capacity comes on line. The South Africans may also hope that when the chips are down the United States will continue cooperation rather than push the country toward less efficient but more autonomous and unsafeguarded nuclear operations. In this situation it is unclear which country has the most leverage with the other. The part of the American strategy that sees cooperation as necessary to prevent proliferation actually vitiates the part that sees the threat to withdraw cooperation as a way of compelling agreeable South African behavior.

Western leverage would be increased to the degree that other suppliers joined in applying pressure—for example, if France had threatened to cancel the sales for the Koeberg reactors. In 1977 Prime Minister Raymond Barre justified the sale by saying that South Africa already had nuclear capability and the reactors would not add to it.[11] Even if France had reneged, South Africa could buy reactors somewhere else. The nuclear suppliers' guidelines do not constrain sales of reactors the way they do sales of more sensitive nuclear equipment. Restraint would have to be nearly universal to be effective. Moreover, pressure from suppliers strengthens incentives to expand or improve sensitive parts of the fuel cycle indigenously. The American refusal to supply highly enriched uranium for the Safari research reactor after 1975, which forced the reactor to function at half of capacity or less, simply encouraged plans to rely on internal enrichment.[12]

Conclusions

The United States could undertake more active measures than those just discussed. It could threaten reprisals for South African development of nuclear weapons: severance of diplomatic relations; pressure on American corporations to curtail operations in South Africa; a trade embargo akin to that imposed on Cuba; diplomatic support for South Afri-

11. Jim Hoagland, "French Leader Confirms S. African Nuclear Ability," *Washington Post,* February 18, 1977.
12. "South Africa Becomes Self-Reliant in Fuel," *Nuclear Engineering International* (August 1979), p. 7; Robert I. Rotberg, *Suffer the Future: Policy Choices in Southern Africa* (Harvard University Press, 1980), p. 148.

can external enemies such as the South West Africa People's Organization (SWAPO); or a tacit threat of covert support to internal black forces against the regime. Opposition in the United States, however, as well as prudence on other grounds, makes most of these measures unlikely. It is also uncertain how much political capital and how much of its modest stock of influence the American government will want to expend on the nuclear issue. Other problems, such as Namibia, will probably take precedence as long as nuclear matters are not critical. Given the limited military utility of a bomb, it would probably be easy for the United States to prevent Pretoria from getting one if nonproliferation were the first or only U.S. priority in the area. But it is not, and the political price that could assuredly buy Pretoria off is prohibitive because of American ideals and interests in black Africa. Only an administration much more liberal and activist than Carter's would coerce South Africa on a broad front; a more conservative president would probably reduce the recent level of pressure.

Nuclear cooperation is the one tangible and credible card that can be played. But this card may be ineffective if South Africa chooses to pay the price and continue to maintain its current degree of autonomy and secrecy, or it may lead to costs in other areas of diplomacy if anti-apartheid countries insist on a nuclear cutoff. Preventing one of these drawbacks requires accepting the other. To prevent the first, South Africans must be convinced that a quid pro quo is in their interest because developing a bomb would produce few gains and substantial losses. A difficult situation would arise if Pretoria were to offer some kind of firm, declared assurance of nonproliferation in exchange for continued cooperation and supply but refused to submit to full-scope safeguards. The United States could then withdraw and terminate the nuclear relationship. This would make those who favor a nuclear embargo happy, but it might push Pretoria closer to a bomb. Then more active threats would become necessary to deter the regime from deploying weapons or to deal with it if it did. The continuing dilemma is that the best way to prevent South Africa's white government from getting the bomb is to offer it something for not doing so, but offering anything significant is almost out of the question because that would constitute support of apartheid.

Hoping that South African authorities will continue to believe that more would be lost than gained by a nuclear explosion is a passive policy.

An active policy, however, designed to reduce the odds of proliferation by further reducing the apparent gains, would require subordinating other policy interests. If nonproliferation is worth that price, the choice is between using more carrots or more sticks. If other interests take precedence or U.S. policymakers are against taking the risk that carrots or sticks might have the wrong effect, then rhetoric on the nuclear issue should de-escalate to a level commensurate with a passive policy—Pretoria should not be continually reminded how much the United States fears its nuclear option if it is apparent that the United States will not act decisively to eliminate it. Putting the nuclear option issue in line behind Namibia, apartheid, and other concerns and deemphasizing its import does not necessarily require admitting that an overt weapons program would be tolerated. Studied nonchalance about the matter, coupled with vague low-key statements (to the effect that the South African government could not rationally see any benefits in proliferation and would invite unspecified but severe problems and sanctions if it did develop a nuclear force) would be a reasonable form of calculated ambiguity. Such ambiguity might well be the proper reply to South Africa's own calculated ambiguity, stabilizing rhetorical deterrence between Washington and Pretoria.

CHAPTER EIGHTEEN

Influencing Incentives and Capabilities

THE principal conclusion to be drawn from the country and regional case studies presented in this book is that every country is different, both in the forces that determine its policies on nuclear issues and in its susceptibility to U.S. influence. This lack of uniformity makes it difficult for the United States to formulate and execute a successful policy to check the spread of nuclear weapons. Measures that will produce desired results in one situation may not do so in another and may not even be available. Pursuing the goal of nonproliferation involves a greater sacrifice of other goals in some countries than it does in others. Nonproliferation can therefore be given high priority in policy toward some countries but must be subordinated to other goals in other areas. And because of differences in its own ability to influence events, the United States can act alone in a few countries but must seek the cooperation of others in other situations.

Whether the United States adopts a unilateral or multilateral approach, it must constantly seek the proper balance between effectiveness and consistency. If nonproliferation policy is not adjusted to the circumstances of individual countries, it may fail; on the other hand, too much differentiation among countries can be viewed as unjust discrimination and be self-defeating. This problem has its diplomatic counterpart. The more the United States emphasizes its nonproliferation goals and the harder it tries to create an international consensus in support of those goals, the less freedom it has to vary its policies toward individual countries.

The problem of pursuing the goal of nonproliferation in a complex and diverse world can best be appreciated by reviewing the various measures available to the United States. These measures are of two kinds: those designed to reduce incentives to acquire nuclear weapons and those designed to limit capabilities to make such weapons.

Measures to Reduce Incentives

For all the countries examined in this study, concern about national security is an existing or potential incentive to acquire nuclear weapons. In some cases, this concern is reinforced by the desire to gain international prestige or to win popular approval at home. The aspirations of technological or military elite groups may also be a pro-nuclear force in a few situations, although this is difficult to document.

Whatever the incentives of another country to acquire nuclear weapons, one course open to the United States is to offer counterincentives, both positive and negative. Positive inducements—such as increases in economic aid or concessions in some other aspect of bilateral relations—are not likely to be cost-effective.[1] Unless the inducement is linked specifically to nuclear policy, there can be no assurance that it will reduce the risk of proliferation. And if it is so linked, it becomes a bribe that is likely to lead to demands for further payments or concessions. Moreover, an expensive precedent is set for other countries that have—or can feign—an interest in nuclear weapons.

Negative counterincentives can be effective if the target country is heavily dependent on the United States and if it has no readily available alternative means of support. For instance, the fear of suspension of U.S. shipments of arms or nuclear fuel and equipment would work strongly against any decision by the leaders of South Korea or Taiwan to develop nuclear weapons. Where dependence is not so great, however—as in the case of Pakistan—the actual termination of arms shipments may not change nuclear policies. In some conceivable situations, the threat of sanctions of one kind or another could have an effect opposite to the desired one by arousing national indignation over U.S. infringement of sovereign rights.

1. Military aid is a special case, and its possible utility as a counterincentive is discussed later in this chapter.

Another approach for the United States is to seek to eliminate or weaken the underlying cause of another country's interest in nuclear weapons. This approach would be most feasible if the incentive for acquiring nuclear weapons was concern about national security. Dealing with a desire for international prestige or domestic approbation would be much more difficult, as would frustrating or diverting the aspirations of a technological or military elite. It is therefore fortunate that national security is by far the most important existing and potential motivation for acquiring nuclear weapons. Security assurances, moreover, can often be tailored to the circumstances of individual countries without raising questions of international equity or consistency. Concern about national security typically arises from disputes between neighboring countries. By helping to settle such disputes, the United States can hope to reduce any interest that the parties may have in nuclear weapons. Carrying out this strategy in specific situations can, however, be difficult. For example, the disagreements between Seoul and Pyongyang and between Taipei and Peking seem unlikely to be resolved soon by any means, including mediation by a third party.

The U.S. success in bringing about a peace treaty between Egypt and Israel has presumably reduced any latent Egyptian desire to possess nuclear weapons and made it less likely that the Israeli nuclear capability will surface. But the impact of the treaty on other Arab states—such as Iraq and Libya—may have been to heighten their interest in nuclear weapons. The United States may therefore have to deal one day with the unacknowledged Israeli capability or see the Middle East become the scene of a dangerous nuclear confrontation.

Where international disputes resist diplomatic solutions, U.S. defense policy can often provide effective support for nonproliferation policy. Through security commitments (or less formal assurances), force deployments, and arms transfers, the United States may be able to reduce the anxiety about security that creates an interest in nuclear weapons.

The United States has formal security commitments to six of the countries examined in this study—Japan, South Korea, Pakistan, Iran, Brazil, and Argentina—and a less formal, but nevertheless firm, commitment to ensure the survival of Israel. When the defense treaty with the Republic of China on Taiwan was terminated at the end of 1979, only a congressional expression of "grave concern" for Taiwan's security remained.

Several of the U.S. security commitments are accompanied by problems. The commitment to Pakistan does not apply to an attack by Pakistan's major enemy, India, which greatly reduces its relevance to Pakistan's nuclear policy. Whether the new revolutionary government in Iran will have much interest in a security relationship with the United States is uncertain but unlikely, to judge from present circumstances. And despite U.S. backing, Israel apparently has created an unacknowledged nuclear weapons capability.

New bilateral security commitments in the regions examined in this study do not appear to be promising means of supporting U.S. nonproliferation policy. India and the more militant Arab states would probably reject such a commitment if it were offered. Some of the conservative Arab states may be receptive in the future, but a commitment to any of them would have to be framed in a way that did not conflict with existing U.S. obligations to Israel, and this would weaken the new commitment's effect on the nuclear policy of the recipient.

The United States could conceivably become a guarantor, either alone or jointly with other powers, of a comprehensive Arab-Israeli settlement. The parties to the settlement might then feel more secure and their incentives to acquire (or, in the case of Israel, openly possess) nuclear weapons reduced. The prospects for such a settlement are not bright, however, and other conceivable occasions for multilateral security commitments (for example, in connection with an India-Pakistan agreement or an accommodation between North and South Korea) appear even more remote.

The deployment of U.S. armed forces plays a critical role in determining the credibility of American security commitments and therefore their effectiveness in reducing incentives to acquire nuclear weapons. Force deployments can also reassure countries to which the United States has made no commitment (for example, the Arab countries bordering on the Persian Gulf) by reinforcing their confidence in the international status quo. In some situations, however, deployments that reassure one country may have the opposite effect on that country's potential adversary, making the net effect of deployments on proliferation incentives unpredictable.

Strategic deployment must be perceived by U.S. allies and others as ensuring a stable state of mutual deterrence between the United States and the Soviet Union. Confidence in the U.S. ability to counter Soviet conventional power at the regional level is essential in both Northeast Asia and the Middle East.

The naval and air forces deployed by the United States in the western

Pacific are especially important in the case of Japan, which must maintain its belief that an autonomous defense policy is not in its best interest. Otherwise it may have to deal someday with the question of acquiring nuclear weapons.

In the Middle East, the chief question concerns the relative capabilities of the United States and the Soviet Union in an emergency to quickly project sufficient military power into the area to affect the local power balance. The traditional advantage of the United States has deteriorated, largely because of rising Soviet capabilities and restrictions on U.S. use of facilities in NATO countries.

The most important U.S. deployments at the local level are to South Korea. The 1977 decision (suspended in 1979) to withdraw all U.S. ground combat troops shook South Korean confidence in the stability of peace on the peninsula and increased interest in nuclear weapons. Any future U.S. withdrawals should be handled with great care to avoid adding to incentives to acquire such weapons.

Only in the cases of South America and South Asia are U.S. deployments of questionable relevance to nonproliferation policy. Brazil and Argentina do not at present need the reassurance that deployments can provide. Deployments in the Indian Ocean are not particularly reassuring to Pakistan, given the qualified nature of the U.S. security commitment, and they have in the past aroused strongly negative reactions in India.

Sales of conventional weapons for cash or through foreign military sales credits can to some extent bolster feelings of national security and reduce incentives to acquire nuclear weapons. In some situations, conventional arms are direct substitutes for nuclear weapons. (This is the case with the heavy artillery and antitank weapons that would be used by South Korean forces against attacking North Koreans.) But arms transfers usually affect attitudes toward nuclear weapons through their general contribution to the defense capabilities of recipients.

In principle, arms transfers could be used to extract promises not to acquire nuclear weapons. Although this approach at first seems appropriate for nations that have not adhered to the Treaty on the Non-Proliferation of Nuclear Weapons, explicit deals of this nature would set dangerous precedents and confront the United States with demands for arms as the price of giving up plans to develop nuclear weapons. Nor, probably, are such deals necessary. Arms transfers create a dependence on the United States for replacements and spare parts, which gives it an influence on nuclear issues that can be more powerful than any contractual rights.[2] The United States could, if necessary, threaten to end arms transfers if the recipient developed nuclear weapons.

A fundamental question concerning the use of arms transfers to check the spread of nuclear weapons is how much is enough. Presumably, the larger the transfers, the greater the results in reducing incentives to acquire nuclear weapons and in increasing U.S. leverage with recipients. But this does not answer the question of how far to go. In many cases other considerations, not directly related to proliferation, will argue in favor of restraint. The effect of arms transfers on the economies of recipients can be important. Also, the United States is committed to the objective of reducing the global traffic in arms.

As with deployments, arms transfers that can be presumed to have a desirable effect on the nuclear policies of the recipient can have the opposite effect on a neighboring country. Large arms sales to Pakistan, for instance, could make it more likely that India would develop and deploy a military nuclear capability. Thus, although U.S. defense policy affects U.S. nonproliferation goals largely through its direct impact on individual countries, possible interactions among countries must also be taken into account. If, however, one party to a dispute has clearly embarked on a nuclear weapons program, providing the other party with military support might keep it from taking the same path. (This situation could conceivably arise someday in the relationship between Brazil and Argentina.)

Similarly, the failure of U.S. nonproliferation policy in one country could have negative repercussions on the nuclear policies of other countries. The basis for the traditional fear that proliferation anywhere increases the risk of proliferation everywhere is limited, but specific connections between countries do exist. There can be no doubt, for example, that China's acquisition of nuclear weapons encouraged India to move in the same direction and that the Indian nuclear test created in Pakistan a strong interest in acquiring nuclear weapons. And if South Korea were to lose confidence in the U.S. security commitment and develop nuclear weapons, Japan would feel threatened and consider acquiring a balancing capability. Taiwan would not feel directly threatened but would be influenced by the South Korean example. The U.S. response to the South Korean

2. There may of course be relationships, such as that with Israel, in which the United States chooses not to exert its full influence.

action would be particularly important. If the United States did not apply sanctions, including suspension of arms shipments, Taipei would revise downward its estimate of the cost of developing its own nuclear weapons.

Defense policy cannot do everything, of course, nor can nonproliferation be the only consideration that shapes it. Relying heavily on the instruments of defense policy—security commitments, force deployments, and arms transfers—to deal with proliferation problems in all areas in which they arise could lead to a dangerous skewing of global strategy and to a wasteful misallocation of scarce defense assets. Moreover, extending security commitments indiscriminately would put the United States in impossible positions—regionally, by guaranteeing antagonists against one another, and globally, by becoming transparently overextended. Despite its limitations, U.S. defense policy must be judged moderately effective in supporting nonproliferation policy in two important areas, the Middle East and Northeast Asia.

In the Middle East, the informal security commitment, massive arms transfers, and a strong U.S. naval presence in the Mediterranean have made it easier for Israel to refrain from proclaiming its apparent nuclear weapons capability—an action that would be sure to arouse a strong interest in nuclear weapons in several Arab countries. Security assistance to Egypt (and to a lesser extent to Jordan and Syria) has helped substantiate the U.S. claim to a mediating role in the Arab-Israeli dispute. U.S. influence in the Middle East rests principally, however, on the fact that its ability to project military power into much of the region is superior to that of the Soviet Union. A continued decline in capabilities would reduce the capacity of the United States to work effectively for a stable peace in that part of the world and, insofar as improved prospects for peace reduce incentives to acquire nuclear weapons, would weaken its nonproliferation policy.

In Northeast Asia, the United States must try to maintain a proper relationship between defense and nonproliferation policies. The U.S. disengagement in Southeast Asia and the improvement of relations with China are bringing about changes in defense policy that have already increased the interest of South Korea and Taiwan in nuclear weapons. At least some of the U.S. tactical nuclear weapons in Korea should remain there. Clarifying U.S. defense policy in the area of Taiwan should be given high priority.

Measures to Limit Capabilities

Limiting the capabilities of states that do not now have nuclear weapons to produce such weapons requires two kinds of action: blocking the construction of facilities specifically dedicated to the production of nuclear weapons or explosive devices and preventing the misuse of civil nuclear energy facilities for military purposes.

The United States has sponsored two international efforts designed to raise obstacles to both the construction of facilities dedicated to producing nuclear weapons and the misuse of civil nuclear facilities: the nonproliferation treaty, which came into effect in 1970, and the guidelines issued by the London nuclear suppliers' group in 1978.[3] The United States has also from time to time acted unilaterally in an effort to limit capabilities to make nuclear weapons.

The country and regional case studies presented in this book throw light on both the past effectiveness of U.S. actions to limit nuclear capabilities and the feasibility of other possible future actions.

Facilities Dedicated to Nuclear Weapons

Article II of the NPT commits nonnuclear weapons states adhering to the treaty not to acquire nuclear weapons. No known violation of this provision has occurred. A number of important countries, however, have not adhered to the treaty. At least two of them, Israel and India, have facilities that can produce the explosive component of nuclear weapons. South Africa may make a third, although the evidence is not clear. And Pakistan's recently revealed effort to build a uranium enrichment plant (which would have no apparent civil use unless Pakistan acquired light water reactors) raises a question about its intentions.

The guidelines agreed to by the nuclear suppliers' group are in part an effort to make up for the incomplete coverage of the NPT. The guidelines—which are not legally binding—specify that certain items on a

3. For the text of the NPT, see Mason Willrich, *Non-Proliferation Treaty: Framework for Arms Control* (Charlottesville, Va.: Michie Co., 1969), pp. 187–96. The "Guidelines for the Export of Nuclear Material, Equipment or Technology" are reproduced in *Nuclear Power and Nuclear Weapons Proliferation,* Report of the Atlantic Council's Nuclear Fuels Policy Working Group, vol. 2 (Washington, D.C.: Atlantic Council, 1978), pp. 63–75.

"trigger list"[4] should not be exported without assurance that they would be used for peaceful purposes. The guidelines also state that such items should normally be placed under International Atomic Energy Agency safeguards.

The combined effect of the NPT and the guidelines is to make it more difficult, though by no means impossible, for a nonweapons state to build facilities for the manufacture of nuclear weapons or explosive devices. Most, possibly all, of the countries examined in this study could acquire a nuclear weapons capability if they were intent on doing so and willing to accept the costs. Some countries would have to make a major effort to circumvent controls on trade in sensitive items and technology, as Pakistan apparently has done successfully in preparing to build a centrifuge enrichment plant. Others could rely to a considerable extent on their own technical and industrial resources, as India did in developing its nuclear explosive device.

Tighter controls should make it more difficult for a given nonweapons state to build nuclear weapons facilities. Whether the various supplier nations would agree to strengthen the guidelines and make them legally binding is uncertain, however. Even if this could be achieved, no impenetrable barrier to the transfer of sensitive nuclear technology could be established. An inevitable consequence of the spread of civil nuclear energy facilities is a continual increase in the technological capabilities of more and more countries.

The fact that efforts to limit capabilities to build weapons facilities cannot be completely successful does not mean that they should be abandoned. Instead it is imperative to reduce incentives to acquire nuclear weapons.

Civil Nuclear Energy Facilities

No country has thus far acquired a nuclear weapons capability by diverting civil nuclear energy facilities to military purposes.[5] The possibility of such diversion has, however, been a matter of international concern since nuclear fission was first exploited as a source of energy. The United

4. The list includes, among other items, reactors, reprocessing plants, enrichment plants, and critical components of such facilities.
5. India is a borderline case in two respects. The plutonium for its explosive device was obtained from a research reactor, not a power reactor, and the Indian government insists that the device was not a weapon.

States has from the beginning insisted on the safeguarding of facilities and materials supplied to other countries under agreements for cooperation in the field of atomic energy. When the IAEA was established in 1957, it was made a party to these agreements and given responsibility for the administration of safeguards.

Article III of the NPT internationalized the system of safeguards by requiring nonnuclear weapons states adhering to the treaty to accept safeguards on "all source or special fissionable material." All parties to the treaty undertook not to supply such material, or equipment for its processing, use, or production, to any nonnuclear weapons state except under safeguards. This last provision has had the effect of applying safeguards to many facilities in countries that have not adhered to the NPT. Moreover, the provision has been reinforced by the guidelines, which were subscribed to by France, the only major nuclear supplier not a party to the NPT.

The system of safeguards could be made more nearly universal by inducing more countries to sign and ratify the NPT, or if they were not willing to do that, to accept full-scope safeguards—that is, safeguards on all of their nuclear facilities. For a variety of reasons brought out in the country case studies, it seems unlikely that the treaty will gain many more adherents. The United States and some other suppliers have therefore been placing greater emphasis on full-scope safeguards.[6] This effort (by West Germany) has succeeded in the case of Brazil but has thus far failed in some other important instances, including India and Argentina.

The establishment of nuclear-weapon-free zones can in principle be used to extend the coverage of safeguards, as well as to reinforce the NPT's effort to check the spread of nuclear weapons. The establishment of such zones in South Asia, the Middle East, and Latin America would clearly be useful. One is less needed in Northeast Asia because all the nonnuclear weapons states in that area have adhered to the NPT.[7]

Prospects for creating a nuclear-weapon-free zone in South Asia will remain poor as long as India continues to insist that all of Eurasia be in-

6. The Nuclear Non-Proliferation Act of 1978, subject to specified exceptions, makes the acceptance of full-scope safeguards a condition of continued nuclear exports to nonnuclear weapons states (sec. 306).

7. The United States and South Korea would presumably not support the creation of such a zone as long as U.S. tactical nuclear weapons remain in South Korea.

cluded in the zone. Establishing a nuclear-free zone in the Middle East could be a means of dealing with the unacknowledged Israeli nuclear weapons capability. However, priority must probably be given to the resolution of other more pressing issues between Israel and the Arab countries. The most promising area for creating a nuclear-free zone is Latin America. The United States should do what it can to bring the Treaty of Tlatelolco, which calls for such a zone, into full effect.

The U.S. government does not consider the universal application of safeguards sufficient protection against the misuse of civil nuclear energy facilities for military purposes. Safeguards are designed to provide timely warning of the diversion of nuclear material. They can be expected to work when they are applied to reactors and related facilities containing natural uranium, lightly enriched uranium, or spent nuclear fuel. Reprocessing plants that produce plutonium and enrichment plants that can produce weapons-grade uranium are another matter. Misuse of such plants could occur with little or no warning. U.S. nonproliferation policy has therefore recently emphasized checking the spread of reprocessing and enrichment plants, especially the former. Plans to reprocess spent fuel from U.S. commercial reactors have been suspended indefinitely, and a strong effort has been made to get other countries to do likewise. Because the economics of fast breeder reactors depend on reprocessing, the United States has also urged that the construction of such reactors on a commercial scale be deferred.

The United States has not relied solely on persuasion to gain support for its policies. On occasion, it has used its legal rights under bilateral agreements to restrict the reprocessing of spent fuel of U.S. origin. Moreover, the Nuclear Non-Proliferation Act of 1978 established tighter rules for the export of nuclear materials and called for the renegotiation of bilateral agreements to increase U.S. controls. At the same time, the United States took the lead in organizing the International Nuclear Fuel Cycle Evaluation, which was designed to create a broader international consensus on the relationship between civil nuclear energy and the possible spread of nuclear weapons capabilities.

Many countries do not share U.S. fears concerning the spread of reprocessing and enrichment plants to more countries. The desire to reprocess spent nuclear fuel is widespread, both as a means of facilitating the disposal of radioactive waste and as a means of obtaining plutonium to be recycled as nuclear fuel. Concrete evidence in support of this is provided by several of the countries examined in this study:

—Japan has built a pilot reprocessing plant, has plans for commercial reprocessing and enrichment plants, and has contracted for the reprocessing of substantial quantities of spent fuel in England and France.

—South Korea and Taiwan were induced to abandon reprocessing projects only by U.S. pressure.

—India has two small reprocessing plants.

—Pakistan is attempting to build both a reprocessing plant and an enrichment plant.

—South Africa has been developing an enrichment capability.

—Brazil has contracted to buy both reprocessing and enrichment facilities from West Germany.

—Argentina is building a reprocessing plant.

The United States clearly will not find it easy to achieve its goals of deferring the reprocessing of spent fuel and checking the spread of sensitive fuel cycle facilities to more nonnuclear weapons states.

Problems of the 1980s and Beyond

The year 1980 is an important one for U.S. nonproliferation policy. The International Nuclear Fuel Cycle Evaluation (INFCE) ended in February, and the second conference to review the nonproliferation treaty will open in August. The INFCE was not intended to arrive at specific agreements on solutions to problems of nuclear energy policy, and it did not do so. Thus the United States faces the problem of how best to build on its analytical achievements. Coming so soon after the INFCE, the NPT review conference presents both the opportunity to achieve further international understanding and the danger of divisive controversy over the future of nuclear energy.

The United States also faces a number of specific problems that may come to a head in the near future. Among these are how to deal with Pakistan's evident intention to acquire at least a near-nuclear weapons capability, whether to continue to supply India's Tarapur reactor with fuel if India does not accept full-scope safeguards, and what criteria to apply in ruling on applications to ship spent fuel of U.S. origin from Japan to reprocessing plants in France and the United Kingdom. Some of the renegotiations of bilateral agreements, required by the 1978 Nuclear Non-Proliferation Act, may also soon reach critical junctures. The next few years promise to be a time in which U.S. nonproliferation policy will be so buffeted by immediate events and crises that dealing with fundamental problems will be difficult.

One such problem, to which there can never be a final solution, is that of priorities. In bilateral dealings with other nations, how much damage to other U.S. interests should be accepted to achieve nonproliferation goals? There can be no one answer to this question, but too much variation in U.S. responses to challenges to its nonproliferation policy can create difficulties.[8] In principle, the problem of consistency of response could be made more manageable by developing multilateral sanctions, but the feasibility of such an approach in the near future cannot be rated very high. Reaching agreement on significant sanctions for violators of the NPT would be hard enough; doing so in the case of potential proliferators that have not adhered to the NPT would be even more difficult.

The question of priorities arises in a multilateral context in the field of energy policy. The United States is sometimes accused of inconsistency in advocating the development of substitutes for imported oil and at the same time interfering with efforts to exploit allegedly more efficient methods of producing nuclear energy.

Another fundamental problem, which may become more acute, is that of discrimination between different categories of countries. The distinction between states that have nuclear weapons and states that do not lies at the heart of the NPT. The nonweapons states adhering to the NPT gave up their right to acquire nuclear weapons but received explicit recognition in article IV of their "inalienable right . . . to develop research, production and use of nuclear energy for peaceful purposes without discrimination and in conformity with articles I and II" of the treaty. To the extent that the United States is perceived as violating the letter or spirit of this commitment, its nonproliferation policies will encounter resistance. Drawing new distinctions between categories of nonnuclear weapons states could be particularly controversial.

To deal successfully with the problems that lie ahead, the United States may well have to take the lead in constructing new international arrange-

8. For example, the restrained U.S. reaction to India's nuclear test explosion (and the virtual ignoring of Israel's unacknowledged capability) must complicate efforts to induce Pakistan to stop work on enrichment and reprocessing facilities.

ments to channel the growth of civil nuclear energy.[9] Such a regime would build on the major elements of the present regime: the NPT and the IAEA safeguards. Countries not willing to adhere to the NPT might in some cases be induced to accept full-scope safeguards, and the effectiveness of safeguards might be strengthened by seeking wider agreement on the rules of trade in nuclear materials and technology.[10]

Steps could also be taken to strengthen the assurance of nuclear fuel supply, on the ground that anxiety about supply provides incentives to build national reprocessing and enrichment facilities. If establishing a nuclear fuel bank—the United States has proposed that one be created to assume the function of supplier of last resort—proves to be impracticable, agreement might be sought on a system whereby fuel suppliers would guarantee one another's supply contracts against specified contingencies.

Reducing national inventories of spent fuel would be desirable for nonproliferation because of the plutonium contained in spent fuel and because mounting stocks of spent fuel increase the pressure for reprocessing. Providing storage for spent fuel will increasingly become a problem for many countries, so some would be happy to have it taken off their hands, although others would want to be assured that they could eventually recover the plutonium and residual uranium in spent fuel or be paid for it. An ideal solution would be to require the return of spent fuel to the country of origin.[11] This is the Soviet practice. It is unlikely to be adopted generally by other suppliers, although its application in sensitive areas, such as the Middle East, would be highly desirable.

The United States has made a limited offer to accept other countries' spent fuel on a voluntary basis.[12] It would be useful to act on this offer and to get other suppliers to do likewise. But popular misgivings in the United States and other supplier countries are likely to severely limit this means of reducing inventories of spent fuel in fuel-importing countries.

9. The possible nature of such arrangements is considered in detail in another Brookings study that is nearing completion.

10. The guidelines agreed to by the nuclear suppliers' group could provide a starting point for such an agreement.

11. Insofar as spent fuel from the dominant light water reactors is concerned, the countries of origin are by definition enrichers and already have the means of producing the explosive component of nuclear weapons.

12. Remarks of the President at the Plenary Session of the International Nuclear Fuel Cycle Evaluation, White House press release, October 19, 1977.

Another possible outlet for spent fuel would be to build multinational storage facilities. The need is most likely to arise first in Northeast Asia. South Korea and Taiwan would definitely be interested in a regional spent fuel storage depot, possibly as a first step in establishing a regional nuclear service center. Japan would be more cautious and, for political reasons, would want at least the United States and possibly other Pacific countries to participate in the enterprise. The need for a multinational storage facility is much less and the prospects for cooperation in establishing it are less bright in the other regions examined in this study.

As the world enters the 1980s, enrichment and reprocessing pose the most difficult questions for the United States. The two principal problems for nonproliferation policy are whether the U.S. effort to defer all reprocessing should be continued and where the line against the further spread of national enrichment and reprocessing plants should be drawn.

The argument for holding out against reprocessing is essentially that the United States still can exert effective influence on the nuclear energy policies of other noncommunist countries and that in time those countries will come around to the U.S. point of view. This influence of course derives largely from the United States' legal control over the disposition of a large part of the spent fuel accumulating in noncommunist nations and from its dominant position in the supply of enrichment services. The hope that others will share its opposition to reprocessing rests on the judgment that the fast breeder reactors under development in several countries will prove not to be competitive with other sources of energy. If no breeders are installed, the major prospective need for plutonium will disappear along with the strongest argument for reprocessing.

The contrary argument is, first, that U.S. leverage is declining as its dominance in supplying enrichment services is eroded by others and that in any case full use of U.S. leverage would be too costly politically.[13] Second, the countries developing breeders are not likely to abandon them lightly after years of effort and heavy investments of both money and prestige. If necessary, those countries may rationalize the breeders on

13. In 1978 the United States had 93 percent of the commercial enrichment capacity outside the Soviet Union. By 1985 the U.S. share is expected to fall to 64 percent. "Uranium Enrichment Present Position," paper prepared by the United States of America for Working Group 3–Supply Assurances, International Nuclear Fuel Cycle Evaluation Program (March 24, 1978), pp. 4–5.

grounds of energy security, even though they may not be competitive in purely economic terms.[14] It may therefore be prudent to use such leverage as is now available to achieve international support for restrictions on the spread of national reprocessing and enrichment plants and for the establishment of an international plutonium management system.

Confining national enrichment and reprocessing plants to states with nuclear weapons is politically impossible. Such facilities already exist elsewhere, and extending the discrimination inherent in the NPT to these important areas of nuclear technology would certainly be unacceptable to the nonnuclear weapons states. Drawing a new line between advanced industrialized countries with large civil nuclear energy programs and all other nonweapons states would not be feasible, either. Of the countries examined in this study, only Japan would benefit from such an approach. The others would resent and resist it.

An approach that is not explicitly discriminatory would be to try to discourage the construction of small reprocessing and enrichment plants because they are demonstrably inefficient economically. To the extent that this approach succeeded, the number of sensitive fuel cycle facilities would be smaller than would otherwise be the case—a definite gain for nonproliferation.

Countries, such as Japan, that have large civil nuclear energy programs might well support this approach. The cooperation of other countries with smaller programs, such as South Korea and Taiwan, might also be obtained, especially if they were given the opportunity to participate in multinational reprocessing and enrichment enterprises.[15] The nuclear policies of the new leaders in Iran are uncertain, but there is no apparent reason for their opposing a large plant policy. Iran is already an investor in Eurodif, which is building a large enrichment plant in France.

Several of the countries examined in this study, however, either have or plan to build small reprocessing or enrichment plants, or both. In this category are India, Pakistan, South Africa, Brazil, and Argentina. It might be possible to induce Brazil and Argentina to join in a binational re-

14. The fate of fast breeder reactors is not all that is involved. Japan is well along in the development of an advanced thermal reactor designed to use mixed oxide fuel (uranium oxide and plutonium oxide).

15. South Korea and Taiwan would probably be satisfied to do without national reprocessing and enrichment for a considerable period if their nuclear fuel supply was assured and if they were given help in solving the problem of storing spent fuel.

processing enterprise (which would probably be of medium size rather than large). Brazil might conceivably also give up its plans for an enrichment plant and join in a multinational enterprise (probably in Europe) that employed a more efficient technology than the jet-nozzle process that Brazil has contracted to buy from West Germany.[16] Obtaining the cooperation of India, Pakistan, or South Africa in a large plant policy appears unlikely at present.

With the exception of Libya, which is getting a power and desalinization reactor from the Soviet Union, the Middle Eastern and North African countries west of Iran have not yet entered the age of civil nuclear energy. Because of the potential volatility of this part of the world, the United States and other suppliers would be wise to insist on a no-reprocessing commitment in selling reactors and fuel there.

Participation in large multinational enrichment and reprocessing enterprises could provide an alternative to small national facilities. The advantage of a multinational facility is that the partners in such an enterprise would presumably watch one another and prevent any of their number from misusing the facility for military purposes. This advantage is only partly lessened by the possibility that multinational facilities would be a means of transmitting sensitive technology to countries that had not previously possessed it. The problem, however, is only one of time. Experience has shown that barriers against the international dissemination of technology are eventually circumvented.

Even if the number of new reprocessing plants could be limited, and even if some of those that were built were under multinational control, the need for an international plutonium management system would still exist. In part, this means safeguarding reprocessing plants and other facilities handling plutonium. It also means establishing both international policies governing the use of plutonium and machinery for carrying out those policies. The objective should be to strike a balance between economic and security goals. Economically important uses of plutonium should be approved, but exposure of plutonium in transit and at fuel cycle facilities should be minimized. Use of plutonium in research projects (other than those involving explosive devices) should probably be approved. The recycling of plutonium as fuel in fast breeder reactors should also be

16. Argentina is committed to heavy water reactors and does not need enrichment services.

approved or the rationale for such reactors would be destroyed. The most difficult and controversial problem is posed by the present generation of thermal reactors. To permit thermal recycling of plutonium would involve excessive exposure of this potentially dangerous substance along many transport lines and at many nuclear facilities scattered widely around the world.[17]

International policies on the use of plutonium might best be applied by requiring that all separated plutonium be placed in depositories controlled by the IAEA.[18] Authority for this step can be found in a thus-far unused provision of the IAEA statute.[19] Withdrawals from depositories would be allowed only for approved uses.

Reaching agreement on the location and management of plutonium depositories would be a complex process, but there is no reason to assume that the problems could not be solved if the question of what uses to approve could be settled. The real sticking point would be thermal recycling of plutonium. Countries, including most of those examined in this study, that have no plans to install breeders could be expected to resist giving up the option of thermal recycling, even though it is at best marginally economic at present uranium prices. They might be more disposed to agree, however, if they were provided with a market for any plutonium separated from their spent fuel.

Other inducements (and at least the implicit threat of restrictive leverage) would probably also have to be offered to bring some countries into the international plutonium management system. Under the best of circumstances, there might well be some holdouts. Countries that saw a national reprocessing capability as a means of moving closer to the acquisition of nuclear weapons would try to stay out. Other countries might see the new system as a threat to their national sovereignty and choose an independent path. Whether enough countries could be brought into the

17. The advanced thermal reactors being developed in Japan are an intermediate case. They are designed to burn plutonium and, by analogy with the breeder, plutonium recycling in them might be permitted.

18. This has been suggested by the IAEA Secretariat and others. IAEA Secretariat, "International Management and Storage of Plutonium and Spent Fuel," July 1978. See also Russell W. Fox and Mason Willrich, "International Custody of Plutonium Stocks: A First Step Toward an International Regime for Sensitive Nuclear Energy Activities," Working Paper of the International Consultative Group on Nuclear Energy (Rockefeller Foundation and Royal Institute of International Affairs, November 1978).

19. Statute of the International Atomic Energy Agency, article XII, sec. A.5.

system to make it worthwhile could be determined only by making the attempt.

The United States cannot expect to be totally successful in its efforts to prevent the further spread of nuclear weapons. Its ability to influence the nuclear policies of many countries is limited, and the need to pursue other goals simultaneously often prevents giving the goal of nuclear non-proliferation top priority. It can, however, realistically hope to slow the rate at which other nations acquire either a near-nuclear weapons capability or the weapons themselves.

The United States does have effective leverage with some potential proliferators. Moreover, by reducing anxiety about security it can sometimes substantially reduce incentives to acquire nuclear weapons. Dealing with the near-nuclear problem requires broad cooperation with other nations. The United States should take the lead in developing new forms of international cooperation that will make the misuse of sensitive civil nuclear energy facilities less likely.

Index

Abu Dhabi, 344
Acheson, Dean, 262n
Adelman, Kenneth L., 294n, 295n, 298n
Advanced thermal reactors, 19, 20
Afghanistan: crisis over Pushtunistan, 126–27; Soviet invasion, 126, 130, 361, 363
Agency for the Prohibition of Nuclear Weapons in Latin America (OPANEL), 256
Ahmad, Aziz, 100
Ahmad, Mohammed, 93n
Ailleret, Charles, 149
Aircraft: adapted for nuclear-capable delivery system, 276; Argentina, 276; Brazil, 276; China, 122; Israel, 232; Japan, 11; ROK, 54; South Africa, 293; Soviet Union, 10–11; U.S. sales to India, 165; U.S. sales to Pakistan, 347, 350, 354
Air Self Defense Force, Japan, 11, 14
Algeria: nuclear-capable delivery system, 231; radical coup, 198; relations with other Arab states, 191
Ali, Khalid, 114n
Ali, Mehrunnisa, 344n
Ali, Salamat, 103n, 222n
Allen, James H., 93n, 96n, 101n, 104n, 285n, 289n
Amazon Pact, 266
Amin, Hafizullah, 127
Anderson, Jack, 134
Angola, 294n, 295, 296, 302
Angra reactor, 245, 383, 389, 391
Apartheid, 283, 301, 305, 398
Arab states: capacity for nuclear tech-

nology, 180; conflict with Israel, 177, 178, 183–91; conflicts among, 177–79, 191–93; conservative-radical split, 192; controlling nuclear forces in, 232–33; conventional arms status, 200–02; covert nuclear programs, 204; internal instability, 178–79, 182–83, 198–200, 375–76; military strength, 185–86; nuclear terrorist threats from, 200; nuclear weapons potential, 234–36; potential for nuclear cooperation among, 217–20; technical skills, 215, 217, 218, 219–20; third world nuclear exports to, 220–25. See also Middle East; individual Arab countries
Argentina, 3; arms buildup, 267; Atucha reactor, 247, 248, 391; defense expenditures, 267–68; denial of nuclear supplies and technology to, 385–86; energy program, 258–61; foreign agreements for nuclear reactors, 247–50; foreign policy, 251–54; GNP, 251; military balance with Brazil, 268–69; national defense policies, 261, 264–67; national goals, 250–51, 254; nuclear-capable delivery system, 276; nuclear safeguards, 386–88; as nuclear supplier, 224, 271–72, 278; as nuclear user, 270–71; nuclear weapons options, 242, 269–70, 274–77; opposition to NPT, 254–55, 257, 279, 389; population, 251; potential nuclear testing by, 274; and Treaty of Tlatelolco, 255–56, 258; and U.S., 253, 262, 384, 390–95

Arms control, 147–49
Aronson, Shlomo, 188, 189, 190, 205, 226, 237n
Assad, Hafiz al-, 199
Aswan Dam, 211, 214
Atkinson, Bob, 294n
Atomic Energy Commission, India, 138, 140, 331
Atomic Energy Commission, U.S., 211
Atomic Energy Council, ROK, 80
Atomic Energy of Canada, Ltd., 67
Atoms for Peace, 88, 99, 213, 377
Atucha reactor, 247, 248, 391
Australia, agreements with Japan, 30, 46
Ayub Khan, Mohammed, 113, 361
Aziz, Qutubuddin, 361n

Baker, Pauline H., 290n
Baluchistan, 126, 132–33
Bangladesh, 119, 126
Barber, Richard J., 99n
Barber, Simon, 109n
Barnds, William J., 121n, 126n, 129n, 341n
Barre, Raymond, 404
Baruch plan, 2
Batista, Paulo Nogueira, 244, 245
Beaton, Leonard, 152n
Bechtel Corporation, 379
Becker, Abraham S., 198n
Becker aerodynamic jet-nozzle process, 243, 278, 289
Benjamin, Milton R., 98n, 102n, 250n, 304n, 403n
Benoit, Emile, 152n, 155n
Betts, Richard K., 294n, 297n, 355n, 365n
Bhabha, Homi, 87, 88n, 91, 95, 111, 119, 137
Bhargava, G. S., 99n, 120n, 121n, 162n, 163n, 340
Bhatia, Shyam, 91n, 101n
Bhutto, Mir Murtaza, 128n
Bhutto, Zulfikar Ali, 110; and China, 349; on nuclear guarantees, 113–14, 356–57; nuclear program, 113, 141; ouster, 126, 330; on relations with India, 128
Bianchi, Mario, 124n
Binder, David, 103n, 339n, 378n, 381n
Birkby, Carel, 286n
Bissell, Richard E., 292n
Blood, Archer K., 347n, 353n

Borders, William, 108n, 340n, 347n, 361n, 363n
Boskma, P., 289n
Botha, Pieter W., 291, 294
Bracken, Paul, 168n
Bradford, Peter, 332
Bradsher, Henry S., 301n
Braibanti, Ralph, 129n
Branigan, William, 194n, 325n
Braun, Dieter, 183n
Braunthal, Gerald, 138n
Bray, Frank T. J., 137n, 163n
Brazil, 3; Angra reactor, 245, 383, 389, 391; civil nuclear program, 242–47; defense expenditures, 267–68; denial of nuclear supplies and technology to, 385–86; energy program, 258–61; foreign policy, 251–54; GNP, 251; military balance with Argentina, 268–69; in multinational nuclear enterprises, 423; national defense policies, 261, 264–67; national goals, 250–51, 254; nuclear agreements with West Germany, 220, 224, 243–47, 272–73, 377–84; nuclear-capable delivery system, 276; nuclear safeguards, 386–88; as nuclear supplier, 224–25, 271–73, 278; as nuclear user, 270–71; nuclear weapons options, 242, 269–70, 274–77; opposition to NPT, 254–55, 257, 279, 389; population, 251; potential nuclear testing by, 274; ratification of Treaty of Tlatelolco, 255–56, 258, 270; relations with U.S., 252, 378–84, 390–95
Brennan, Donald G., 162
British Nuclear Fuels, Ltd. (BNFL), 29, 68, 209
Brody, Richard, 183n
Brown, George S., 72n
Brown, Harold, 172, 197, 374, 395
Brown, Warren, 301n
Brzezinski, Zbigniew, 186n, 373n
Buchan, Alastair, 152n
Burnham, David, 379n
Burns, John F., 284n, 403n
Burrell, R. M., 133n
Burt, Richard, 114n, 115n, 207n, 303n, 334n, 347n, 350n, 403n
Bustin, Edouard, 292n, 299n, 300n

Cahn, Anne Hessing, 105n
Callaghan, James, 108
Canada: nuclear agreements with India, 95, 97–98, 107–08, 110; nuclear

agreements with Japan, 30; nuclear agreements with Pakistan, 100, 335; nuclear safeguards and, 330; ROK uranium purchases from, 49
Canadian deuterium and uranium reactor (CANDU), 17n; for India, 88n, 96, 109, 329; for Pakistan, 100; proposed for Argentina, 248; for ROK, 48
Canadian General Electric Company, 100
Carlton, David, 294n
Carter administration: and apartheid, 301; arms to Egypt and Israel, 202; on commercialization of plutonium breeder, 371; efforts to prevent global plutonium leasing, 86; and India, 125; suspension of arms sales to South Africa, 293
Carter, Jimmy: and Brazil–West Germany nuclear agreement, 380–84; deferred withdrawal of troops from ROK, 51; Middle East policy, 374; and nuclear exports to India, 331–34; and Nuclear Non-Proliferation Act of 1978, 30; order on nuclear exports environmental impact, 330; pledge on nuclear weapons use, 342–43; on plutonium as energy source, 28; on South African nuclear testing, 301; on U.S. relations with Taiwan, 72
Castelo Branco, Humberto, 265, 266, 270
Central Intelligence Agency, 291, 349n, 353n
Central Treaty Organization (CENTO), 359, 360, 361
Centrifuge enrichment process, 19, 289
Cervenka, Zdenek, 287n, 289n, 290n, 402n
Chagla, M. C., 356
Chamberlain, Donald F., 108n
Chari, P. R., 299n, 333n
Chatterjee, Basant, 356n
Chiang Ching-kuo, 70
Chien, Frederick, 70
China, People's Republic of, 2, 8; and India, 120–21, 339; "no-first-use" pledge, 122; nuclear explosion, 137; and Pakistan, 349; reaction to ROK nuclear weapons acquisition, 58–60; satellite launching, 137; and Soviet Union, 37–39; and Taiwan, 37–38, 71–77, 78; and U.S., 40–41
Chopra, Maharaj J., 97n, 112n, 362n

Choudhury, G. W., 113n, 361n
Chou En-lai, 78n
Christopher, Warren, 115n, 381, 382
Chubin, Shahram, 142n, 158n, 170n, 183n
Chu, David S. L., 68n, 69n
Chungshan Institute of Science and Technology, Taiwan, 79–80
CIRUS reactor, 95, 204
Civil nuclear energy, 1; adaptations for military, 85, 415–18; in Argentina, 260; in Brazil, 242–47, 260; cost effectiveness, 90, 209–10; as cover for military program, 204–05; energy saving from, 86–87; in Japan, 15–20, 27; plans for channeling, 419–20; in ROK, 47–50; safeguards for, 2, 27, 44, 416–17; in Taiwan, 66–69
Claiborne, William, 157n
CNEA. See National Atomic Energy Commission, Argentina
Cohen, Barry, 293n
Cohen, Stephen P., 130n, 136n, 139n, 140n, 165n, 345n
Compagnie Générale des Matières Nucléaires (COGEMA), 29, 209, 211
Conant, Melvin A., 336n
Cordesman, Anthony H., 185n
Coredif, 336
Cottrell, Alvin J., 133n, 343n, 359n
Couto e Silva, Golbery do, 265n
Crocker, Chester, 286n, 287n, 292n
Cuba: role in Middle East, 195, 199; and South Africa, 294; and Treaty of Tlatelolco, 255, 257, 288
Culwick, A. T., 296n

Dal, Pratap C., 163n
Das, Sitanshu, 130n
Daud Khan, Muhammed, 126
Dayan, Moshe, 186, 187
Defense expenditures: Argentina, 267–68; Brazil, 267–68; Egypt, 230; India, 125, 155; Iran, 158; Israel, 230; Jordan, 230; Pakistan, 124; Syria, 230
de Guiringaud, Louis, 288
de Onis, Juan, 383n
Desai, Manilal Jagdish, 123–24
Desai, Morarji, 98n, 138, 339; on nuclear explosion, 112, 323; opposition to nuclear weapons program, 123–24, 139, 356; on safeguards, 108, 130; on U.S. nuclear exports to India, 331–34

Desalinization. *See* Water desalinization projects

Developing countries: economic rationale for nuclear energy programs, 86; need for breeder reactors, 89; nuclear exports to Arab nations, 220–25; scientific and technology equality for, 87–88

Dhan, Ram, 342

Doder, Dusko, 351n, 361n

Dougherty, James E., 115n, 343n

Duchêne, François, 373n

Dunn, Lewis A., 105n, 115n, 160n, 167n, 168n, 327n, 346n, 350n

Dwivedi, O. P., 88n, 90n

Ebinger, Charles K., 100n, 102n, 110n, 112n, 113n, 114n, 346n, 349n

Egypt, 3; arms buildup, 201, 202; defense budget, 230; nuclear-capable delivery system, 231; nuclear energy research, 177; peace treaty with Israel, 178, 372–73, 409; planned nuclear development, 206–07; radical coup, 198; relations with other Arab states, 191; reprocessing agreement with U.S., 211; water desalinization, 214

Eisenhower, Dwight D., 213, 359

El-Khawas, Mohamed A., 293n

Endicott, John E., 21n, 27n, 31n, 33n, 34

Epstein, William, 106n, 255n, 400n

Erdman, Paul, 236n

Eshkol, Levi, 214

Euratom, 27

Eurodif, 104, 336

Evron, Yair, 201n, 373n

Farrell, William E., 297n

Fast breeder reactors: future role of, 423–24; India's, 90, 96; proposed Japanese, 19, 20

Fialka, John J., 303n

Ford administration: and nuclear exports, 378, 402; and nuclear safeguards, 371

Ford, Gerald R., 27

Foreign aid, U.S. restrictions on, 352–53

Fourie, Deon, 295n

Fox, Judith B., 93n, 96n, 101n, 104n, 285n, 289n

Fox, Russell W., 424n

France, 2; cost of weapons program,

230; Dimona reactor, 205, 220, 234, 368; nuclear assistance to Iraq, 134, 368; nuclear deterrence, 161; plutonium reprocessing agreement with Japan, 29–30; plutonium reprocessing agreement with Pakistan, 101–02, 328; reactor sales to South Africa, 403, 404; role in Middle East, 195

Freed, Kenneth J., 353n

FROG rocket, 231

Frye, Alton, 355n

Fukuda, Takeo, 28

Furlong, R. D. M., 343n, 359n

Gall, Norman, 110n

Gallois, Pierre, 149–50, 231

Gandhi, Indira, 124, 137, 138; defeat of, 337; and nuclear tests, 111, 113, 334; return to power, 143; and U.S., 119

Gandhi, Mohandas K., 136

Geisel, Ernesto, 243, 244

Gelb, Leslie H., 347n

General Agreement on Tariffs and Trade, 253–54

Gervasi, Sean, 293n

Gilinsky, Victor, 328, 332

Gillette, Robert, 90n

Giscard d'Estaing, Valéry, 102, 297

Glenn, John H., 329

Glennon, Michael J., 358n

Global bipolarity, 147

Goheen, Robert F., 362

Gold, Fern Racine, 336n

Goldschmidt, Bertrand, 336

Gompert, David C., 146n

Goshko, John M., 361n

Gromyko, Andrei, 166n

Gross national product (GNP): Argentina, 251; Brazil, 251; India, 118, 152n, 155

Ground Self Defense Force, Japan, 12, 14

Gupta, Bhabani Sen, 109n, 137n, 138n, 140n

Gutteridge, William, 294n

Gwertzman, Bernard, 343n, 403n

Haddad, Naim, 134

Handa, Rohit, 120n

Handel, Michael I., 373n

Hansen, Bert, 198n

Harrison, Selig S., 127n, 139n

Hasan, Khurshid, 360n

Heavy water reactors: Argentina, 247;

India, 90, 96; proposed for Pakistan, 102; proposed for ROK, 48, 49; Taiwanese interest in, 67
Heikal, Mohamed, 115, 184, 192n, 199n, 206n
Henderson, P. D., 88n
Hoagland, Jim, 288n, 404n
Hoogendoorn, Jan C., 286n
Horton, Frank P., III, 139n, 347n
Hovey, Graham, 301n, 383n, 384n
Howe, Marvine, 379n
Huntington, Samuel P., 136n
Hyder, Tariq Osman, 89n

India, 1, 3; alliance ties with superpowers, 117; atomic energy research, 95–97; and China, 339, 355–56, 412; conventional defense system, 121–22; cost of nuclear force, 150–51, 154–57; criticism of NPT, 88, 106–07, 112; defense budget, 125, 155; as disarmament exponent, 119; economic rationale for nuclear program, 89, 91; and foreign nuclear guarantees, 355–56; GNP, 118, 152n, 155; leadership changes, 116; nuclear agreements with foreign countries, 97–98, 107; nuclear capability, 89, 117–18; nuclear expenditures, 89–90; nuclear explosion, 107–08, 111–13, 114, 118, 119; nuclear exports, 223–24; and nuclear-free zone, 342; and nuclear safeguards, 98, 108–09, 111, 130, 330, 333; nuclear weapons options, 123; opinions on nuclear weapons, 136–41; and Pakistan, 126–27, 128–31, 339–41; plutonium needs, 90–91, 99; prospects for arms control in, 148–49; security threats to, 119–23, 136, 355–56; self-sufficiency of nuclear program, 88–89, 90–91, 96–97; Sino-Pakistani relations, 361; and Soviet Union, 355–56, 362–63; space program, 153n; thorium resources, 90, 95; and U.S., 125, 330–34, 347–48, 352; utility of nuclear force, 161–65
Indo-Pakistani war, 119, 120, 127
Institute of Nuclear Energy Research (INER), Taiwan, 67; military influence on, 79–80; research, 68
Institute of Space and Aeronautical Science, Japan, 20
Inter-American Treaty of Reciprocal Assistance. See Treaty of Rio de Janeiro
Intermediate-range ballistic missiles, 122, 161
International Atomic Energy Agency (IAEA): and Brazil–West Germany agreement, 380; and India, 109; international safeguards, 2, 27, 44, 205, 220, 256, 328, 369, 386, 388, 389, 415; Japan's participation in, 45; objectives, 417; on Pakistan's nuclear program, 93, 94; and peaceful explosions, 257; proposed plutonium depositories controlled by, 424; ROK's participation in, 50; second conference of, 1980, 418; South Africa's expulsion, 399; uranium projections, 288
International Development Agency, 352–53
International Nuclear Fuel Cycle Evaluation (INFCE), 2, 18n, 29, 371; Japan's participation in, 45; on reprocessing, 327; ROK's participation, 50; South African SWU capacity, 289–90
Iran, 3; alliance ties with superpowers, 117; conflicts with Iraq, 133, 194–95; cost of nuclear force, 152–53, 154, 157–58; decisionmaking process, 142; defense budget, 158; Khomeini government, 92, 103, 194, 325; leadership changes, 116; NPT ratification, 106, 115; nuclear agreements with foreign countries, 335–36; and nuclear guarantees, 359–60; and nuclear safeguards, 110–11; and Pakistan, 343–44; prospects for arms control, 148–49; rivalry with Arab states, 179; security interests, 132–33; shah's nuclear policy, 92, 104, 110–11, 115, 325; and Soviet Union, 135; strategic role in Middle East, 193–95; uncertain future of nuclear program, 86, 91–92, 103–05, 143–44; uranium sources, 92; utility of nuclear force, 169–72
Iranian Atomic Energy Organization, 103, 104
Iraq: conflicts with Iran, 133; conventional arms buildup, 201; French nuclear assistance, 136, 368; internal instability, 198, 199; NPT ratification, 133; nuclear agreement with Brazil, 272–73; nuclear-capable de-

livery system, 231; nuclear energy research, 177; planned nuclear development, 207; relations with other Arab states, 191–93
Irredentism, 126
Isotope separation plants, 209
Israel, 1, 3, 134; arms buildup, 180, 201; conflict with Arab nations, 177, 178, 183–91, 372–73; defense budget, 230; Dimona reactor, 205, 220, 234, 368; erosion of Western support, 185, 196; military strength relative to Arabs, 185–86; nuclear-capable delivery system, 231–32; nuclear technology, 209; nuclear weapons options, 180, 188–90, 204–05, 226–27, 234–35, 367–68; peace treaty with Egypt, 178, 372, 373, 409; planned nuclear development, 207; proposed alliance with U.S., 187; proposed settlements with Arabs, 186–87, 188–90; refusal to sign NPT, 64; security threats to, 184, 297; and South Africa, 297–98, 299; water desalinization, 214

Jabber, Paul, 189, 205
Jack, Brian, 55n
Jackson, James O., 359n
Jaipal, Rikhi, 87n, 89, 107, 112, 342n
Jalloud, Abdel Salem, 206
Japan, 3, 7; civil nuclear energy, 15–20, 27, 319; conventional defense system, 35–36; defense of, 7, 10–14; dependence on imported oil, 16; in multinational uranium ventures, 45–46; mutual security treaty with U.S., 10, 33, 40, 43, 311; neutrality, 37; NPT ratification, 8, 26–27; nuclear drift, 44; nuclear policy, 25–27; nuclear ship program, 24–25, 34; nuclear weapons options, 9, 31–44; participation in INFCE, 45; plutonium agreements, 28–29; proposed enrichment and reprocessing plants, 46; public opinion on nuclear weapons, 31–32; reaction to ROK status, 38–39, 41–42, 60–61, 320–22, 412; satellite launches, 20–23; and Sino-Soviet dispute, 37–40; and Sino-U.S. relations, 40–41; strategic deterrence of SLBMs, 33–36; uranium, 16–19; and U.S. defense policy, 310–12; U.S. nuclear umbrella, 25, 36, 43, 312

Jasani, Bhupendra, 289n
Jaster, Robert S., 290n, 399n
Jayagopal, Jayashree, 123n
Jericho ballistic missile, 231
Jha, L. K., 356
Johnson, Lyndon B.: reaction to China's nuclear explosion, 355; Water for Peace program, 213, 214
Johnson, Stuart E., 10n, 54n, 73n
Jones, David C., 312n
Jordan: defense budget, 230; internal instability, 192, 201; relations with other Arab states, 191–92

Kahan, Jerome H., 275n
Kahn, Herman, 160n, 167n, 350n
Kandell, Jonathan, 101n, 382n, 383n
KANUPP reactor, 100, 335
Kapur, Ashok, 107n, 108n, 121n, 123n, 137n, 138n, 139n, 140n, 363n
Karmal, Babrak, 127
Kashmir, 340–41
Kaufman, Michael T., 127n, 399n
Kavic, Lorne J., 118n, 142n, 347n
Kemp, Geoffrey, 137n, 158n, 163n, 274n
Kerr, Malcolm H., 198n
Khalilzad, Zalmay, 92n, 93, 94, 100n, 101n, 102n, 113n, 127n, 165n, 167n, 210n, 344n, 346n, 361n
Khan, Abdul Qader, 102, 105
Khan, Asghar, 328
Khan, Munir, 113
Khomeini government, 133; nuclear policy, 92, 103, 134–35
Kissinger, Henry A., 119, 141, 325, 363n, 380
Knight, Albion W., 295n
Kohl, Wilfred L., 136n
Korea. See North Korea; Republic of Korea
Korea Electric Company, 48, 49, 319
Korea Nuclear Fuel Development Institute, 49
Koven, Ronald, 134n
Kraftwerk Union, 103, 335; contracts with Argentina, 247–48, 250, 384; contracts with Brazil, 273, 381
Kratzer, Myron B., 331n, 402n
Kraus, Charles A., 384n
Kuwait, 177; planned nuclear development, 207; relations with other Arab states, 191, 192

Lahore Atomic Energy Center, 100
Lance missile, 232

Larus, Joel, 285n, 399n
Latin America: nuclear-free zone, 255; regional conflicts, 241–42, 278. *See also* individual countries
Lawrence, Robert M., 285n, 399n
Lebanon: internal instability, 193, 198; relations with other Arab states, 191
Lee, B. W., 50n
Lewis, Bernard, 185
Lewis, Flora, 166n
Lewis, William H., 293n
Liberal Democratic Party (LDP), Japan, 26, 31
Liberia, 296
Libya: nuclear-capable delivery system, 231; nuclear energy research, 177; plans for nuclear development, 208; radical coup, 198; relations with other Arab states, 192; stockpiling of Soviet arms by, 202; water desalinization, 214, 423
Light water reactors (LWRs), 17; Brazil, 243; India, 96; multinational ventures, 45–46; need for low enriched uranium, 329; proposed for Iran, 104, 335; proposed for Japan, 19; proposed for Pakistan, 102, 334–35; proposed for ROK, 48, 49; proposed for Taiwan, 67
London nuclear suppliers' group, 44, 104, 108, 330
Long, F. A., 97n
Lovett, Robert A., 263n
Luck, Edward C., 349n

McCain, John, 296
Machel, Samora, 300n
McLaurin, R. D., 193n, 199n
Maddox, John, 123n
Madero, Carlos Castro, 247, 248, 249, 273n
Mandelbaum, Michael, 146n
Mantel, Robert, 158n
Marder, Murray, 301n
Maritime Self Defense Force, Japan, 10, 14
Martin, David C., 293n
Martin, H. J., 291
Marwah, Onkar, 88n, 89, 90n, 95n, 119n, 138, 139n, 152n, 153n, 155, 156n, 172, 245n, 292n, 364n
Mattos, Carlos de Meira, 266n, 270n
Maynard, Harold W., 164n
Mecham, L. Lloyd, 262n

Medium-range ballistic missiles: China, 122; India, 153, 164
Mellor, John W., 97n, 112n, 118n, 148n
Meyer, Charles A., 388n
Middle East: cost ineffectiveness of nuclear energy in, 209–10, 371; cost of nuclear weapons programs, 229–31; efforts to increase stability in, 372–75; nuclear-capable delivery systems, 231–32; nuclear-free zone, 342, 368; nuclear weapons options, 188–89, 226–28; plutonium recycling costs, 211; role of outside powers, 178, 181, 195–97, 366–67, 372–76, 411, 413; rules on access to nuclear explosives, 367–72; water desalinization projects, 212–15. *See also* Arab states; individual countries
Milenky, Edward S., 251n
Miller, Dane Lee, 24n
Mirchandani, G. G., 139n
Misra, K. P., 139n
Mohan, C. Raja, 112n
Mondale, Walter F., 380–81, 382
Montes, Oscar A., 270n
Moodie, Michael L., 137n
Moorer, Thomas H., 389n
Morrison, Barrie, 95n, 107n, 137n, 153n, 351n
Mossavar-Rahmani, Bijan, 92n
Mozambique, 294, 295
Mughisuddin, Mohammed, 193n, 199n
Mukerjee, Dilip, 346n
Murphy, Caryle, 286n
Murray, Roger, 399n

Namboodiri, P. K. S., 11n, 130n
Nanda, B. R., 109n
Nandy, Ashis, 138n
Nasser, Gamal Abdel, 193
National Atomic Energy Commission, Argentina (CNEA), 247, 250
National Resources Defense Council, 330
National Space Development Agency (NASDA), Japan, 20, 21
Nayar, Baldev Raj, 118, 148n, 362n
Nehru, B. K., 356
Nehru, Jawaharlal, 107, 136, 138
Niesewand, Peter, 110n, 153n
Nigeria, 293, 294
Nixon administration, arms sales to South Africa, 293
Nixon doctrine, 117, 358

Nixon, Richard M., 78n; initiative toward China, 361, 364
Nonproliferation policy, U.S., 1, 3; balanced aid and, 363–64; controlling military assistance, 346–51, 353–54, 394, 410–13; controlling nuclear fuel supplies, 329–38, 385–86, 416–17, 420–22; controlling weapons sales, 367–72; counterincentives, 408–13; diplomacy, 338–45, 365, 395; direct intervention, 364–65, 376; economic assistance, 345–46, 353–54; ineffectiveness in South Asia, 323–24; Japan, 309–12, 322; limited nuclear technical assistance, 352–53, 365, 385–86; near-nuclear weapon development, 318–20; nuclear cooperation, 390–91, 398, 401–06, 424–25; nuclear guarantees, 354–63; preventing access to fissionable material, 324–29; priorities, 419; problems, 396, 407–08; for ROK, 313–14, 322; safeguards, 385, 386–88; security assurances, 372–75, 391–95, 409–13; storage controls, 389, 420–21; for Taiwan, 314–18, 322. See also Nuclear Non-Proliferation Act of 1978; Treaty on the Non-Proliferation of Nuclear Weapons; Safeguards, nuclear
Noorani, A. G., 119n, 355n, 356n
North Atlantic Treaty Organization (NATO), 117, 169, 196, 375; coordinating use of nuclear weapons, 233; Soviet Union versus southern flank members, 179; versus Warsaw Pact forces, 52, 128, 166
North Korea: potential reaction to ROK nuclear weapons acquisition, 57–58; ROK nuclear deterrent against, 52–53
NRC. See Nuclear Regulatory Commission
Nuclear deterrence: arguments to counter, 146; proportional, 149–50, 160; stable, 147; by uncertainty, 160
Nuclear drift, 44
Nuclear energy, civil. See Civil nuclear energy
Nuclear explosions: by India, 107–08, 111–13, 114, 118, 119; IAEA safeguards and, 257; peaceful uses, 212, 273–74, 279; possible South African, 284, 300–04
Nuclear Fuel Complex, India, 96

Nuclear Non-Proliferation Act of 1978, 323, 329; provisions, 30, 61n, 352, 403, 416n, 417, 419
Nuclear Regulatory Commission (NRC), 329, 331, 334
Nuclear technology: dissemination under Atoms for Peace, 213; overlap in civilian and military, 203; safeguards as condition for export of, 371; special enrichment, 209; U.S. restrictions on, 337; U.S. secrecy on, 2
Nuclear waste disposal, 417
Nuclear-weapon-free zones: Africa, 400; Middle East, 342, 368; Southeast Asia, 342
Nuclear weapons programs: conventional defense versus, 150, 157; cost, 150–57, 229–31; cover development, 204; guarding of, 370; objectives, 226–28; types, 228–29; varied postures, 160–61
Nye, Joseph, 332
Nyerere, Julius, 284

Oberdorfer, Don, 97n, 108n, 115n, 222n, 354n, 365n
Okawa, Yoshio, 45n
Okimoto, Daniel I., 25n, 26n
Omang, Joanne, 330n
Oren, Stephen, 127n, 133n
Organization of African Unity (OAU), 292, 400
Organization of American States (OAS), 241, 263
Organization of Petroleum Exporting Countries (OPEC), 93–94
O'Toole, Thomas, 98n, 304n, 402n
Ottaway, David B., 297n
Overholt, William H., 90n, 115n, 346n

Page, Donald M., 95n, 107n, 137n, 153n, 351n
Pakistan, 3; alliance ties with superpowers, 117; and China, 361; cost of nuclear force, 150–51, 153–54, 156–57; defense expenditures, 124; disincentives for nuclear force, 131–32, 156–57; economic justification for nuclear program, 93–94; foreign arms sales to, 346–50, 353–54; and foreign nuclear guarantees, 356–58, 360–62; incentives for nuclear force, 94, 125–31, 156; and India, 114, 339–41, 412; and Iran, 343–44; leadership changes, 116; nuclear

agreements with foreign countries, 100–03, 335; nuclear exports, 221–23; and nuclear safeguards, 100, 109–10, 111; nuclear technology, 209; nuclear weapons capability, 99–100, 102–03; official opinions on nuclear weapons, 141–42; OPEC aid to, 93–94, 344–45; opposition to NPT, 106, 113; plan for nuclear testing, 114–15; prospects for arms control, 148–49; reprocessing facilities, 325–28; security threats to, 126–27, 128–31, 136; and Soviet Union, 127, 131, 360–61; uncertain future of nuclear program, 143–44; uranium deposits, 93; and U.S., 360, 362–63, 410, 412; utility of nuclear force, 166–69

Pakistan Atomic Energy Commission (PAEC), 93, 99–100, 335

Palestine Liberation Organization, 217, 375

Palit, D. K., 114n, 130n

Palkhivala, Nani A., 109n

Pan Heuristics, 86, 87, 94, 154

Pannikar, K. M., 344n

Park Chung Hee, 51n

Park, Richard L., 165n

Patil, R. L. M., 285n

Pearton, Maurice, 293n

Perón, Juan, 252

Peterson, Harold F., 262n, 264n

Pfaltzgraff, Robert L., Jr., 137n, 163n, 274n

Pierre, Andrew J., 136n, 349n

Plutonium reprocessing, 2, 50; Brazil, 244–45; economics of, 211; India, 90–91, 98–99; international fuel bank for, 336; international rules governing, 208–09; Japan, 17–19, 20; multinational cooperation, 50, 325–26, 390, 422–24; national decisions, 418; Pakistan, 101–02, 325–28; ROK, 50; U.S. policy, 27, 28, 353, 417

Pollack, Jonathan D., 122n

Poulose, T. T., 112n, 123n, 140n

Power, Paul F., 98n, 112n, 333n

Pushtunistan, 126–27

Qaddafi, Muammar, 192, 198, 199, 206, 369

Qattara project, 212

Quanbeck, Alton H., 34n

Quandt, William B., 227n

Quester, George H., 78n, 105n, 112n, 115n, 138n, 298n, 356n

Ra'anan, Uri, 137n, 163n, 274n

Ram, Mohan, 124n, 141n, 163n, 351n

Rao, R. Rama, 123n

Ray, Dixy Lee, 378

Reactors: Angra, 245, 383, 389, 391; Atucha, 247, 248; CANDU, 48, 88n, 96, 100, 109, 248, 329; CIRUS, 95, 204; Dimona, 205, 220, 234, 368; KANUPP, 100, 335; RAPP, 109; Safari, 285, 398, 402. See also Advanced thermal reactors; Fast breeder reactors; Heavy water reactors; Light water reactors

Record, Jeffrey, 169n

Republic of China (ROC). See Taiwan

Republic of Korea (ROK), 3; civil nuclear energy program, 47–50, 65; conventional defense, 54–55; defense problems, 7–8; deterrence capability, 52–53, 55–56; foreign reaction to nuclear weapons acquisition, 57–61, 65; and Japan, 38–39, 41–42, 320–22, 412; and North Korea, 52–53, 57–58; NPT ratification, 8, 50–51; nuclear fuel supply problem, 49–50; nuclear weapons options, 63–64; participation in IAEA and INFCE, 50; tank force, 54; uranium reprocessing potential, 62–63; uranium supply, 49; and U.S. defense policy, 313–14; and U.S. nuclear weapons, 8, 51, 56–57

Ribicoff, Abraham A., 329, 402n

Roett, Riordan, 252n

Rogers, Barbara, 287n, 289n, 290n, 402n

Rogerson, Anthony C., 139n, 347n

Rondeau, Jacques A., 296n

Rood, Harold W., 87n, 88n, 97n

Rosen, Steven J., 189, 205, 232n

Rotberg, Robert I., 285n, 290n, 291n, 301n, 404n

Rousseau, P. E., 286n

Roux, A. J. A., 289, 291

Rowen, Beverly, 75n

Rowen, Henry S., 166n, 183n

Sadat, Anwar, 198, 199

Saeki, Kiichi, 373n

Safari reactor, 285, 398, 402

Safeguards, nuclear: and Brazil, 246; as condition for nuclear exports, 369, 371; effectiveness, 369–71, 417; IAEA, 2, 27, 44, 205, 220, 256, 328, 369, 386, 388, 389, 415; and India, 98, 108–09, 111; and Iran, 110–11;

and Pakistan, 100, 109–10; Treaty of Tlatelolco, 256
Safran, Nadav, 191–92, 217n
SALT. *See* Strategic arms limitation talks
Sandoval, R. Robert, 168n
Sarabhai, Vikram A., 88n, 138
Sato, Eisaku, 25
Saudi Arabia: conventional arms status, 201, 202; defense budget, 230; relations with other Arab states, 191–92; and U.S., 185
Sawhny, Rathy, 344n
Schaerf, Carlo, 294n
Schlesinger, James R., 51n, 171
Schmidt, Helmut, 378, 381, 382
Schulz, Ann, 88n, 119n, 292n, 364n
Scud missile, 231, 232, 237
Self Defense Forces (SDF), Japan: capability, 10; public opinion polls on, 32; Standard Defense Force Concept and, 14
Separative work unit (SWU): Japanese capacity, 19; South African capacity, 289, 290
Sethna, H. N., 95n, 106, 331
Seth, S. P., 97n, 98n, 137n
Shahi, Agha, 114
Shastri, Lal Bahadur, 111, 355
Shearer, Lloyd, 297n
Sherwani, Latif Ahmed, 360n, 361n
Silveira, Azeredo da, 379, 380
Singer, Fred, 374n
Singh, Charan, 124
Singh, Sampooran, 152n
Smith, Colin, 101n
Smith, Gerard, 364–65, 398
Smith, J. P., 134n
Smith, Terence, 297n, 384n
Snider, Lewis W., 191n
Sondhi, M. L., 107n, 112n, 120n, 123n
South Africa, 3; arms buildup, 292–93; attempts at détente by, 296–97, 302; declining Western support, 297; economic incentives for nuclear energy, 285–87; enrichment capability, 288–89; French reactor sale to, 403, 404; and Israel, 297–98; and NPT, 291, 398–400; nuclear capability, 283, 284; nuclear cooperation with U.S., 398, 401–06; nuclear self-sufficiency, 290, 400–01; as nuclear supplier, 225, 290; nuclear weapons options, 299–300, 305; possible nuclear explosion, 284, 300–04; research reac-

tors, 285, 398, 402, 404; security threats to, 291–92, 294–95; SWU capacity, 289, 290; UN arms embargo against, 292, 293, 294, 298; uranium resources, 287–88; Western influence on, 304–05
South African Atomic Energy Board (AEB), 285, 291
South African Nuclear Fuels Corporation, 287
South Atlantic Treaty Organization, proposed, 267, 297
Southeast Asia Treaty Organization (SEATO), 360
South West Africa People's Organization (SWAPO), 298, 405
Soviet Union, 2, 8; air force, 10–11; amphibious lift capability, 12; and China, 37–39; ground forces in Siberia, 12; and India, 98, 355–56; and Iran, 135; Japan's strategic deterrence of, 33–36; nuclear umbrella for allies, 117; opposition to IAEA, 108; Pacific fleet, 10; possible reaction to ROK nuclear weapons acquisition, 58–59; potential threat to South Africa, 295; potential presence in South America, 391–92; role in Middle East, 185, 193–95, 202, 237; Scud missiles, 231, 232, 237
Space Activities Commission, Japan, 23
Spence, J. E., 285n, 291n, 399n
Standard Defense Force Concept, Japan, 13–15
Stanley, John, 293n
Stetson, John C., 359
Stobbs, John J., 93n, 96n, 101n, 104n, 285n, 289n
Strategic arms limitation talks (SALT), 147, 339
Strauss, Lewis L., 213, 214
Submarine-launched ballistic missiles: India's, 165, 167; and Japan, 34–36
Subrahmanyam, K., 88, 110, 119n, 139, 155n, 364
Surface-to-air missiles, 11n, 228, 394
Switzerland, nuclear technology for Argentina, 248, 249
SWU. *See* Separative work unit
Syed, Anwar H., 126n, 156n
Symington amendment, 353
Syria, 177; conventional arms buildup, 201–02; defense budget, 230; internal instability, 198, 199; nuclear-capable delivery system, 231; planned nu-

clear development, 208; relations with other Arab states, 191–93

Tahir-Kheli, Shirin, 100n, 119n, 129, 130n, 131n, 141n, 156n, 328n, 335n, 345n
Taipower. *See* Taiwan Power Company
Taiwan, 3; and China, 37–38, 72–77; civil nuclear energy program, 66–69, 81; foreign reaction to nuclear weapons acquisition, 78–79; near-nuclear policy, 80; NPT ratification, 8, 70; nuclear energy research, 68; nuclear weapons capability, 69–70; nuclear weapons options, 70–71; offshore islands, 76; purchase of uranium and enrichment services, 68–69; reaction to ROK and Japan nuclear weapons development, 321–22; regional approach to fuel management, 68–69; risk of U.S. sanctions against, 315, 317–18; security threats to, 7, 8, 37–38, 71–77, 298; and South Africa, 297–99; and Soviet Union, 71, 72, 78; suspension of nuclear fuel reprocessing in, 79; and U.S., 72, 78, 80, 81, 187n, 314–18, 409
Taiwan Power Company, 67, 68, 319
Tank forces: Israel, 180; ROK, 54
Tanzania, 284, 293
Taraki, Nur Mohammed, 127
Tarapur power project, India, 91, 96, 329, 331–34
Tattinger, Pierre Christian, 297
Tavora, Virgilio, 244n
Taylor, David, 286n
Teltsch, Kathleen, 342n
Teng Hsiao-ping, 339
Third world. *See* Developing countries
Thomas, K. T., 112n
Thorium-based breeders, 90
Thornton, Richard C., 348n, 362n
Tikka Khan, 114n
Tokai-Mura plutonium reprocessing plant, 28–29
Tomura, Tetsuo, 49n
Treaty for the Prohibition of Nuclear Weapons in Latin America. *See* Treaty of Tlatelolco
Treaty of Rio de Janeiro: provisions, 262–63; relevance to nuclear weapons, 263–64; U.S. obligations under, 393, 394, 395–96
Treaty of Tlatelolco: Cuba and, 255, 257; provisions, 256–57, 387–88; ratification, 255–56, 384; safeguards, 386; U.S. and, 377
Treaty on the Non-Proliferation of Nuclear Weapons (NPT), 2, 411; future agreements, 418–20, 422; guidelines, 414–15; opposition to, 64, 88, 106–07, 112, 113, 226, 254–55, 257, 291, 389; provisions, 203; ratification, 8, 26, 51, 70, 106, 133, 225–26. *See also* Safeguards, nuclear
Trombay chemical separation plant, India, 97
Trumbull, Robert, 335n
Tucker, Robert, 188, 189, 190, 205
Turkey, 193–95

Ullman, Richard H., 187n
United Kingdom, 2; agreement with Japan on plutonium reprocessing, 29–30; arms embargo against South Africa, 293; role in Middle East, 195
United Nations: arms embargo against South Africa, 292, 293, 294, 298; Atoms for Peace, 88, 99, 213, 377; conference on apartheid, 301; Eighteen-Nation Disarmament Committee, 254; and nuclear guarantees, 357; proposed nuclear-free zone for Middle East, 342; Treaty of Rio de Janeiro and charter of, 263
United States: and Argentina, 253, 262; armed forces deployment, 410–11; arms sales, 346–50; and Brazil, 252; and China, 40–41; and civil nuclear energy, 419–20; and Egypt, 211; and India, 112–13, 119–20, 330–34, 346–50; legislation on nuclear exports, 203n; mutual security treaty with Japan, 10, 33, 40, 43; nuclear cooperation with South Africa, 398, 401–06; nuclear umbrellas, 25, 36, 43, 117, 312, 355; and Pakistan, 346–50, 360, 362–63, 410, 412; policy on reprocessing nuclear energy, 28–30, 353, 417; relations with West Germany over nuclear transfers, 377–84; restrictions on foreign aid, 352–53; and ROK, 8, 49, 51, 61, 65; role in Middle East, 184, 185, 187, 196–97, 366–67, 372–75, 409; as supplier of enriched fuel, 329; and Taiwan, 72, 78, 80, 81, 409. *See also* Nonproliferation policy, U.S.
Uranium: Iran and, 92; isotope sepa-

ration plant, 209; Japan and, 16–19; monopoly on enrichment, 89; Pakistan and, 93; ROK and, 49, 62–63; South Africa and, 287–88
Urenco, 244

Vajpayee, Atal Bihari, 334, 339
Vance, Cyrus R., 72, 382, 383, 384
Van Cleave, William R., 87n, 88n, 97n
Vidal, David, 384n
Visser, Andries, 291
Vorster, John, 284, 301, 302, 399

Wagner, Abraham R., 193n, 199n
Walcott, John, 293n
Walker, Walter, 293n
Walsh, Edward, 301n, 336n
Walters, Ronald W., 284n
Wariavwalla, B. K., 137n
Warner, Edward L., III, 139n, 347n
Warnke, Paul C., 349n
Warsaw Pact, 117, 196, 233; versus NATO forces, 52, 128, 166
Water desalinization projects, 212–15, 423
Water for Peace program, 213, 214
Weinraub, Bernard, 380n, 381n
West Germany: nuclear agreement with Brazil, 220, 243–47, 272–73, 373–84; nuclear agreement with Iran, 335; nuclear exports, 220, 224; relations with U.S. over nuclear transfers, 377–84

Whitaker, Arthur P., 253n
Whiting, Allen S., 121n
Whitney, Craig R., 378n, 381n, 382n, 383n
Wilcox, Wayne, 155n, 363n
Williams, Shelton L., 106n, 124n
Willrich, Mason, 402n, 414n, 424n
Wilson, George C., 165n, 351n, 353n, 360n
Winchester, Simon, 98n, 108n, 340n
Wohlstetter, Albert, 63n, 69n, 101n, 106n, 154n, 183n, 203n, 207n
Wohlstetter, Roberta, 88n, 91n, 107n, 108n, 205n, 220n
Wolfowitz, Paul, 212n, 214
Wood, Archie L., 34n
Wriggins, W. Howard, 129n

Yager, Joseph A., 10n, 54n, 73n
Yahya Khan, 119
Yemen: internal instability, 192, 198; relations with other Arab states, 191
Yiftah, Shimon, 213n
Young, Andrew, 302, 403
Yuenger, James, 359n
Yugoslavia, 337–38

Zabih, Sepehr, 142n
Zia ul-Haq, Mohammed, 102, 103, 105, 109, 114, 127, 129, 156
Ziring, Lawrence, 129n